THE DOCTRINE OF THE KNOWLEDGE OF GOD

A THEOLOGY OF LORDSHIP

A SERIES BY JOHN M. FRAME

Also available in the series:

The Doctrine of God

THE DOCTRINE OF THE KNOWLEDGE OF GOD

JOHN M. FRAME

P&R
PUBLISHING
P.O.BOX 817 • PHILLIPSBURG • NEW JERSEY 08865-0817

Manufactured in the United States of America.

Library of Congress Cataloging-in-Publication Data

Frame, John M., 1939-
The doctrine of the knowledge of God.

(A Theology of lordship)
Bibliography: p.
Includes indexes.
1. God—Knowableness. 2. Knowledge, Theory of (Religion) 3. Apologetics—20th century. I. Title. II. Series.
BT102.F75 1987 231'.042 87-16894
ISBN 0-87552-262-9

Contents

Analytical Outline

Preface

This book was written as a text for my course at Westminster Theological Seminary in California called The Christian Mind. The course, an introduction to theology and apologetics, begins with a brief introduction to the Reformed faith, which is followed by a unit on the Word of God, and ends with discussions of some problems of apologetics (e.g., the existence of God, the problem of evil). In between those two units—Word of God and problems of apologetics—comes a section on the theology of knowledge (Christian epistemology if you will), which is the subject of this volume.

The arrangement of my course will explain why in this book I am so dogmatic as to assume Reformed theology without argument, especially on matters such as biblical inerrancy. I trust that in the future I may be able to publish materials that cover the other areas of my course. If the reader is not sympathetic to my general theological views, however, I do ask his patience; he may well find that some of this material will be helpful to him nevertheless. Also, I hope that this book will help some readers from other theological orientations to see an orthodox, Reformed position "from the inside." I hope to show such readers, in some measure, the richness of the theological resources available to Reformed orthodoxy and thereby to make that position more attractive to them. Thus, rather indirectly, this book constitutes a sort of argument for my theological position—to those readers willing to give me some benefit of the doubt.

Indeed, readers of all theological positions will have to give me some of that benefit! As I read over the manuscript, there seems to be something in it to create difficulties for almost every kind of reader. Some of it is far too difficult for those without theological training (e.g., the sections on anti-abstractionism and the basis of logic); other parts may seem too simple for those *with* theological training (e.g., the material on apologetic method). Some parts merely gather together traditional ideas that have been stated by other authors (e.g., Van Tillian presuppositionalism, Van Til's rationalist-irrationalist dialectic). Other parts are rather new, at least in an orthodox context (theology as application, multiperspectivalism, appreciation for subjectivism, anti-anti-abstractionism, critiques of biblical and systematic theology, polemic against the ideal of total precision in theology, attack on word-level criticism, attack on "logical order," etc.). Thus I manage to offend both the traditionalists and the avant-garde.

Also, I keep feeling that at most points in the book more argument would be helpful. Yet the book is already terribly long, and one of my theses is that theological argument has to start and stop somewhere. Not everything can be argued to everyone's satisfaction. I do believe that for those readers willing to give me the benefit of the doubt, the book is sufficient to present at least the main lines of an adequate argument for its positions. For those who are not willing to give me that benefit—well, I may not be the one suited to help you.

Another group I possibly may have offended is women readers or at least women (and men) who share certain current feminist ideas about the use of language. On the one hand, our language is changing somewhat in a nonsexist direction, and I have often found myself writing "human beings" or "persons," rather than "men," in certain contexts. On the other hand, I confess that I have not always avoided the generic masculine pronouns; I have not always written "he or she" in place of the traditional "he" when referring to an indefinite subject. I have, for example, referred to "the theologian" as "he," rather than as "he or she" or (as often in recent publications) as "she."

My practice does not reflect a belief that women cannot be theologians. Quite the contrary. For according to this book, everyone is a theologian! I do believe that only men are called to the teaching eldership of the church, but the interest of this book is broader than that. Why, then, do I resist, to some extent, the trend toward "nonsexist" language? (1) To use "he or she" in place of "he" as a generic pronoun still sounds awkward to me. Possibly that will change in ten or twenty years, but I am writing in 1986. (2) The English language is complete without the new circumlocutions. The generic use of the masculine pronoun does not exclude women. (Look up *he* in the dictionary.) Thus the new language is linguistically superfluous. (3) Theologically, I believe that God ordained man to represent woman in many situations (cf. 1 Cor. 11:3), and so the generic masculine pronoun has an appropriateness that is more than merely linguistic. Not that it would be wrong to replace it with "he or she" for some purposes; it would be wrong, however, to condemn the older language. (4) I realize that language changes and that one must, to some extent, "go with the flow." I resent attempts, however, to change language in the interest of a political ideology, especially one that I do not entirely agree with! I feel an obligation to accept linguistic change when it arises out of the "grass roots," out of some cultural consensus. When people try to impose it through political pressure, however, I believe that I have a right, for a time at least, to resist. (5) Are women offended by the generic pronouns? I doubt that many of them are. Probably the ones offended are mostly "professional" feminists. I do not believe, in any case, that women have a *right* to be offended, for the generic language, in fact, does not exclude them (see *(2)*, above). Furthermore, I think that the professional feminists themselves are guilty of insulting women when they claim that this language is offensive. For they are saying, in effect, that women do not understand the English language, because they are offended by language which, according to the dictionary, is nonoffensive. (6) Most importantly, this is not a book about "women's issues," and therefore I do not want to use locutions that will distract the reader's attention, making him (or her!) think about women's rights when I want him to think about, for example, situational justification.

For many readers, this book will be a reference text. Few will bother to read it all the way through (though I may force my students to do so!). That is fine, but such readers should recognize that the book is a connected argument and that material toward the end may be a trifle bewildering (though not entirely unhelpful) to one who has not read the preceding sections. But such directions may be superfluous. Most readers, I trust, read with common sense.

I wish to acknowledge the help of many who have contributed to my thinking in general and to this book in particular. Thanks to my mother and (now deceased) father who tolerated a lot of theological nonsense from me in my formative years. To Bob Kelley and Alberta Meadowcroft, who first excited my fascination with God, with Jesus Christ, and with the Christian life. To John Gerstner, who first introduced me to serious and rigorous theological thinking and who showed me that such thinking was possible within, even demanded by, an orthodox Christian confession. To Pastor Ed Morgan, Dr. Donald B. Fullerton, and the Princeton Evangelical

Fellowship, who challenged me to study Scripture in depth, reminding me that God's answers are the most important in all areas of life. To two Princeton professors: Dennis O'Brien, a slightly unorthodox Roman Catholic who started me thinking in a "perspectival" direction, and the late Walter Kaufmann, who for all his militant anti-Christianity managed to teach me that philosophy and theology could be fun. To Cornelius Van Til, the chief intellectual influence of my seminary years and beyond. To other seminary professors, especially Edmund P. Clowney, Meredith G. Kline, and John Murray, who showed me riches in the Scriptures beyond my most fantastic imaginings. To Paul Holmer, my advisor at Yale, who planted many seed thoughts in my head (doubtless he will be appalled to discover what I have done with them!). To many students and colleagues with whom I have had profitable discussions, especially Greg Bahnsen, Vern Poythress, Jim Jordan, Carl Ellis, Susanne (Klepper) Borowik, and Rich Bledsoe. To John Hughes, who painstakingly edited and typeset this volume and made a great number of valuable suggestions. To Lois Swagerty and Jan Crenshaw, who typed portions of the manuscript. To all the Dombeks and all the Laverells, whose Christian friendship nurtured and strengthened me in many ways. To the faculties and boards of the Westminster Theological Seminaries (of Philadelphia and Escondido) for their many encouragements and for their patience in accepting me for so many years as a (relatively) unpublished professor. To Dick Kaufmann, whose precious ministry of the gospel has constantly renewed my faith. To my dearest Mary, the kindest, sweetest, most godly human being I know, whose love has sustained me and has motivated me to persevere in my work. And finally, "to him who loves us and has freed us from our sins by his blood, and has made us to be a kingdom and priests to serve his God and Father—to him be glory and power for ever and ever! Amen" (Rev. 1:5, 6).

INTRODUCTION

Epistemology and the Theological Curriculum

Calvin's *Institutes* begins not with a discussion of scriptural authority or of the doctrine of God, as have most Reformed theologies since Calvin, but with a discussion of the "knowledge of God." The topic with which an author begins a book is not necessarily "central" or "foundational" to his thinking, but clearly the *Institutes* begins with a subject very close to Calvin's heart. In the *Institutes*, "knowledge of God" is both basic and distinctive, since there is very little that compares with it in the writings of Calvin's predecessors or successors. The point is not that in his historical context only Calvin wrote extensively about knowing God. Many people wrote on this subject as they considered the knowability and incomprehensibility of God, human reason, faith, illumination, revelation, Scripture, tradition, preaching, the sacraments, prophecy, the Incarnation, and so forth. And of course many people wrote about salvation, which (as we shall see) is virtually equivalent to the "knowledge of God," viewed from a certain perspective. Yet it seems that Calvin was uniquely fond of the phrase "knowledge of God," and that fondness signals a preference that is more than merely linguistic. For Calvin, "knowledge of God" was a "foundational" concept, a concept by means of which he intended to bring all of his other concepts into focus, a concept by which he sought to make all his other concepts understood. The "knowledge of God" is not the only "central" concept in Calvin, nor is it necessarily the most important. Unlike many modern writers, Calvin was not a "theologian of" this or that (the Word, personal encounter, self-understanding, crisis, process, hope, liberation, covenant, the Resurrection, or even "knowledge of

God"). Yet Calvin recognized "knowledge of God" as one important *perspective* through which the whole Bible can be helpfully understood, as one useful means of summing up the whole biblical message, as well as being a key to certain specific areas of biblical teaching.

Where did Calvin get this remarkable idea? Doubtless through his own study of Scripture. We tend to forget how often in Scripture God performs His mighty acts so that men will "know" that He is Lord (cf. Exod. 6:7; 7:5, 17; 8:10, 22; 9:14, 29f.; 10:2; 14:4, 18; 16:12; Isa. 49:23, 26; 60:16; etc.). We tend to forget how often Scripture emphasizes that although in one sense all people know God (cf. Rom. 1:21), in another sense such knowledge is the exclusive privilege of God's redeemed people and indeed the ultimate goal of the believer's life. What could be more "central" than that? But in our modern theologizing—orthodox and liberal, academic and popular—this language does not come readily to our lips. We speak much more easily about being saved, born again, justified, adopted, sanctified, baptized by the Spirit; about entering the kingdom, dying and rising with Christ; and about believing and repenting than we do about knowing the Lord. For Calvin, there was no such reticence. He was quite at home with the scriptural language; he made it truly his own. And in doing so, he unlocked a rich treasury of biblical teaching of which we are largely ignorant today.

But we do hunger for it. Questions about knowledge—epistemological questions—are a preoccupation of our time. The basic questions raised by Hume and Kant have made modern philosophers (as well as scientists, theologians, artists, sociologists, psychologists, etc.) deeply obsessed by the problems of what we can know and how we can know. Such topics also frequently dominate discussions among nonacademic Christians: How can I know that the Bible is true? How can I know that I am saved? How can I know God's will for my life? How can we, with twentieth-century American biases and prejudices, really know what Scripture means? The biblical doctrine of the knowledge of God was not concocted as an answer to Hume and Kant or to modern skepticism in general or to ancient skepticism, for that matter. It primarily addresses questions of a different sort. But it *does* also address the modern questions in a powerful way.

And there are signs that God (in His mysterious historical slowness, which is never too late) is teaching these truths again to His church. Many useful articles have been written in biblical journals and dictionaries about the concept of "knowledge" in Scripture. And there are even some books on this topic (see the Bibliography). F. Gerald Downing's *Has Christianity a*

Revelation?[1] (he answers, No) goes to some rather absurd extremes but along the way says some very helpful things about revelation and knowledge in Scripture. Cornelius Van Til's apologetic has taken some giant steps toward reforming our Christian epistemology and theological method. These developments, however, have not profoundly affected the contemporary teaching of systematic theology or the preaching and popular theologizing of our day.

Therefore as part of a solution, following Calvin (but departing from much Reformed theology since his time), I have introduced a formal unit on the "knowledge of God" as part of my teaching in systematic theology. The idea came to me ten years ago, when Westminster Seminary determined to combine its first-semester theology course (which includes units on Introduction to Theology, The Word of God, and Revelation, Inspiration and Inerrancy) with its first-semester apologetics course. Both courses were deeply concerned with epistemology. In the theology course, we asked about the nature of theology and about theological method and structure, as well as about God's self-communication to us in nature, Word, and Spirit. In the apologetics course, we dealt with the unbeliever's knowledge of God, its differences from the believer's knowledge, and the means by which God replaces the former with the latter. Therefore it seemed pedagogically sound to introduce a unit on epistemology into the combined theology-apologetics course, and it seemed an ideal means to reintroduce into our "system" much of the biblical teaching on the knowledge of God. And incidentally, it also seemed a useful method of presenting some fresh ideas on what it ought to mean in our day to be "Reformed," to be followers of Calvin. Those purposes, then, define what my class lectures and what this book intend to do.

But where should the epistemology unit be placed in the larger structure of the theology-apologetics course that includes the "Word of God" and various apologetic topics? Generally, questions of theological encyclopedia (i.e., Where in our system do we discuss x—before what and after what?) bore me; they are not nearly as important as some people make them out to be. Most often, they are questions about pedagogy much more than they are questions of theological substance; the answers depend as much on the nature of a particular audience or situation as on the nature of the biblical truth itself. There is no *one point* in the theological system at which epistemology must be discussed. My decision to discuss epis-

1. London: SCM Press, 1964.

temology after the introductory unit on the Word of God, however, is based on the following lines of thought.

One could argue that the doctrine of the knowledge of God ought to be a student's first introduction to systematic theology. After all, it seems that one must know what knowing is before one goes about the business of knowing specific things. One must know what theology is before one can do theology. Right? Well, yes and no. On the one hand, there is certainly much virtue in the idea of discussing epistemology toward the beginning of a student's theological course of study, since it does provide him with concepts and methods that will enrich the rest of his study. On the other hand, the lack of philosophical, linguistic, and catechetical background of many seminary students makes me wonder if first-year students are ready to tackle an area of study as difficult as this can be. And more seriously, there is a sense in which students are not ready to define "theology" until they have done it, just as they are not ready to define "knowledge" until they have done some knowing. Contrary to our intellectualist prejudices, the practice of something generally precedes its definition. (People were writing poetry and thinking logically long before Aristotle defined poetry and formulated a logic.) Can you do theology without knowing what theology is? Of course, just as you can tell time without having a definition of "time," just as you can walk or eat or breathe without being able to give precise definitions of those activities. And sometimes we *must* do something before we can define it. It is scarcely conceivable that anyone could define "seeing" without ever having seen anything. And if a blind man were able, through reading in braille dictionaries, to define sight, imagine how much deeper his understanding of it would be after his sight were restored. A student is not ready, in my view, to appreciate definitions of "theology" or of the "knowledge of God" unless he has already done some theology and unless he already knows God!

Thus I place this unit second—after the unit on the Word of God. That satisfies the legitimate desire to have it toward the beginning of the curriculum (though it does not solve the problem of the inadequate background of many students), and it does give the students some experience in doing theology before they learn, in a formal sense, what theology is. Furthermore, this procedure has the advantage of supporting a major theme of our study: the knowledge of God is a human response to God's Word and is justified by its conformity thereunto. Word of God, then knowledge of God; that is the order both in experience and in our curriculum.

Within the class unit and within this book, the structure looks like this: Part One: The Objects of Knowledge (What do we know?); Part Two: The

Justification of Knowledge (On what basis do we know?); Part Three: The Methods of Knowledge (How do we know?). These questions are not independent. To answer one, you must have some answers in the other areas, too. For example, if you are going to define the objects of knowledge (Part One), you cannot do so unless you do it on the right basis (Part Two), using a proper method (Part Three). In theology, as in other disciplines, it very often happens that questions are interdependent in this way. This does not mean, however, that we must know all the answers before we can know any. God has revealed His truth clearly, and all of us have some knowledge in each area on which we can build. We will begin with the first question, use it to help us answer the second, then find that the second question gives us a fuller understanding of the first one, and so forth. The interdependence of the questions will thus help our study, not hinder it.

One last introductory comment: the material in this book is not intended to do all the work of a philosophical epistemology. Of course, there will be some overlap between this book and works on the theory of knowledge, but I do not intend to go into detail on topics such as the relations between sense data, a priori concepts, sensation, perception, abstraction, and so forth. Studies of such topics have their place (which is *not* to serve as our ultimate source of epistemological certainty), and they can be valuable, especially when developed on Christian assumptions. But our purposes are different.

PART ONE

THE OBJECTS OF KNOWLEDGE

What is the "object" of the knowledge of God? In knowing God, what do we know? Well, *God*, of course! So what remains to be said? Much.

In the first place, it is important that we be clear on what kind of God we are seeking to know. There are many different kinds of knowledge, and differences in the justification and methods of knowledge are often based on differences in the objects that we know. We come to know our friends in different ways from the ways that we come to know the Middle Ages; knowing the population of San Diego is different from knowing Bach's Brandenburg Concerti. Our criteria, methods, and goals in knowing will depend on what we seek to know. Knowing God is something utterly unique, since God himself is unique. Though many beings are called gods by men, there is only one living and true God, and He is radically different from anything in creation. We are not seeking to know just any god; we are seeking to know the Lord Jehovah, the God of Scripture, the God and Father of our Lord Jesus Christ. Thus we must spend a bit of time in the "doctrine of God," even though, as I indicated in the preface, in my teaching and writing that topic follows the doctrine of the knowledge of God, the topic of this book.

In the second place, we do not come to know God, or anything else, in a vacuum. In knowing God, we come to know His relations to the world and to many things in the world, especially to ourselves. We cannot know God without understanding some of those relations: the biblical God is the

God of the covenant, the Creator and sustainer of the world, the Redeemer and judge of men. So we cannot know God without knowing other things at the same time, hence the plural *objects* in the title of this section. And, quite importantly, we cannot know other things rightly without knowing God rightly. Thus theistic epistemology, the doctrine of the knowledge of God, implies a general epistemology, a doctrine of the knowledge of everything. And so in this section we will have to discuss, at least in a limited way, all the "objects" of human knowledge.

A word to some of you who have studied epistemology before: by beginning this book with a discussion of the "objects" of knowledge, I am not intending to erect some great wall of separation between "subject" and "object." To do so would be to destroy all knowledge and would be entirely contrary to Scripture. You will see that I am in greater danger of relating subject and object too closely than I am of illegitimately "dichotomizing" them. Still, one has to start somewhere; he cannot relate everything to everything else all at once, for otherwise he would be God. Thus I start with the "object" of knowledge, and in time we shall see how intimately that object is bound up with the knowing subject. If someone argues that even to distinguish these is to presuppose some illegitimate separation, I reply that that is nonsense. One may make a distinction without separating at all in any meaningful sense, for example, between morning star and evening star, between California and the Golden State.

In this section I shall discuss (1) God, the Covenant Lord, (2) God and the World, and (3) God and Our Studies. In those three chapters we will discuss God, His law, creation, man as God's image, and the "objects" of knowledge in theology, philosophy, science, and apologetics. In each of these disciplines we will ask what it is that we seek to know.

CHAPTER ONE

God, the Covenant Lord

Who is this God that we seek to know? Scripture describes Him in many ways, and it is dangerous to seize on any of them as being more basic or more important than others. In seeking to summarize Scripture's teachings, however, we can certainly do worse than to use the concept of divine "lordship" as our point of departure. "Lord" (*Yahweh* in Hebrew) is the name by which God identified himself at the beginning of His covenant with Israel (Exod. 3:13-15; 6:1-8; 20:1f.). It is the name (*kurios* in Greek) that has been given to Jesus Christ as head of the New Covenant, as head of His redeemed body (John 8:58; Acts 2:36; Rom. 14:9). The fundamental confessions of faith of both testaments confess God—Christ—as Lord (Deut. 6:4ff.; Rom. 10:9; 1 Cor. 12:3; Phil. 2:11). God performs His mighty acts "that you may know that I am the Lord" (cf. Exod. 7:5; 14:4, 18; the references in the Introduction; and Pss. 83:18; 91:14; Isa. 43:3; 52:6; Jer. 16:21; 33:2; Amos 5:8). At critical points in redemptive history, God announces "I am the Lord, I am he" (Isa. 41:4; 43:10-13, 25; 44:6; 48:12; cf. 26:4-8; 46:3f.; Deut. 32:39f., 43; Ps. 135:13; Hos. 12:4-9; 13:4ff.; Mal. 3:6, which allude to Exod. 3:13-15). In such passages, not only "Lord" but also the emphasis on the verb "to be" recall the name-revelation of Exodus 3:14. Jesus also frequently alludes to the "I am" in presenting His own character and office (John 4:26; 8:24, 28, 58; 13:19; 18:5ff.; cf. 6:48; 8:12; 9:5; 10:7, 14; 11:25; 12:46; 14:6; 15:1, 5). One of the most remarkable testimonies to Jesus' deity is the way in which He and His disciples identified Him with *Yahweh* of Exodus 3—a name so closely associated with God that at one point the Jews became afraid even to pronounce it. To summarize those points: throughout redemptive history, God seeks to identify himself to men as Lord and to teach and demonstrate to them the meaning of that concept. "God is Lord"—that is the message of the Old Testament; "Jesus Christ is Lord"—that is the message of the New.

A. THE BIBLICAL CONCEPT OF LORDSHIP

What is divine lordship? Little can be learned from the etymologies of *Yahweh*, *adonai*, or *kurios*. For one thing, those etymologies are uncertain (especially that of *Yahweh*), and furthermore, etymology is not always a reliable guide to meaning. The English *nice*, for example, comes from the Latin *nescius*, which means ignorant; the meanings of the two words are very different! Meanings of words are discovered through an investigation of their use, and such investigation does prove fruitful in the study of the lordship vocabulary in Scripture. My own study can be summarized as follows.

(1) Lordship and Covenant

First of all, lordship is a covenantal concept. "Lord" is the name God gives to himself as head of the Mosaic Covenant and the name given to Jesus Christ as head of the New Covenant (on this, see the passages cited earlier). We may, therefore, define divine lordship as covenant headship.

Covenant may refer to a contract or agreement among equals or to a type of relation between a lord and his servants. Divine-human covenants in Scripture, of course, are of the latter type. In the most prominent ones, God as covenant Lord selects a certain people from among all the nations of the earth to be His own. He rules over them by His law, in terms of which all who obey are blessed and all who disobey are cursed. Yet the covenant is not merely law; it is also grace. It was God's grace, or unmerited favor, by which the covenant people were chosen. And since all men are sinners, it is only by God's grace that there will be any covenant blessing. Even the reprobate—those who do not receive blessing—are vessels of grace, means that God uses to fulfill His gracious purposes (Rom. 9:22-23).

In a broad sense, all of God's dealings with creation are covenantal in character. Meredith Kline[1] and others have observed that the creation

1. See Meredith G. Kline, *Images of the Spirit* (Grand Rapids: Baker Book House, 1980).

narrative in Genesis 1 and 2 is parallel in important respects to other narratives that describe the establishment of covenants. During the creation week, all things, plants, animals, and persons are appointed to be covenant servants, to obey God's law, and to be instruments (positively or negatively) of His gracious purpose. Thus everything and everybody is in covenant with God (cf. Isa. 24:5: all the "inhabitants of the earth" have broken the "everlasting covenant"). The Creator-creature relation is a covenant relation, a Lord-servant relation. When the Lord singled out Israel as His special people to be Lord over them in a peculiar way, He was not giving them an absolutely unique status; rather, He was calling them essentially into the status that all men occupy yet fail to acknowledge. Israel, to be sure, was given certain unique privileges (the land of Palestine, the institutions of sacrifice, prophet, priest, king, etc.), and God used Israel in a unique way to bring redemption (Christ) to the world. Thus Israel had certain unique responsibilities, portraying to the world through its diet, clothing, calendar, and so forth, the nature of the redemption to come. But essentially, Israel was simply a servant of God, like everyone else. This is only to say that God is Lord of all, that in all His relations with the world He speaks and acts as Lord.

(2) Transcendence and Immanence

If God is covenant *head*, then He is exalted above His people; He is transcendent. If He is *covenant* head, then He is deeply involved with them; He is immanent. Note how beautifully these two concepts fit together when understood biblically.

Historically, terrible problems have developed with concepts of transcendence and immanence. The transcendence of God (His exaltation, His mysteriousness) has been understood as God's being infinitely removed from the creation, being so far from us, so different from us, so "wholly other" and "wholly hidden" that we can have no knowledge of Him and can make no true statements about Him. Such a god, therefore, has not revealed—and perhaps cannot reveal—himself to us. He is locked out of human life, so that for practical purposes we become our own gods. God says nothing to us, and we have no responsibilities to Him.

Similarly, the concept of immanence has been distorted in non-Christian thought, even in some would-be Christian theologies. Immanence has been understood to mean that God is virtually indistinguishable from the world, that when God enters the world He becomes so "worldly" that He cannot be found. The "Christian atheists" used to say that God abandoned His divinity and no longer exists as God. Less "radical" thinkers, like Barth and Bultmann, argued that though God still exists, His activity cannot be identified in space and time, that it affects all times and places equally and none in particular. Thus, in effect, there is no revelation; we have no responsibility before God.

Those false concepts of transcendence and immanence fit together in a peculiar way: both satisfy sinful man's desire to escape God's revelation, to avoid our responsibilities, to excuse our disobedience. Yet at bottom they are inconsistent with one another. How can God be infinitely far removed from us and wholly identical to us at the same time? Furthermore, neither of those concepts is even coherent. If God is "wholly other," then how can we know or say that He is "wholly other"? What right do we have to do theology at all if that is the case? And if God is indistinguishable from the world, why should the theologian even bother to speak of God? Why not simply speak of the world? Is it faith that validates such talk? Faith based on what? Can such faith be more than an irrational leap in the dark?

But if transcendence is covenant headship, and if immanence is God's covenant involvement with His people, then we are on solid ground. We are using concepts taught in Scripture, not ones invented by unbelieving philosophers. We are contemplating relations that however mysterious they may be (and they are mysterious) are nevertheless closely analogous to interpersonal relations in everyday life (father-son, ruler-citizen, husband-wife).

The differences between biblical and nonbiblical thought on these questions may be clarified (for some!) by figure 1.

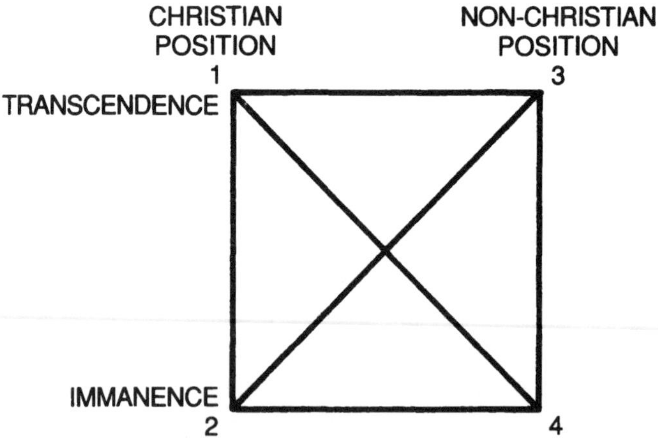

Fig. 1. The square of religious opposition.

The four corners represent four assertions:

1. God is head of the covenant.
2. God is involved as Lord with His creatures.
3. God is infinitely far removed from the creation.
4. God is identical to the creation.

Assertions *1* and *2* are biblical assertions, *3* and *4* are unbiblical. The first assertion represents a biblical view of divine transcendence, the second a biblical view of divine immanence. The third assertion represents a nonbiblical view of transcendence, the fourth a nonbiblical view of immanence. So the two sides distinguish a Christian from a non-Christian approach to the questions of God's immanence and transcendence. The upper half of the square deals with the concept of transcendence, the lower half with immanence. The diagonal lines indicate direct contradictions, showing precisely how the two positions differ: *1* asserts that God is distinct from creation as Lord, *4* denies any distinction at all; *2* asserts a meaningful involvement, *3* denies it. The horizontal lines indicate linguistic similarity: both *1* and *3* can be expressed as views of "transcendence," "exaltation," "mystery," and so forth; both *2* and *4* can be described as forms of "involvement," "immanence," and so forth. Thus there is plenty of room for misunderstanding. Although the two views are diametrically opposed, they can be confused with one another. Even biblical passages can be used in confusing ways. Passages on God's greatness, exaltation, incomprehensibility, and so forth can be applied either to *1* or *3*, passages on the divine nearness to either *2* or *4*. This shows why *3* and *4*, which are essentially non-Christian philosophical speculations, have gained some acceptance among theologians and churches. We must labor mightily to clarify these differences and to attack ambiguity if we are to speak clearly into the modern theological climate.

Vertical lines 1-2 and 3-4 represent the internal structure of each system. As we have seen, 3-4 is inconsistent at a basic level, though 1-2 presents a meaningful, coherent analogy with ordinary experience as interpreted by Scripture.

(3) Control, Authority, Presence

Let us explore a bit further the concepts of transcendence (covenant headship) and immanence (covenant involvement). Divine transcendence in Scripture seems to center on the concepts of control and authority. Control is evident in that the covenant is brought about by God's sovereign power. God brings His covenant servants into existence (Isa. 41:4;

43:10-13; 44:6; 48:12f.) and exercises total control over them (Exod. 3:8, 14).[2] As Lord, He sovereignly delivers them (Exod. 20:2) from bondage and directs the whole natural environment (cf. the plagues in Egypt) to accomplish His purposes for them. Authority is God's right to be obeyed, and since God has both control and authority, He embodies both might and right. Over and over, the covenant Lord stresses how His servants must obey His commands (Exod. 3:13-18; 20:2; Lev. 18:2-5, 30; 19:37; Deut. 6:4-9). To say that God's authority is absolute means that His commands may not be questioned (Job 40:11ff.; Rom. 4:18-20; 9:20; Heb. 11:4, 7, 8, 17, passim), that divine authority transcends all other loyalties (Exod. 20:3; Deut. 6:4f.; Matt. 8:19-22; 10:34-38; Phil. 3:8), and that this authority extends to all areas of human life (Exod.; Lev.; Num.; Deut.; Rom. 14:32; 1 Cor. 10:31; 2 Cor. 10:5; Col. 3:17, 23). Control and authority—these are the concepts that come to the fore when the Lord is presented to us as exalted above creation, and they are as far removed as possible from any notion of God as "wholly other" or as "infinitely distant."

God's immanence may be further described as "covenant solidarity." God elects His covenant people and identifies their goals with His. The heart of the relation is expressed by the words "I will be your God and you shall be my people" (Lev. 26:12; cf. Exod. 29:45; 2 Sam. 7:14; Rev. 21:27). He names himself as their God—"God of Israel"—thus identifying himself with them. To despise Israel is to despise God, and vice versa. In that way, God is "with them" (Exod. 3:12), near them (Deut. 4:7; cf. 30:14), Immanuel (cf. Gen. 26:3; 28:15; 31:3; 46:4; Exod. 3:12; 33:14; Deut. 31:6, 8, 23; Judg. 6:16; Isa. 7:14; Jer. 31:33; Matt. 28:20; John 17:25; 1 Cor. 3:16ff.; Rev. 21:22). Therefore we will sometimes describe God's "covenant solidarity" as a "presence" or "nearness," and this nearness, like God's exaltation, is a defining characteristic of God's lordship (Exod. 3:7-14; 6:1-8; 20:5, 7, 12; Ps. 135:13f.; Isa. 26:4-8; Hos. 12:4-9; 13:4ff.; Mal. 3:6; John 8:31-59; cf. Lev. 10:3; Ps. 148:14; Jonah 2:7; Rom. 10:6-8; Eph. 2:17; Col. 1:27). To emphasize the spiritual nearness between himself and Israel, God draws near to them in a spatial sense: on Mount Sinai, in the cloud and pillar in the wilderness, in the land of promise, in the tabernacle and temple. And He draws near in time, as well; He is "now" as well as "here." When the people are tempted to think of the covenant as an artifact of the distant past, God reminds them that He is the same today as

2. Cf. Exod. 33:18; 34:6; and Geerhardus Vos, *Biblical Theology* (Grand Rapids: Wm. B. Eerdmans Pub. Co., 1959), 129-34.

He was yesterday. He is the God of the present and future, as much as He is the God of Abraham, Isaac, and Jacob; He is the God who is ready now to deliver (cf. Exod. 3:15; 6:8; Isa. 41:4, 10, 13; Deut. 32:7, 39f., 43; Ps. 135:13; Isa. 26:4-8; Hos. 12:4-9; 13:4ff.; Mal. 3:6; John 8:52-58). Thus God's lordship is a deeply personal and practical concept. God is not a vague abstract principle or force but a living person who fellowships with His people. He is the living and true God, as opposed to all the deaf and dumb idols of this world. Knowledge of Him, therefore, is also a person-to-person knowledge. God's presence is not something that we discover through refined theoretical intelligence. Rather, God is unavoidably close to His creation. We are involved with Him all the time.

As controller and authority, God is "absolute," that is, His power and wisdom are beyond any possibility of successful challenge. Thus God is eternal, infinite, omniscient, omnipotent, and so on. But this metaphysical absoluteness does not (as in non-Christian thought) force God into the role of an abstract principle. The non-Christian, of course, can accept an absolute only if that absolute is impersonal and therefore makes no demands and has no power to bless or curse. There are personal gods in paganism, but none of them is absolute; there are absolutes in paganism, but none is personal. Only in Christianity (and in other religions influenced by the Bible) is there such a concept as a "personal absolute."

Control, authority, personal presence—remember that triad. It will appear often in this book, for I know of no better way to summarize the biblical concept of divine lordship. And since lordship itself is so central, we will be running into this triad again and again. I will refer to those three ideas collectively as the "lordship attributes" of God. Remember, too, the concept of God as transcendent and immanent and as personal absolute (i.e., absolute personality). We will find these categories very useful in summarizing the Christian world view and in contrasting it with the non-Christian one.

It is also important that we see the three lordship attributes as forming a unit, not as separate from one another. God is "simple" in the theological sense (not compounded of parts), so there is a sense in which if you have one attribute you have them all. All of God's attributes involve one another, and that is definitely the case with the lordship triad. God's control, according to Scripture, involves authority, for God controls even the structure of truth and rightness. Control involves presence, for God's power is so pervasive that it brings us face to face with Him in every experience. Authority involves control, for God's commands presuppose His full ability to enforce them. Authority involves presence, for God's commands are clearly revealed and are the means by which God acts in our midst to bless and curse. Presence involves control, lest anything in heaven or earth should keep us from God or Him from us (John 10; Rom. 8). Presence involves authority, for God is never present apart from His Word (cf. Deut. 30:11ff.; John 1:1ff.; etc.; and see my unpublished *Doctrine of the Word of God*).

To summarize, knowing God is knowing Him as Lord, "knowing that I am the Lord." And knowing Him as Lord is knowing His control, authority, and presence.

B. LORDSHIP AND KNOWLEDGE

How does the character of God as Lord affect the way in which we know Him? Let us consider several implications of the foregoing discussion.

(1) Knowability and Incomprehensibility

a. *Everyone Knows God*

Because God is Lord, He is not only knowable but *known* to all (Rom. 1:21). The "agnostic" who says that he does not know if God exists is deceiving himself and may be seeking to deceive others. God's covenantal presence is with all His works, and therefore it is inescapable (Ps. 139). Furthermore, all things are under God's control, and all knowledge, as we will see, is a recognition of divine norms for truth; it is a recognition of God's authority. Therefore in knowing anything, we know God. Even those without the Scriptures have this knowledge: they know God, they know their obligations to Him (Rom. 1:32), and they know the wrath that is on them because of their disobedience (Rom. 1:18).

But in a more profound sense, only believers know God, only Christians have a knowledge of God that is the essence of eternal life (John 17:3; cf. Matt. 11:27; John 1:14; 1 Cor. 2:9-15; 13:12; 2 Cor. 3:18; 2 Tim. 1:12, 14ff.; 1 John 5:20). When this knowledge is in view, it may be said by comparison that unbelievers are ignorant, that they do *not* know God (1 Cor. 1:21; 8:2; 15:34; Gal. 4:8; 1 Thess. 4:5; 2 Tim. 3:7; Titus 1:16; Heb. 3:10; 1 John 4:8).

Although non-Christians know God, they frequently try to deny that He is known or even knowable. They wish to avoid being confronted by the glory of God, by His demands, and by His judgment; they want no part of His love. Denial of God's knowability stems from a personal, moral situation; views about God—Christian and non-Christian alike—always arise from one's personal relation to God, from a person's ethical and religious orientation.

We can also understand the non-Christian's position by seeing how it is related to his views of transcendence and immanence, as we noted earlier. On the one hand, if God is so far away that He cannot be identified (i.e., transcendent), then of course He cannot be known. On the other hand, if God is so close to the world that He cannot be distinguished from it (i.e., immanent), then again we are ignorant of God. Or perhaps it might be said that since God is so immanent, so "near us," we can know Him perfectly well, with unaided human reason, perhaps (i.e., rationalism), or by some sort of mystical intuition. But the god that is known through such methods will not be the God of Scripture; he will be a god of man's own devising—subject to man's control, yielding to man's own methods of knowing, subject to man's criteria. Thus both the non-Christian transcendence and immanence standpoints deny the knowability of the biblical God. Metaphysics and epistemology are correlative; the nature of God determines His knowability. Once you deny the lordship of God, you will not be able to defend His knowability. Only if God is who Scripture says He is may we claim to know Him. And if He is Lord, then His control, authority, and presence in the world make Him unavoidably knowable, as we have seen.

When non-Christians argue that God is unknowable, they generally appeal to the limitations implicit in human knowledge. They claim, with Hume, that our knowledge is limited to sense perception or, with Kant, that we can only know "appearances" or "phenomena," not reality itself. Or, with more recent (but currently unfashionable) positivism, they argue that we know only what can be established by a certain kind of scientific method. Thus God either must be unknowable (the non-Christian transcendence standpoint), or He must fit within the realms of finite sense-perception—"phenomena" or science—and thus be less than the biblical God (the non-Christian immanence standpoint); or else we must bounce arbitrarily back and forth between these two positions (the approach of modern dialectical theology and philosophy).

It is certainly true that our knowledge is finite. The agnostic has recognized that in some measure, though he illegitimately uses it for his own purposes.[3] But the limitations of human knowledge are, we will see, very

3. We will discuss the limitations of our knowledge in the next section.

different from the kinds of limitations supposed by Hume, Kant, and the positivists. For now, however, we should simply remind ourselves who the Lord is. Because He *controls* all things, God enters His world—our world—without being relativized by it, without losing His divinity. Thus in knowing our world, we know God. Because God is the supreme *authority*, the author of all the criteria by which we make judgments or come to conclusions, we know Him more certainly than we know any other fact about the world. And because God is the supremely *present* one, He is inescapable. God is not shut out by the world; He is not rendered incapable of revealing himself because of the finitude of the human mind. On the contrary, all reality reveals God. The agnostic argument, then, presupposes a nonbiblical concept of God. If God is who Scripture says He is, there are no barriers to knowing Him.

b. *Limitations on Our Knowledge of God*

The fact that God is Lord also implies that our knowledge is not on a par with His. As the servant comes to know his Lord, he becomes more and more aware of how little he knows, of how much God transcends the reach of a servant's mind.

Our limitations are of several kinds. First (as we have mentioned), sin motivates fallen people to distort the truth, to flee from it, to exchange it for a lie, and to misuse it. This is one potent source of falsehood and ignorance in our thinking, even in the redeemed mind. Because of Christ, Christians have that problem under control (Rom. 6:14), but it will not completely disappear until the Last Day.

Second, errors in our knowledge arise from immaturity and weakness. Even if Adam had not fallen, the acquisition of knowledge would not have taken place all at once. It would have been a historical process, part of the "subduing of the earth" (Gen. 1:28; cf. 2:19f.). Even Jesus "grew" in wisdom and stature (Luke 2:52) and "learned" obedience (Heb. 5:8) in His life as a perfect man. Certainly, then, even apart from sin, human knowledge may be incomplete; we may be ignorant in comparison to what we may know later. Thus I see no reason why even an unfallen race may not have proceeded by the method of trial and error in the continuing quest for knowledge. Error as such need not cause pain or wrongdoing; to make an honest mistake is not in itself sinful. Thus unfallen Adam might have been wrong about some things. And it is much more likely that *we* will make mistakes, because our weakness and immaturity are compounded with the sin of our hearts. Unfallen Adam could not have made a mistake about his present duty before God, but he might have made other kinds of mistakes, even about theological formulations.[4]

But those limitations are only the beginning. For even a perfect creaturely knowledge, that is, the knowledge of a sinless, mature creature who possesses as much information as a creature could possess, would be a limited knowledge. To be a creature is to be limited in thought and knowledge, as in all other aspects of life. We are limited by our Creator, our Lord. We have a beginning in time, but He does not. We are controlled by Him and subject to His authority; we are the objects of ultimate covenant blessing or cursing, and so the nature of our thought should reflect our status as servants. Our thinking should be "servant-thinking."

For those reasons, theologians have spoken of God's "incomprehensibility." Incomprehensibility is not inapprehensibility (i.e., unknowability), because incomprehensibility presupposes that God is known. To say that God is incomprehensible is to say that our knowledge is never equivalent to God's own knowledge, that we never know Him precisely as He knows himself.

In the 1940s there was a debate within the Orthodox Presbyterian Church about the concept of God's incomprehensibility. The major opponents were Cornelius Van Til and Gordon H. Clark.[5] Neither man was at his best in this discussion; each seriously misunderstood the other, as we will see. Both, however, had valid concerns. Van Til wished to preserve the Creator-creature distinction in the realm of knowledge, and Clark wished to prevent any skeptical deductions from the doctrine of incomprehensibility, to insist that we really do know God on the basis of revelation. Van Til, therefore, insisted that even when God and man were thinking of the same thing (a particular rose, for example), their thoughts about it were never *identical*—God's were the thoughts of the Creator, man's of the crea-

4. Is it sinful to hold the wrong view about limited atonement, for example? Holding a wrong view about this (or any doctrine) would be sinful only if (1) the person has the Bible in his own language, presented at a level suited to his mental capacity, (2) he has had the time and resources to come to a correct conclusion, and (3) he has nevertheless willfully rejected the truth (at some level of his thinking). We should be gentle with those who differ from us; they may not be rebellious or sinful in their disagreement, only immature (in other respects they may surpass us). And, of course, we must always recognize the possibility that *we* may be wrong, that a brother or sister who disagrees may have something to teach us.

5. See the "Minutes of the Fifteenth General Assembly" (1948) of the OPC for a committee report on this question. Other minutes during that general period also refer to the controversy. Van Til presents his account in his (unpublished) *Introduction to Systematic Theology*, 159-93. Fred Klooster analyzed the debate in *The Incomprehensibility of God in the Orthodox Presbyterian Conflict* (Franeker: T. Wever, 1951), a helpful book but not sufficiently sensitive to the ambiguities of the language used in the debate.

ture. Such language made Clark fear skepticism. It seemed to him that if there was some discrepancy between man's "This is a rose" and God's (concerning the same rose), then the human assertion must somehow fall short of the truth, since the very nature of truth is identity with God's mind. Thus if there is a necessary discrepancy between God's mind and man's at every point, it would seem that man could know nothing truly; skepticism would result. Thus the discussion of incomprehensibility—essentially a doctrine about the relation of man's thoughts to God's being—turned in this debate more narrowly into a discussion of the relation between man's thoughts and God's thoughts. To say that God is incomprehensible came to mean that there is some discontinuity (much deeper in Van Til's view than in Clark's) between our thoughts of God (and hence of creation) and God's own thoughts of himself (and of creation).

My contribution to this discussion will be to offer the reader a list of discontinuities between God's thoughts and ours that I believe can be substantiated from Scripture, a list of continuities between the two that ought to be acknowledged, and a list of alleged relations between the two that seem to me to be stated ambiguously and that therefore are capable of being affirmed in one sense and denied in another.

(i) *Discontinuities*. Scripture teaches the following discontinuities between God's thought and ours.

1. God's thoughts are uncreated and eternal; ours are created and limited by time.

2. God's thoughts ultimately determine, or decree, what comes to pass. God's thoughts cause the truths that they contemplate; ours do not. This is the lordship attribute of control in the realm of knowledge.

3. God's thoughts, therefore, are self-validating; they serve as their own criteria of truth. God's thoughts are true simply because they are His. None of us can claim to have such self-attesting thoughts. Our thoughts are not necessarily true, and when they are true, it is because they agree with the thoughts of someone else, namely God, who furnishes the criteria for our thinking. This is the lordship attribute of authority in the area of knowledge.

4. God's thoughts always bring glory and honor to Him because God is always "present in blessing" to himself. Because God is "simple," His thoughts are always self-expressions.[6] Our thoughts are blessed only by vir-

6. See my (unpublished) *Doctrine of the Word of God*. God's thinking and speech are divine attributes and therefore (by the doctrine of simplicity) are identical to God himself. They express, therefore, everything that God is.

tue of God's covenantal presence with us. This is the lordship attribute of presence as applied to knowledge. Note that in *1-4*, "incomprehensibility" is an aspect of God's lordship. All the divine attributes can be understood as manifestations of God's lordship, as applications of divine lordship to different areas of human life.

5. God's thoughts are the originals of which ours, at best, are only copies, images. Our thoughts, therefore, would not exist apart from God's covenantal presence (see *4* above).

6. God does not need to have anything "revealed" to Him; He knows what He knows simply by virtue of who He is and what He does. He knows, then, at His own initiative. But all of our knowledge is based on revelation. When we know something, it is because God decided to let us know it, either by Scripture or by nature. Our knowledge, then, is initiated by another. Our knowledge is a result of grace. This is another manifestation of the lordship attribute of "control."[7]

7. God has not chosen to reveal all truth to us. For example, we do not know the future, beyond what Scripture teaches. We do not know all the facts about God or even about creation. In the OPC debate, the difference between God's knowledge and ours was called a "quantitative difference"—God knows more facts than we do.[8]

8. God possesses knowledge in a different way from us. He is immaterial and therefore does not gain knowledge from organs of sense perception. Nor does He carry on "processes of reasoning," understood as temporal sets of actions. Nor is God's knowledge limited by the fallibilities of memory or of foresight. Some have characterized His knowledge as an "eternal intuition," and however we may describe it, it clearly is something quite different from our methods of knowing. In the OPC debate, this discontinuity was called a difference in the "mode" of knowledge.[9]

7. Cf. Van Til, *Introduction*, 165 (top).

8. Clark expressed this idea by saying that God (more precisely, God's essence) is incomprehensible except as God reveals truths concerning His nature. Van Til rightly replied that apart from revelation, God is not only incomprehensible but inapprehensible (i.e., unknowable; ibid., 168f.). The proper conclusion, then, would be to say that Clark failed to distinguish adequately between incomprehensibility and inapprehensibility or to say that he has an inadequate concept of incomprehensibility. Van Til, however, assumed that Clark was willing to make such a distinction. He understood Clark to say that God is incomprehensible but not inapprehensible apart from revelation, and thus he charged Clark with holding that God is knowable apart from revelation. But I find no evidence that warrants such an interpretation of Clark. Van Til's argument here is ingenious, but it is a misunderstanding of Clark's position.

9. Clark affirmed the difference in mode, as well as the "quantitative difference" between God's knowledge and ours (see *7* above). Van Til, however, replied "that if one does not know anything of God's mode of knowing then one can know nothing of God's being"

9. What God does reveal to us, He reveals in a creaturely form. Revelation does not come to us in the form in which it exists in God's mind. Scripture, for example, is in human, not divine, language. It is "accommodated," that is, adapted in some measure to our ability to understand, though it is not exhaustively understandable to us even in that accommodated form.[10]

10. God's thoughts, when taken together, constitute a perfect wisdom; they are not chaotic but agree with one another. His decrees constitute a wise plan. God's thoughts are coherent; divine thinking agrees with divine logic. That is not always true of our thoughts, and we have no reason to suppose that even as we deal with revelation we may not run into truth that our logic cannot systematize, that it cannot relate coherently with other truth. Therefore we may find in revelation what Van Til calls "apparent contradictions."[11]

11. Discontinuity 7 is affected by the progress of revelation: the more God reveals, the more facts we know, though we never reach the point where we know as many facts as God. The other discontinuities, however, are not at all affected by revelation. No matter how much of himself God reveals, there always remains an "essential disproportion between the infinite fullness of the being and knowledge of God and the capacity and intelligence of the finite creature."[12] Thus even what God has revealed is in important senses beyond our comprehension (cf. Judg. 13:18; Neh. 9:5; Pss. 139:6; 147:5; Isa. 9:6; 55:8f.). According to these passages, there is not merely a realm of the unknown beyond our competence, but what is within our competence, what we know, leads us to worship in awe. The hymn of wonder in Romans 11:33-36 expresses amazement not at what is unrevealed but precisely at what is revealed, at what has been described in great detail by the apostle. The more we know, the more our sense of wonder ought to increase, because increased knowledge brings us into greater contact with the incomprehensibility of God.[13] It was this "essential dis-

(ibid., 170). This, too, seems to reflect a misunderstanding of Clark, who according to Van Til's own account said that the mode is different, not that the mode is unknowable.

10. Cf. ibid., 165.

11. I will say more on these later, when we take up the subject of logic. My pamphlet *Van Til the Theologian* (Phillipsburg, N.J.: Pilgrim Publishing, 1976) attempts to give an analysis of this subject.

12. For this formulation and others in this section I am indebted to my colleague Norman Shepherd's lectures on the Doctrine of God. For the uses made of this indebtedness, I take full responsibility.

13. There are (at least) two passages in Scripture that seem to suggest that the difference between divine and human knowledge is temporary, a difference to be remedied by further revelation. In Matthew 11:25-27 Jesus says that it is the prerogative of the Son to reveal the

proportion" between Creator and creature that sometimes in the OPC controversy was described as a "qualitative difference" between divine and human knowledge, as distinguished from the "quantitative difference" described above in 7.

12. And doubtless, there is much more; we cannot exhaustively describe the differences between God's mind and ours—if we could, we would be divine. Thus we must add an "et cetera" to the eleven differences that we have already enumerated. This "et cetera" seems to have been another part of what was meant in the OPC controversy by the phrase "qualitative difference." At one point in that controversy, the Clark party challenged the Van Til party to "state clearly" what the qualitative difference was between God's thoughts and man's. The Van Til group replied that to accept that challenge would be to retract their whole position; if we could "state clearly" this qualitative difference, the difference would no longer exist. Again, I think, there was some mutual misunderstanding. At one level, it is possible (and necessary) to state clearly the nature of the difference. The difference is the difference between Creator and creature in the world of thought; it is a difference between divine thinking and human thinking, between the thoughts of the ultimate Lord and the thoughts of His servants. The implications of this basic difference can also be spelled out to some extent, as I have sought to do above. Insofar as they were asking for that kind of information, the demand of the Clark group was legitimate. But we must remember that the concept of incomprehensibility is self-referential, that is, if God is incomprehensible, then even His incomprehensibility is incomprehensible. We can no more give an exhaustive explanation of God's incomprehensibility than we can give of God's eternity, infinity, righteousness, or love.

(ii) *Continuities*. Scripture teaches the following continuities (the ways that divine and human thought are alike) between God's thought and ours. Failure to consider this side of the truth will lead us into skepticism.

knowledge that He has in distinction from all creatures, and in 1 Corinthians 13:12 (cf. 2:6-17) Paul says that in the consummation we will know "even as" God has known us. Here we should note that there certainly is one sense in which revelation diminishes the distance between our knowledge and God's (see 7 above) and that Scripture often speaks in broad, general terms, without making distinctions that may be found elsewhere on its pages. Note Hodge's comment on 1 Corinthians 13:12: "As we are required to be perfect as our Father in Heaven is perfect, Matt. 5:48, so we may be said to know even as we are known. We may be perfect in our narrow sphere, as God is perfect in His; and yet the distance between Him and us remains infinite. What Paul wishes to impress upon the Corinthians is that the gifts in which they so much prided themselves were small matters compared to what is in reserve for the people of God."

If knowledge of any sort is to be possible, there must be some sense(s) in which man's thought can "agree" with God's, in which we can think God's thoughts after Him.

1. Divine and human thought are bound to the same standard of truth. As Van Til puts it, "The Reformed faith teaches that the reference point for any proposition is the same for God and for man."[14] I prefer the term "standard" to the more ambiguous "reference point." God's thoughts are self-validating; man's are validated by God's. Thus they are both validated by reference to the same standard, divine thought. Man's thoughts are true insofar as they conform to God's norms for human thinking. "For human thinking," of course, reminds us of those discontinuities we discussed earlier. And it must also be emphasized that our thought is subject to the norm, not identical with it, as is God's. Yet both divine and human thinking must accord with norms, and in both cases those norms are divine.

2. Divine and human thought may be about the same things, or as philosophers say, they may have the same "objects." When a man thinks about a particular rose and when God thinks about it (He is always thinking about it, of course, since He is always—eternally—omniscient), they are thinking about the same thing. Sometimes those objects are "propositions," assertions of fact. Van Til says, "That two times two are [sic] four is a well known fact. God knows it. Man knows it."[15] Paul believed Christ was risen; God believes the same thing. Now of course we must keep our discontinuities in mind. God's belief in the Resurrection is the belief of the Creator, the Lord. It is not the same as Paul's belief, therefore, in *every* respect. But it has the same *object*; it affirms the same truth. To deny this is to render impossible any talk of "agreement" between God and man. If God and man cannot think about the same things, how can they agree about them? Furthermore, denying this leads to manifest absurdity. For example, if I believe in the Resurrection, then God must not believe in it.[16]

3. It is possible for man's beliefs, as well as God's, to be true. A true belief is a belief that will not mislead. God's beliefs do not mislead Him, and

14. *Introduction*, 171; cf. 165.

15. Ibid., 172.

16. The reader may well ask why I am belaboring such an obvious point. The reason is that some disciples of Van Til have been so zealous for divine incomprehensibility that they have gone far beyond Van Til himself, overstating their point to dangerous and preposterous lengths. Jim Halsey, for example, in his article "A Preliminary Critique of 'Van Til: the Theologian'," *WTJ* 39 (1976): 129 takes issue with my statement that God and man can have the same beliefs and think about the same things. Does he really mean to imply that God disbelieves in the Resurrection? It is hard for me to believe that any Reformed writer could hold such a nonsensical position. Either I have misunderstood him or he has expressed himself most unclearly. More on Halsey at a later point.

true human beliefs do not mislead human beings. But there is a difference: a belief adequate to direct or lead a human life will not be adequate for God. God's life, however, is sufficiently like its image, human life, so that both God's beliefs and man's may be meaningfully described as true. A proposition that is true for humans plays a role in human life similar to the roles that propositions that are true for God play in His life. If there is no truth, or if man's truth is "wholly different," wholly disanalogous, from God's, then knowledge is impossible.

4. Just as God is omniscient, so man's knowledge in a certain sense is universal. Van Til says, "Man knows something about everything."[17] Because we know God, we know that everything in the universe is created, subject to His authority, and filled with His presence. Because all things are known to God, He can reveal knowledge to us about anything. Therefore all things are potentially knowable, though nothing can be known by us precisely as God knows it.

5. God knows all things by knowing himself, that is, He knows what He knows by knowing His own nature and plan. As we said earlier (discontinuity 6, above), God does not need to have anything "revealed" from outside of himself. Our thinking, as we noted, is very different in this respect, yet in a certain sense it is also similar. We, too, gain our knowledge by knowing ourselves—by knowing our own sensations, thoughts, actions, and so forth. Everything "from outside" must enter our minds if we are to know it. In a sense, then, all knowledge is self-knowledge. Unlike God's, our knowledge does not originate from within, though its inward character bears a significant resemblance to the inwardness of God's knowledge.

6. God's knowledge is self-validating, self-attesting, as we have seen (discontinuity 4, above); ours is not. Because we are God's image, however, there is some reflection in us of God's self-attestation. Because everything we know must enter our consciousness (see 5, above), even the norms by which we think must be adopted by us if we are to use them. We think on the basis of norms that we have chosen but that does not make us autonomous. The norms originate in God and proclaim His ultimate authority (not ours), and we are obligated *to choose* the ones that are truly authoritative. Thus the norms that we obey on any occasion will be the ones that we have chosen.

7. God's thoughts are ultimate creators. They cause the truths that they contemplate, but ours do not (discontinuity 2, above). Nevertheless, our thoughts are also creative in a sense. We are secondary creators. On the

17. *Introduction*, 164; cf. 166.

one hand, when we refuse to think according to God's norms, we are at the same time refusing to live in His world and devising a world of our own to replace it. On the other hand, when we think obediently, we are recreating for ourselves what God has created for us. As Romans 1 teaches, fallen man exchanges the truth for a lie. Adopting a lie affects not only the contents of our heads but every area of our lives. Fallen man lives as if this were not God's world; he lives as if the world were his own ultimate creation. And having abandoned the criteria furnished by revelation, the only criteria by which he can distinguish truth and falsehood, he has no way of correcting his mistake. On the basis of his false criteria, his false world seems to be the real world, the only world that there is. Thus in an important sense, the sinner is a "secondary creator," one who chooses to live in a world—a dream world—that he has invented. The believer, too, is a secondary creator, one who adopts God's world as his own (see 6, above).

Why speak of "creation" here? Why not merely say that men "interpret" the data of creation in different ways? Certainly it is true that this activity can be characterized as "interpretation." But if we leave the matter there, we may falsely suggest that believer and unbeliever are merely organizing or analyzing data that in themselves are neutral, that their analyses or interpretations can be compared with data that in themselves are uninterpreted and capable of being understood either way. That supposition, however, is false. The facts of creation are not raw data or brute facts that are subject to mutually contrary interpretations. They are preinterpreted by God. As Van Til says, "God's interpretation logically precedes . . . all facts."[18] Therefore human interpretation is never merely the interpretation of facts; it is always also a reinterpretation of God's interpretation. To deny God's interpretation is not merely to adopt an alternative but equally valid interpretation; it is to reject the facts as they truly are; it is to reject reality. There is no such thing as "brute fact" by which fallen man can seek to validate his interpretation over against God's. Fallen man can only reject the facts and seek to live in a world of his own making. Similarly, the believer, in working out a faithful interpretation of the facts, is not merely "interpreting" data but is affirming creation as it really is; he is accepting creation as the world that God made, and he is accepting the responsibility to live in that world as it really is. Thomas Kuhn, in his *The Structure of Scientific Revolutions* (Chicago: University of Chicago Press, 1962), argues that when there are no "brute facts" to adjudicate rival understandings, the activity of interpretation is much like that

18. Van Til, *Christian Theistic Evidences* (unpublished syllabus), 51.

of creation. Although I reject Kuhn's relativism (as a nontheist, he assumes that we have no criterion beyond our systems to regulate facts), the concept of "re-creation" that is implicit in his view does not seem too strong.

Talk about "secondary creation" and "secondary self-attestation" (see 6, above) might be frightening to those who do not have a Reformed understanding of what the Bible teaches. To make human beings creators or attesters in any sense might seem to detract from the ultimate causality and authority of God. We must not forget, however, that not only is the Lord authoritative and in control but He is also covenantally present. Because He perfectly controls our interpretative work, all of our thinking is a revelation of Him and a manifestation of His presence. Thus we do not need to fear that the work of the human mind necessarily competes with the authority of God, because the Lord reveals himself in and through our thinking. Human freedom, then, need not block out God's revelation. Thus we need not fear thinking and knowing. And so a Reformed, or Calvinistic—not an Arminian—understanding of what the Bible teaches champions the true freedom of human thought. If true, the Arminian's boast that he is able to think autonomously ("freely") would imply only that human thought is in bondage to the random forces of chance, when in reality (according to a Reformed understanding of the Bible) that is not the case. When we think in obedience to God's Word, we know that our very thinking processes will reveal God to us. Our minds image God, even in His sovereign attributes of control and authority.

(iii) *Problem areas*. But there are some problem areas. We have seen that God's thoughts are unlike ours in certain respects and like ours in others. I have, however, purposely avoided the use of certain language commonly used in discussing these issues. Those familiar with these discussions will wonder why I have not commented, for example, on the questions of whether we can know "God in himself." Well, my position is that this and other expressions are ambiguous and therefore certain assertions containing them ought to be affirmed in one or more senses and denied in others.

Let us now examine some of these problem areas.

1. Do we have an "adequate" idea of God? Van Til[19] and Bavinck[20] say No, but that notion seems irrational. Surely, we want to say, though God

19. *Introduction*, 183.

20. H. Bavinck, *The Doctrine of God* (Grand Rapids: Wm. B. Eerdmans Pub. Co., 1951), 33.

is incomprehensible, at least we have an "adequate" knowledge of Him, a knowledge that is sufficient for our needs. Well, the problem is a simple case of ambiguity. In classical theology, *adequatio* meant something much more than *adequate* generally means to us, something more like *comprehension*. Van Til and Bavinck are thinking more of the classical *adequatio* than of the contemporary use of *adequate*.

2. Do we know the "essence" of God? It has been common in theology to deny that we do. Thus Bavinck says, "Calvin deemed it vain speculation to attempt 'an examination of God's essence.' It is sufficient for us 'to become acquainted with His character and to know what is conformable to His nature'."[21] Van Til, however, says that we know something about everything, including the essence of God, though we cannot comprehend it. Thus Van Til teaches that with regard to knowledge of God's "essence," we are basically in the same position that we are in with regard to all of our other knowledge of God. There is no special problem in knowing God's "essence." Now we must be careful here. In such situations of theological perplexity, we are often tempted to respond to the sounds of words, rather than to their meanings. To some it sounds rationalistic to claim knowledge of God's essence; to others it sounds irrationalistic to deny it. But a theologian must learn to analyze first and to react later. Actually the idea of "essence" is not entirely clear.

Essence, in general, is the quality or qualities by which something is defined, the quality or qualities that make something what it is. In theology we define justification as the imputation of Christ's righteousness and the forgiveness of sins. Many things are true about justification, but it seems that those two phrases somehow specify what justification "really" is, what its essence is. What is the difference between a defining quality (an "essential" quality) and a nonessential quality? That is a difficult question to answer, but (ignoring some of the problems) let me suggest four criteria for an "essential quality." (a) An essential quality is one that is in some sense real, not merely apparent—perhaps even what is "most real" about something. We seem to feel that when we get to the "essence" of anything, we are getting to what it "really" is. (b) An essential quality is one that is necessary to the being of the thing, so that the thing could not be what it is without that attribute. A triangle, for instance, cannot be a triangle without being three-sided. Three-sidedness is "necessary" to triangularity. "Having an area of three square feet" is not necessary in this sense. (c) An essential attribute is distinctive to the type of thing being defined.

21. Ibid., 25.

Triangles are three-sided, but no nontriangles are three-sided. (d) An essential quality must be important to our understanding of the thing defined; one might even argue that it should be the most basic quality for our understanding. Three-sidedness, we generally feel, is the "most basic" fact for our understanding of triangularity.

In the light of that discussion, do we know the "essence" of God? We certainly know a number of divine attributes, or qualities. God is a spirit, infinite, eternal and unchangeable in His being, wisdom, and so forth. Certainly these attributes are real (see *(a)*, above). Although there are differences between God's thoughts and ours, we dare not make those differences so great that they rob us of the reality of God. When we say that God is eternal, we are talking about how He really and truly is, not merely about how He appears to us. We are talking about Him in a human way but in a way that is true; God has certainly given us the power to speak truly about Him. Furthermore, at least some divine attributes, such as eternality, are necessary (see *(b)*, above). God would not be God if He were not eternal. Eternality is also distinctive of God (see *(c)*, above), for in an important sense God alone is eternal.[22] And surely, eternality is also important to our understanding of God (see *(d)*, above), though it is dangerous to make judgments about what attribute or attributes of God are "most" important.[23]

With respect to the most natural meaning of *essence*, then, Van Til is correct. We can know God's "essence" as much as we can know anything else about God (within the limitations we noted earlier); there is no reason to draw any limitations about "essence" that we have not already drawn about other knowledge of God. Perhaps the polemic against seeking to know God's "essence" is more broadly intended to discourage speculation (assertions not warranted by Scripture), specifically about the nature of God. Certainly, people do often speculate when they seek to answer questions about God's nature and attributes. And often the quest for God's "essence" becomes an attempt to weigh the importance of various attrib-

22. In another sense, we can have a life that Scripture calls "eternal," but that is different from the eternity that is distinctive of the Creator.

23. In one sense, all necessary attributes of God are equally important because they are all "coterminous with" one another; they represent the whole being of God as seen from different perspectives. In another sense, it is difficult to determine what is most important "for our understanding" of God. Subjective considerations that raise questions about the whole idea of "essence" certainly enter in here. Perhaps what is "essential" has as much to do with our subjective need as it has to do with "objective reality." Yet as we have seen, essence (see *(a)*, above) is often thought to be, among all possible predications of a subject, a paradigm of objectivity.

utes against one another—generally a wholly fruitless pursuit. Although it is proper to warn ourselves against such error, there are better ways to formulate that warning than by generally condemning inquiry about God's essence.

3. Do we know "God in himself" or only "God in relation to us"? Theologians are often terribly adamant in denying that we know "God in himself." Unfortunately, they often fail to clarify the meaning of that rather ambiguous phrase. Even Bavinck, one of the greatest Reformed theologians, is confusing on this matter. On page 32 of *The Doctrine of God* he says, "There is no knowledge of God as he is in himself," but on page 337 he announces, "Thus far we have dealt with God's being as it exists in itself," and on page 152 he tells us that God does not change, though His relations to creatures change—thus assuming that we have some knowledge of God's change-ability apart from His relations to us.

Let us examine various things that might be meant by "knowledge of God in himself." (a) Knowing God without any admixture of human interpretation. Such knowledge, of course, is impossible to man, because all human knowledge involves human interpretation. (b) Knowing God in a "purely theoretical" way, without any reference to our practical needs or concerns. Later, I will argue that there is no such thing as "purely theoretical knowledge" in this sense. All knowledge is practical because it meets human needs. Certainly the knowledge of God in Scripture has this character. Thus there is no knowledge of "God in himself" in this illegitimate sense. Calvin seems to have this sort of point in mind in III, ii, 6 of the *Institutes*, though he has a less technical concept of "theoretical" than I presently have in view. (c) Knowing God without revelation. Clearly such knowledge does not exist for man. Calvin often has the concern of bringing all of our thinking into subjection to revelation. Note the context of I, x, 2. (d) Knowing God as He knows himself. As we have argued, this too is excluded. John Murray argues that when Calvin denies knowledge of God *apud se* ("in himself") he means that we do not know God as God knows himself. He distinguishes *apud se* from *in se*, which (he argues) would have a broader meaning. (e) Knowing God exhaustively. This, too, is excluded by our previous argumentation. (f) Knowing God's essence. See 2, above. (g) Knowing facts about God (e.g., His eternality), which would be true even if He had not created the world. In that sense we can know "God in himself." We know these facts because Scripture reveals them. That is what Bavinck had in mind on page 337. (h) Knowing God as He really is. Yes! Although modern theologians have sometimes used Calvin's statement in I, x, 2 to encourage a denial of God's knowability, such a thought never crossed Calvin's mind. Scripture, at any rate, is clear: God is both knowable and known. He is known truly, known as He really is. Some people have argued that because our knowledge of God comes through revelation and then through our senses, reason, and imagination, it cannot be a knowledge of God as He really is but only of how He appears to us. It is certainly true that we know God as He appears to us, but must we therefore assume that these appearances are false, that they do not tell us the truth? We would assume that only if we were to buy the Kantian presupposition that truth is always relativized when it enters our consciousness, that reality is forever hidden from us. But that is an unscriptural concept. In Scripture, reality (God in particular) is known, and our senses, reason, and imagination are not barriers to this knowledge; they do not necessarily distort it.[24] Rather, our senses, reason, and imagination are themselves revelations of God—means that God uses to drive His truth home to us. God is Lord; He will not be shut out of His world.

We should learn several lessons from this discussion. Ambiguities in theological terms are rampant. We should avoid emotional reactions to the sounds of theological expressions. We should try to unravel ambiguities in terminology and determine what expressions mean before we adopt or attack them. When an expression can have many meanings, such as "God in himself," we should carefully distinguish the meanings to determine in what senses we can accept it and in what senses we cannot.

4. Does a piece of human language have the same "meaning" for God that it has for man? For Clark, it was important to say, for example, that the statement "2 + 2 = 4" has the same meaning for God that it has for man. The alternative, he argued, was skepticism: "Thou shalt not kill" might mean to God "Thou shalt plant radishes," that is, divine-human communication would be impossible. His point is persuasive, but some clarifications are needed about the meaning of *meaning* (a topic that I will address later). The meaning of *meaning* has been the subject of much controversy in our century. I believe that *meaning* is best employed to designate that *use* of language that is authorized by God.[25] If we assume that view, then various theologically significant conclusions follow, as we will see later. One of those conclusions is that learning meaning is a matter of degree. Each piece of language has a multitude of uses, and we learn these by degrees—one by one, better and better. Knowing the meaning of a sen-

24. They do distort it when they are sinfully employed.

25. Of course God does not give us special revelations about the meanings of words (generally speaking), but He expects us to use our language properly, that is, truly, clearly, and lovingly by studying language in the context of His creation.

tence like "2 + 2 = 4" is not something that occurs once-for-all in completed fashion, so that one either does or does not know the meaning. Rather, we learn more and more about the meaning (i.e., the uses) of "2 + 2 = 4" as we grasp more and more of its implications, its relations to other statements, its applications to technology, and so forth. God, of course, knows the meanings of all words, phrases, and statements exhaustively. He knows all of their uses, both actual and potential; He can use our language better than any of us can. And of course, at a deeper level, we must say that God's knowledge of our language is different from our own knowledge of it because His is the knowledge of the Creator, the Lord of language (cf. the discontinuities discussed earlier).

Van Til's basic concern in the context of the incomprehensibility of God is with our understanding of Scripture. Can we say that we have "fully" understood a passage when we have exegeted it correctly? Van Til says No[26] for essentially the reasons that I noted above. God's knowledge, even of human language, is of a fundamentally different order from ours. Does that mean that Scripture is unclear or even unintelligible? If so, we would have to say that God failed in His attempt to communicate! No, Scripture is clear enough, so that we have no excuse for disobedience. We know the language well enough (note the emphasis on degree) to use Scripture as God intended. But because human language is so rich and because God's knowledge of it is so comprehensive, Scripture will always contain depths of meaning beyond our understanding. Are these depths of meaning irrelevant to us because they are beyond our understanding? No. Nothing is more important in Scripture than the sense of mystery that it conveys, the attitude of awe that it evokes from its readers.

Even for "2 + 2 = 4," we can say that God knows depths of meaning that we do not know, not to mention the other discontinuities implicit in the Creator-creature distinction. But God also surely knows the same limited levels of meaning that we know, and within that sphere He communicates with a clarity that leaves us without excuse.

5. Is all language about God figurative rather than literal? Question 4 dealt with God's use of human language; this one deals with our use of it. Here we are asking whether words must have different senses when applied to God than in other uses. We all know that Scripture uses figures of speech in referring to God—God's "hand," "eye," and so forth. Some have held the view that all human language about God is figurative. They argue that human language is an earthly language, a language that refers

26. *Introduction*, 181ff.

primarily to finite, temporal realities. If such language is to refer to God, it must be used in a way that is different from its natural use, that is, it must be used "figuratively" or "analogically."

But that is another problem that is too large for us to discuss in detail here. It has been one of the chief problems of the philosophy of religion, especially since the time of Thomas Aquinas. Many different kinds of analogies have been distinguished from one another. Certain basic points, however, need to be taken into account.

(a) *Different referents, not different meanings*. It is certainly true that words have a significantly different *reference* when they are applied to God. Divine righteousness, for example, is significantly different from human righteousness. But the meaning of a term is not its referent.[27] *Chair* does not vary in meaning because it is used to refer to different chairs or to different kinds of chairs. If one is to show that *righteousness* has a figurative meaning when applied to God, then he will have to show not merely that God's righteousness is different from ours but also that the difference is of such a sort as to require a figurative use.

(b) *Distinction imprecise*. The differences between "literal" and "figurative" uses are imprecise. The "literal" use of a term is its "standard" or primary use. But it is not always possible to distinguish sharply between a "standard" and a nonstandard use.

(c) *Human language refers naturally to God*. A Christian epistemology will reject the premise that human language necessarily refers primarily to finite reality, because this premise is based on what we have called a non-Christian view of transcendence—that God is not clearly revealed in creation. On a Christian basis we must say that God made human language for His own purposes, the chief of which was to relate us to himself. Human language is (perhaps even chiefly, or "primarily") a medium by which we can talk to one another about God. Set free from that false premise, we can see all sorts of terms as having primary ("literal") reference to God, rather than to the creation. *God, righteousness, love*, and so forth are suitable candidates. Why should we not think of human righteousness as being modeled on God's, rather than the other way around? That is, in fact, the pattern indicated in Scripture. We should also note that all languages have religious vocabularies, and there is no evidence that these terms developed as a sophisticated extrapolation of previously existing naturalistic vocabularies. Religious language is a natural part of human discourse, be-

27. When Pompeii was destroyed, the meaning of *Pompeii* remained.

cause God is as involved in human life as are tables, chairs, birds, and trees.

(d) *Some God-language clearly literal.* Certain terms clearly refer to God literally, not figuratively. For example, take negative attributes such as "God is not a liar." What in that sentence could possibly be construed as figurative? *Not*, clearly, has its usual sense. *Liar* is also literal; we are distinguishing God from literal liars, not, in this case, figurative ones. As another example, take *love*. Surely, as we noted (see *(a)*, above), there are many different referents here, that is, between divine and human love. Insofar as *love* has value here, however, it attributes to God what one would expect of human love at its best: self-giving, helping, commitment, sympathy, and so forth. It is surely not like the attribution of arms and eyes to God, for we can meaningfully say that God does not "really" have arms and eyes, but we cannot make a similar disclaimer about God's love. God's love is more than our language can grasp, but surely it is not less. To say that *love* applies to God only in a figurative sense has the force of diminishing content without adding anything.

(e) *Van Til on "analogy."* Van Til does teach that all of our thinking about God is "analogical," but in his vocabulary *analogical* means "reflective of God's original thought."[28] Because both "literal" and "figurative" language can be "analogical" in Van Til's sense, his view of analogy does not resolve the question before us. As far as I know, Van Til nowhere comments on the question of whether or not language about God can be literal.

(f) *Never compromise God's knowability.* We must be careful, here as elsewhere, about drawing such sharp distinctions between God's thought and ours that we compromise His knowability. Even where figurative expressions are used about God, they may convey truth. The figurative character of some language in Scripture does not rob that language of meaning. "God is a rock" is true, and it conveys meaning that could not have been conveyed by a literal expression. God has made rocks, and He has ordained them from before the foundation of the world to reflect His strength and constancy. The rock is a revelation of God, and it is for that reason that it is a suitable figure.[29] Such language is not a mere expediency

28. *Reflective* has two senses here. In one sense, all human thought reflects God; in another sense, only obedient, believing thought does. This distinction corresponds to the traditional Reformed distinction between "wider" and "narrower" senses of the image of God. Unbelieving thought does not image God's truth and goodness (except in ironic ways), but it does reflect God in its skillfulness. See our later discussion of the unbeliever's knowledge.

29. See Kline, *Images*, for biblical data about the whole creation as an image of God.

that God is forced to use despite its falsehood. As John Murray says, "We know God by means of analogy, but what we know is not a mere analogy, but the true God."[30]

6. Does God's "thought-content" always differ from man's? *Content* played a crucial role in the OPC controversy. Van Til's followers insisted that when a man thinks about a particular rose, for example, the "content" in his mind always differs from the "content" in God's mind when He thinks about the same rose.[31] It would be a mistake for us to assume that *thought-content* has a perfectly clear meaning and then to leap on one bandwagon or another. In my booklet *Van Til the Theologian*, I argue that the idea of "thought-content" is ambiguous.[32] In some senses, I would argue, Van Til is right; in others, Clark. (a) *Content* can refer to *mental images*. I think Van Til has this in mind, for example, on page 184 of *Introduction*: "When man says that God is eternal, he can, because of his own limitations, think of God only as being very old. He can think of eternity only in terms of endless years." That statement is false, unless "think of" refers to imaging of some sort, the imagining of what it would be like for us to be eternal. If imaging is not in view, then there certainly are ways in which we can think of eternity as other than endless time. Otherwise, how do theologians (including Van Til) come to define eternity as supratemporal? If *content* in the controversy means "mental images," then the whole argument is speculative and foolish. We have no ground for supposing that God thinks in anything like our mental images. (Even we can think without using images.) And even if He does, there is no reason to suppose that God's images are the same as ours or that they are not.

(b) *Content* can refer to the *objects of thought*. To say that God and man have the same "thought-content," then, would simply mean that God and man are thinking about the same things. If this is the meaning of *thought-content*, then obviously God and man have common thought-content. I

30. Paraphrased from Murray's unpublished "Lectures on the Doctrine of God." He is, I think, using *analogy* in the traditional linguistic sense, not in Van Til's sense described above in *(c)*.

31. Cf. Van Til, *Introduction*, 172, on the proposition "2 x 2 = 4." Van Til denies that "there must be identity of content between the divine and human minds on such a proposition."

32. Interestingly, Van Til confirms the ambiguousness of this concept in a different context. On page 194 of *Introduction*, he argues that Christians and non-Christians do not agree on any "thought content" about God. On page 195, however, he argues vigorously that the non-Christian's knowledge of God is an actual thought content, with which, presumably, the Christian would agree. And even more remarkably, on pages 194 and 195, "thought content" is contrasted with "mere formality," rendering the latter expression similarly ambiguous.

have thoughts about my typewriter; surely God also has thoughts about it![33]

(c) *Thought-content* could refer to *beliefs* or *judgments of truth*. Certainly it is possible for God and man to have the same "thought-content" in that sense; Scripture constantly urges us to agree with God's judgments. Van Til's concept of "analogical reasoning" is inconceivable without reference to such sameness.

(d) *Content* could also refer to the *meanings* associated with words in the mind. On this point, see problem areas 4 and 5.

(e) *Content* can refer to the *fullness* of one's understanding. On this interpretation, clearly there is always a divine-human difference, because God's concept of anything is always richer and fuller than any human's concept of the same thing.

(f) Finally, *content* can refer to all of the *attributes* of the thought under consideration. Because God's thoughts are all divine in quality and because none of ours are (see above under "discontinuities"), in this respect there is always a difference in content between God's thoughts and ours. Nevertheless, the ambiguities we have discerned in the expression "thought-content" ought to convince us against any undefined use of it. I am sure that confusion over the meaning of this phrase was a significant hindrance to mutual understanding between the Clark and Van Til groups.

7. Is there a "qualitative difference" between God's thoughts and ours? *Qualitative difference* was the great rallying cry of the Van Til forces against the Clark party. On the one hand, Clark (we are told) held that there was only a "quantitative difference" between God's thoughts and ours, that is, that God knew more facts than we do. On the other hand, Van Til be-

33. Jim Halsey ("Critique," 129) actually takes issue with my statement that God and man can have the same beliefs and think about the same things. I confess that this leaves me entirely baffled. With regard to God's beliefs and objects of thought, I am willing to posit the same differences that I have posited elsewhere, that is, God's beliefs are the beliefs of the Creator and therefore original as opposed to derivative, and so forth. But for Halsey to deny the continuity that I assert makes no sense at all to me. I believe that Jesus rose from the dead. Does Halsey mean to say that God does not affirm that fact? It is hard for me to believe that any Reformed scholar could maintain anything so absurd. Halsey's concern, of course, is to insist upon the Creator-creature distinction at every point; thus the idea of "sameness," in his view, must be rejected all along the line. In my view, however, this is an extremely mechanical approach, oblivious to the different kinds of "samenesses" there are. Furthermore, merely to reject the concept of "sameness" across the board creates serious theological problems. If the wrong sort of "sameness" threatens the Creator-creature distinction, denial of all sameness threatens the presence of God in our world, for it renders impossible the thought that God and man ever dwell in the same universe, share the same history, or enter into meaningful relationships with one another.

lieved that the difference was "qualitative." I am willing to affirm that there is a qualitative difference between God's thoughts and ours, but I am not convinced of the value of the phrase in the present controversy. What is a "qualitative difference"? Most simply defined, it is a difference in quality. Thus a difference between blue and green could be a "qualitative difference." Such a usage, of course, is totally inadequate to do justice to the Creator-creature distinction, which the Van Til forces were trying to do. In fairness, however, we should also recognize that in English *qualitative difference* generally refers to *very large* differences in quality, not differences like that between blue and green. We tend to speak of "qualitative differences" where the differences are not capable of quantitative measurement. But even on such a maximal definition, the phrase still denotes differences *within* creation; it does not uniquely define the Creator-creature distinction. I therefore tend to avoid the phrase, though I have no objection to it. Although it is appropriate to use a superlative term like this to describe the Creator-creature relation, we should cure ourselves of the notion that *qualitative* automatically takes us outside of the sphere of intracreational relations and that no other terms may be substituted for it in such a context.[34] Rather than using *qualitative difference*, I prefer to use terms that are more directly related to the covenantal terminology of Scripture, for example differences between Creator and creature, Lord and servant, Father and son, original and derivative, self-attesting and attested by another. In some contexts, those terms can also designate intracreational relations; all terms in human language can apply to something or other within creation. But when they refer to the divine-human difference, they are no less clear than *qualitative difference*, and in most respects, they are clearer. The suggestion that *qualitative difference* somehow designates a larger difference than these other terms or that it is more appropriate than the biblical terms to denote the difference in view is entirely groundless. It was most unfortunate that *qualitative difference* became a kind of partisan rallying cry in the OPC controversy. For such work the phrase is entirely unsuited.

Let us summarize our discussion of the incomprehensibility of God. The lordship of God must be recognized in the area of thought, as well as in all other aspects of human life. We must confess that God's thoughts are wholly sovereign and therefore sharply different from ours, which are the thoughts of servants. God's being, too, is quite beyond our compre-

34. This notion seems to pervade Halsey's article. He continually suggests that since I do not speak of "qualitative differences," I must hold that the differences in view are merely "quantitative." That suggestion is entirely false.

hension, but we must not interpret God's incomprehensibility in such a way that we compromise the knowability of God or the involvement of God with us in the process of thinking and knowing. God is revealed, and we know Him truly, but it is in that revelation and because of that revelation that we stand in wonder. The "Clark Case" is a classic example of the hurt that can be done when people dogmatize over difficult theological issues without taking the trouble first to understand one another, to analyze ambiguities in their formulations, and to recognize more than one kind of theological danger to be avoided.

(2) Knowing as a Covenant Relationship

We have been considering the implications of God's lordship for our knowledge of Him. We have seen how His lordship implies His knowability and, at the same time, His incomprehensibility. Now we want to ask more specifically, What kind of knowledge is consistent with God's lordship? Above all, we must recognize that human knowledge of God is covenantal in character, as all human activities are. Knowing is the act of a covenant servant of God. That means that in knowing God, as in any other aspect of human life, we are subject to God's control and authority, confronted with His inevitable presence. As we learned in our discussion of God's incomprehensibility, we dare not aspire to the kind of knowledge that God has of himself; we must be satisfied with the kind of knowledge that a servant may have of his Lord, even when that knowledge is a knowledge of mystery or of our own ignorance. Let us now look at this "servant-knowledge" in more detail. I will suggest that servant-knowledge is a knowledge *about* God as Lord and a knowledge that is *subject to* God as Lord.

a. *A Knowledge About God as Lord*

Knowing God is knowing Him as Lord, knowing His name *Yahweh* (Exod. 14:18; 33:11—34:9; 1 Kings 8:43; 1 Chron. 28:6-9; Pss. 83:18; 91:14; Prov. 9:10; Isa. 43:3; 52:6; Jer. 9:23; 16:21; 33:2; Amos 5:8). As we saw earlier, God performs mighty acts "so that men may know that I am the Lord." This emphasis is prominent in the covenant treaty documents of Scripture.[35] At the very beginning of the treaty, the Great King pro-

35. Meredith Kline in his *Treaty of the Great King* (Grand Rapids: Wm. B. Eerdmans Pub. Co., 1963) has identified certain parts of Scripture (e.g., Exod. 20:1-17, the Book of Deuteronomy) as having the form of Hittite "suzerainty treaties," wherein a powerful king would impose his will on a lesser king. These documents generally included: (1) identification of the

claims His lordship: "I am the Lord thy God."

Knowing God as Lord involves knowing that *control*.[36] As mentioned earlier, God makes himself known through His mighty works, both in nature (Rom. 1:18-20) and in history (Pss. 106:2, 8; 145:4, 12; Matt. 11:20f.; 2 Cor. 12:12; Heb. 2:4). These may be works of judgment (Exod. 14:18) or of grace (Matt. 5:45; Acts 14:17; Matt. 11:20f.) It also involves knowing His *authority*, knowing *that* He is the ultimate authority and knowing *what* He commands us to do. According to Genesis, Adam's first experience was to hear God's commands (Gen. 1:28f.; cf. 2:16f.). Man has never been without knowledge of God's will. Even unregenerated people know what God requires (Rom. 1:21, 32, possibly 2:14f.), and the redemptive covenants always involve renewed applications of God's statutes (Exod. 33:13; 34:5f.; 1 Chron. 28:6-9; Jer. 9:24). Furthermore, knowing God's authoritative will involves knowing that God is *present* as the one who unites us to Him in a covenant relationship. Adam walked and talked with God in the Garden of Eden, and even the unbeliever sees God clearly (Rom. 1:19f.). All men are in God's image (Gen. 1:27ff.; 9:6; 1 Cor. 11:7; James 3:9), and so they know God as He is reflected in their own lives; God is so close that He is inescapable. In redemption, God draws near to His people anew, addresses them intimately (cf. the "I-thou" language of the Decalogue, as if God were addressing only one person), and dwells with them and blesses them (Deut. 33:13).

b. A *Knowledge Subject to God as Lord*

To say, however, that knowing is covenantal is more than to say it is *about* the covenant. Knowing the Lord is not merely knowing about God's lordship, though it certainly is that. Knowing is a process that itself is *sub-*

great king—his name, (2) historical prologue—the past relations between the great king and the lesser king, focusing on the ways in which the former has helped the latter, (3) laws—(a) fundamental covenant allegiance, called "love," and (b) detailed commandments for the lesser (vassal) king to obey, (4) sanctions—blessings promised for obedience, curses for disobedience, (5) covenant administration—use of the documents, succession arrangements, and so forth. In the Decalogue and in Deuteronomy, God is the Great King, Israel the vassal. Kline argues that the Decalogue covenant is in fact the original part of the canon and that as God inspired additional Scripture, the additions continued to perform essentially the same functions: identification of the name of the Lord, covenant history, covenant law, covenant sanctions, and covenant administration.

36. Remarkably, the treaty pattern (both biblical and extrabiblical), as described by Kline, follows the control-authority-presence pattern closely. Following His name-identification, the Lord describes His mighty works in the historical prologue (control), gives His laws (authority), and pronounces the blessings and cursings (presence). The "covenant administration" section, then, deals with the promulgation and enforcement of the covenant history, law, and sanctions.

ject to God's lordship. Like all other processes, human knowledge is under God's control, subject to His authority, and exposed to His presence. Thus God is involved in our knowing, just as He is involved in the things we know about. The process of knowing itself, apart from any information gained by it, is a revelation of God. As we come to know about God, we inevitably come to know Him. Let us consider the lordship attributes in this regard.

(i) *Knowledge under God's control.* First, our knowledge of God is always based on revelation. In our coming to know God, it is He who takes the initiative. He does not wait passively for us to discover Him, but He makes himself known. Furthermore—at least in the postfall context[37]—this revelation is gracious; we do not deserve it, but God gives it as a "favor" to us as part of His redemptive mercy (Exod. 33:12f.; 1 Chron. 28:6-9; Prov. 2:6; Isa. 33:5f.; Jer. 9:23f.; 31:33f.; Matt. 11:25-28; John 17:3; Eph. 4:13; Phil. 1:9; Col. 1:9f.; 3:10; 2 Tim. 2:25; 2 Peter 1:2f.; 2:20; 1 John 4:7). This process not only involves revelation in an objective sense (i.e., God creating the world and inspiring the Bible so that they reveal Him to an open heart), it also involves revelation in a subjective sense, what the Bible calls "illumination" or "enlightenment"—the work of the Holy Spirit that opens our hearts, so that we acknowledge, understand, and rightly use His truth (2 Cor. 4:6; Eph. 1:18; Heb. 6:4; 10:32; cf. 1 Thess. 1:5). Thus the origin of knowledge is trinitarian: The Father knows all and reveals truth to us by the grace of His Son through the work of the Spirit in our hearts. Note how each person of the Trinity is involved in the knowing process (cf. 1 Sam. 2:3; Ps. 73:11; Isa. 11:2; 28:9; 53:11; Matt. 11:25f.; Eph. 1:17; Col. 2:3). Thus it is all of God, all of grace. We know God because He has first known us as His children (cf. Exod. 22:12; 1 Cor. 8:1-3; Gal. 4:9).[38]

(ii) *Knowledge subject to God's authority.* In Scripture knowledge is very closely linked with righteousness and holiness (cf. Eph. 4:24; Col. 3:10). These "go together" (1 Cor. 8:1-3; 1 John 4:7f.). Knowledge of God, in

37. Before the fall there was grace in the sense of undeserved blessing but not in the sense of a remission of wrath.

38. The natural question at this point is If knowledge is a product of redemptive grace, then how can the unregenerate be said to know God at all? The answer is that there are two kinds of "knowledge of God," knowledge in faith and knowledge in unbelief. We will deal with "knowledge in unbelief" later. Here we will only speak about the believer's knowledge.

the fullest sense, is inevitably an *obedient* knowledge. Let me sketch five important relations between knowledge and obedience.

1. *Knowledge of God produces obedience* (John 17:26; 2 Peter 1:3, 5; 2:18-20). God's friends necessarily seek to obey Him (John 14:15, 21; etc.), and the better they know Him, the more obedient they become. Such a relation to God is inevitably a sanctifying experience; being near Him transforms us, as the biblical pictures of God's glory being transferred to His people, of His Spirit descending on them, and of their being conformed to His image indicate.

2. *Obedience to God leads to knowledge* (John 7:17; Eph. 3:17-19; 2 Tim. 2:25f.; 1 John 3:16; cf. Ps. 111:10; Prov. 1:7; 15:33; Isa. 33:6).[39] This is the converse of the previous point; there is a "circular" relation between knowledge and obedience in Scripture. Neither is unilaterally prior to the other, either temporally or causally. They are inseparable and simultaneous. Each enriches the other (cf. 2 Peter 1:5f.). In my view, some Reformed "intellectualists" (Gordon Clark has applied this label to himself) have failed to do justice to this circularity. Even in the writings of J. Gresham Machen, one often finds the slogan "life is built upon doctrine" used in a way that distorts the fact that in some senses the opposite is also true. It is certainly true that if you want to obey God more completely, you must get to know Him; but it is also true that if you want to know God better, you must seek to obey Him more perfectly.[40]

This emphasis does not contradict our earlier point that knowledge is by grace. Knowledge and obedience are *given* to us simultaneously by God on the basis of Jesus' sacrifice. Once they are given, God continues to give them in greater and greater fullness. But He uses means; He uses our obedience as a means of giving us knowledge, and vice versa.

3. *Obedience is knowledge, and knowledge is obedience*. Very often in Scripture, *obedience* and *knowledge* are used as near synonyms, either by being set in apposition to one another (e.g., Hos. 6:6) or by being used to define one another (e.g., Jer. 22:16). Occasionally, too, *knowledge* appears as one term in a general list of distinctly ethical categories (e.g., Hos. 4:1f.) and so is presented as a form of obedience (cf. Jer. 31:31f.; John 8:55 [note the context, esp. vv. 19, 32, 41]; 1 Cor. 2:6 [cf. vv. 13-15; "mature" here is an ethical-religious quality]; Eph. 4:13; Phil. 3:8-11; 2 Thess. 1:8f.; 2

39. The "fear of God" is that basic attitude of reverence and awe that inevitably carries with it a desire to do God's will.

40. The circle goes even farther: knowledge originates in God's grace and leads to more grace (Exod. 33:13), which leads to more knowledge. In this case, however, there is a "unilateral" beginning. Grace originates knowledge, not vice versa.

Peter 1:5; 2:20f.). In these passages, obedience is not merely a consequence of knowledge but a constitutive aspect of it. Without obedience there is no knowledge, and vice versa.[41]

The point here is not that *obedience* and *knowledge* are synonymous terms, interchangeable in all contexts. They do differ. *Knowledge* designates the friendship between ourselves and God (see below), and *obedience* designates our activity within that relation. But these two ideas are so inseparable from one another that often they can legitimately be used as synonyms, each describing the other from a particular perspective.

4. *Thus obedience is the criterion of knowledge.* To determine if someone knows God, we do not merely give him a written exam; we examine his life. Atheism in Scripture is a practical, not merely a theoretical, position; denying God is seen in the corruption of one's life (Pss. 10:4ff.; 14:1-7; 53). Similarly, the test of Christian faith or knowledge is a holy life (Matt. 7:21ff.; Luke 8:21; John 8:47; 14:15, 21, 23f.; 15:7, 10, 14; 17:6, 17; 1 John 2:3-5; 4:7; 5:2f.; 2 John 6f.; Rev. 12:17; 14:12). The ultimate reason for that is that God is the real, living, and true God, not an abstraction concerning whom we can only theorize, but one who is profoundly involved with each of our lives. The very "I am" of *Yahweh* indicates His presence. As Francis Schaeffer says, He is "the God who is there." Thus our involvement with Him is a practical involvement, an involvement with Him not only in our theoretical activity but in all of life. To disobey is to be culpably ignorant of God's involvement in our lives. So disobedience involves ignorance and obedience involves knowledge.[42]

5. *Therefore it is clear that knowledge itself must be sought in an obedient way.* There are commandments in Scripture that bear very directly on how we are to seek knowledge, that identify the differences between true and false knowledge. In this connection, we should meditate on 1 Corinthians 1-2; 3:18-23; 8:1-3; and James 3:13-18. When we seek to know God obediently, we assume the fundamental point that Christian knowledge is a knowledge under authority, that our quest for knowledge is not autonomous but subject to Scripture. And if that is true, it follows that the truth

41. F. Gerald Downing in his *Has Christianity a Revelation?* (London: SCM Press, 1964) equates knowledge with obedience in such a way that he actually denies the existence of a revealed knowledge of God in the conceptual sense of *knowledge*. In my opinion, he presses his case much too far (see, for example, his exegesis of Phil. 3:8ff., which is somewhat bizarre). But he makes many useful suggestions, and the book is very helpful in combating our traditional picture of "knowledge" as something merely intellectual. ("Merely" can be such a helpful word in theology! If Downing had said that knowledge is not *merely* intellectual, he would have said something true and helpful.)

42. A number of ideas in this paragraph come from Shepherd's lectures, cited earlier.

(and to some extent the content) of Scripture must be regarded as the most certain knowledge that we have. If this knowledge is to be the criterion for all other knowledge, if it is to govern our acceptance or rejection of other propositions, then there is no proposition that can call it into question. Thus when we know God, we know Him more certainly, more surely than we know anything else. When He speaks to us, our understanding of His Word must govern our understanding of everything else. This is a difficult point because, after all, our understanding of Scripture is fallible and may sometimes need to be corrected. But those corrections may be made only on the basis of a deeper understanding of Scripture, not on the basis of some other kind of knowledge.

It is at this point that we introduce ourselves to the term for which Van Til's apologetics is best known, the term *presupposition*. A presupposition is a belief that takes precedence over another and therefore serves as a criterion for another. An ultimate presupposition is a belief over which no other takes precedence.[43] For a Christian, the content of Scripture must serve as his ultimate presupposition. Our beliefs about Scripture may be corrected by other beliefs about Scripture, but relative to the body of extrascriptural information that we possess, those beliefs are presuppositional in character. This doctrine is merely the outworking of the lordship of God in the area of human thought. It merely applies the doctrine of scriptural infallibility to the realm of knowing. Seen in this way, I really cannot understand why any evangelical Christian should have a problem in accepting it. We are merely affirming that human knowledge is servant-knowledge, that in seeking to know anything our first concern is to discover what our Lord thinks about it and to agree with His judgment, to think His thoughts after Him. What alternative could there possibly be? Would anyone dare to suggest that though we commit ourselves unreservedly to Christ, there is no place for such commitments in our intellectual work? Thus this doctrine of presuppositions purely and simply asserts the lordship of Christ over human thought. Anything less than this is unacceptable to Him.

(iii) *Knowledge exposed to God's presence.* We commonly distinguish between knowledge of facts ("knowing that . . ."), knowledge of skills

43. Some may feel that this definition of *presupposition* has too much of an intellectualistic ring. Of course, in this context we are concerned mainly with beliefs, propositions, and so forth. But I would certainly want to stress that "presuppositions" are rooted in "basic commitments" of the heart. Whether we use the term "presupposition" as defined above or whether we define it as "basic commitment" and find another term to employ in the narrowly epistemological context does not seem to me to be a very important problem.

("knowing how . . ."), and knowledge of persons ("knowing whom . . .").[44] These three are related, but they are not identical with one another. Knowing a person involves knowing facts about him (contrary to some "personalistic" theologians), but one can know facts about someone without knowing him, and vice versa. A political scientist may know many facts about the president of the United States without being able to say that he "knows" the president. The White House gardener may know far fewer facts and yet be able to say that he knows the president quite well.

All three kinds of knowledge are mentioned in Scripture, and all are important theologically. A believer must know certain facts about God—who He is, what He has done. Note the importance of the "historical prologue" within the covenant structure: the Lord begins the covenant document by telling what He has done. The covenant begins in grace. Those who disparage the importance of factual knowledge in Christianity are in fact disparaging the message of grace (cf. Ps. 100:3; Rom. 3:19; 6:3; 1 John 2:3; 3:2—random examples of factual knowledge that is vital to the believer). Furthermore, a believer is one who learns new skills—how to obey God, how to pray, how to love—as well as skills in which believers differ from one another—preaching, evangelizing, diaconal service, and so forth (cf. Matt. 7:11; Col. 4:6; 1 Tim. 3:5). But (and perhaps most importantly) Christian knowledge is knowledge of a person. It is knowing God, Jesus Christ, and the Holy Spirit.[45]

Sometimes in the Scriptures, "knowing" a person refers mainly to knowing facts about him, but most often it means being involved with him either as a friend or as an enemy (cf. Gen. 29:5; Matt. 25:24; Acts 19:15; 1 Cor. 16:15; 1 Thess. 5:12. The common use of *know* to refer to sexual intercourse should also be noted at this point, e.g., Gen. 4:1). When Scripture speaks of God "knowing" men, generally the reference is not to factual knowledge at all (since it goes without saying that God knows the facts). In such contexts, *knowing* generally means "loving" or "befriending" (note Exod. 33:12, 17; Ps. 1:5f.; Jer. 1:5; Amos 3:2; Nahum 1:7;

44. Knowledge of things might be a fourth category. Often when we talk about knowing things (bananas, Switzerland, the price structure of the grain market), we are thinking about factual knowledge. Other times, or perhaps always to an extent, we are thinking of an acquaintance somewhat analogous to the knowledge of persons. I do not think it would be edifying to try to sort out those questions now.

45. Although the three kinds of knowledge are distinct, each involves the others. You cannot know a person without knowing some facts about him and having some ability to relate meaningfully to him, and so forth. One can, therefore, describe Christian knowledge under three "perspectives": as learning facts and mastering the implications and uses of those facts (Gordon Clark) or as developing skills in using facts in our relations with one another and with God or as learning to know God, in which context we learn facts and skills.

Matt. 25:12; John 10:14, 27). This is frequently an important exegetical point, especially in Romans 8:29. The statement there that God "foreknew" certain persons cannot mean that He knew that they would believe, and thus it cannot teach that predestination is based on God's foresight of man's autonomous choices. Rather, the verse teaches that salvation originates in God's sovereign knowledge (i.e., love) of His elect. Hence Scripture almost never speaks of God "knowing" an unbeliever; the only examples I can find of that (John 2:25; 5:42) clearly refer to factual knowledge.

Man's knowledge of God, then, is very similar to God's knowledge of man. To know Him is to be involved with Him as a friend or as an enemy. For the believer, to know Him is to love Him—hence the strong emphasis on obedience (as we have seen) as a constitutive aspect of the knowledge of God. Here, however, we wish to focus on the fact that the God whom we know and whom we love is of necessity present with us, and therefore our relationship with Him is a truly personal one. The intimacy of love assumes the present reality of the beloved. We can love someone at a distance but only if that person plays a significant, continuing role in our thoughts, decisions, and emotions and in that sense is near to us. But if God controls all things and stands as the ultimate authority for all of our decisions, then He confronts us at every moment; His power is manifest everywhere, and His Word makes a constant claim on our attention. He is the most unavoidable reality there is and the most intimate, since His control and authority extend to the deepest recesses of the soul. Because of the very comprehensiveness of His control and authority, we may not think of God as far away. (Earthly controllers and authorities seem far away precisely because their authority and control are so limited.) Thus God is not merely a controller or authority, He is also an intimate acquaintance.

The covenantal language of Scripture brings out this intimacy. God speaks to Israel using the second person singular, as if the whole nation were one person; God uses the language of "I and thou." He proclaims to His people blessings and curses, the mark of His continuing (priestly) presence. As the history of redemption progresses, the covenant relationship is described in terms of marriage (Hosea; Eph. 5; etc.), sonship (John 1:12; Rom. 8:14-17; etc.), and friendship (John 15:13-15).[46]

46. Some writers find great "progress" being made here, from legal-covenantal categories to intimate-personal ones. I, however, see these latter metaphors as the natural outworking of the intimacy already involved in the covenant relationship. What could be more intimate than the relationship assumed in Deuteronomy 6:5? The idea that law is necessarily something cold and impersonal stems from modern humanistic thinking, not from Scripture.

The sense of the believer doing all things not only to the glory of God but in God's presence (*coram deo*) has been a precious truth to Reformed people. God not only controls and commands, but in all of our experience He is, ultimately, the "one with whom we have to do." Nothing can be farther from the deterministic, impersonalistic, intellectualistic, unemotional brand of religion represented in the popular caricature of Calvinism.

In summary, "knowledge of God" essentially refers to a person's friendship (or enmity) with God. That friendship presupposes knowledge in other senses—knowledge of facts about God, knowledge of skills in righteous living, and so forth. It therefore involves a covenantal response of the whole person to God in all areas of life, either in obedience or in disobedience. It involves, most focally, a knowledge of God's lordship—of His control, His authority, and His present reality.

EXCURSUS: WISDOM AND TRUTH

The biblical concepts of wisdom and truth are similar to the concept of knowledge in important ways. Although *knowledge* broadly designates the covenantal friendship (or enmity) between God and man, *wisdom* focuses on the element of know-how, or skill. A wise man is one who has the ability to *do* something—not just a factual knowledge of something but also the ability to *use* his knowledge correctly. That use may be in various areas, for example, Bezalel the son of Uri was "filled with the Spirit of God and with wisdom" (NIV reads "skill," "ability") to do the craft work for the tabernacle (Exod. 31:1-6). But more often, *wisdom* has a moral-religious connotation, so that we may define it as "the skill of godly living" (cf. esp. James 3:13-17). We can see, then, how wisdom, like knowledge, involves an understanding of God's lordship as well as actual obedience to the Lord (Prov. 9:10; cf. 1:7).[47] We can also see that wisdom, like knowledge, is a gift of God's grace and has a trinitarian origin: God the Father is the source of wisdom, in the Son are hidden all the treasures of wisdom, and the Spirit is the Spirit of wisdom. Wisdom is communicated by the Word and by the Spirit (cf. Exod. 28:3; 31:3; Deut. 34:9; Prov. 3:19; 8:30; 28:7-9; 30:5; Jer. 8:8f.; Acts 6:3; 1 Cor. 1:24, 30; 2:6-16; Col. 2:3; 3:16; 2 Tim. 3:15).

Truth is used in various senses in Scripture. We may distinguish a "metaphysical" sense (the true is the absolute, the complete, as opposed to the

47. *Wisdom* and *knowledge* are nearly synonymous in Proverbs and in other biblical wisdom literature.

relative, the partial, etc.—John 6:32, 35; 15:1; 17:3; Heb. 8:21; 1 John 5:20), an "epistemological" sense (the true is the correct—Deut. 17:4; 1 Kings 10:6; Eph. 4:24—i.e., "propositional truth"), and an "ethical" sense ("walking in" truth, i.e., doing right—Neh. 9:33; Pss. 15:2; 25:5; 26:3; 51:6 [note the parallel with wisdom]; 86:11; Ezek. 18:9; Hos. 4:1; John 3:20f.; Gal. 5:7; 1 John 1:6).[48] Truth, like knowledge and wisdom, comes by grace, by trinitarian communication, by Word and by Spirit (Dan. 10:21; John 8:31f.; 14:6; 17:17 [cf. vv. 6, 8; 2 Sam. 7:28; Ps. 119:142, 160]; Rom. 2:8; 2 Cor. 4:2; 6:7; Gal. 2:5; Eph. 1:13; Col. 1:5; 2 Thess. 2:12; 1 Tim. 3:15; Jas. 3:14; 1 Peter 1:22; 2 Peter 2:2; Rev. 6:10; 15:3; 16:7).

Although the biblical concepts of wisdom and truth are not precisely synonymous with "knowledge," they corroborate certain emphases made in our discussion of knowledge. Although both wisdom and truth are significantly related to propositional or conceptual knowledge, neither can be fully explained by propositional categories. Being "wise" or "knowing the truth" in the fullest biblical sense is not merely knowing facts about theology (nor is it a kind of mystical knowledge devoid of propositional content). Wisdom and truth, like knowledge, are given by God's grace and in the deepest senses of the terms, involve obedience and intimate, personal involvement between Creator and creature.

C. THE UNBELIEVER'S KNOWLEDGE

We are now faced with a problem. If *knowledge* in Scripture not only involves factual knowledge but also is (1) a gift of God's redemptive grace, (2) an obedient covenantal response to God, and (3) a loving, personal involvement, how can the unbeliever be said to know God at all? We have seen that according to Scripture, the unbeliever does know God (Rom. 1:21), but how can that be?

Well, Scripture also tells us that unbelievers do not know God (cf. the passages listed earlier). Evidently, then, there is a sense (or senses) in which they do know Him and a sense (or senses) in which they do not. We now must try to sort out some of these distinctions.

48. Regarding this threefold distinction, see John Murray, *Principles of Conduct* (Grand Rapids: Wm. B. Eerdmans Pub. Co., 1957), 123-28, and Vos, *Biblical Theology*, 382f.

(1) SIMILARITIES

In important ways, the unbeliever's knowledge is like the believer's. Surveying the outline of the last section, we can say (1) that God is knowable but incomprehensible to believer and unbeliever alike and (2) that in both cases the knowledge can be described as covenant knowledge. Both believer and unbeliever know *about* God's control, authority, and presence. The knowledge of the unbeliever, like that of the believer, is a knowledge that God is Lord (cf. passages mentioned earlier). And both forms of knowledge are *subject to* God's control, authority, and presence. The unbeliever, like the believer, knows God only on God's initiative, though he refuses to obey that authority. His knowledge is not only a knowledge about God, but a knowledge of God himself (Rom. 1:21). Indeed, it is a confrontation with God as present, though he experiences the presence of God's wrath (Rom. 1:18), not His redemptive blessing (cf. Exod. 14:4, where the Egyptians' knowledge of God occurs in the midst of the experience of judgment).[49]

(2) DIFFERENCES

The essential differences may be derived from the preceding discussion. The unbeliever's knowledge entails (1) a lack of saving grace, (2) a refusal to obey, and (3) a lack of redemptive blessing. But we must be more specific. How do these differences affect the consciousness of the unbeliever and his expression of that consciousness as he lives, makes decisions, argues, philosophizes, theologizes, and so forth? Let us examine various possibilities.

a. *Revelation Makes No Impact on the Unbeliever*

We might be tempted to say that the unbeliever's "knowledge" consists simply in the fact that he is surrounded by God's revelation, though that revelation makes no impact whatever on his consciousness. On such a view, we could certainly say that in a sense God has revealed himself to everyone. We could also speak emphatically about the effects of depravity on knowledge. So depraved is the sinner that he banishes God from his mind altogether; God's revelation has absolutely no impact on his thinking.[50] I find this view inadequate for the following reasons. (1) According

49. Of course, the unbeliever does experience the blessing of God's "common grace" (Matt. 5:45ff.; Acts 14:17ff.)—God's nonredemptive kindnesses by which He seeks to draw men lovingly toward repentance and faith.

50. In some translations of the Bible, Romans 1:28 suggests something like the following.

to this view, we could speak of God's revealing himself to fallen man, but we certainly could not speak of fallen man's having knowledge of God. But Scripture portrays unbelievers as knowing God. (2) Scripture represents unbelievers, and even devils, as constantly interacting with God's revelation. God is not only revealed to them but "clearly seen" (Rom. 1:20). They "know" God (Rom. 1:21), and they "exchange the truth for a lie" (Rom. 1:23, 25). But how can one exchange something that has never entered his mind? According to Scripture, unbelievers also speak truly of God, as we will see.

b. *The Unbeliever Ought to Know but Doesn't*

Jim S. Halsey (mentioned earlier in another connection) suggests in his book *For a Time Such as This*[51] that the unbeliever ought to know from nature alone that the true God is the Creator of the world, that His providence is over all His works, and so forth. He adds, "The above, it should be carefully noted, are conclusions to which every man ought to come; it is not to be implied, however, that any man actually can come to them. . . . 'Ought' does not necessarily imply ability."[52] Halsey's point is that the unbeliever's knowledge is only potential, not actual, that though he is obligated to know, he does not actually know. Van Til also talks that way on occasion, but I am convinced that such expressions are inadequate. Essentially, it is the same position as *a* above—the unbeliever does not really know; he is merely obligated to know. But Scripture says that the unbeliever does know, as we have seen. Furthermore, neither Halsey nor Van Til holds this position consistently, as we will see.

c. *He Knows God "Psychologically"*

On page 65 of his book, Halsey suggests another formulation: the unbeliever knows God in a "psychological," not in an "epistemological," sense.[53] It is a bit unclear to me what Halsey means by "epistemological," but in the following pages he repeatedly relates it to "interpretative activity." Thus, he seems to argue, the unbeliever knows God, but his inter-

The unbeliever does not want to have God in his consciousness, and so his consciousness is devoid of God. However, *epignosei* in Greek means much more than "consciousness," and in any case the rejection envisaged in the verse is a deliberate act that presupposes at one point a knowledge of God; the unbeliever is rejecting something he knows.

51. Nutley, N.J.: Presbyterian and Reformed Pub. Co., 1976.

52. Ibid., 63.

53. Van Til uses some of the same terminology, as Halsey points out, but I'm not sure he uses it as Halsey does. In any case, it is clear (see below) that Van Til (in contrast with Halsey) does not regard this distinction as a definitive solution to the problem.

pretative activity always denies God. However, (1) this view contradicts *b*, which Halsey apparently also wishes to hold. According to this view, the unbeliever's knowledge is not only potential, but actual, even if only "psychological." In his book, Halsey shows no awareness of any problem here. (2) What does it mean to speak of a knowledge in man ("psychological") that is completely devoid of "interpretation." Does not all knowledge involve "interpretation" in some sense? Does not knowledge necessarily involve an "interpretation" of what is known? I confess that I do not find this view to be intelligible.

d. *He Represses His Knowledge Psychologically*

Some students of Reformed apologetics have been tempted to think of the matter in somewhat Freudian terms, that is, the unbeliever "represses" his knowledge to such an extent that it becomes wholly subconscious or unconscious.[54] This view, unlike the others, presents a somewhat intelligible sense in which we can speak of an unbeliever's "knowledge" but at the same time regard his depravity as so radical that it banishes the knowledge of God from "consciousness." The problem here, however, is that Scripture speaks of unbelievers—and even devils!—as (at least sometimes) conscious of the truth and willing to affirm it (see Matt. 23:3f.; Mark 1:24; Luke 4:34; 8:28; John 3:2; Acts 16:17; James 2:19).

e. *His Agreements With Believers Are "Purely Formal"*

Every now and then, Van Til refers to "agreements" between believers and unbelievers as being "purely formal," that is, the two use the same words to express utterly different meanings.[55] Certainly situations like this do arise, for example when heretical theologians use *revelation* to refer to their own religious insights. Clearly this is one way in which unbelief suppresses the truth. It would be wrong, however, to generalize and to say that all agreements between unbelievers and Scripture have this character. (1) If that were true, the unbeliever could not be said to have knowledge; his "knowledge" would be only apparent. If I say "2 + 2 = 4" but mean by it "2 + 2 = 7," I have not expressed any knowledge, only error. But without genuine knowledge, Romans 1 tells us, the unbeliever could excuse himself. (2) Scripture does not present the statements of Satan or of unbe-

54. Van Til occasionally speaks this way. Note his frequent refrain that the unbeliever knows the truth "deep down," and sometimes his language is even more psychologistic than that. However, I do not think this representation is consistent with other things that Van Til says, nor do I think it is at all central to his perspective.

55. Cf. Van Til, *Introduction*, 92, 113; *Defense of the Faith* (Philadelphia: Presbyterian and Reformed Pub. Co., 1955, 1967), 59.

lievers as only *formally* true (see the list under *d* above). Such statements are an artful mix of truth and error. (3) If unbelievers spoke only formal truth, then communication with them would be impossible; a Christian could not speak to them of trees because to them *tree* would not refer to trees. (4) I doubt that there is any such thing as a *purely* formal agreement. Even the decision to "use the same words" in a conversation (about trees or God) is a decision that presupposes more than a formal knowledge of truth. Even when the modern theologian uses *revelation* to refer to his own religious insights, he shows that he knows something about his religious insights, about the potentialities of *revelation*, and about the truth that he artfully seeks to avoid.

f. *His "Knowledge" Is Always Falsified by Its Context*

Or should we say that the unbeliever accepts propositions that are true in isolation but falsified in the context he supplies for them?[56] For example, the unbeliever says truly that "the rose is red," but the statement becomes false when seen in the unbeliever's overall framework of thought, that is, "the not-created-by-the-triune-God rose is red because of chance." And since statements are properly understood "in context," rather than "out of context," we can say that properly understood, all the unbeliever's statements are false. Well, it is true that a normally true statement can be used to communicate falsehood when put into a false context. And it is certainly true that the antitheistic framework (which every unbeliever adopts) is a false context. But the idea that true sentences used as part of a false system thereby become false themselves is a kind of idealistic theory of language that has no Christian basis and would be rejected by almost all linguists, including idealist ones! We may legitimately assert that unbelievers do sometimes repress the truth by trying to integrate it into a comprehensive framework that is false, but (as in *e*) we should not generalize so much that we say that all unbelievers always do that. To say that (even accepting the questionable linguistic premises) would be to deny to the unbeliever anything that could legitimately be called "knowledge."[57]

g. *His Knowledge Only Exists When He Is Unreflective*

Somewhat related to the above (and to *c*) is Van Til's willingness to say that unbelievers speak truth when they are unreflective but not in their

56. Cf. Van Til, *Introduction*, 26.

57. Thus when Van Til says that the unbeliever's knowledge is "true as far as it goes," we should not use that as a pretext for jumping into an idealist theory of language that, as I understand him, Van Til repudiates.

"systems of thought."[58] There is some point to this. Typically, non-Christian philosophers seek to use their philosophies to articulate and to inculcate their opposition to the truth; they seek to make their unbelief plausible, to show how the facts are best dealt with on an unbelieving basis. Since they tend to devote more effort and energy into suppressing the truth in their theoretical work than in their practical life, one would expect that they would be more off guard in practical situations, that they would be more inclined then unwittingly to acknowledge God. Well, I think this is usually the case, but certainly this is nothing more than a rough-and-ready generalization. We have no basis for denying exceptions to this rule, and we certainly have no justification for locating here the basic difference between believing and unbelieving knowledge. Would anyone suggest that an unbelieving philosopher is *necessarily* less depraved in his personal than in his professional life? And if he knows any truth at all, how can we claim that such knowledge will not influence his scholarship, as it influences his ordinary life? Scripture certainly never draws any line of this sort between life and theory. On the contrary, in Scripture thinking is part of life and is subject to the same moral and religious influences that rule the rest of life.

h. *He Doesn't Believe Enough Propositions*

Gordon H. Clark, in his *Religion, Reason and Revelation*[59] (87-110) and in the *Johannine Logos*[60] (69-90), seeks to define saving faith as assent to certain propositions. He rejects the traditional Reformation position that faith as "trust" (*fiducia*) is more than "assent." An unbeliever, then, is simply one who has failed to assent to the requisite number of propositions. The devils in James 2:19, Clark argues, believe that God is one but fail to believe other propositions and therefore are lost. Clark is willing to describe this position as a form of "intellectualism," and so it is. We should not forget, however, Clark's strong insistence that the will is very much involved in assent and that in fact it is unwise to make any sharp distinction between will and intellect. Will is active in all intellectual acts, and vice versa. Furthermore, Clark's notion of "assent" is a robust one. To assent, in his view, is not merely to have ideas "flitting about in the brain," as Calvin liked to say, but to accept a proposition wholeheartedly

58. In a student paper, I criticized Van Til for claiming that the unbeliever "knew nothing truly." He wrote in the margins several times that in his view the ignorance of unbelievers is focused "in their system," cf. Van Til, *Introduction*, 81-84, 104.

59. Philadelphia: Presbyterian and Reformed Pub. Co., 1961.

60. Nutley, N.J.: Presbyterian and Reformed Pub. Co., 1972; cf. Gordon H. Clark, *Faith and Saving Faith* (Jefferson, Md.: Trinity Foundation, 1983).

enough to act on it. Thus Clark is not blind to the scriptural connection between knowledge and obedience. Although his view has a much more intellectualistic cast than the more traditional one, we could not seriously maintain that Clark's "assent" is less rich than the Reformation *fiducia*. My problem with Clark's view, rather, is that it overlooks some complications in the *psychology of belief*.

(i) Clark does recognize at one point that beliefs can be more or less strong, but this principle plays little role in his analysis. Generally speaking, for Clark either one believes a proposition or one does not, and the strength of that belief does not enter the analysis. But the question of relative strength of belief is quite relevant to our present concerns. A relatively weak belief may have very little influence on conduct and thus be far from the biblical *fiducia*. For example, a man may know that his son has left skates on the driveway but will give that knowledge so little attention that he trips over the skates and falls. But if that is the case, then surely faith must be analyzed in terms not only of assent but also of *strength of assent*. Merely to speak of assent here will not give us the kind of wholehearted commitment to the truth that Clark advocates. And I rather suspect that this is part of the reason why the Reformers were not satisfied to define faith as assent.

(ii) Once we recognize the importance of discussing the strength of belief in this connection, it becomes easier for us to see how a person can have *conflicting* beliefs. Often a person will believe inconsistent groups of propositions, and he must be taught that these beliefs are indeed inconsistent. The most relevant example here is the case of self-deception. Someone knows that roulette is a losing proposition, but he somehow persuades himself that this is not true, at least for him, right now. And yet "deep down inside," he continues to know the truth. He believes it, yet does not believe it. The situation is paradoxical, and the psychology of it is difficult to construe, yet it happens all the time.[61] It becomes a bit more intelligible when we construe the two beliefs in terms of their relative strengths. The man's self-deceptive conviction that he can beat the odds governs his conduct up to a point. It keeps him at the tables. But after the evening is over and he surveys his losses, he may "wake up," he may reprove himself, since he "knew all along" that the odds were against him. And perhaps even at the roulette wheel he has misgivings. So the fact is that both beliefs, contradictory as they are, govern his actions, attitudes, and thoughts

61. For an excellent analysis of self-deception by a Christian philosopher and theologian, see the (unpublished) doctoral dissertation on the subject by Greg L. Bahnsen (University of Southern California, Philosophy Department).

to some extent. Thus faith must involve not only assent, and that of a certain strength, but also the relative absence of contrary assents. Unbelief, then, may be compatible with some degree of assent to the truth of Scripture, perhaps even to all the truth of Scripture, provided that this assent is a weak assent, coupled with contrary assents that hold dominion over the person. (Cf. Rom. 6:14. The difference between believer and unbeliever is not that the believer is sinless but that sin has no "dominion" over him.)

(iii) The necessity of this sort of analysis is especially apparent with regard to the devils' knowledge (James 2:19). On Clark's view, the devils' knowledge is defective because they believe certain propositions but not others. But what propositions do they fail to believe? That God is sovereign? That Christ is divine? Speculations of this sort are rather implausible because in Scripture the devils are presented as highly intelligent beings who, generally speaking, know more about God's plans than human beings do. It makes much more sense to think of them as believing and disbelieving at the same time, with the disbelief in control of their behavior. Furthermore, the unbelief of the devils is surely not due to a mere lack of intelligence or information. It is a culpable disbelief. But what is a culpable disbelief if not a disbelief of what one *knows* to be true? The same, indeed, is the case with the human unbeliever. Thus unbelief is not merely lack of assent to certain propositions but lack of assent of a certain strength, coupled with contrary assent(s) of a certain strength. It is a state of mental (and therefore practical) conflict. It is belief in the truth, dominated by belief in a lie. Therefore it is irrationality, foolishness, stupidity, to use language warranted by Scripture. Let us not seek to make Satan wiser than he is; he, too, is a fool.

And there is a further question. Is it legitimate to analyze faith in terms of assent, as long as we add comments about the strength of assent and about contrary assents? Clark's analysis does, as we have seen, do justice to the biblical conjunction of faith (knowledge) and obedience. We could, perhaps, also argue that he does justice to the element of friendship (knowledge of the person) that we have found to be so central. Although friendship is not reducible to factual knowledge, it is certainly true that one who wholeheartedly believes all the propositions of God's Word will be a friend of God. Assent, obedience, and friendship—you cannot have one without the others. Since each implies the others, any one of them could be used to define faith. So "assent" is adequate (with the qualifications made earlier), but it is neither the only possible analysis nor necessarily the best. The intellectualistic connotations of *assent*, which Clark rightly finds so valuable in combating the antitruth mentality of our day, also tend to mislead people into thinking that our relation with God is essentially theoretical or academic in character. The term, as Clark uses it, does not warrant such confusion, but it might cause it. And more seriously, Clark does not seem to recognize the fact that other perspectives (e.g., obedience, friendship) are at least equally adequate ways of characterizing faith. These are the concepts that are reflected in the term *fiducia*. Thus even if (as Clark says) faith is not something "more" than assent, at least it certainly has aspects other than the intellectual aspect suggested by *assent*. And we can see, then, why the Reformers felt the need for something "more."

i. *His Knowledge Is "Intellectual" but Not "Ethical"*

We move on to another possible analysis. Why shouldn't we simply say that the unbeliever can know God in an intellectual, but not in an ethical, sense? That is to say, he can know plenty of propositions about God, but he does not act on them, does not obey God. That is the sort of analysis favored by Reformed thinkers like John H. Gerstner[62] who seek to do justice to the doctrine of total depravity and at the same time to maintain that there is no fundamental difference between Christian and non-Christian reasoning. The difference, they would maintain, is ethical, not epistemological. This position certainly evokes a biblical picture. Scripture often portrays unbelievers as those who know but fail to act properly on that knowledge (see Matt. 23:2f.; Luke 12:47f.; Rom. 1:18-21; 2 Thess. 1:8; James 2:19f.). But Scripture, as I understand it, does not permit such a sharp dichotomy between the ethical and the epistemological. Knowledge, as we have seen, is a part of life, and therefore must be achieved and maintained in a way that honors God. That is to say that there is an ethics of knowledge. There are right and wrong ways to think and learn. And if depravity is total, if it extends to all areas of life, then the unbeliever is one who *thinks* wrongly. And when people think wrongly, they come to wrong conclusions. Their thinking is foolish and stupid, to use biblical language. "Israel does not know," says God in exasperation (Isa. 1:3). Disobedience itself, we must say, is an ignorant, stupid response to God, and stupid even in an "intellectual" sense. If God is who He is and we are who we are, then it makes no sense at all to disobey. Renowned intellectual unbelievers are truly intelligent in the sense that they make extremely sophisticated and ingenious use of their mental powers, but they are stupid in that they reject the obvious.

62. See R. C. Sproul, John H. Gerstner, and A. Lindsley, *Classical Apologetics* (Grand Rapids: Zondervan Publishing House, 1984).

Having said all that, I must agree with Gerstner that an unbeliever may know all sorts of true propositions about God. The trouble is, though, that as part of his disobedience he will also advocate many false propositions about God. In fact, he will advocate propositions that contradict the true propositions that he holds. In his mind there will be "conflicting assents" (cf. *h*, above). And the habits of thought that lead to this falsehood must be challenged head-on. The biblical picture is authentic. Unbelievers are people who "know but fail to act," and part of that "failure to act" is a failure to think as God requires.

j. *My Formulation*

So we come to the analysis that I consider the most adequate. Let's take it in several steps. (1) All unbelievers know enough truths about God to be without excuse and may know many more, as many as are available to man. There is no limit to the number of true, revealed propositions about God that an unbeliever can know. (2) But unbelievers lack the obedience and friendship with God that is essential to "knowledge" in the fullest biblical sense—the knowledge of the believer. Yet at every moment, they are personally involved with God as an enemy. Thus their knowledge of Him is more than merely propositional. (3) The unbeliever's disobedience has intellectual implications. First, it is itself a stupid response to God's revelation. (4) Second, disobedience is a kind of lying. When we disobey God, we testify to others and to ourselves that God's Word is untrue.[63] (5) Third, disobedience involves fighting[64] the truth—fighting its dissemination, opposing its application to one's own life, to the lives of others, and to society. Sinners fight the truth in many ways. They (a) simply deny it (Gen. 3:4; John 5:38; Acts 19:9), (b) ignore it (2 Peter 3:5), (c) psychologically repress it, (d) acknowledge the truth with the lips but deny it in deed (Matt. 23:2f.), (e) put the truth into a misleading context (Gen. 3:5, 12, 13; Matt. 4:6), and (f) use the truth to oppose God. We should not fall into the trap of assuming that all sinners always use the same strategy. They do not always deny the truth in word or repress it into their subconscious. (6) Fourth, lying and fighting the truth involve affirmations of falsehoods. We must not assume that every sentence uttered by an unbeliever will be false;

63. I take *katechon* in Romans 1:18 to mean "hindering," "holding back" (cf. John Murray, *The Epistle to the Romans* [Grand Rapids: Wm. B. Eerdmans Pub. Co., 1960]). The *en* may be instrumental: "hindering the truth by his unrighteousness." The point is that disobedience itself is an attack on the truth. It is not only "intellectual" unbelievers who attack the truth of Christianity. "Practical" unbelievers do too, by living in disobedience. Their very disobedience is a lie, an assault on the truth.

64. I.e., "hindering."

unbelievers can fight the truth in ways other than by uttering falsehoods. Yet disobedience always involves the acceptance of atheism, whether so stated in words or merely acted on in life (there is no significant difference between denying God's existence and acting as if God does not exist). (7) Fifth, these falsehoods may conflict with true beliefs that the sinner holds. At some level, every unbeliever holds conflicting beliefs, for example, God is Lord and God is not Lord. (8) Sixth, these falsehoods affect every area of life, including the epistemological. Thus the unbeliever has false notions even about how to reason—notions that may conflict with true notions that he also holds. (9) Seventh, the believer and the unbeliever differ epistemologically in that for the believer the truth is dominant over the lie, and for the unbeliever vice versa. It is not always clear which is dominant, which is to say that we do not have infallible knowledge of another's heart. (10) Finally, the unbeliever's goal is an impossible one—to destroy the truth entirely, to replace God with some alternative deity. Because the goal is impossible, the task is self-frustrating (see Ps. 5:10; Prov. 18:7; Jer. 2:19; Luke 19:22; Rom. 8:28; 9:15f.). The unbeliever is condemned out of his own mouth for he cannot help but affirm the truth that he opposes. And because the unbeliever's views are false, even his limited success is possible only because God allows it (see Job 1:12; Isa. 10:5-19). Adding to the fact that the unbeliever frustrates himself, God also frustrates him, restraining him from accomplishing his purposes (Gen. 11:7) and using him to accomplish God's purposes instead (Ps. 76:10; Isa. 45:1f.; Rom. 9:17). Thus the unbeliever's efforts accomplish good in spite of himself.

k. *A Disclaimer*

The last paragraph represents the most adequate view of the matter that I know of. Yet the question remains a very mysterious one. Scripture says that the unbeliever knows and that he does not know. Scripture does not give us an epistemological elucidation in as many terms; that elucidation must be drawn carefully out of what Scripture says about other matters. And much more work remains to be done before we will have a formulation that is credible to the church (even the Reformed churches) generally. Van Til is at his best in his *Introduction to Systematic Theology* (24-27) where he admits the difficulty of the questions (something he does not often do) and rests content with a description of the natural man as "a mixture of truth with error" (27). I will continue to assume the truth of the analysis under *j* above, but I would not advise anyone to be dogmatic about the details. Certainly they should not be used as tests of orthodoxy.

(3) The Logic of Unbelief

Having surveyed the similarities and differences between believing and unbelieving knowledge of God, we shall now examine the general structure of unbelieving thought. What does the unbeliever believe? Well, obviously unbelievers differ among themselves about many things. But is there anything they all have in common? Yes, they all disbelieve! So we ask: What are the implications for knowledge of unbelief in the God of Scripture? Does that unbelief in and of itself impose any structure on a person's thoughts?

If the biblical God does not exist, there are two alternatives: either there is no god at all, or something other than the biblical God is god. On the one hand, if there is no god at all, then all is chance, all thinking is futile, and all ethical judgments are null and void. I shall therefore call that the irrationalist alternative. Irrationalism results not only when the existence of any god is denied but also when a god is affirmed and yet thought to be so distant or mysterious (or both) that he can have no practical involvement with the world. Irrationalism, parasitically, lives off of certain truths: that man is small, that the mind is limited, that God is far above us and incomprehensible. Thus irrationalism often enters theology masquerading as a respect for God's transcendence. We therefore described this position earlier as a "non-Christian view of transcendence."

On the other hand, if the unbeliever chooses to deify something in the world, something finite, then a kind of rationalism results. Man's mind either is the new god or is considered competent to discover it autonomously, which is the same thing. This is what we earlier described as a "non-Christian view of immanence," and it too masquerades as biblical truth, trading on biblical language about the covenant nearness of God, about His solidarity with the world.

Both rationalism and irrationalism are futile and self-defeating, as sin must always be. If irrationalism is true, then it is false. If all thinking is the product of chance, then how can it be trusted even to formulate an irrationalism? Rationalism flounders on the truth that is obvious to everyone: the human mind is not autonomous, not suited to be the final criterion of all truth. We are limited. The rationalist can defend his position, then, only by limiting his rationalism to certain truths of which he thinks there is no question—that we exist, that we think, and so forth. Then he seeks to deduce all other truth from those statements and to deny the truthfulness of anything that cannot be so deduced. But the result of this is that the mind turns out to know only itself or, more precisely, to know only its thinking. Thought is thought of thinking. Only that can be known for certain. Once some more specific content is specified, certainty disappears. Thus the consistent rationalist will deny that there is anything, ultimately, except "pure thought," "pure being," and so forth. All else is illusion (but how is that illusion to be explained!?). But what is a "pure thought" that is not a thought of something? Does that idea have any meaning at all? It is a pure blank. The knowledge of which rationalism boasts turns out to be a knowledge of . . . nothing!

Thus in the end, rationalism and irrationalism, so contrary to one another in mood and style, turn out to be identical. Rationalism gives us a perfect knowledge—of nothing. Irrationalism leaves us ignorant—of everything. Both are self-refuting for neither can give an intelligible account of itself. The irrationalist cannot consistently affirm his irrationalism. The rationalist, similarly, cannot affirm his rationalism; he can affirm only "pure thought," without specifying any content to it.

And so it is not surprising that rationalists and irrationalists borrow ideas from one another to avoid the destructive consequences of their own positions. The rationalist, when he seeks to get some content into his "pure being," resorts to irrationalism. The irrationalist can assert his irrationalism only on a rationalist basis—the basis of his own autonomy.

Thus these positions destroy themselves and one another, and yet they also need one another. They provide many tools for the Christian apologist, and it is quite proper for the Christian apologist to confront the rationalist with his dependence on irrationalism, and vice versa and to show how each position is self-destructive. But of course, unless this destructiveness is replaced by the truth, our witness will be no help.

CHAPTER TWO

God and the World

A. THE COVENANT LAW

So far most of this book has dealt with God as the object of human knowledge. In this and the following sections, we will continue to consider "the objects of knowledge" by discussing God's law, the world, and ourselves as objects of knowledge.

The present section is somewhat redundant because we have already discussed the knowledge of God's authority, and there is no important difference between knowing God's authority and knowing God's law. Indeed in an important sense, the Word of God (and hence the law, a form of the Word) is divine. God's speech has divine attributes (Gen. 18:14; Pss. 19:7ff.; 119:7, 86, 89, 129, 137, 140, 142, 160; Isa. 55:11; Luke 1:37; John 17:17), functions as an object of worship (Pss. 9:2; 34:3; 56:4, 10; 68:4; 119:120, 161f.; 138:2; Isa. 66:5), and is called divine (John 1:1; Rom. 10:6-8; cf. Deut. 30:11ff.).[1] Thus we cannot know God without knowing His Word, and we cannot know the Word without knowing God.

Still, I have some systematic reasons for including here a special section on knowing the covenant law.[2] To know God's authority, control, and

1. I argue this point, and other points in this chapter, at length in my *Doctrine of the Word of God*, which I hope to publish eventually.

2. There has been some discussion recently of the fact that *Torah* in the Old Testament is often, at least, better translated "instruction" than "law." Some take this fact as justification for relaxing the traditional emphasis in Reformed theology on the *normativity* of God's commands, the requirement of absolute obedience. In reply we may note the following. (1) Whatever we may say about *Torah*, we must also do justice to that great redundant collection of other "norm-terms" in Scripture: "statutes," "commandments," "testimonies," and so on

presence, involves knowledge of His law, His world, and ourselves. This triad deserves some analysis. To know God is to know His law. God himself necessarily acts as law to all being other than himself. To be Lord is to be the giver and ultimate enforcer of ultimate law. Thus Scripture speaks of God's nature as word, as name, as light. To obey the law is to obey God himself. God's law, therefore, is divine—divine in authority, power, eternity, and ultimacy. We cannot know God without knowing Him as law. God's law, then, is God himself; God himself is law to His creation. And that law is also revealed to us through creaturely media: nature, history, conscience, theophany, prophecy, Scripture. The law in these "forms" is no less divine than in its essential identity with God.

Knowing God, therefore, involves knowing His law and obeying it. To know God (in the "fullest" sense) is to know God obediently, to know Him as He wants to be known. And there are divine laws that govern knowledge. The obedient believer is one who counts the Word of God as the surest truth he knows, as his "presupposition," because the deepest commitment of his heart is to serve the God of the Word. The unbeliever is one who rejects that presupposition, though also holding it after a fashion (see above). The commitment of his heart is to oppose God, and so he seeks to escape his responsibility to obey any scriptural law, including the norms for knowledge. But he cannot succeed. Indeed, he cannot even attack the law without assuming its truth, and thus his thinking is muddled.

Therefore it is possible and useful to regard epistemology as a branch of ethics, though this is not the only way to classify epistemology. (Different classifications have value for different purposes; there is no one "right" classification.) Ethics, we may say, deals with the norms, or laws, for human life in general. Epistemology deals with the norms that govern thought. By seeing epistemology as a branch of ethics, we remind ourselves in the most vivid way that knowing is not autonomous; it is subject to God's authority, as is all of human life. This procedure also reminds us that knowing, thinking, theorizing, and so forth are indeed parts of human life as a whole. Although that point seems obvious, often we fail to consider that theory is part of practice, that thinking is one kind of doing, that knowing is one kind of achievement. Often we are inclined to put "epistemological" activities into some special kind of category, wherein they furnish the norms for all the rest of life and are themselves subject to no

(see, e.g., Ps. 119). (2) Deuteronomy 4:1-14; 6:1-9; 8:1-9, and many other passages make it clear that God's Word (even understood as "instruction") demands absolute obedience. In the New Testament, see Matthew 4:4; John 14:15, 21; Romans 4:16-25; 1 Corinthians 14:37f., and elsewhere. God's Word is *normative* instruction.

norm at all. No! Thought is not an activity that lifts us above the normal level of our humanity. It is an ordinary part of human life, subject to the same law as the rest of life, and no more autonomous than any other human activity. Indeed, I will show that far from determining the whole course of human life, thought is as dependent on our other activities as they are on it.

Epistemology, then, analyzes the norms for belief. It tells us what we ought to believe, how we ought to think, what justifications ought to be accepted. Those "oughts" are ethical oughts.

B. THE WORLD, OUR SITUATION

Knowing God involves knowing His world for several reasons. (1) Just as knowing God's authority involves knowing His law, so knowing God's control involves knowing His "mighty works," that is, His works of creation, providence, and redemption. The world itself is a mighty work of God, and the whole course of nature and history comes under that category as well. (2) Furthermore, we know God by means of the world. All of God's revelation comes through creaturely means, whether events, prophets, Scripture, or merely the human eye or ear. Thus we cannot know anything about God without knowing something about the world at the same time. Also, (3) God wants His people to apply His Word to their own situations, and this implies that He wants them to understand their own situations. We have a divine warrant for studying the world. To know God obediently, then, we must know something about the world as well.

The converse is also true. We cannot know the world without knowing God. As we have seen, God is "clearly seen" in the creation. Although God is not part of creation, He is part of the world in the sense of "our situation"; He is the most significant fact of our experience. He is present with and near to the world that He has made.

C. OURSELVES

On the first page of his *Institutes*, Calvin observes that the knowledge of God and the knowledge of self are interrelated. We might expect Calvin (as a good Calvinist!) to add that of course of the two, the knowledge of God "comes first." Remarkably, however, Calvin says instead that he doesn't know which comes first. This comment I take to be enormously perceptive. The best way to look at the matter is that neither knowledge of God nor knowledge of self is possible without knowledge of the other, and growth in one area is always accompanied by growth in the other. I cannot know myself rightly until I see myself as God's image: fallen, yet saved by grace. But also I cannot know God rightly until I seek to know Him as a creature, as a servant. The two kinds of knowledge, then, come simultaneously, and they grow together. The reason for this is not only that each of us is part of the "situation" that is essential to the knowledge of God (see above) but also the additional fact that each of us is made in God's image. We know God as He is reflected in ourselves. Furthermore, all the information we receive about God, through nature, Scripture, or whatever source, comes to us through our eyes, ears, minds, and brains—through ourselves. Sometimes we dream fondly of a "purely objective" knowledge of God—a knowledge of God freed from the limitations of our senses, minds, experiences, preparation, and so forth. But nothing of this sort is possible, and God does not demand that of us. Rather, He condescends to dwell in and with us, as in a temple. He identifies himself in and through our thoughts, ideas, and experiences. And that identification is clear; it is adequate for Christian certainty. A "purely objective" knowledge is precisely what we don't want! Such knowledge would presuppose a denial of our creaturehood and thus a denial of God and of all truth.

D. RELATIONSHIPS BETWEEN OBJECTS OF KNOWLEDGE

We have seen that knowledge of God involves (and is involved in) knowledge of His law, the world, and ourselves. It is also important to see that the latter three forms of knowledge are involved in one another because of their mutual coordination in God's plan.

(1) The Law and the World

a. *The Law Is Necessary to Understand the World*

All of our knowledge is subject to law, and so all knowledge of the world ("things," "facts") is subject to the norms of God's Word. The law itself is a fact—part of our experience that we must take careful account of—and it is a fact that governs our interpretations of other facts. Hypotheses or interpretations that on careful analysis are found to contradict Scripture can have no standing in Christian thought. In rejecting the law, the unbeliever inevitably misinterprets the facts.

b. *The World Is Necessary to Understand the Law*

God reveals His law through the world, through natural revelation, as we see in Romans 1:32 (in context). The law revealed in nature does not go beyond the law of Scripture; Scripture is sufficient to reveal God's will (2 Tim. 3:17). Yet through different media, those without Scripture do have access to essentially the same divine law as is found in Scripture.

But the world also helps us to understand the law in another sense. The law was designed to be used in the world. God revealed His law to be used, to be applied to the situations of human life. To use the law, some knowledge of the world is necessary. God commanded Adam not to take the fruit of the tree of the knowledge of good and evil. That command assumed considerable knowledge on Adam's part. It assumed that he knew what a tree was, the difference between fruit and leaves, how to eat a fruit, and so forth. None of that information was included in the divine command; God assumed that Adam had other means of obtaining that information. I doubt, in fact, if it would have been possible for all the relevant information to be specified in human language, even by the voice of God. If God had told Adam what a tree was, what a fruit was, what eating was, and so forth, it would still have been necessary for Adam to relate those definitions to his own experience, to recognize that in fact *this* object is a fruit. No matter how elaborate a linguistic explanation is, it is always the responsibility of the hearer to relate the explanation to the situation in which he is living and thus to understand the language. No one else can do it for him; no one else can understand language for someone else. Therefore any law will require knowledge of the world if it is to be properly applied. Thus the common "moral syllogism": Disobeying authorities is wrong, transgressing the speed limit is disobedience to the authorities, therefore transgressing the speed limit is wrong. To apply the commandment against disobeying authorities to the "situation" of the speed limit, we need extrabiblical knowledge.

I would even maintain that the *meaning* of the law is discerned in this process of application. Imagine two scholars discussing the eighth commandment. One claims that it forbids embezzlement. The other thinks he understands the commandment but can't see any application to embezzlement. Now we know that the first scholar is right. But must we not also say that the first scholar understands the *meaning* of the commandment better than the second? Knowing the meaning of a sentence is not merely being able to replace it with an equivalent sentence (e.g., replacing the Hebrew sentence with the English sentence "Thou shalt not steal"). An animal could be trained to do that. Knowing the meaning is being able to *use* the sentence, to understand its implications, its powers, its applications. Imagine someone saying that he understands the meaning of a passage of Scripture but doesn't know at all how to apply it. Taking that claim literally would mean that he could answer no questions about the text, recommend no translations into other languages, draw no implications from it, or explain none of its terms in his own words. Could we seriously accept such a claim? When one lacks knowledge of how to "apply" a text, his claim to know the "meaning" becomes an empty—meaningless—claim. Knowing the meaning, then, is knowing how to apply. The meaning of Scripture is its application.

The interesting result of that line of reasoning is that we need to know the world to understand the meaning of Scripture. Through study of the world, we come to a greater and greater knowledge of the meaning of the law. Adam was told to replenish the earth and subdue it. That "subduing," however, entailed a bewildering variety of tasks. From our vantage point, we can see that it entailed the development of hydroelectric power and cathode rays and miniaturized transistors. But Adam didn't know all that. The meaning of "subduing" would grow on him gradually. He would see a rock and ask, "How can I use this in subduing the earth?" He would study it, analyze it, and try various projects with it. Eventually, he would find a use for it and thus learn something more of the meaning of "subdue."

This need to gain extrabiblical knowledge to understand the Bible is not an onerous necessity. It is a natural, normal part of our task, and God expects us to do it. He expected Adam to get the information necessary to understand, and Scripture regularly demands its application to current issues. The Pharisees were reproved because they failed to apply the Old Testament Scriptures properly to events of their own time, namely the ministry of Jesus (cf. Matt. 16:3; 22:29; Luke 24:25; John 5:39f.; Rom. 15:4; 2 Tim. 3:16f.; 2 Peter 1:19-21).

Thus every fact tells us something about God's law. Everything we learn about eggs or petroleum or solar energy or cold fronts—all of this information shows us something of how we may glorify God in the use of His creation. It helps us exegete 1 Corinthians 10:31—and much more.

And now I can make an even more surprising statement: just as the law is a fact, so the facts are laws in a sense; they have normative force. Why? Because as we have seen, the facts determine the meaning of the laws. To discover the meanings of the facts is at the same time to discover the specific applications of the laws—applications that are as binding as the laws themselves. In studying the world, we discover in more and more detail what our obligations are. Or, to put it differently, the law itself commands us to live wisely—to live according to an understanding of reality. It commands us to be governed by the facts, to take account of what is. Thus the law *gives* to the facts a normative status.

To say all of this is not to break down the important distinction between scriptural and extrascriptural considerations. Only the former are infallible, divine norms. There is, in other words, an important difference between the Scriptures on the one hand and the reasoning by which we determine applications of Scripture on the other. We discover the applications through fallible means, but of course that is true with respect to all exegesis, all understanding of Scripture. But once we discover a true application of Scripture, that application is unconditionally binding. No one has the right to say, for example, "I won't steal, but I will embezzle, since the prohibition of embezzling is only an 'application'."

Knowing the world, then, involves knowing the law, and vice versa. God's laws are facts, and His facts are laws. Ultimately, knowing laws is the same thing as knowing facts. The two represent one process as seen from different "perspectives." If Scripture is applied to the world, and if the world is understood in the light of Scripture, then there will be no conflict between "facts" and "law." The two will be one.

c. *The Non-Christian Loses the Facts and the Law*

But what is true for the Christian is not true for the non-Christian. Lacking faith in the biblical God, non-Christian philosophers have regularly sought to find some other basis for certainty, often through "facts" or "law." As Van Til points out, many, especially in the empiricist tradition, have sought to find in "fact" a kind of bedrock on which the whole edifice of knowledge can be built. On the one hand, according to empiricists, all ideas about criteria, law, and norms must be verified on the basis of "fact." But then, what kind of "facts" are we talking about? Facts, apparently, that themselves are beyond all law, that we can discover without obeying any norms at all, and by which all norms can be judged. But such facts would be "brute" facts—facts devoid of any sense. On the other hand, the rationalist tradition recognizes that we cannot identify facts at all without presupposing some criteria of facticity. So the rationalists seek to find the "bedrock" in law—in those principles by which we identify and interpret the facts. But this "law," then, must be superior to all factual knowledge, and thus it cannot be known as a fact. Its meaning cannot be determined by facts, as is the case with the Christian view of law. The result is that this "law" becomes an empty shell, a principle with no applications, a form of words with no meaning. The problem in both cases is idolatry—an attempt to deify "fact" or "law." Once we try to make a god out of "fact," we lose factuality altogether. And once we try to make a god out of "law," we lose all normativity. The "factualist," in this case, is what we earlier called an "irrationalist"; the advocate of law is the "rationalist."

(2) THE WORLD AND THE SELF

a. *Self-Knowledge and Knowledge of the World Are Correlative*

Human beings are, first of all, creatures of God and therefore part of the "world." We are among the "facts" to be learned. And as part of that created system of facts, we come to know ourselves as we interact with other persons and things, especially with God and His Word but also with other creatures. It is hard to imagine what a "pure thought of the self"—a thought merely of the self and not of anything else besides—would be like. On the one hand, the self "in itself" is, like God, mysterious. We know ourselves in knowing other things. Every thought of a tree is a thought of me thinking of the tree. We know ourselves in seeing reflections of ourselves in mirrors, in hearing the sounds we make, in experiencing the effects of our decisions. But in important ways, the self is elusive. We can no more gaze upon the self itself than the eye can look directly at itself (without a mirror). We know ourselves by knowing the world.

On the other hand, the reverse is also true. We come to know the world by knowing ourselves. All knowledge, in a sense, is self-knowledge. Unlike God, of course, our knowledge is never absolutely self-attesting; our knowledge is attested, or validated, by God's prior knowledge. Furthermore, there is a sense in which God's self-knowledge is self-sufficient: He knows all things by knowing himself and His plans. He knows all things absolutely by knowing himself. But since we are not the creators and determiners of the world, that is not true of us. We know because someone outside of us—God—has given us revelation. Still, because we are God's image, there is a sense in which all knowledge is self-knowledge, even for us. All our information reaches us by our own faculties—our eyes, ears, brains, intuition, and so forth. To know a fact is to know something about the content of our own experience, our thinking, our capacity to understand.

And so we come to the famous problem of the "relation of the subject and object." Throughout the history of philosophy, this topic has caused all sorts of perplexities. It seems either that the self disappears into the world or the world disappears into the self ("solipsism"—the view that nothing exists except the self). Non-Christian philosophers have been utterly unsuccessful at maintaining a workable balance here. It seems either that the world is something utterly alien to the self, so alien that it can hardly be known or spoken of ("transcendence"), or that it is identical to the self, so that there is no world to speak of, only self ("immanence"). Some, in desperation, seek a special kind of knowledge that allegedly "transcends the subject-object distinction," but they are unable to state coherently what that knowledge is or how it is to be obtained. Their claim is essentially a claim to know the unknowable, to achieve, by a mystical leap, access to the transcendence that is unknowable by ordinary means.

The Christian does not entirely escape the difficulties involved in an adequate formulation of the subject-object distinction, but he knows by faith, by divine revelation, that he is not the only being in the universe. He is not divine and therefore cannot exist alone; something does exist beyond himself. He also knows that he is not a mere "object," a mere thing among other things. He need not fear vanishing into the world, for the human self is the image of God—distinct from all other creatures and created for dominion over the earth. Only divine revelation can justify our affirming both of these principles simultaneously. Otherwise, nothing prevents our losing either the world or ourselves. If the non-Christian does maintain the reality of these two poles, he does not do so on the basis of his antitheistic theories but under the pressure of God's revelation.

It is interesting that the problems involved in knowing the self are rather similar to those involved in knowing God. In both cases, the knowledge is "indirect"—that is, through means; and in both cases the knowledge is "direct"—that is, the object is always present in and with the means. On the one hand, if we merely listed the "facts" that appear in our sense experience, we would not list the self, for the self is neither seen nor heard. The same is true of God. Even when He speaks "directly" (as on Mt. Sinai), He appears in created media (on Mt. Sinai it was smoke, fire, and sound waves). On the other hand, God is so intimately involved with the facts that no fact can be accounted for apart from Him. And the same is true of the self. This is, I believe, part of the likeness between God and man. It is useful in apologetics (cf. Alvin Plantinga, *God and Other Minds*[3])

3. Ithaca, N.Y., and London: Cornell University Press, 1967.

to point out that if belief in God is irrational, belief in the human mind is also irrational.

Another implication of what I am saying is this. Only the Christian has the conceptual resources for distinguishing between persons and things, a distinction that is necessary if we are to raise a credible protest against the dehumanization of our age. At the same time, the unity between self and world must also be appreciated. One never finds a "bare world," uninterpreted by the self, nor does one find a "bare self," devoid of any environment. The search for one or the other is a non-Christian search; it is an attempt to find some ultimate point of reference other than God's revelation. That search, as we have seen, is futile. Self and world are experienced together; the two are aspects of a single organism of knowledge. The self is known in and through the facts; the world is known in and through my experience and thought. Although self and world are different, knowing the self and knowing the world are ultimately identical. The two are the same process, seen from different perspectives.

b. *Facts and Their Interpretations Are Inseparable*

For similar reasons, the common distinction between "fact" and "interpretation" must be rethought in the light of Scripture. It will serve us adequately if we think of "facts" as the world seen from God's point of view (or, perhaps, when truly seen from a human point of view) and "interpretations" as our understanding of those facts, whether true or false. Often in philosophy, however, the "fact" is thought to be a kind of reality-in-itself, a reality totally devoid of any interpretation—divine or human—by which all attempts at interpretation are to be tested. In reply, (1) we must insist that there are no facts utterly devoid of interpretation; there are no "brute facts," to use Van Til's terminology. All facts have been interpreted by God, and since all things are what they are by virtue of God's eternal plan, we must say that "the interpretation of the facts precedes the facts" (Van Til). The idea of "brute fact" is an invention intended to furnish us with a criterion of truth other than God's revelation. Yet, as with all other such substitutes, it cannot even be made intelligible. A "fact" devoid of any normative interpretation would be a fact without meaning, without characteristics—in short, a nothing. (2) We must insist also that human interpretation is involved in any knowledge of facts. We can have no knowledge of facts devoid of human interpretation, for knowing itself is interpretation. We have no access to reality apart from our interpretative faculties. To seek such access is to seek release from creaturehood (see above). We cannot step outside of our own skins. The desire for a "fact" totally devoid of human interpretation that can serve as an authoritative criterion for all interpretations is a non-Christian desire, a desire to substitute some other authority for the Word of God. And we can see, again, that this desire leads to unintelligible nonsense, to a "fact" that cannot be known or interpreted as a fact. No! It is better to recognize frankly that all statements of fact are interpretations of reality and that all true interpretations are factual. When we speak of "checking out the facts," we are talking about comparing ideas (interpretations) of which we are unsure with ideas (interpretations) of which we are more sure. But we never dig deep enough to reach some "bedrock" of pure facticity—facts undefiled by any interpretative activity. Such facts, by definition, could not be known at all, because knowledge itself is always interpretation.

Thus it is not surprising that though people do seek to make their interpretations cohere with "the facts," they determine what the facts are by reference to their system of interpretation (cf. Thomas Kuhn, *The Structure of Scientific Revolutions*[4]). And that is as it should be. Determining what the facts are and determining the best system of interpretative "understandings" are not two processes (with one of them utterly "prior to" the other) but the same process seen from different perspectives. It is perfectly true to say that our knowledge (even of theology) must be "based on the facts." But it is equally true to say that our factual judgments must be "based on" an adequate interpretation of our situation.

Some apologists have dreamed that the whole edifice of Christianity could be established by reference to something called "the facts," which could be understood apart from any Christian commitment. John W. Montgomery, for example, argues that way in his *Faith Founded on Fact*.[5] But what constitutes a fact for Montgomery (e.g., the Resurrection) will not be accepted as a fact by everyone (e.g., Rudolf Bultmann). It is possible to disagree about what the facts are on philosophical or theological grounds! Thus the choice of facts is dependent on the choice of a theology, not merely the other way around. And without a theology or philosophy—without a framework for the facts—and without a methodology, it is impossible to conceive of any fact being identified or grasped. Thus Montgomery's dream will not come true. The basis of Christianity and of all thought is God's revelation. The "facts" are the facts of that revelation, interpreted by God, known and therefore already interpreted by man.

4. Chicago, Ill.: University of Chicago Press, 1962.
5. Nashville and New York: Thomas Nelson Publishers, 1978.

There are no facts devoid of such interpretation, and if there were, they could not be known, let alone used as the basis of anything.

(3) The Law and the Self

Similar comments may be made here. The self is not the law, nor is the law the self, but knowing the self and knowing the law are essentially the same process, since we cannot know the one without knowing the other.

Non-Christian philosophy confuses law and self, as it confuses facts and law, and world and self. As in the other cases, it either isolates these from one another or identifies them. Law is identified with self, for example, in existentialism, where the doctrine of autonomy appears in the most vivid way. Sartre believed that self is the only law there is. But this means, in effect, that there is no law at all and that the self, being utterly the product of chance, loses its personhood, its selfhood. In idealism, however, the self is reduced to an instance of a universal law. Thus the individuality of the self is destroyed and the law itself becomes (contrary to the wishes of the idealists) totally abstract—a law that is not about anything except itself. The law—to be a law on such views—must be radically distinct from its subjects. And the subjects, the selves, must be totally autonomous, distinct from law; or they must be their own law, which is the same thing.

In Christianity, we distinguish self and law by revelation, not by first isolating them from one another and then trying somehow to get them together. Self and law are discovered at the same time, for each is necessary to the understanding of the other. The law tells us of ourselves, and a study of ourselves reveals applications of the law (see above; as facts are in a sense normative, so also is the self). The law is inscribed on us and within us because we are God's image. And as we are renewed in the image of Christ, we come to reflect God's righteousness more and more, so that we become more and more a source of revelation—to ourselves and to others—of God's law.

E. PERSPECTIVES

In the last section, I argued that although law, world, and self are distinct "objects" of knowledge, they are so closely related to each other that knowing law, world, and self are all the same process, seen from different "perspectives." More needs to be said about these perspectives. I suggested earlier in this chapter that it would be profitable for us to view epistemology as a subdivision of ethics, describing our obligations in the realm of knowledge, answering questions like What ought we to claim knowledge of? and How ought we to seek knowledge?—questions using the ethical "ought." In making ethical decisions, we meet again the factors we have been discussing—the law, the situation, the self. Every ethical decision involves the application of a law (norm, principle) to a situation by a person (self). Thus in counselling people with problems, we generally seek to ascertain three things: (1) What was the situation (the problem)? (2) How are you responding to it? (3) What does Scripture say? For the Christian, as we have seen, these questions are interdependent. The individual and the Scripture are part of the situation, the situation and the Scripture are parts of the person's experience, and an analysis of the situation and person helps to show us what Scripture says (i.e., how it applies in this case). In non-Christian ethics, however, these three factors tend to get separated or totally lost in one another. Kant's ethics makes much of the moral law (and to some extent of the self), but on his theory, the situation makes no significant contribution to the ethical decision. For John Stuart Mill, however, right behavior may be calculated almost entirely on the basis of situational factors. And for Sartre, only the ethical self seeking authenticity deserves any attention. Non-Christian ethics tends to absolutize or to eliminate one factor or another, because it seeks to find some absolute reference point outside God's revelation and because it has no resources for showing how all these factors work together. Scripture, however, tells us that God is in control, is the authority, and is present; therefore the situation, law, and person are part of an organic whole, together revealing God's lordship.

Thus I would maintain that Christians should not follow non-Christian models, advocating an "ethics of law" as opposed to a "situation ethic" or an "ethic of authentic existence." Rather, the Christian ethic should present law, situation, and ethical subject in organic unity. A Christian understanding of law will be essentially the same as a Christian understanding of situation and of person. The three will be "perspectives" on one another and on the whole. Each will include (not exclude) the others; thus each will cover the same ground with a different emphasis. I call these three "perspectives" normative (the law), situational (the facts, the world), and existential (the person). The normative perspective studies Scripture as the moral law that applies to situations and persons; without these applications, the law says nothing. The situational perspective studies the world as a field of ethical action, particularly those situations that we find ethically problematic. But in doing so, it accepts the biblical description of the world and the reality of persons in the world. The existential perspective studies the ethical subject—his griefs, his happiness, his capacities for making decisions—but only as interpreted by Scripture and in the context of his situational environment.

The same "perspectives" may be used with regard to epistemology. The normative perspective focuses on God's authority as expressed through His law. That authority is self-attesting; it cannot be tested by any higher criterion. Man was made to think in accordance with God's law, but he rebelled. Although fallen man seeks to repress his knowledge of the law, he continues to know it and even uses it to survive in God's world. The redeemed come once more to accept, even to delight in, God's law. It becomes their fundamental "presupposition," though they will not hold it with absolute consistency until their glorification on the Last Day. The law is comprehensive, governing all areas of life, and any assertion that conflicts with it must be rejected as false.

The situational perspective focuses on the law as revealed both in Scripture and in the creation generally. God commands us to understand the creation well enough to apply Scripture to all areas of life. Knowledge of creation is necessary if we are to apply Scripture properly. Every fact poses ethical questions (for example, How do I use this to the glory of God?) and suggests answers (in the example, qualities of the object that indicate God-honoring uses for it). The situational perspective, therefore, will analyze what we know about the world, to suggest a biblical understanding of it.

The existential perspective focuses on the law as revealed in man as God's image. We get to know the law better as we come to know ourselves better. Furthermore, we learn how regeneration and sanctification (i.e., obedience) are essential to knowledge in the fullest sense and how these interact with law and situation to lead us into truth.

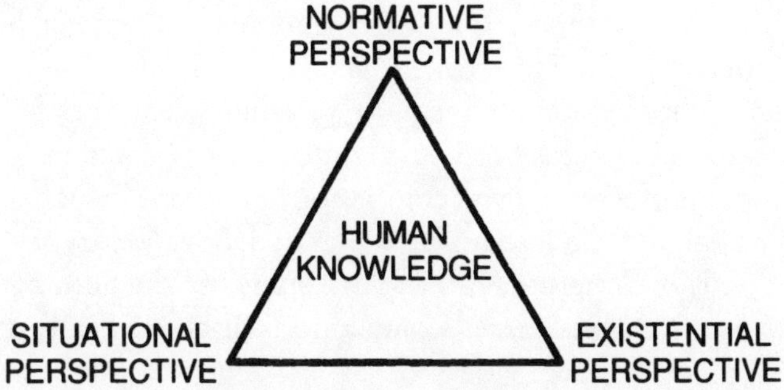

Fig. 2. Human knowledge can be understood in three ways: as knowledge of God's norm, as knowledge of our situation, and as knowledge of ourselves. None can be achieved adequately without the others. Each *includes* the others. Each, therefore, is a "perspective" on the whole of human knowledge.

CHAPTER THREE

God and Our Studies

A. THEOLOGY

We not only speak of knowing God and the law but also of "knowing theology." What are we claiming to know when we claim to "know theology"; or, to put it differently, what is the object of theological knowledge? What is it that theology claims to know? Theology has often been equated (as in Abraham Kuyper, *Principles of Sacred Theology*)[1] with the knowledge of God in some sense. I don't object to that equation, but I think there is some value in specifying more precisely the kind of knowledge of God that is in view. In what follows I shall argue that we may helpfully define theology as "the application of God's Word by persons to all areas of life."

First, a word about definitions. There is no one "right" definition of theology. Language is a flexible organism, and it can tolerate numerous varying definitions of terms, as long as speakers make reasonable efforts to make themselves clear. This doesn't mean that all definitions are equally valid. If one defines *ashtray* to mean "typewriter," he serves no good purpose and is especially likely to cause confusion. But there may be two or more definitions of a term, even conflicting definitions, which are of more or less equal validity. So if someone wants to define *theology* as "a study of God" or "study of Scripture" or even as a study of "the faith aspect of human existence" (Dooyeweerd),[2] complaints will be minimal, unless they

1. Grand Rapids: Wm. B. Eerdmans Pub. Co., 1965, 228-340.

2. See Herman Dooyeweerd, *In the Twilight of Western Thought* (Nutley: N.J.: Presbyterian and Reformed Pub. Co., 1968), 132-56.

refuse me the right to use *theology* or some other term to denote *my* concept of theology.

Generally speaking, *theology* refers to study of, knowledge of, speaking of, teaching of, learning about God. That's the "ball park" in which a definition ought to be sought if we are to use the term in a historically responsible way. Within that general area, however, there have been many different accounts of the concept.

(1) Schleiermacher

Schleiermacher, for example, said that "Christian doctrines are accounts of the Christian religious affections set forth in speech." No doubt it is a good thing to describe the Christian religious affections (feelings, intuitions, and sensitivities), and I have no strong objection to the use of *theology* to denote such accounts. What is objectionable, however, is that Schleiermacher intended for these accounts to replace what was more commonly called theology, namely the exposition of scriptural teachings. He intended to replace Scripture with human feeling (*Gefuhl*) as the final authority for theology, the definitive interpretation of our situation and the ultimate power for spiritual growth. By his definition, therefore, Schleiermacher sought to promulgate his general "subjectivism"; and, wishing to distance myself from that very subjectivism, I will not be using Schleiermacher's definition.

(2) Hodge

On the other side, we come to a definition that might be described as "objectivist." Charles Hodge, the great nineteenth-century Reformed theologian of Princeton Theological Seminary, argued that theology is necessary to put biblical truth into a different form. Scripture contains "facts," and the theologian gathers these facts, as a scientist gathers the facts of nature, and formulates "laws" about them. "Theology, therefore," Hodge said, "is the exhibition of the facts of scripture in their proper order and relation, with the principles or general truths involved in the facts themselves, and which pervade and harmonize the whole."[3] Hodge was not satisfied, as was Schleiermacher, to describe human subjective states; he wanted theology to describe the truth—what is the case apart from our feelings—the "objective" truth. He wanted to set forth the facts as they

3. *Systematic Theology* (Grand Rapids: Wm. B. Eerdmans Pub. Co., 1952), I, 19.

are (objectively), in their proper order (the objective order), not merely an order that reinforces our feelings, with those principles or general truths that are really (objectively) involved in the facts.

Hodge was certainly closer to the truth than Schleiermacher, since Hodge was concerned to distinguish true and false in theology and to determine truth on the basis of Scripture. Hodge's formulation, however, raises a number of problems.

a. *Theology and Natural Science*

Hodge makes too much out of the parallel between theology and the natural sciences. Certainly there are "facts" in the Bible that theologians ought to investigate. But these facts (as earlier I pointed out with respect to facts in general) are not "brute facts," facts devoid of interpretation, nor are they facts like quasars or electrons, which passively await the advance of science before they can be described in human language. No, the Bible is *language*. It describes itself. Not only is it preinterpreted by God (as all facts are), but it also interprets and describes its own facts. And Scripture's self-interpretations and self-descriptions are infallible and normative; in the most important sense, they cannot be improved upon. Now certainly Hodge knew all of that, but he should have taken more account of the implications of Scripture's uniqueness for the nature of theology. The job of the theologian cannot be to give the first or most definitive description of Scripture in human language. Why? Because Scripture has already done that. So what is the job of the theologian? If he is to be a "scientific examiner of Scripture," much more ought to be said about how his "scientific method" differs from the methods of the other sciences.

b. *Intellectualism and Theology*

Hodge also errs in the direction of a too intellectualist concept of theology, again because he was somewhat misled by the theology-science analogy. He saw theology largely as an exercise in theory construction, in description of facts, in the accurate statement of "principles" or "general truths." But why should theology be seen in such academic terms? Scripture is not merely a body of factual statements but is full of other kinds of language: imperatives, interrogatives, promises, vows, poetry, proverbs, emotive language, and so forth. The purpose of Scripture is not merely to give us an authoritative list of things we must believe but also to exhort us, command us, inspire our imaginations, put songs in our hearts, question us, sanctify us, and so on. Surely the work of teaching in the church is not only to list what people must believe but also to communicate to them all the other content of Scripture. Why should theology restrict itself to academic theorizing? Now doubtless some argument could be given for such a restriction. Someone might argue, for example, that theology should declare the propositional content of Scripture and that some other discipline, like preaching, should concern itself with the other aspects of Scripture. Later, I shall argue against this sort of proposal. But Hodge, so far as I can see, offers no argument at all. The problem is that in this context he was thinking of Scripture as a "body of facts" and neglecting the fact that it is also language. With a mere "body of facts," about all one can do is to describe and analyze. But with language, one needs to do much more.

c. *Scripture, Facts, Order, and Relations*

I am also disturbed by Hodge's statement that theology exhibits the facts of Scripture "in their *proper* order and relation" (emphasis mine). Again, Hodge neglects the fact that Scripture is language as well as fact and that therefore Scripture has already exhibited, described, and explained the facts in an orderly way (cf. Luke 1:3). Why, then, do we need another order? And more seriously, why should the order of theology (as opposed, presumably, to the order of Scripture) be described as the "proper" order? Is there something "improper" about the order of Scripture itself? I suspect that this wording is something of a slip of the pen; Hodge would never have wished to be known as a critic of Scripture. But the relationship between the order of theology and the order of Scripture itself remains a mystery. And it is a mystery that ought to be cleared up, since the perfection and normativity of Scripture are at stake.

The way out of this bind is to recognize that Scripture is language, that it has its own rational order, that it gives a perfect, normative, rational description and analysis of the facts of redemption. It is not the job of theology to supply such a normative description and analysis; that account has been given *to* theology by revelation. Theology, then, must be a *secondary* description, a reinterpretation and reproclamation of Scripture, both of its propositional and of its nonpropositional content. Why do we need such a reinterpretation? *To meet human needs*. The job of theology is to help people understand the Bible better, not to give some sort of abstractly perfect account of the truth as such, regardless of whether anyone understands it or not. Rather, the job of theology is to teach people the truth of God. Although Scripture is clear, for various reasons people fail to understand and use it properly. Theology is justified not merely by its correspondence with the truth—if that were the criterion, theology could do no better than simply to repeat Scripture—but theology is justified by the help it brings to people, by its success in helping people to use the truth.

That, at least, is the view that I will argue more systematically in the next section. And I honestly believe that if Hodge were alive today and were confronted with this argument, he would accept it, for the alternative would be to claim that Scripture is somehow inadequate and that theology must correct Scripture's inadequacies. Yet Hodge never formulated the matter as I have, probably because he did not want to allow any element of subjectivity into his formulation of the nature of theology. He was afraid of the ghost of Schleiermacher. He was afraid that if he made theology a reinterpretation of Scripture to meet human needs, those human needs would in some measure determine the structure and content of Scripture and thus replace Scripture as man's authority. If that was Hodge's motive, then it is understandable and, in part, laudable. Although Hodge was concerned with the authority and sufficiency of Scripture when contrasted with the authority and sufficiency of human religious feeling, he failed to realize that to systematically exclude human *need* from a structural role in theology is precisely to lose the authority and sufficiency of Scripture. If theology is a purely "objective" discipline where the scientist determines "the truth as it really is" apart from any human need, then he cannot help but be in competition with Scripture. He will be seeking a better formulation than Scripture itself contains or at least a better "order."

"Objectivism" continues to be a danger in orthodox Christian circles. It is all too easy for us to imagine that we have a higher task than merely that of helping people. Our pride constantly opposes the servant model. And it is all too easy for us to think of theological formulations as something more than truth-for-people, as a kind of special insight into God himself (which the biblical writers would have written about, had they known as much as we). But no, theology is not "purely objective truth"; as we saw earlier, there is no such thing as purely objective truth, or "brute fact." Our theologies are not even the best formulation of truth-for-people for all times and places; Scripture is that. Our theologies are merely attempts to help people, generally and in specific times and places, to use Scripture better.

An adequate concept of theology, then, will be a concept that does justice to the interdependence of the three "perspectives" on knowledge that we discussed earlier. It will involve the application of Scripture (normative perspective) by persons (existential perspective) to situations (situational perspective). It will not seek to replace Scripture or to improve on it but to use Scripture in the situations of human life. To such a concept of theology we now turn.

(3) A "Covenantal" Definition

I would suggest that we define theology as "the application of the Word of God by persons to all areas of life." The meaning of this definition ought to be fairly clear, except for *application*. I would define *application* as "teaching" in the New Testament sense (*didache*, *didaskalia*), a concept represented in some translations by *doctrine*. Teaching in the New Testament (and I think also in the Old) is the use of God's revelation to meet the spiritual needs of people, to promote godliness and spiritual health. Often *teaching* in the New Testament is coupled with an adjective like *hugiainos* (healthy), or *kalos* (good or beautiful), or with some other indication that the teaching is conducive to spiritual health. Naturally, then, *teaching* is not a mere description of human religious feelings (Schleiermacher), nor is it an attempt to formulate the truth in some merely "objective" sense (which was the tendency of Hodge's position, though surely he would have rejected the bad implications of it). It is not a narrowly intellectualist or academic discipline. And though there are "specialists" of a sort (the "teachers" of the New Testament), there are also important senses in which all Christians teach (Heb. 5:12) by word and deed, and even in their singing (Col. 3:16). And this concept of theology coordinates the three perspectives of knowledge that we have discussed; it is based on the Word of God (normative), and it applies that Word to situations (situational) on a person-to-person basis (existential).

Besides being a clear alternative to the two other definitions, this definition has many advantages. (1) It gives a clear justification for the work of theology. Theology is not needed to remedy formal (Hodge?) or material (Schleiermacher) defects in Scripture but to remedy defects in ourselves, the hearers and readers of Scripture. (2) Theology in this sense (as opposed to theology in other senses) has a clear scriptural warrant: Scripture commands us to "teach" in this way (cf. Matt. 28:19f. and many other passages). (3) Despite its focus on human need, this definition does full justice to the authority and sufficiency of Scripture. *Sola scriptura* does not require that human needs be ignored in theology, only that Scripture have the final say about the answers to those needs (and about the propriety of the questions presented). (4) Theology is thus freed from any false intellectualism or academicism. It is able to use scientific methods and academic knowledge where they are helpful, but it can also speak in nonacademic ways, as Scripture itself does—exhorting, questioning, telling parables, fashioning allegories and poems and proverbs and songs, expressing love, joy, patience . . . the list is without limit. (5) This definition enables us to make use of data from natural revelation and from man himself, not artificially separating the three "perspectives."

But why should we use *application* in this definition? If *application* means "teaching," then why not simply speak of "teaching"? Well, we could. There is nothing sacrosanct about *application*. I chose it to discourage a certain false distinction between "meaning" and "application" that I believe has resulted in much damage to God's people. Over and over, preachers (and others) try to proclaim the "meaning" of the text and then its "application"—the first part is "what it means," the second "what it means to us." Sometimes we are told that we must understand "what it means" before we can understand "how it applies." The meaning "comes first," the application is "based on" the meaning. Various disciplines are even distinguished in this way but not always very consistently. Sometimes we are told that Bible "translations" give us "the meaning" but "paraphrases" give us "the application." Alternatively, sometimes we are told that both translations and paraphrases give the meaning, and the exegete or interpreter gives the application. Or still differently, the exegete gives the meaning and the theologian gives the application; or the theologian gives the meaning and the preacher provides the application. One gets the impression rather quickly that though many people are sure that the meaning-application distinction is important, they aren't very certain where one ends and the other begins.

Could the distinction be saved by making it more precise? Let's try. Let's use the example of the eighth commandment. (1) The "text" would be the Hebrew words. (2) The "translation" would be "Thou shalt not steal." (3) The "interpretation" would be "Don't take anything that doesn't belong to you." (4) Then one could think of various "application-formulations" such as "Don't embezzle," "Don't cheat on your income tax," "Don't take doughnuts without paying," and so forth. (5) Then beyond the application-formulation would be the "practical" application, the application-in-real-life—the actual decisions that we make not to embezzle, cheat, and so forth.

Yet even this more precise way of speaking breaks down in the final analysis because all four transformations of the text *(2-5)* can be described as "meaning" and all can be described as "application." Something of the meaning is lacking if we have only *(2)* and *(3)* and not *(4)* and *(5)*. Similarly, even at stages *(2)* and *(3)* application is going on. "Meaning," clearly, is found at stage *(2)*: the translation gives the meaning of the Hebrew. (In an important sense, surely, it is found even at stage *(1)*; every text means what it says). But it is also found at stage *(3)*; in fact it is usually "interpretation" that people are asking for when they ask for "meaning." But what of *(4)*? Let us imagine two scholars who agree on the translation "Thou shalt not steal" but disagree on application-formulations. For example, one believes that stealing is wrong but thinks the text permits one to embezzle from his employer. The other disagrees. Shall we say that both understand the "meaning" equally well but differ on the "application?" Surely not. Clearly the two differ, not only concerning the "application" but also about the meaning of the text. "Steal" to the one has an entirely different meaning from that understood by the other. And surely, if both agree on a translation *(2)* but one actually embezzles and the other does not *(5)*, though both profess to be bound by the text, the difference in behavior manifests a difference in understanding.

"Meaning," then, is found at all five points, and so is "application." Remember, "application" is the use of Scripture to meet some human need. One may meet such needs either by simply repeating the Hebrew text (to a Hebrew scholar! *(1)*) or by translating (*(2)*) or by interpreting (*(3)*) or by formulating a policy (*(4)*) or by carrying out a policy (*(5)*). The important point is that at every one of those stages some human need is being met. None of those activities presents us with a "purely objective" truth that is removed from all human questions and concerns. Every request for "meaning" is a request for an application because whenever we ask for the "meaning" of a passage we are expressing a lack in ourselves, an ignorance, an inability to use the passage. Asking for "meaning" is asking for an application of Scripture to a need; we are asking Scripture to remedy that lack, that ignorance, that inability. Similarly, every request for an "application" is a request for meaning; the one who asks doesn't understand the passage well enough to use it himself.

At each stage, then, meaning is found; and at each stage, application is made. There is, in fact, no important distinction to be made at all between *meaning* and *application*, and so I shall use them interchangeably. To find "meaning" is to ask a question of Scripture, to express a need, and to have that need met. To "apply" is to learn more of what is in the text, to see more of its potential, its powers, its wisdom. I understand the distinction between meaning and application as a remnant of objectivism, as an attempt to find somewhere a "bedrock" of pure facticity (meaning) on which all other uses of the text are to be based. But the true bedrock of the meaning of Scripture is Scripture itself, not some product of man's ingenuity;

and we have seen elsewhere what happens when people try to replace the true bedrock with a false one: the notion of "brute fact" appears—long enough to destroy itself. No, the work of theology is not to discover some truth-in-itself in abstraction from all that is human; it is to take the truth of Scripture and humbly to serve God's people by teaching and preaching it and by counselling and evangelizing.

This, indeed, is the picture that Scripture itself presents. As we saw earlier, we learn the meaning of Scripture as we apply it to situations. Adam learned the meaning of "subdue the earth" as he studied the creation and discovered applications for that command. A person does not understand Scripture, Scripture tells us, unless he can apply it to new situations, to situations not even envisaged in the original text (Matt. 16:3; 22:29; Luke 24:25; John 5:39f.; Rom. 15:4; 2 Tim. 3:16f.; 2 Peter 1:19-21—in context). Scripture says that its whole purpose is to apply the truth to our lives (John 20:31; Rom. 15:4; 2 Tim. 3:16f.). Furthermore, the applications of Scripture are as authoritative as the specific statements of Scripture. In the passages referred to above, Jesus and others held their hearers responsible if they failed to apply Scripture properly. If God says "Thou shall not steal" and I take a doughnut without paying, I cannot excuse myself by saying that Scripture fails to mention doughnuts. Unless applications are as authoritative as the explicit teachings of Scripture (cf. *The Westminster Confession of Faith*, I, on "good and necessary consequence"), then scriptural authority becomes a dead letter. To be sure, we are fallible in determining the proper applications; but we are also fallible in translating, exegeting, and understanding the explicit statements of Scripture. The distinction between explicit statements and applications will not save us from the effects of our fallibility. Yet we must translate, exegete, and "apply"—not fearfully but confidently—because God's Word is clear and powerful and because God gives it to us for our good.

So the whole process from translation to application-in-life could be called "interpretation" or "finding the meaning," or it could be called "application." And other names might also be found. I don't have strong feelings about which term should be used, but I do feel that it is good to use one term to describe the whole process to indicate that the same things are being done all along the line. And my personal preference is for *application*, for if we define theology as "application," we are less likely to draw that fatal dichotomy between "meaning" and "application."

One final note. By defining theology as application, I am not seeking to disparage the theoretical work of theologians. Theory is one kind of application. It answers certain kinds of questions and meets certain kinds of human needs. I am, however, seeking to discourage the notion that theology is "properly" something theoretical, something academic, as opposed to the practical teaching that goes on in preaching, counselling, and Christian friendship. Once we see the essential similarity of "interpretation" and "application," we will see that it is arbitrary to restrict the work of theology to the theoretical area or to think that the more theoretical a piece of Christian teaching is, the more "theological" it is. Furthermore, we shall see that it is arbitrary to insist that theology be written in a formal, academic style. Rather, theologians ought to make broad use of human language—poetry, drama, exclamation, song, parable, symbol—as Scripture itself does.

B. PHILOSOPHY AND SCIENCE

a. *Philosophy*

It is difficult for me to draw any sharp distinction between a Christian theology and a Christian philosophy. Philosophy generally is understood as an attempt to understand the world in its broadest, most general features. It includes metaphysics, or ontology (the study of being, of what "is"), epistemology (the study of knowing), and the theory of values (ethics, aesthetics, etc.). If one seeks to develop a truly Christian philosophy, he will certainly be doing so under the authority of Scripture and thus will be applying Scripture to philosophical questions. As such, he would be doing theology, according to our definition. Christian philosophy, then, is a subdivision of theology. Furthermore, since philosophy is concerned with reality in a broad, comprehensive sense, it may well take it as its task to "apply the Word of God to all areas of life." That definition makes philosophy identical with, not a subdivision of, theology.

If there are any differences between the Christian theologian and the Christian philosopher, they would probably be (1) that the Christian philosopher spends more time studying natural revelation than the theologian, and the theologian spends more time studying Scripture, and (2) that the theologian seeks a formulation that is an application of Scripture and thus absolutely authoritative. His goal is a formulation before which he can utter "Thus saith the Lord." A Christian philosopher, however, may have a more modest goal—a wise human judgment that accords with what Scripture teaches, though it is not necessarily warranted by Scripture.

A Christian philosophy can be of great value in helping us to articulate in detail the biblical world view. We must beware, however, of "philosophical imperialism." The comprehensiveness of philosophy has often led philosophers to seek to rule over all other disciplines, even over theology, over God's Word. Even philosophers attempting to construct a Christian philosophy have been guilty of this, and some have even insisted that Scripture itself cannot be understood properly unless it is read in a way prescribed by the philosopher! Certainly, philosophy can help us to interpret Scripture; philosophers often have interesting insights about language, for example. But the line must be drawn: where a philosophical scheme contradicts Scripture or where it seeks to inhibit the freedom of exegesis without scriptural warrant, it must be rejected.

b. *Science*

Scientists study various areas of the creation. A Christian who is a scientist will do this under the authority of God's Word and thus will be doing theology (i.e., applying Scripture) much of the time. Since Scripture is not given to us as a comprehensive catalogue of scientific principles, however, much of the scientist's time will be spent in the study of God's revelation in nature. To the extent that he is consistent with his Christian commitment, such a scientist will presuppose in his study of nature the truth of the teachings of Scripture, especially as they bear on his work as a scientist. Although Scripture is not intended primarily as a textbook of physics or biology or psychology, it says many things relevant to those disciplines, not only about the broad realities of creation, fall, and redemption but also on more detailed matters such as the biological uniqueness of man, the genuineness of guilt-feelings, the legitimacy of making value-judgments in the study of human cultures, and the chronology of the history of Israel, to name but a few examples.

A Christian who is a scientist should also be critical of the theories of other scientists, not only on the usual logical, methodological, and mathematical grounds but also on religious grounds. Scientists who develop theories on the presupposition of autonomy ought to be called to account. It is usually easier and more effective for Christians who are scientists to do this than it is for Christian theologians. It has been rather common lately for non-Christian biologists and geologists to recommend the theory of evolution on the ground that the only alternative is biblical creationism. In effect, they are admitting that their view is biased by religious assumptions. That fact ought to be proclaimed loud and long. And it is only one example of the kind of critique that we should be carrying out. Though not written from a Christian perspective at all, Thomas Kuhn's *The Structure of*

Scientific Revolutions[4] is extremely helpful in destroying the myth of the alleged "objectivity" of science. Non-Christian science is widely deified and worshipped, but it is more vulnerable now than it ever has been for the last four hundred years.

C. APOLOGETICS

Apologetics may be defined as the application of Scripture to unbelief and as such may be seen as a subdivision of theology. It is important to understand that that definition makes apologetics a part of theology, not a "neutral basis" for it. Too often writers on such matters have assumed that the work of the apologist is to reason with the unbeliever, using criteria and presuppositions that are acceptable both to belief and unbelief. On the basis of such reasoning, it is supposed, the apologist establishes the existence of God, the substantial truth of the gospel, and the authority of Scripture. Once these points are established, the rest of the Christian body of doctrine can be based on the exegesis of Scripture. So the transition from apologetics to systematic theology is a transition from neutral reasoning to reasoning under scriptural authority. This common view, however, must be rejected as unsound. "Neutral" reasoning, reasoning not subject to scriptural authority, is forbidden to us, even at the "preliminary" stage. (One should say, rather, *especially* at the "preliminary" stage, for it is at that stage that the framework is established to which all subsequent conclusions must conform.) Reasoning, even with unbelievers, must be obedient and godly, as foolish as that may seem to the unbelieving mind. Only such reasoning is capable of maintaining and defending the truth. For the unbeliever's own good, we must not—at this point especially—compromise the only message that is capable of saving him. And in the final analysis, "neutrality" is not only forbidden; it is impossible. One is either for God or against Him; to abandon the authority of God's Word is to adopt the authority of the would-be autonomous man and the Devil's lie.

But if apologetics is not "neutral," then there is no particular reason to say that it furnishes a "basis" or "presupposition" for theology. It is probably more illuminating to put it the other way around: theology supplies the presuppositions for apologetics. Theology formulates the truth that the apologist is to defend and describes the kind of reasoning that the apologist must practice. Insofar as the apologist (reasoning non-neutrally) establishes

4. Chicago: University of Chicago Press, 1962.

such truths as the existence of God and the authority of Scripture, one may say that he is developing a "basis" for theology, but only insofar as he is himself a theologian. It is best to say that the basis of theology is the Word of God. There is no other discipline or body of knowledge that mediates between the Word and the theologian, any more than there is a realm of "brute fact" or "abstract law" to which recourse must be made.

Appendix A

PERSPECTIVALISM

I have argued that the knowledge of God's law, the world, and the self are interdependent and ultimately identical. We understand the law by studying its relations to the world and the self—its "applications"—so that its meaning and its application are ultimately identical. Thus all knowledge is a knowledge of the law. All knowledge also is a knowledge of the world, since all our knowledge (of God or the world) comes through created media. And all knowledge is of self, because we know all things by means of our own experience and thoughts. The three kinds of knowledge, then, are identical but "perspectivally" related; they represent the same knowledge, viewed from three different "angles" or "perspectives."

I assume that all of this will sound rather strange to some Reformed ears. We are used to placing the law of God (Scripture) in a privileged position, so that our knowledge of Scripture determines our knowledge of self and world, but not vice versa. Well, I am a staunch defender of biblical inerrancy and sufficiency. Certainly Scripture does have a privileged position. What Scripture says must govern our thinking about the world and the self—and about Scripture, too. The reciprocity works this way. We come to know Scripture through our senses and minds (self) and through Scripture's relations with the rest of the world. But then what we read in Scripture must be allowed to correct the ideas we have formed about these other areas. Then as we understand the other areas better, we understand Scripture better. There is a kind of circularity here, a "hermeneutical circle," if you will, but that does not prevent Scripture from ruling our thoughts; it merely describes the process by which that rule takes place.

Strange as all of that may sound to Reformed people, I insist that this approach is nothing less than generic Calvinism. It is in the Reformed faith that nature as revelation is taken most seriously. Since God is sovereign and present, all things reveal Him. And it is Reformed theology that makes the fullest use of the biblical concept of God's image, that man is revelational. Thus on the first page of the *Institutes*, Calvin speaks of the interdependence of the knowledge of God and the knowledge of self and then, surprisingly to some of us, states that he does not know which comes first! Thus in Van Til's *Introduction to Systematic Theology*, there are four chapters on general revelation, interrelating the revelation from nature, from man, and from the divine voice: "Revelation about Nature from Nature," "Revelation about Nature from Man," "Revelation about Nature from God," "Revelation about Man from Nature," and so forth. I suspect that only a Reformed theologian could write that way. I seek only to carry this development one step further.

Appendix B

ENCYCLOPEDIA

There are those, such as the great Dutch thinkers Kuyper and Dooyeweerd, who believe that "encyclopedia of the sciences" is terribly important. In "encyclopedia of the sciences," an attempt is made to state the proper subject matter of each science and its relation to all the others. One almost gets the impression that for some Dutch thinkers this is the supreme problem of philosophy—perhaps the only problem—so that once one determines the relationships of the sciences, no more problems remain. Among these thinkers there is also the tendency to think that there is only one right way to classify the sciences and that the definitions of the sciences ought to be as precise as possible.

I question all of those assumptions. It seems to me that there may be many legitimate ways to organize the subject matter of the universe for study, just as there are many ways of cutting a cake for purposes of eating and just as there are many ways of dividing up the color spectrum for purposes of description. (In some languages there may be five colors, in others eight, and so forth; and the color terms of one language often overlap the color terms of another.) I also question the importance of this and the need for enormous precision. Interestingly, Van Til, Dutchman though he is, seems to be closer to my view than to those of Kuyper and Dooyeweerd. In the *Introduction to Systematic Theology* (3), Van Til recognizes mutual dependence of different disciplines, as opposed to the Dutch tendency to want to establish unequivocal priorities between one discipline and another. He argues that the distinction between "dogmatic theology" and "systematic theology" is unimportant (ibid.), and he recognizes that a discipline may deal with one thing "primarily" and something else "secondarily" (1, 2).

My fear, in relation to the intense concern with encyclopedia among some thinkers, is that that concern represents in part a search for a kind of unequivocal "bedrock," an ultimate priority, an absolute "starting point" other than Scripture. Dooyeweerd finally locates his "Archimedean point" in the human heart, which is thought in some odd sense to transcend time. Kuyper never resolved the question of "priority" in that sort of decisive way. But in Van Til we have found a thinker who does not need to find some form of human thought that is "prior to" all others, since he is far more self-conscious about the implications of the primacy of Scripture itself. If we find our "starting point" in Scripture, then it really doesn't matter so much which science is based on which. The important thing is that all are based on the teachings of Scripture, and beyond that they can work out their interrelations as seems wise. Nor is it so terribly important that each discipline have absolutely precise boundaries that dare not be transgressed by another. If Scripture is our authority, we need not fear flexibility in this area. Scripture gives its believers a comprehensive vision that transcends interfield "boundaries."

APPENDIX C

MEANING

The "meaning of meaning" is a subject that has frequently been discussed by linguists, philosophers, theologians, and others. As with most terms, there is no single correct definition of *meaning*. Some types of definitions, however, promote misunderstandings and others help to alleviate them. In that regard, we will compare several approaches to the "meaning of meaning." My discussion in this appendix is indebted to William P. Alston's *Philosophy of Language*,[1] though I have made some adaptations.

In his *Foundations of the Theory of Signs*,[2] Charles W. Morris distinguished between syntactics, semantics, and pragmatics as elements of the theory of signs. Morris defined syntactics as "the study of the syntactical relations of signs to one another in abstraction from the relations of signs to objects or to interpreters."[3] Semantics, he said, "deals with the relation of signs to their designata and so to the objects which they may or do denote."[4] And Morris said that pragmatics deals with "the relation of signs to their users."[5] By means of those categories, we may distinguish various possible concepts of *meaning*.

1. William P. Alston, *Philosophy of Language* (Englewood Cliffs, N.J.: Prentice Hall, 1964).

2. Charles W. Morris, *Foundations of the Theory of Signs* (Chicago: University of Chicago Press, 1938).

3. Ibid., 13.

4. Ibid., 21.

5. Ibid., 29.

(1) SYNTACTIC

Often when we ask for the meaning of a word or phrase, what we want is a synonymous expression. Because synonymy is *sameness* of meaning, it is tempting to equate meaning with synonymy. If meaning is synonymy, then the meaning of an expression is the set of expressions that are synonymous with it. Such an approach seems to have the advantage of allowing meanings to be determined by "pure syntax"; the meaning of an expression can be determined without knowing anything about its referents or the uses of its terms. That advantage, however, is illusory. The concept of synonymy itself carries us beyond pure syntax; we cannot know if two words are synonyms unless we know something about their referents or the ways they are used. For that same reason, we cannot derive an adequate definition of *meaning* from *synonymy*. For example, we can know that *amare* and *aimer* are synonyms, without knowing the meaning of either.

(2) SEMANTIC

Some scholars have argued that the meaning of a word is an object to which it refers, its referent. If that were true, then the meaning of a sentence would be a state of affairs asserted by the sentence. Five considerations show why such a theory is incorrect. (a) Two expressions may have the same referent but different meanings (in some normal senses of *meaning*). For example, *Scott* and *the author of Waverly* have the same referent, but they are neither interchangeable nor identical in meaning. (b) An expression may vary in its reference from one object to another but maintain the same meaning, for example, personal pronouns. (c) *Meaning* and *referent* are generally not interchangeable. The referent of *Pompeii* is the town of Pompeii, but that town is not the meaning of *Pompeii*. When Pompeii was destroyed, the meaning of *Pompeii* did not perish! (d) Not all words are used to refer. According to this theory, what would be the meaning of *and*, *Oh!*, and *if*? What would be the meanings of sentences that do not assert states of affairs but that ask questions or that issue commands? (e) The very concept of reference leads us beyond semantics. How do we teach referents to someone who is just learning to talk? By pointing ("ostensive definition")? But how do we then teach the meaning of the pointing gesture (which certainly is part of language)? Not by pointing at anything! There is no thing you could point to to define the act of pointing. Without some knowledge of or competence in the *pragmatics* of language, one cannot learn referents. And so we move on.

(3) PRAGMATIC

There are six subtypes in this category.

a. *Behavioral*

In *Language*,[6] Leonard Bloomfield defined the meaning of an expression as "the situation in which the speaker utters it and the response which it calls forth in the hearer." Bloomfield took his cue from the stimulus-response relationship that behavioral psychologists emphasized. He understood linguistic expressions as a type of stimulus, presented in a particular situation, that evokes a particular response from its hearers. Similarities of situation and response, however, do not seem to correlate very well with similarities of meaning, as *meaning* is generally used. On the one hand, words with different meanings can be spoken in similar situations and provoke similar responses. On the other hand, two expressions with the same meaning, even two identical expressions, can be uttered in different situations and/or provoke quite different responses.

b. *Mental Image*

Sometimes we may be tempted to equate the meaning of an expression with a mental image the speaker or hearer associates with it. It is not the case, however, that *carrot*, for example, always indicates the presence of a carrot image in the mind of the speaker or evokes such an image in the mind of the hearer. Furthermore, the presence or absence of such images is entirely irrelevant to determining the meaning of an expression, as Wittgenstein showed in *Philosophical Investigations*.[7]

c. *The Speaker's Intention*

This is one of the more plausible candidates for a definition of *meaning*. Often we clinch an argument about the meaning of an expression by saying, "This is what the speaker (or writer) intended." Nevertheless some qualifications are in order. (a) If *intention* refers to a hidden psychological state of the author, then we have no more access to that than we have to his mental images (see *(3)*, *B* above). And such a hidden psychological state is as irrelevant to determining what an author or speaker means as are his mental images. *Intentions*, of course, may be defined to refer to something other than psychological states, to something objective that it is pos-

6. Leonard Bloomfield, *Language* (London: Allen and Unwin, 1935), 139.

7. Ludwig Wittgenstein, *Philosophical Investigations* (New York: Macmillan, 1958), 175ff., passim.

sible for us to discover, at least provisionally. But such definitions of *intention* make the search for an author's intention identical with a search for something else, such as *d* or *f* below. (b) What people say is often different from what they intend to say. If someone intends to say "noetic effects of sin" but says "poetic effects of sin," does "poetic" *mean* "noetic"? Surely not. I believe that the biblical writers did not make such mistakes, although because of textual corruption, errors of this kind do sometimes appear in copies of Scripture. The biblical writers, however, do say *more* than they consciously intended to say. Did Moses intend for the story of Abraham and Hagar to be used as an allegory (Gal. 4:21-31)? Did David realize how much he was saying about Jesus in Psalm 110? The exegete must, therefore, take into account the intention of the *divine* author, as well as the intention of the human author. But how do we do that? Other accounts of meaning provide more concrete guidance than do theories based on intention.

d. *The Understanding of the Original Audience*

Often we determine meaning by asking, How would this expression have been understood by its original hearers? Although that is a useful question, it is not adequate as a criterion of meaning for the following reasons. (a) Hearers and readers of language often *misunderstand* one another. Therefore if we ask how the original audience understood an utterance, we might be led astray. And even when the original hearers are on the right track, they often fail to understand the fullness of meaning that prolonged reflection on the utterance might reveal. Should we seek to determine the meaning of Jesus' parables, for example, by asking how His disciples initially would have understood them? (b) In the area of biblical exegesis, we must remember that the divine author of the text intends to address not only the original hearers and readers but us as well (Rom. 15:4). The intended audience of Scripture spans many centuries and cultures.

e. *Verification*

The logical positivist philosophers argued that "the meaning of a statement is the method of its verification." It is true that sometimes when we are confronted with a difficult expression, it is helpful to ask, How would we establish its truth or falsehood? Sometimes such questions help to determine meaning. (a) Verifiability, however, is a guide to meaning only for indicative expressions, for expressions that claim to state facts. Verifiability does not help determine the meaning of questions, exclamations, commands, and so forth. (b) The concept of verifiability has been philosophically controversial. Many philosophers have attempted to define it precisely, and all have failed.[8] Because the concept of verifiability has been used to challenge the meaningfulness of religious statements, it has also been criticized on theological grounds.[9] (c) In most cases, as George Mavrodes has pointed out,[10] we must know the meaning of an expression *before* we can learn how to verify it. Therefore meaning seems to be independent of the method by which one would verify a statement.

f. *Use*

Wittgenstein argued that in many, though not all cases in which we use *meaning*, the meaning of an expression is its use. He compared words to tools that were suited to do different jobs in society. Thus the meaning of a piece of language can be found by discovering what job the language performs. But some clarification is necessary. Wittgenstein and Ryle thought of "use" (as opposed to mere "usage") as a normative concept: the "use" does not tell us how people *actually* use an expression but how they *ought* to use it. But how do we discover such norms? Whose use is to be normative in our judgments about meaning? The speaker's? That of the original hearers? Ours? From a Christian perspective, norms are applications of God's Word. Unless God has spoken, there can be no norms. Thus we must say that the meaning of an expression is its *God-ordained* use. Of course God does not give us a dictionary that teaches us how to use words! Rather, the meaning of an expression is the meaning it has when used with understanding and responsibility. That does not mean, however, that blasphemy and lies are meaningless; usually there is continuity between the irresponsible and responsible uses of words. Sinful speech often imitates godly speech, using God-ordained meanings to speak against the Lord. But godly speech is the norm. Ungodly speech is meaningful only in a parasitic way; it borrows norms from the godly. That is the account of meaning that I find most helpful—a Wittgensteinian "use view" that is grounded in distinctively Christian norms. That helps to explain my earlier statement: "Meaning is application."

In summary we can say the following.

1. To ask for the meaning of an expression is to ask for an application. When we ask to know the meaning of a word or sentence, we are ex-

8. See Carl Hempel, "The Empiricist Criterion of Meaning," in A. J. Ayer, ed., *Logical Positivism* (Glencoe, Ill.: The Free Press, 1959), 108-29 and my *Christianity and the Great Debates*, 20-22.

9. See my "God and Biblical Language," in J. W. Montgomery, ed., *God's Inerrant Word* (Minneapolis: Bethany Fellowship, 1974), 159-77.

10. George Mavrodes, *Belief in God* (New York: Random House, 1970), 47f.

pressing a problem. We are indicating that we are not able to *use* the language in question. That problem may be relieved in a wide variety of ways: synonymous expressions, ostensive definition, references to mental images, intentions, methods of verification, and so forth may all be of help. The goal, however, is not merely to supply one of those; the goal is to relieve the problem, to help the questioner use the language in question.

2. As meanings are applications, so applications are meanings. One does not know the meaning of a text or piece of language if he cannot use it in some way. Scripture makes it clear that those who are unable to *apply* God's Word do not *truly* understand it. To understand God's Word, we must be able to apply it to situations that are not explicitly mentioned in the text itself (see Matt. 16:3; 22:29; Luke 24:25; John 5:39f.; Rom. 15:4; 2 Tim. 3:16f.; and 2 Peter 1:19-21, which indicates that Scripture is to be used to combat contemporary false teachers).

3. Some people find this account too subjective and would like meaning to be the objective *basis* for all application. Christians have a healthy resistance to subjectivism! And true enough, application must be the application *of* something! But in my view, the objective basis of application must be the text itself, nothing more and nothing less. I am flexible on matters of definition. If someone wishes to define *meaning* as the text itself, then I can accept a distinction between meaning and application. Meaning is the text, and application is our use of the text. Those definitions are, however, entirely contrary to normal usage, and that is why I shun them. What we must categorically reject, however, is some mysterious, intermediary thing called "the meaning" that stands *between* the text and its application. Instead of increasing the objectivity of our knowledge, such an intermediary is a subjective construct that inevitably clouds our understanding of the text itself.

4. That sort of subjectivity is especially evident in the theological context. Suppose that there is something called "the meaning" of Scripture that is distinct from the text and from the applications of Scripture. Where would that meaning come from? In theology, who supplies the meaning? The exegete? The biblical theologian? The systematic theologian? The Christian philosopher? All of those have, at various times, claimed to supply the fundamental meaning of Scripture that all other forms of theology were supposed to seek to apply. But those various claims cancel one another out. No, the objective basis of theology is the text of Scripture, not any product of theological endeavor. *Sola scriptura.*

Appendix D

FACT AND INTERPRETATION

Fact has meant various things in the history of philosophy. To some, a fact is simply a matter that is agreed upon in a particular context of discussion. To others, facts are the ultimate building blocks from which the world itself and human knowledge of the world are constructed.

In this book a fact is, first of all, a state of affairs. A state of affairs is not a thing. States of affairs include things, together with their properties and relations to other things. Although things can be designated by nouns, states of affairs can only be represented by sentences or clauses. *Chair* designates a thing. *The chair is blue* asserts a state of affairs. *Chalk* designates a thing. *The chalk is to the right of the eraser* asserts a state of affairs. Thus *fact* is often followed by a "that clause." We speak of the "fact that" the chair is blue or the "fact that" the chalk is to the right of the eraser.

That distinction has played an important role in philosophical controversy. Aristotle's *Metaphysics* describes the world as a collection of *things*, or "substances," made of form and matter. Wittgenstein's *Tractatus Logico-Philosophicus*,[1] however, teaches that "The world is the totality of facts, not of things" (section 1.1). According to Wittgenstein, even if we knew all the things in the world, we would not know the world, because we would not know how the things were actually related to one another. We would not know what was *happening* to those things. Whitehead and his followers, the process philosophers and theologians, carry the debate one step further. Just as things are intelligible only in the context of facts,

1. Ludwig Wittgenstein, *Tractatus Logico-Philosophicus* (London: Routledge and Kegan Paul, 1961).

they argue, facts are intelligible only in the context of processes. We will not at this point, however, enter that particular debate, for our present concern is with facts.

Fact can also be shorthand for *statement of fact*. Some forms of language—indicative sentences and clauses—assert that some state of affairs exists, that so-and-so is the case. Statements of fact, of course, may be true or false. Thus they may turn out, in one sense, not to be factual.

In this book when I say that "fact and interpretation are one," I am using *fact* in the second sense as *statements* of fact. It would not be true to say that facts in the sense of states of affairs are identical with our interpretations of them, but facts in the sense of statements of fact *are* interpretations. To make a statement of fact is to offer an interpretation of reality. There is no significant difference between a statement of fact and an interpretation of reality.

Remember, too, that all of our perceptions of the world are influenced by our interpretations;[2] there is no knowledge of facts that is not influenced by our interpretative activity. The Christian knows by faith that this world is not of his own making, that there is a "real world"—a world of facts—that exists apart from our interpretation of it. But in actual life we only encounter the world through the mediation of our interpretations, and so the world we live in is to some extent of our own making. That helps to explain my emphasis in this book on human beings as secondary creators. What prevents us from constructing an absolutely *crazy* world? Only our faith. Only our faith assures us that there is a "real world" that exists apart from our interpretation. Only God's revelation provides us with a sure knowledge of that world and so serves to check our fantasies. Non-Christians, then, have no safeguards against such craziness, except for their tendency to live parasitically off Christian capital.

2. Cf. Thomas Kuhn, *The Structure of Scientific Revolutions* (Chicago: University of Chicago Press, 1962).

PART TWO

THE JUSTIFICATION OF KNOWLEDGE

In Part One we considered the general nature of the knowledge of God and its "objects"—the question of *what* we know. Now in Part Two we will consider the basis or justification of knowledge. How may a claim to knowledge be justified? What *right* do we have to believe what we do?

As before, in this part of the book we are primarily concerned with the knowledge of God. But the knowledge of God is intimately related to other forms of knowledge. We know God through the created world, and we know the created world by means of God's self-revelation. Thus in considering the knowledge of God, we will have to look at knowledge in general.

CHAPTER FOUR

The Problem of Justification

A. DOES KNOWLEDGE NEED JUSTIFICATION?

We have defined the knowledge of God as a covenantal friendship. "Intellectual knowledge," knowledge of facts about God, is one aspect of that friendship for those who have reached an age of intellectual accountability. If we love God, we will seek to praise Him for His perfections and wonderful acts. To do that, we must know *about* His nature and acts, and we must continually seek to know more and more about them.

Knowledge in the "intellectual" sense is often defined as "justified, true belief." Obviously, any claim to knowledge expresses a *belief*, and no such belief qualifies as "knowledge" unless it is *true*. Furthermore, such a belief will not be knowledge if it merely *happens* to be true. Imagine an astrologer who correctly predicts the outcome of a presidential election. He had a "true belief" about the election. Did he thereby *know* the election's outcome in advance? Generally, we would say No. The astrologer had true belief, not knowledge. Why not? Because he just *happened* to be right. He had a true belief, but he had no adequate *justification* for that belief. He believed the truth, but he did so on inadequate grounds; he believed the truth, but he was not *justified* in believing the truth.

The knowledge of God in Scripture also involves justified belief. In Scripture faith is not a "leap in the dark" but is grounded in God's clear revelation of himself in nature, man, and the Bible, as we saw in Part One. The God of the Bible proves himself faithful and worthy of trust. There is no need, then, for Christians to be "fideists," people who renounce reason in religious matters.[1]

Therefore (although the point has been disputed by some philosophers) I believe that justification is an essential component of knowledge. That does not mean, however, that every demand for justification is legitimate. A child believes that there is a bird outside his window. If you ask him to justify that belief, he would probably be unable to. Does that mean that his belief is unjustified or groundless? Certainly not! Many of our beliefs are held in this sort of way: we believe them, we have a right to believe them, but we cannot articulate our reasons for believing them. Surely George Mavrodes is right when he argues that it is possible to "have a reason" for a belief without being able to "give a reason" for it.[2] Indeed, few of us could justify *any* of our beliefs in the way demanded by some philosophers! Sometimes philosophers seem to be telling us that we cannot have any justified belief unless we have a fully articulated *philosophy* of belief, an epistemology. But surely that, too, is wrong. If we must be able to give a reason for every belief, then we must be able to give a reason for every reason, and so the process of justification would require infinite chains of reasoning. Justification would be a hopeless task.

Epistemology, then, should be seen in perspective. It is a useful discipline, but it is not absolutely necessary for everyone's walk with God. There are additional reasons, too, why epistemology is a subordinate or secondary concern. (1) As Mavrodes argues, epistemological questions frequently depend on "substantive" or "content" questions. For example, the epistemological question of whether God's existence can be proved depends on the substantive question of whether God exists.[3] (2) Furthermore, we cannot prove the existence of God or of anything else unless we have some knowledge that will serve as premises for the proofs. Thus a person cannot, Mavrodes argues, "learn everything he knows from proofs."[4] (3) There is also the consideration that epistemology is simply too technical and too intricate (and therefore too uncertain) a discipline to

1. Van Til's critics typically claim that he is a fideist. But there is nothing in his writings to justify that claim, and Van Til often attacks fideism. See *Christian Theistic Evidences*, 34f.; *Common Grace and the Gospel* (Nutley, N.J.: Presbyterian and Reformed Pub. Co., 1972), 184; *The Defense of the Faith* (Philadelphia: Presbyterian and Reformed Pub. Co., 1955, 1967), 41, 100f., 199; *Why I Believe in God* (Philadelphia: Great Commission, n.d.), 16.

2. George Mavrodes, *Belief In God* (New York: Random House, 1970), 11ff.

3. Ibid., 41ff.; cf. 72ff., 76f., 95ff., 112ff.

4. Ibid., 41f. Recall also what I said in the Introduction to this book about how one must frequently have experience in doing something before he can devise a definition for it, and that applies to theology in particular.

serve as the foundation of all knowledge. Right now I believe that there is an evergreen tree outside of my window. To some epistemologists, however, that belief is subject to doubt. Maybe so; but epistemological theories are *also* subject to doubt. And when I consider all the complicated ways that epistemological theories can be mistaken, I cannot imagine any epistemologist ever persuading me that my belief about the evergreen tree is false. There must be something wrong with any theory that requires me to abandon such a belief. Epistemology, then, just does not have enough credibility to govern all my beliefs about everything. On the contrary, epistemological theories must *respect* my fundamental beliefs and build on them.

Often the search for a "foundation" or "justification" of knowledge is also *theologically* objectionable. That may sound strange. Is it not true that Christians, more than anyone else, have a right and a duty to be concerned about "justification"? Yes, in one sense, as we will see. Christians have an obligation to conform all their ideas and decisions to the Word of God. But often the search for "foundations" and "justifications" is precisely the result of an ungodly *dissatisfaction* with Scripture. Occasionally, some Christians feel that the Bible is not sufficient to serve as an *ultimate* standard of judgment, and so they believe that they need something else to serve as such a standard. They may attempt to identify their ultimate standard as something *in* Scripture (e.g., a "central theme," perhaps), or in something that is humanly derived *from* Scripture (e.g., "the meaning" of Scripture, understood as a system of exegesis or theology—see Part One), or in something that is *extrascriptural* (e.g., a philosophical epistemology). And so once again we see that though justification is a necessary aspect of knowledge, the demand that we *give* a justification, especially justification of a certain sort, is often illegitimate, as is the demand that we support our beliefs by reference to an epistemological theory.

What, then, is epistemology good for? Well, it is useful to become as self-conscious as we can be about our reasons for believing what we believe. When we are not aware of our reasons for believing something, it is difficult to analyze and to evaluate that belief, and it is certainly difficult to argue it with someone else. It is proper, then, for us to spend some time thinking about the justification of knowledge, but we should avoid becoming epistemological fanatics.

B. PERSPECTIVES ON JUSTIFICATION

In Part One, I discussed law, object, and subject (self) as elements of every piece of knowledge. Knowledge always involves a subject who knows an object according to some standard or criterion (law). I also argued in Part One that though law, object, and subject are distinct from one another, they are also inseparable: we cannot know one of them without knowing the others. Thus all of our knowledge is knowledge of the world (object); all of it is knowledge of self; and all of it is knowledge of God's standard. These distinctions, then, generate three "perspectives" on knowledge. When we think about knowledge as a knowledge of the world, we are examining it under the "situational" perspective. Knowledge as self-knowledge constitutes the "existential" perspective. And knowledge as a knowledge of law or criterion constitutes the "normative" perspective.

These perspectives are not distinct "parts" of knowledge. They are "perspectives"; each describes the *whole* of knowledge in a certain way. The existential perspective describes *all* knowledge as self-knowledge, the situational perspective as knowledge of the world, and the normative perspective as knowledge of law.

The structure of this book is based on that triad. Part One dealt with the "objects" of knowledge, with knowledge from the "situational perspective." Part Three will deal with the "methods" of knowledge, how we as subjects go about knowing—the "existential perspective." The present section, which discusses the justification and criteria of knowledge, focuses on the "normative perspective." The reader, however, should remember that these perspectives, precisely because they are perspectives, are not sharply separable. Thus we cannot understand the justification of knowledge (normative) unless we also understand something about the world (situational) and ourselves (existential). Recall again Mavrodes's points about how epistemological questions are subordinate to content questions ("situational questions," in my vocabulary). He also has some useful observations about how epistemological questions are "person-variable" ("existential"), a topic that we will discuss later. Mavrodes would not deny, I think, that the opposite points can also be made: person and content questions cannot be answered without criteria, though those criteria may not always be of the sort demanded by epistemologists (see A above). Thus as we discuss justification, we will have to consider objects and subjects, as well as criteria. To put it differently, the criteria of knowledge *include* the objects and subjects in a certain way. God's normative revelation comes to us through every object and subject, as well as through the special medium of Scripture. And objects and subjects are themselves normative in a sense: knowledge "must" (a normative "must") rightly represent its object, and it "must" be suited to its subject.

Therefore although the "justification of knowledge" focuses on the normative perspective, it must pay attention to the "normative functions" of all three perspectives. We will, then, distinguish three kinds of justification. (1) Normative justification will warrant a belief by demonstrating that it accords with the "laws of thought" (meaning in this context God's laws for human thought). (2) Situational justification will warrant a belief by demonstrating that it accords with "evidence" (i.e., the facts of creation—natural revelation—interpreted in accordance with Scripture). And (3) existential justification will warrant a belief by demonstrating its capacity to serve the needs of the subject as those needs are defined by Scripture. Because the three perspectives cohere, they will lead to the same results.

C. ETHICS AND KNOWLEDGE

It is useful to see epistemology as a subdivision of ethics. In ethics, as in epistemology, we are concerned about "justification"—the justification of human intentions, attitudes, decisions, and behavior. Ethical justification may be achieved in three ways that correspond to our system of triads. Ethical philosophers have sought to justify an act (1) by showing that it accords with an ethical standard (normative ethics, which traditionally has been called "deontologism"), (2) by showing that it produces desirable consequences ("teleological" or "utilitarian" ethics, which focuses on our "situational perspective"), and (3) by showing that it is the product of a good motive ("ethics of self-realization" or "existential" ethics). A Christian ethic should recognize some validity in each of those approaches. Because of the centrality of Scripture, certainly in Christianity there is a place for normative ethics. But if we allow Scripture to govern our thinking about these matters, then Christian ethics should also be concerned about the consequences of and the motives for our actions. Christians are to seek to glorify God in all that they do (1 Cor. 10:31, i.e., consequences), and they are always to act out of love and faith (Rom. 14:23; 1 Cor. 13:1-13, i.e., good motives).[5]

5. There is more discussion of these matters in my *Doctrine of the Christian Life*, an ethics text that I hope to publish someday.

To ask a person to justify a *belief* is to ask an ethical question. It is to ask what *ethical right* that person has to believe such and such; it is to ask whether and why we are *ethically obligated* to believe it. What is the "pressure" we feel to accept a justified belief? It is not a physical pressure, like a drug that causes hallucinations in the brain. At least we hope not! Nor is it merely the desire to believe what is convenient or in our best interests. Many justified beliefs are not convenient, and many unjustified beliefs are. The pressure, I think, can be understood only as *moral* pressure, as the pressure of conscience. After all, believing is one human activity among other human activities, and like all of those activities, believing is subject to ethical evaluation. Beliefs can be responsible or irresponsible, obedient or disobedient to God. Thus we sense an *obligation* to accept justified beliefs and to act on them, to live "according to truth." We can resist that obligation, we can dull our conscience in that regard, but that obligation always remains in effect.

Thus the three epistemological perspectives are identical to the three ethical perspectives. When we investigate the normative perspective of knowledge, we are asking what we *ought* to believe in the light of God's revealed norms. When we investigate the situational perspective of knowledge, we are asking, in effect, what beliefs are most conducive to the goals of God's kingdom. And when we investigate the existential perspective of knowledge, we are asking what beliefs are the most *godly*, arising from the best heart-motives.

The correlation between ethics and epistemology underscores our emphasis on the centrality of presuppositions. If I am right, *every* belief presupposes an ethical value judgment. When a person claims to know something, he is also claiming to be under a certain ethical obligation, to have a certain ethical right. But if knowledge claims presuppose value judgments in that way, then there is no such thing as ethically or religiously "neutral" knowledge. There are two kinds of knowledge claims: those which assume godly ethical standards and those which do not.

D. TRADITIONAL EPISTEMOLOGIES

In this section I will describe certain "tendencies" that have appeared throughout the history of epistemology. I refer to them as "tendencies" rather than as "views," because they have rarely, if ever, been held in "pure" form. Most philosophers, especially the greatest philosophers, have tried to combine elements of more than one of these tendencies. Nevertheless, these tendencies are clearly distinguishable; even if they have not been held by anyone, they have been disputed by many! It is not important to my argument that the following enumeration be the best possible classification of such tendencies or an exhaustive classification of them. It is sufficient for us to recognize that these three tendencies have existed and have influenced Christian and non-Christian thinking alike.

The first tendency, *rationalism*, or *a priorism*, is the view that human knowledge presupposes certain principles that are known independently of sense-experience and by which knowledge of our sense-experience is governed.[6] The second tendency, *empiricism*, is the view that knowledge is based on sense-experience. And the third tendency, *subjectivism*, is the view that there is no "objective" truth but only truth "for" the knowing subject, verified by criteria internal to the subject. These three tendencies correspond to the normative, situational, and existential perspectives, respectively. To the rationalist, knowledge is conformity of the mind to laws, to norms of thought. To the empiricist, knowledge is correspondence of an idea to an object. And to the subjectivist, knowledge is a state of the subject's consciousness.

That those tendencies reflect my "three perspectives" is interesting, but it should not be surprising. Any epistemology must do justice to subject, object, and criterion. When, like the majority of famous philosophers, people try to do epistemology without God, they must find an absolute somewhere else than in God. For such people it is tempting to try to make absolute, that is, to deify, one of the three elements of human knowledge—the subject (subjectivism), the object (empiricism), or the law (rationalism)—and to call the other two elements into question. In such epistemological systems there is no God to guarantee that the three elements will cohere, and so the philosopher must be prepared to make choices among those elements when there are, as in his assumption there will be, irresolvable conflicts.

No philosopher has succeeded in being a consistent rationalist, empiricist, or subjectivist, though a few have tried. Parmenides came close to being a consistent rationalist, John Stuart Mill a consistent empiricist, and Protagoras and other Sophists consistent subjectivists. But the failures of such attempts have become well known in the philosophical literature. The greatest philosophers, like Plato, Aristotle, Aquinas, and Kant, did

6. This is a somewhat different concept of "rationalism" from that used in Part One. In Part One *rationalism* referred to a characteristic of all non-Christian thinking, and, in a different sense, to a characteristic of Christian thought as well. Here, *rationalism* refers to a particular *school* of epistemology.

not try to achieve epistemological purity in terms of our categories. Instead, such philosophers have sought to do justice to divergent epistemological concerns. But that too has proved to be a difficult task. Rationalism, empiricism, and subjectivism simply cannot be reconciled, and I believe that it is impossible, without Christian commitment, to reconstruct these approaches sufficiently to make them adequate. Nevertheless, it is not surprising that philosophers have tried to combine these inconsistent tendencies, for each seems to arise out of legitimate concerns that will become evident as we look more closely at each of these approaches in turn.

(1) Rationalism

The rationalist's chief concern is *certainty*. To the rationalist, sense-experiences seem uncertain and problematic, as do subjective states. Thus, he thinks, there must be an alternative—some form of knowledge that is not derived from sense-experience and that is not distorted by human subjectivity. Such knowledge, the rationalist believes, is in fact available. It is a knowledge of *criteria*.

For example, we have experienced a great many "circular" objects, none of which, however, is *perfectly* circular. In all of them there are defects, tiny in some, more obvious in others. Thus we have never experienced a perfect circle. Yet somehow, mysteriously, we know what a perfect circle is. We can test circles to see how close or how far removed from perfection they are, because somehow we have in our minds a *criterion* of circularity.

Plato, a rationalist, more or less, concluded from such evidence that there was a whole world of perfect objects (which he called "forms") that serve as criteria for the objects of our knowledge, and he argued that we must know the forms with greater certainty than we know anything else. The criterion of circularity, for example, cannot be problematic, changeable, and fallibly apprehended, as are the circles of our experience. Our knowledge of that criterion, therefore, must come from a source other than sense-experience. And so Plato speculated that we came to know criteria in a previous life when we lived in the world of forms, without the encumbrance of a material body to inhibit our knowledge.

Regardless of Plato's speculations about preexistence, rationalists believe that criteria play a unique role in the fabric of human knowledge. We do not derive criteria *from* sense-experience, they argue; we bring them *to* sense-experience. They are "a priori" (from before), that is, *presupposed* in any analysis of experience.

So we have our criteria; what next? Generally, rationalists have argued that our knowledge is built up by a deductive process. We start with the criterial truths and then derive consequences from them by deductive logic. Why *deductive* logic? Because only deductive logic preserves the *certainty* that the rationalist craves. If you start with premises that are certain and properly apply the laws of logic to those premises, you will get a conclusion that is also certain. Thus Descartes began with the criterial certainty that he existed as a thinking being, and from that he was able, he thought, to deduce a number of conclusions—the existence of God, the reality of the world, and so forth. Thus the rationalist's goal is to establish a body of knowledge that is totally free from the uncertainties of sense-experience and subjectivity.

All of that must have sounded wonderfully promising to Plato, Descartes, and to other rationalists, but today it merely seems like a historical curiosity. No one now wants to be rationalistic in the way that those older thinkers were. Modern thinkers have found the rationalistic approach inadequate for reasons such as the following.

a. *Innate Knowledge*

The notion that we have a collection of infallible ideas of mysterious origin that do not arise from sense-experience seems mythological to twentieth-century minds, and so alternative accounts of the source of such criteria have been offered. Some have argued that concepts such as "circularity," for example, are the products of linguistic definitions, which, in turn, arise from various human needs (e.g., architecture and navigation) that may be found throughout the whole range of our epistemic faculties, including sense-experience. And they have argued that the concepts used in logic and in mathematics can also be understood in that way.[7] I do not, however, think these alternative approaches are adequate, because they do not account for the *normativity* of the criteria. If there is no normativity, there can be no epistemology (see C above). Nevertheless, I do not think that the need for normativity in knowledge forces us to move in the direction of the rationalists. Scripture tells us that laws, laws of God, are available to all men through the creation (Rom. 1:32, cf. v. 20). I see no reason to deny that sense-experience plays a role in our coming to know these laws. If the derivation of these laws from sense-experience is mysterious,

7. See the discussion of logic and mathematics in Part Three.

then surely there is an equally great mystery in the notion of an innate idea that is not based on sense-experience.

b. *Sensation*

If one argues that sensation is fallible and therefore inadequate as a source or partial source for criteria, then we should reply that rational criteria can be just as fallible as sense-experience and that it is by no means obvious that we should be guided by a philosopher's reasoning in preference to our own sense-experience. Parmenides claimed that reason demanded a motionless universe, thus contradicting all the evidence of sense-experience, but most people have thought their senses were more dependable than Parmenides' reasoning.

c. *Formalism*

After all the arguments have been presented against innate knowledge (see *a* above), there are not many areas where the rationalist's arguments are persuasive, though there are a few. Knowledge of the laws of logic, of our own mental states, and of the existence of objective truth, at least, may plausibly be argued to be a priori ideas (ideas that are independent of sense-experience) that are, perhaps, even innate. We can, however, deduce very little from such a priori ideas. Certainly, we cannot deduce the whole fabric of human knowledge from them or even enough knowledge to constitute a meaningful philosophy. Nothing follows from the laws of logic, taken alone, except possibly more laws of logic. From propositions about our own mental states, nothing follows except further propositions about our own mental states. From the statement "there are objective truths," nothing specific follows, and a statement that tells us nothing specific (which has no "applications") is not a meaningful statement (cf. the discussion of meaning and application in Part One and in Appendix C). Thus if knowledge is limited to the sorts of propositions we have just examined, we will know only about our own minds[8] and not about the real world. We cannot reason from our mental states to the real world because our mental states often deceive us. Thus rationalism leaves us not with the body of certainties that Plato and Descartes dreamed of but with no knowledge at all of the real world. And so in the final analysis, there is no difference between rationalism, on the one hand, and subjectivism and skepticism, on the other.

8. I.e., about logic and mental states.

d. *A Christian Analysis*

From a Christian point of view, it is evident that the rationalist's difficulties have a spiritual origin. The rationalist seeks certainty outside of God's Word. He seeks the ultimate criteria for thought within his own innate ideas and deductive reasoning. In biblical terms, the rationalist's quest is idolatrous because it is the attempt to deify human thought. But when we set up false gods, they inevitably fail us, and so we have seen that human, logical thought is simply incapable of supplying us with an infallible body of knowledge. When it tries to provide certain knowledge, rational thought must restrict its scope to the most abstract truths that in effect provide no knowledge at all about the real world. Thus, using the scheme that we developed in Part One, we can see how non-Christian rationalism becomes irrationalism.

e. *A Second Christian Analysis*

Essentially the same point can be made in somewhat different terms. Van Til says that human thought seeks to relate "unity" to "plurality" in the world. It seeks to unify the particulars by finding patterns among them that help us to understand them. Thus philosophers (especially rationalists) have often sought abstract rational concepts that are broad enough to include many particulars under their scope. *Bear*, for example, includes all the bears in the world; *tree* includes all the trees; *living thing* includes all trees, bears, and much more; and *being* includes everything. The more abstract our concepts become, the less they tell us about the particular things. *Dog* includes more animals than *Welsh corgi*, but it is less descriptive of the animals it designates. *Being* includes everything but says almost nothing about anything. Rationalism seeks the most abstract knowledge possible, but in doing that it finds it can make no specific claims about the world (see c above). The idolatrous quest for exhaustive human knowledge always leads to emptiness, skepticism, and ignorance.

f. *The Paradox of Analysis*

Another way to make the same point has been described as the "paradox of analysis." Pretend that I try to gain knowledge of kangaroos by formulating various equations such as "kangaroo = mammal," "kangaroo = marsupial mammal," "kangaroo = marsupial mammal found in Australia," and so forth. Such a process might be called an "analysis" of the concept "kangaroo." It works fine, until I decide that there must be an absolute identity between the two sides of the equation, which is the desire for perfect or exhaustive knowledge of the kangaroo. When I make that demand, I can satisfy it only by the equation "kangaroo = kangaroo." Although that equation gives me an absolute identity, it gives me absolutely no useful information. The moral is the same: when we seek Godlike, exhaustive, infallible knowledge, we are likely to achieve only total ignorance. Rationalism begets irrationalism.

(2) EMPIRICISM

Empiricism gains its plausibility, I think, from the popular understanding of the scientific method. The common view is that during the ancient and medieval periods, the growth of human knowledge was slow because the methods of acquiring it were based on tradition and speculation. Great thinkers like Bacon and Newton, however, convinced the world of a better way: forget traditions and speculations. Verify your hypotheses by going to the *facts*. Experiment. Observe. Measure. Gradually, observed facts will accumulate into a dependable body of knowledge. Is that not the method that made the modern age a time of enormous scientific advance?

That kind of investigation is successful, the argument goes, because it provides publicly observable checking procedures. If you do not agree with a theory, you can go and check it out. The facts are there for all to see; just compare the theory with the facts.

Although empiricists are not as concerned about certainty as rationalists are, empiricists believe that their procedure is the way for us to achieve as much certainty as is possible. What greater certainty is there than that which arises from direct encounter with the facts of experience? I believe that my shirt is brown. I believe that more certainly than I believe any philosophical epistemology and even more certainly than I believe some propositions of logic and mathematics.

Empiricism, then, seeks to avoid speculation and fantasy and to test all of our ideas by the standard of hard reality—"the facts." Here, then, is another promising program! Unlike rationalism, empiricism has been a very popular movement among twentieth-century philosophers who are concerned to make philosophy measure up to the rigorous standards of modern science. For all that, however, empiricism, like rationalism, has failed to supply us with a basis for knowledge. Consider the following reasons.

a. *Verification*

Do we know something only after we have verified it empirically, after we have checked it directly by looking at the facts? Surely not. We know many things that we have not checked ourselves and *could not* check by ourselves. For me, that knowledge includes propositions about ancient history, about nuclear particles, about heaven and hell, and so forth. In many areas, we accept testimony from those we trust, even though we are unable to verify things for ourselves. As Mavrodes argues,[9] the demand for verification is a demand that is sometimes, but not always, appropriate. It is appropriate when we are in doubt, but to make it a general requirement for knowledge would mean that every verification would have to be verified *ad infinitum*.

b. *Verifiability*

Therefore verification is not essential to knowledge; we may know something without having verified it empirically. But perhaps at least the *possibility* of verification is essential. If verification is not a criterion of knowledge, perhaps *verifiability* is. Some have charged that Christianity cannot *possibly* be verified and therefore is not worthy of serious consideration. That charge, however, is (i) often based on the presuppositions of the logical positivist philosophy[10] and thus is open to criticism on theological lines. And the *type* of verification that logical positivists demand uses the methods of autonomous science, which the Christian cannot accept. (ii) Mavrodes offers a simpler reply: verifiability cannot be a general criterion for knowledge, because often we cannot tell whether a statement is verifiable unless we first ascertain that it is true.[11] (iii) Unlike verification, verifiability cannot serve as a basis for knowledge; at most it can be a necessary condition of it. Even if all knowledge must be verifiable, not all verifiable propositions constitute knowledge. "The moon is made of green cheese" is verifiable but false and therefore not an item of knowledge.

c. *Deception*

Many philosophers have pointed out that our senses deceive us, that it is not as easy as it seems to "check out the facts" by sense-experience.

d. *The Scientific Method*

The "popular understanding of the scientific method" that we mentioned earlier is really a serious oversimplification. Scientists do not just "check out the facts" by means of sense-experience. (i) Generally they use

9. Mavrodes, *Belief*, 75ff.

10. See my "God and Biblical Language," in J. W. Montgomery, ed., *God's Inerrant Word* (Minneapolis: Bethany Fellowship, 1974), 159-77 and my *Christianity and the Great Debates*, so far unpublished.

11. Mavrodes, *Belief*, 76ff.

instruments, rather than their naked senses, because the senses by themselves are generally not sufficiently accurate for scientific purposes. But the instruments that scientists use interpose a great deal of human theoretical ingenuity between the observer and the things he observes. When he uses such instruments, the scientist is not only checking his theory with observations, he is also checking out his observations by means of theory-dependent instruments. (ii) Scientific work does not consist in just making and reporting observations but in *analyzing* and *evaluating* data. (iii) Scientific theories do not merely report observational data; they go beyond it. Scientific laws are usually general; they claim to hold for the entire universe. (iv) What we "see," "hear," "smell," "taste," and "feel" is influenced by our expectations. Those expectations do not come just from sense-experience but from theories, cultural experience, group loyalties, prejudice, religious commitments, and so forth. Thus there is no "purely empirical" inquiry. We never encounter "brute," that is, uninterpreted, facts. We only encounter facts that have been interpreted in terms of our existing commitments.[1] (v) Often, then, scientists do not recognize data that contradict their theories. But even when they do, they do not immediately accept such data as refutations of the theories in question. An apparently contradictory datum constitutes a "problem" to be solved in terms of the theory, not a refutation of it. Only when the problems multiply and alternative theories begin to look more promising will the scientist abandon his theory for another. For all of those reasons, the work of science is far more than merely "checking out the facts." And if scientists are unable to separate theory from fact, nonscientists can hardly be expected to do so. Science does not operate by means of a pure empiricism, and certainly the rest of us cannot be expected to either.

e. *Empiricism Too Limited*

If we consistently followed an empirical approach to knowledge, we would have to abandon many claims to knowledge that otherwise we would make without hesitation. (i) Empiricism cannot justify a *general* proposition, such as "all men are mortal" or "F = MA." Such general propositions always go beyond anything we can observe, because they encompass the whole universe. Similarly, the propositions of logic and mathematics, propositions that claim to be universally true, cannot be established on an empirical basis. (ii) Empiricism cannot justify any statements about the future, for no one has known the future by sense-experience, and

1. See Thomas Kuhn, *The Structure of Scientific Revolutions* (Chicago: University of Chicago Press, 1970).

so empiricism cannot justify scientific prediction. Thus we must either drastically limit the scope of what we call "knowledge" or else abandon empiricism. (iii) As Hume pointed out, empiricism cannot justify any statements about ethical values. Statements about sensible facts do not imply anything about ethical goodness or badness, right or wrong, or obligation or prohibition. But as we have seen above in C, epistemology is a subdivision of ethics, and knowledge depends on our adoption and use of ethical values. If empiricism cannot justify the language about empirical values, then it cannot justify any claim to knowledge. (iv) Therefore empiricism cannot justify empiricism. For empiricism is a view of how one *ought* (an ethical "ought") to justify his beliefs, and on an empiricist basis, we cannot justify from sense-experience the proposition that we *ought* to justify our beliefs in that way.

f. *Knowledge of God*

Empiricism also rules out claims to know God, if God is thought to be invisible or otherwise resistant to empirical "checking procedures." For some empiricists, that fact rules out the knowledge of God. For Christians, it rules out empiricism as a general theory of knowledge.

g. *Facts*

What are the "facts" that empiricists believe we directly experience? These "facts" are difficult to identify, as we have seen. Are there any "facts" about which we can be *certain*? Some people have suggested that if we cannot know the world infallibly through our senses, at least we can know infallibly our own sense-experience! For example, I have a sensation of greenness. That may or may not mean that there is something green in my vicinity; my senses may be deceiving me. One thing that I do know, however, is that I have a green *sensation*. (Sometimes this is called a green "sense-datum.") Well, maybe so. But notice that here the empiricist has shifted his ground pretty drastically. Instead of a claim to know the world *by means of* sense-experience, he now claims to know *only* his sense-experience, *only* his own ideas. Instead of knowing "facts," now we know only a certain type of fact—those about our own subjectivity. And on the basis of those facts, we can determine nothing about the world beyond our own minds. Just as we saw that in the final analysis there is no difference between rationalism and subjectivism, now we see that there is no difference between empiricism and subjectivism.

h. A *Christian Analysis*

Like the problems of rationalism, the problems of empiricism are essentially spiritual. Like rationalists, empiricists have tried to find certainty apart from God's revelation, and that false certainty has shown itself to be bankrupt. Even if the laws of logic are known to us (and it is unclear how they could be on an empirical basis), we could deduce nothing from statements about sensation except, at most, other statements about sensation. Thus, once again, rationalism[13] becomes irrationalism: a bold plan for autonomously building the edifice of knowledge ends up in total ignorance.

(3) SUBJECTIVISM

It seems, then, that we are shut up to subjectivism, both by process of elimination and also because rationalism and empiricism are defensible only in forms that are indistinguishable from subjectivism.

Apart from the problems of rationalism and empiricism, however, subjectivism has much to recommend it. As Mavrodes indicates, proofs of propositions are "person-variable."[14] For example, you can have an argument that is logically valid (the premises imply the conclusion) and sound (the premises are true) that does not persuade the person you are arguing with. In that case, though you have a valid and sound argument, in one sense you have not "proved" your case. Proof, or persuasion, depends on many subtle personal factors that are difficult, if not impossible, to formulate in a general epistemology.

What happens when I am finally persuaded of something? Is there one thing that identifies the moment of persuasion, the moment when a hypothesis becomes a belief or knowledge? That is a difficult question to answer. Could the "one thing" be a sound argument? But as Mavrodes indicates, sound arguments do not always persuade. I may be confronted by a sound argument and still think that it is unsound, because of various objections that occur to me. Yet sometimes as I compare the argument with the objections, at some point I become convinced of the soundness of the argument. The objections become less convincing to me, the argument more so, and at some point I decide to affirm the argument and to reject the objections. What happens to make me do that? It's hard to say. It's just something that happens inside of me—a psychological change, perhaps—a growing friendliness to one conclusion and a hostility toward another. The

13. In the sense of "rationalism" discussed in Part One, empiricism is itself a *form* of rationalism.

14. Mavrodes, *Belief*, 7f., 27ff., 31-41, 80-89, 101-11.

change may have any number of causes. Logical reasoning is one, but what makes the logical reasoning *persuasive* to me? Sense-experience is another, but what makes me accept one interpretation of sense-experience in preference to a different one? Religious presuppositions, group loyalties, aesthetic tastes, socio-economic and racial biases—any number of good or bad factors can influence the process of persuasion.

Thus it seems that in the final analysis, knowledge-claims are psychological states, and each of us evaluates those claims by a wide range of highly personal, individual criteria. There is no "objective" truth, truth that is publicly accessible by universally accepted criteria; there is only truth "for" the individual. Therefore there is no knowledge of an objective truth, only knowledge of my own experience that is based on my own internal criteria.

Or so it seems. But there are problems even with subjectivism!

a. *Inter-Subjective Truth*

Subjectivism cannot be consistently asserted or argued. The subjectivist tries to convince others of his view, and thus he concedes that there is some truth knowable to others besides himself. But his theory denies such inter-subjective truth. He claims to know objectively the truth that there is no objective truth, and that is a self-defeating argument, a kind of contradiction. This argument goes back to Parmenides and Plato and has been used for centuries by rationalists and empiricists against subjectivism and skepticism. Because the subjectivist inevitably asserts his subjectivism in a dogmatic manner, his non-Christian irrationalism reduces to rationalism (just as non-Christian rationalism reduces to irrationalism).

b. *Consistency*

When faced with this contradiction, the subjectivist may choose to become even more irrationalistic. He may reply that he is not asserting that subjectivism is objectively true, only that it is true for him. But here the objector may properly ask if the subjectivist is willing to apply his theory to his *life*. If the subjectivist stops at red lights and seeks to avoid eating poisonous materials, we may conclude that he is really an objectivist at heart. On the other hand, if the subjectivist is willing to live without any objective constraints at all, then he is insane and there is not much that we can say to him, except to bear witness.

c. *Facts and Criteria*

Furthermore even if we concede that truth and knowledge are internal to the subject and that they rest on internal, subjective criteria, we still have not disposed of the claims of rationalism and empiricism. The subjectivist still must face the questions about "facts" and "criteria." Granting that there is no "objective" truth, what are the criteria for an individual's "subjective truth"? Granted that he is "shut up to his inner experience," he must still make a judgment about what in that inner experience will determine his life-decisions. Part of his inner experience, for example, will be the Bible, or a set of images and thoughts about the Bible. The individual must ask whether he will let that Bible rule his life or whether he will let some other element of his experience rule his life. Whether the Bible is an external fact or an internal datum does not matter; it still must be dealt with. And the same is true about the laws of logic, the self, and the facts of the world. The subjectivist must ask how all of those relate to one another. His subjectivism has not freed him in the least from wrestling with these epistemological questions; his subjectivism has not solved any of them. The subjectivist must decide whether to be a subjective-rationalist, a subjective-empiricist, a subjective-subjectivist, or, perhaps, a subjective-Christian! Therefore since the subjectivist move accomplishes nothing, it can hardly be regarded as a meaningful epistemological alternative to rationalism and empiricism. And so the irrationalism of subjectivism manifests itself as just another form of rationalism or empiricism.

d. A *Christian Analysis*

Once again the issues are spiritual. The subjectivist seeks to avoid responsibility to anything outside of himself; he seeks to become his own lord, and that is a form of idolatry. As a god, the self is a failure. And as he flees inside himself to escape responsibility to facts and to criteria, the subjectivist discovers facts and criteria within his own being, staring him in the face, because the true God reveals himself even in the heart of the subjectivist. Even when we seek to flee within ourselves, God is there. His laws and His facts cannot be avoided.

(4) COMBINATIONS

No one, of course, is a pure rationalist, empiricist, or subjectivist. Plato was subjectivistic about the world of sense-experience or "opinion" and rationalistic about the "world of forms." Kant was skeptical about metaphysics and theology, but he combined elements of rationalism and empiricism in his account of mathematics and science. Might one of these more sophisticated epistemologies succeed where the simpler ones fail? I think not. Adding zero to zero makes zero. Combining one bankrupt epistemology with another leads nowhere.

a. *Plato*

Plato was skeptical about the world of sense-experience, but he believed that we could have infallible knowledge of criteria, the forms that exist in another world. Forms are supposed to be the models of which the world of experience is an image, but the world of experience is an *inadequate* image of the world of forms. The world of experience contains imperfections that the forms do not have. After all, then, the forms do not do their job; they do not account for *all* the qualities of the world of experience. The imperfections of this world make the forms imperfect. If the forms were perfect, however, then the imperfect world would not exist; it would be identical to the world of forms. Therefore Plato's attempt to combine rationalism (the forms) with irrationalism (the world of experience) fails. The two cannot coexist in the same universe without destroying one another or without one being turned into the other.

b. *Kant*

Kant was skeptical about "what really is" (the "noumenal" in his terminology) and rationalistic about "appearances" (the "phenomenal"). According to Kant, we cannot know what really is, but we can have a thorough, rational understanding of phenomena. But if we know nothing about reality, how can we even understand what the phenomena "really" are? And if we can distinguish clearly between phenomenal and noumenal, then do we not know something, after all, about the noumenal—namely that it exists? All the traditional arguments against skepticism (see *(3)* above) may be used against Kant's account of the noumenal, and all the traditional arguments against rationalism and empiricism (see *(1)* and *(2)* above) can be used against his account of the phenomenal.

CHAPTER FIVE

Perspectives on Justification

A. NORMATIVE JUSTIFICATION

No Christian should be a rationalist, empiricist, or subjectivist, as these terms have been used historically. Although these three epistemological traditions have been developed primarily by unbelieving thinkers, they do have some positive value. In spite of their unbelieving nature, these positions display a certain knowledge of the truth.

Rationalism recognizes a need for criteria, or standards; empiricism a need for objective, publicly knowable facts; and subjectivism a need for our beliefs to meet our own internal criteria. A Christian epistemology will recognize all of those concerns but will differ from the rationalist, empiricist, and subjectivist schools of thought in important ways. Most importantly, the Christian will recognize the lordship of God in the field of knowledge. God is sovereign, and He coordinates law, object, and subject, so that the three cohere; a true account of one will never conflict with a true account of the others. We do not need, then, to choose one of those three elements, make it the "key" to knowledge, and pit it against the other two. Indeed, in most cases, to seek such a "key" is idolatry; it is an attempt to find an infallible guide other than God's Word in Scripture, to find some other absolute criterion of truth.

But there is no need for Christians to fall into epistemological despair. Although we avoid the rationalistic search for an infallible something beyond Scripture, we need not fall into skepticism, as if that were the only alternative. Because God has revealed himself clearly in Scripture and in creation, we can speak confidently about the justification of our knowledge of Him, a justification that can be described from three perspectives. Under "normative justification," we will consider divine law, God's revelation, as justification for knowledge; and in succeeding sections, we will consider the roles that creation ("situational") and the self ("existential") play in justifying our knowledge of God.

(1) God's Epistemological Authority

We have seen that God's lordship is comprehensive, that it extends to every area of human life, including our thoughts, beliefs, and knowledge. Scripture teaches that sort of lordship in various ways. (a) It teaches that God must prevail in any dispute about His truth or justice. He is not obligated to answer accusations against himself. Indeed, when accused, He turns the tables; He accuses His accusers. In Genesis 3:4, the serpent accused God of lying maliciously, and Adam and Eve accepted the Devil's viewpoint. When God appeared, however, He did not defend himself against the false charge. Instead, He judged His accusers and prevailed against them (vv. 14-19). When by divine order Abraham lifted the knife against his own son (Gen. 22:1-18), God did not explain how He could righteously order a man to kill his own son. Instead, He simply commended Abraham for his obedience.[1]

(b) God rejects the wisdom of the world and calls His people to a special wisdom of His own that is sharply at odds with the world's values. Believers are to stand *for* God's wisdom and *against* false teaching, even under the most difficult challenges.[2] This is a touchy subject for modern people; intellectual authoritarianism is difficult to present attractively! Intellectual freedom, academic freedom, freedom of speech and thought—these are important values in our time. Can modern people be brought to worship a God who is an intellectual authoritarian? That depends, of course, on God and His grace. The fact is, however, that this authoritarianism is the source of true intellectual freedom. Human thinking must be subject to a norm, to a criterion. If we reject God as our norm, we must find another (rationalism) or despair entirely of knowledge (skepticism). Rationalism brings intellectual bondage to human systems, and skepticism is intel-

1. Also see Job 38-42; Isa. 45:9f.; Matt. 20:1-15; Rom. 3:3f., 26, and note how Paul answered doubting questions by first rebuking them with the exclamation *me genoito*, "may it not be!" We will look at those passages more closely in my forthcoming *Doctrine of God* in the section on the problem of evil.

2. See Prov. 1:7 passim; Jer. 9:23f.; 1 Cor. 1:18-2:16; 3:18-23; 8:1-3; 2 Cor. 10:2-5; Gal. 1:8f.; Eph. 3:8f.; Col. 2:2-23; 1 Tim. 1:3-11; 4:1-5; 2 Tim. 3:1-17; James 3:13-17; 2 Peter 1:16-2:22; 1 John 1:20-23; 4:1-6; Jude 3-4; Rev. 2:14-15.

lectual death. When we serve God, however, our minds are set free from human traditions and from the death of skepticism to accomplish their great tasks.

(2) PRESUPPOSITIONS

Earlier we defined an ultimate presupposition as "a belief over which no other takes precedence," or, more profoundly, as a "basic commitment of the heart." Since God is Lord and rules us by His Word, Christians have presuppositions. Our hearts are committed to Him, and no other belief can take precedence over our belief in Him and His Word.

The term "presupposition" may be confusing in some respects. In several recent books, such as Mark Hanna, *Crucial Questions in Apologetics*,[3] and R. Sproul, J. Gerstner, and A. Lindsley, *Classical Apologetics*,[4] *presupposition* seems to designate a mere "supposition," "assumption," or "postulate"—a belief that is chosen arbitrarily, with no rational basis whatsoever. That, however, is neither my concept nor Van Til's. To be sure, many people choose their presuppositions arbitrarily, or at least on insufficient grounds. Unbelievers are in precisely that position. But the idea of arbitrary selection is not a necessary part of the concept of a presupposition. Indeed, the Christian presupposition has the strongest possible rational ground: it is based on God's revelation. In Hanna's terms, it is "veridical knowledge," not a "postulate." It can even be *proved*, by a kind of argument (circular, to be sure, but cogent), as we will see.

Despite that potential for misunderstanding, I still prefer *presupposition* to *starting point*, which is sometimes used by Van Til and others as a synonym for *presupposition. Starting point* is even more ambiguous than *presupposition* and has, I believe, caused quite a bit of confusion in discussions about epistemology and apologetics. A starting point for a discussion can be (a) a point with which one literally *begins* the discussion (e.g., it might be nothing more than a joke or other "icebreaker"), (b) a point that receives major *emphasis* in the discussion, (c) a *hypothesis* that is to be evaluated in the course of the discussion, (d) a *method* by which one intends to present the material, (e) a conviction about what is most *important* (not necessarily the same as *(b)*), (f) a point that is best presented before other points, for example, for *pedagogical* reasons, (g) a necessary or sufficient *condition* of the conclusion to be argued, (h) *data* presented for analysis, or (i) a

3. Grand Rapids: Baker Book House, 1981.
4. Grand Rapids: Zondervan Publishing House, 1984.

presupposition. The last, of course, should not be confused with any of the others. Unfortunately, though, there has been confusion of this sort, both among Van Til's disciples and among his critics.

Non-Christians as well as Christians have presuppositions. Everyone has them because everyone has some commitment that at a particular time (granted, it may change) is "basic" to him. Everyone has a scale of values in which one loyalty takes precedence over another until we reach one that takes precedence over all the rest. That value is that person's presupposition, his basic commitment, his ultimate criterion. Theologically, the point can be expressed this way: when people forsake the true God, they come under bondage to idols. When they reject the true standard, they adopt a false one.

Thus it is wrong to say that Christians are "biased" or "prejudiced" by their presuppositions and that non-Christians are "neutral," "unbiased," and "objective." Both groups are equally biased and equally prejudiced. Jesus said, "He who is not for me is against me" (Matt. 12:30). The non-Christian is as passionately concerned to reject God as the Christian is to love Him. In the Garden, Eve may have thought that she was playing the role of a "neutral" judge who could choose between God's word and Satan's, but in fact her very decision to consider those competing revelations on an equal basis came from a fallen mind. She was not "neutral"; by that time she hated God.

The situation is complicated further in that the unbeliever knows God (as we saw in Part One), and this knowledge influences his thoughts, speech, and actions in varying degrees and ways. In a sense, then, the unbeliever has *two* presuppositions. He presupposes both truth and falsehood, both the reality of God and the unreality of God. His thinking, therefore, is radically contradictory. If, however, we ask what his *ultimate* presupposition is, the most basic commitment of his heart, we would have to say that it is unbelief—a passionate desire to oppose and to frustrate God's purposes.

(3) The Oddness of Religious Language

Philosophers of the school of language analysis have often argued that when compared with other types of language, religious language is rather "odd." There are, of course, some types of religious language that are not odd at all. "Let us turn to hymn number 215" is religious language of a sort, but it is not philosophically problematic. When religious people begin to utter propositions about God, Christ, or salvation—when they begin to use creedal language—however, difficulties start to emerge. Philosophers of the language analysis school note that (a) such religious language tends to be uttered with much more *certainty* than other language, that (b) it does not seem to be open to the kinds of tests (e.g., verification, falsification) to which, for example, the propositions of science are subject, that (c) religious language becomes a defining mark of a community, so that only those who agree with its propositions are allowed to be members in good standing, and that (d) religious language has a strong emotional component; it is embraced with passion, religious fear, wonder, and joy.

In my article "God and Biblical Language,"[5] I argue that the oddness of religious language stems from the fact that such language expresses and applies presuppositional commitments. It is the language of certainty, because it expresses a person's most fundamental commitments, his greatest certainties. It resists what are otherwise normal demands for verification, because it claims to furnish the *standards*, or *criteria*, for verification. It defines the community, because the community exists by virtue of its mutual allegiance to these commitments. And there is a strong emotional element in religious language, because religious commitments govern the whole of one's life, including emotions. That to which we are most firmly committed will be the source of our greatest passions, insofar as we live consistently with our beliefs.

In my article I argue that point at greater length. I summarize the material here to indicate the usefulness of a presuppositional analysis for understanding religion in general and for showing the parallel between Christian and non-Christian religious commitments in particular. For Christian language and the language of other specific religious beliefs are not the only types of religious language that are odd in the ways we have mentioned above. Atheism, humanism, and secularism also use language in those same odd ways. The perfectibility of man, the joys of the secular city, and even the nonexistence of God function as "presuppositions" in my sense.[6] Those presuppositions, like their explicitly religious counterparts, are uttered with certainty, resist verification, create communities of thought, and excite the emotions of those who adhere to them.[7]

5. In J. W. Montgomery, ed., *God's Inerrant Word* (Minneapolis: Bethany Fellowship, 1974).

6. In my article I seek to use such arguments about the oddness of all ultimate-commitment language to turn the tables on critics of Christianity, such as Antony Flew.

7. "God and Biblical Language" also discusses a sense in which religious language is "ordinary," in addition to the sense in which it is "odd."

(4) All Knowing Is Theologizing

The Christian presupposition, God's revelation of himself in Scripture, is the highest "law of thought" for human beings. Scripture, therefore, justifies all human knowledge.

But how does Scripture do that? (a) Some of our beliefs can be justified *explicitly* by scriptural teaching, for example, the belief that God so loved the world that He sent His Son to die for our sins (John 3:16). (b) Other beliefs can be justified as logical *deductions* from biblical premises (cf. my account of logic in Part Three of this book). An example of that would be the doctrine of the Trinity, which (as formulated at Nicaea and Constantinople) is not found explicitly in Scripture but can be deduced from doctrines that are found explicitly in Scripture. (c) Other beliefs can be defended as *applications* of Scripture. "Don't cheat on your income tax" cannot be defended on scriptural premises alone; extrabiblical information is needed about the nature of income tax, though "Don't cheat on your income tax" is clearly an application of the eighth commandment, and thus is part of that commandment's "meaning" (see Part One).

What of (d) beliefs like "Sacramento is the capital of California," which don't seem to fit under any of these categories? Is there any sense in which Scripture warrants them as well? Yes. One element of justification is a belief's *coherence* with Scripture. Scripture has a kind of veto-power over beliefs that are inconsistent with its teachings—such as "Man has evolved." Scripture does not veto beliefs that are consistent with its teachings, and such consistency is a necessary condition of justification. Not all beliefs consistent with Scripture, however, are true. "Escondido is the capital of California" is not inconsistent with Scripture in any obvious way, but it is not thereby true; therefore coherence with Scripture is not *sufficient* to justify a belief. There is a stronger sense, however, in which beliefs in category *(d)* are justified by Scripture. Scripture commands us to use all diligence to discover the truth and to live by it.[8] When we seek to obey this scriptural principle, it leads us to affirm, among other things, that Sacramento is the capital of California. In one sense, then, even beliefs of this sort are applications of Scripture. All knowing is theologizing!

In one sense, then, Scripture is the "foundation" of all human knowledge. The position I am arguing, however, should not be confused with what has been called "foundationalism."[9] Foundationalism is the view

8. See Deut. 17:6f.; 19:15; Matt. 18:16; 1 Thess. 5:21; 1 Tim. 5:19; 1 John 4:1ff.

9. Cf., e.g., N. Wolterstorff, *Reason Within the Bounds of Religion* (Grand Rapids: Wm. B. Eerdmans Pub. Co., 1976), 24ff.

that knowledge begins with a body of propositions that are known with absolute certitude and from which all the rest of our knowledge can be derived by logical deduction (or, perhaps, induction). "Rationalism" and "empiricism," as we earlier discussed them, are forms of foundationalism, the former finding its foundational certitudes in the *a priori* truths of reason, the other finding its foundation in reports of sense-experience. In general, I agree with Wolterstorff's critique of those forms of foundationalism: it is difficult to find enough foundational propositions to build an adequate foundation for knowledge, and most likely it is impossible to deduce or to induce from any proposed foundation an adequate body of certain knowledge. Furthermore, there are many justified, true beliefs (such as the child's belief that there is a bird outside his window) that do not seem to be deducible from any plausible group of "foundational certainties." Rationalism and empiricism also violate my stricture against seeking infallible knowledge outside of Scripture.

Now Wolterstorff also mentions a form of foundationalism in which the Bible serves as the foundation. I agree with the "biblical foundationalists" that the Bible contains knowledge about which we can be certain. Whether Wolterstorff agrees with this I do not know for sure; if he does not, he is wrong. But I would not seek to derive all human knowledge from the Bible, either by a deductive or an inductive process. The process by which Scripture justifies all human knowledge is different, in my view, from either of those two processes. And I would not say that a person must be able to present a biblical rationale to be justified in a belief (see chapter 4, A).

Therefore we do not need to affirm foundationalism, though we should recognize that in an important (nonfoundationalistic) sense, Scripture warrants all human knowledge. Since our knowledge requires that sort of scriptural justification, the denial of scriptural authority effectively leaves human knowledge without any justification. Thus again, in another way, we see how non-Christian rationalism leads to skepticism.

(5) Scripture Justifies Itself

If Scripture is the ultimate justification for all human knowledge, how should we justify our belief in Scripture itself? By Scripture, of course! There is no more ultimate authority, no more reliable source of information, and nothing that is more certain by which Scripture might be tested.

Does Scripture's self-attestation imply that we may not use extrabiblical evidence in arguing for biblical authority? We may use such evidence, and indeed we ought to (see F below). But even as we select, interpret, and evaluate evidence, we must presuppose a biblical epistemology. Therefore, in a sense, our argument for Scripture will always be circular. Even in our use of evidence, Scripture will be, in effect, justifying itself.

(6) Circularity

Thus we face a major problem: since circular arguments are usually considered to be fallacious, how can the Christian justify circularity in his argument for Christianity?

a. *No Alternative to Circularity*

Criticism is effective only when the critic can suggest a better way. But there is no alternative to circularity. First, allegiance to our Lord demands that we be loyal to Him, even when we are seeking to justify our assertions about Him. We cannot abandon our covenant commitment to escape the charge of circularity. Second, no system can avoid circularity, because all systems (as we have seen)—non-Christian as well as Christian—are based on presuppositions that control their epistemologies, argumentation, and use of evidence. Thus a rationalist can prove the primacy of reason only by using a rational argument. An empiricist can prove the primacy of sense-experience only by some kind of appeal to sense-experience. A Muslim can prove the primacy of the Koran only by appealing to the Koran. But if all systems are circular in that way, then such circularity can hardly be urged against Christianity. The critic will inevitably be just as "guilty" of circularity as the Christian is.

b. *Circularity Restricted*

Circularity in a system is properly justified *only* at one point: in an argument for the *ultimate* criterion of the system. The Christian employs circularity in his argument for Scripture, the rationalist in his argument for reason, and the empiricist in his argument for sense-experience, but that does not imply that circularity is permissible in other sorts of arguments. "Paul wrote Second Timothy because Paul wrote Second Timothy" is a circular argument whose circularity is *not* justified. It is possible to argue the Pauline authorship of Second Timothy on the basis of higher and broader principles than the Pauline authorship of Second Timothy. Allowing circularity at one point in a system, therefore, does not commit us to allowing circularity at all points.

c. *Narrow and Broad Circles*

It is important to distinguish between "narrow" and "broad" circles. "Scripture is the Word of God because it is the Word of God" is a "narrow" circle, as is the similar argument "Scripture is the Word of God because it says it is the Word of God." But it is possible to broaden the circle. One way to do so is by bringing more biblical data into the argument. "Scripture is the Word of God because in Exodus, Deuteronomy, and elsewhere God indicates His desire to rule His people by a written text, because in 2 Timothy 3:16 and 2 Peter 1:21 the Old Testament is identified with that covenantal constitution, because Jesus appointed the apostles to write authoritative words," and so forth. Although that argument is still circular (we are listening to what Scripture says about Scripture), it is more persuasive because it offers us more data. And we can broaden the circle even more than that: "Scripture is the Word of God because archaeology, history, and philosophy verify its teachings." If used rightly, that argument will still be circular, because the archaeology, history, and philosophy in view will be *Christian* sciences that presuppose the biblical world view. But that argument will be more persuasive than a *bare* circle. Thus to say that our argument for Christianity is circular need not imply a *narrow* circle. That fact removes some of the sting from our admission of circularity.

d. *Circularity and Persuasion*

But how can a circular argument, even one that is broadly so, be *persuasive*? In several ways. First, a circular argument displays more vividly the *meaning* of the conclusion. When we set forth the biblical and extrabiblical evidence for scriptural authority, for example, the meaning of scriptural authority becomes clearer (see our earlier equation of meaning with application, or use); and the better we understand biblical authority, the more cogent the idea becomes to us. Second, a circular argument sets forth the conclusion together with its true *rationale*, the reasons why it should be accepted. That is all that an argument can do. The unbeliever may not wish to accept that true rationale, but that recalcitrance exists whether the argument is circular or not. Third, even the unbeliever, "at some level of his consciousness," will recognize the truth of the conclusion and of its rationale. That is the message of Romans 1. The unbeliever is made in the image of God and therefore is made to think in God's way. In the present context, circularity is God's way. Thus the unbeliever, at some level of his consciousness, will recognize the persuasiveness of the circular argument for Christianity. Fourth, the circular argument presents a framework for the interpretation of Christianity—a presuppositional methodology, a conceptual scheme—and that is always an aid to understanding the cogency of a position.

e. *Competing Circularities*

The perspective just developed should help us to resolve the issue of "competing circularities." A Muslim argues that the Koran is God's Word because the Koran so testifies. A Christian argues that the Bible is God's Word because the Bible so testifies. How can they resolve that impasse? Are they reduced to shouting at one another? Are we reduced to making an arbitrary choice between the two positions? First, consider that as Christians we do not reject Islam arbitrarily but on the basis of God's revelation, which we know to be true. Second, our rejection of Islam is cogent for the same reasons that Christianity itself is cogent. Third, a broadly circular argument for Christianity will display the internal coherence of the Christian position—the fact that it "holds together" on its own terms—a coherence that can be compared with that of the Muslim or other non-Christian system. The non-Christian will be unable to maintain his system consistently, and he will rely on Christian concepts at crucial points. Fourth, because the Muslim is made in the image of God, at some level he is able to see the cogency of the Christian circle and the implausibility of his own.

Consider an illustration adapted from one of R. M. Hare's. Imagine that you are dealing with a paranoid student who believes that all professors are out to kill him. Everything you say he reinterprets according to his presuppositions and turns into evidence for his position. You say that the professors have been kind and generous to him, but he replies that they are only scheming to gain his confidence so that later they may kill him more easily. Here, again, we have two circularities—yours, and the paranoid's. How do you deal with him? Well, you certainly do not accept *his* circle, nor do you try to fashion a third position, supposedly "neutral," between your truth and his distortion. To rescue someone from quicksand, you must stand on the solid ground. You simply proclaim the truth, together with the arguments for that truth (its rationale). You assume that no matter how ingenious the paranoid may be at assimilating your data into his system, he still "knows" at some level, or at least is capable of knowing, that he is wrong and that you are right. Otherwise, the conversation is totally hopeless. But we know that it is not hopeless; sometimes paranoids do return to reality. Communication *is* possible.

(7) Coherence

I mentioned above ((6), *e*) that a broadly circular argument is persuasive in part because it displays the internal coherence of the system in question. Now I will develop the concept of coherence.

Secular philosophers have sometimes espoused a "coherence theory of truth." That theory means that a system of thought is true if it is internally consistent with itself. The coherence theory of truth is sometimes contrasted with the "correspondence theory" of truth, the belief that truth is a correspondence between idea and reality. Empiricists have tended to favor the correspondence theory, and rationalists have tended to favor the coherence theory. Rationalists (as we have seen) doubt the empiricist claim of access to "facts" through sense experience, and so they seek a kind of truth that can be tested without such access, one that can be tested by reference to our ideas alone. Because our "normative perspective" represents a kind of "Christian rationalism," it is proper for us to consider coherence at this point and correspondence later under the situational perspective.[10]

Certainly, God's truth is coherent. God is a God of order, not chaos. He speaks truth, not falsehood. He cannot lie. He cannot make a promise and then break it. All that He does reflects an infinitely wise eternal plan. Therefore our God is rational and logical. Coherence, then, is a mark of His truth. In Scripture coherence is used as a test of religious truth.[11]

That coherence, however, is not always easy for us to identify. There are "apparent contradictions" in Scripture.[12] Some of these may be resolvable by human logic and ingenuity; some may not be. Therefore it is not likely that Christian theology will ever be successfully formulated as an axiomatic deductive system.

Although we cannot formally demonstrate the *complete* coherence of the Christian system, at least we can show that systems that reject the bib-

10. Basically, my view is that both of these theories, with modifications, can serve as "perspectives" on the idea of truth, though neither ought to function as its sole definition or criterion.

11. See Deut. 18:20-22; Matt. 12:22-28; 1 Cor. 15:12-20.

12. See my discussion of logic in Part Three and my essay *Van Til the Theologian* (Phillipsburg, N.J.: Pilgrim Publishing, 1976), which was also published as "The Problem of Theological Paradox" in *Foundations of Christian Scholarship*, ed. Gary North (Vallecito, Calif.: Ross House Books, 1976).

lical God are not able to maintain intelligibility, let alone coherence. Thus the relative coherence of the Christian system, even if not all the problems are resolved, will be seen as an asset. But the coherence in view must itself be defined in terms of Christian presuppositions. It is not that "coherence" or "logical consistency" is a kind of neutral principle by which all religious claims can be tested. The meaning of "theological coherence" must itself arise from Scripture. Otherwise, it is difficult to escape the objection against the coherence theory that there may possibly be more than one fully coherent system. But if we develop our concept of coherence from Scripture, then we presuppose that competing systems will not, in the final analysis, be proved coherent, that they are unstable in themselves, and that they depend on Christian concepts—"borrowed capital"—for their apparent plausibility. We value coherence because we have been overwhelmed by the divine wisdom displayed in Scripture, not the other way around. To use coherence as a test of truth is simply to display that wisdom in all of its wonderful unity.

(8) CERTAINTY

The rationalist tradition, we may recall, was concerned primarily with attaining certainty. Is our "normative justification" (opposed, but parallel to secular rationalism) able to furnish us with certainty? We have, after all, been stressing the fallibility of human knowledge-claims, the idolatry of trying to find an infallible authority outside Scripture. Does that mean that all of our knowledge is tentative, uncertain? No. God wants us to be certain of the things about which He has instructed us.[13]

The very nature of an ultimate presupposition is that it is held with certainty. An ultimate presupposition is an ultimate criterion of truth, and therefore it is a criterion by which all other alleged certainties are tested. There is no higher criterion by which the certainty of such a presupposition can be called in question. Thus by its very nature, such a presupposition is the most certain thing that we know. And the certainty that belongs to presuppositions also belongs to their implications and applications. Implications and applications constitute the *meaning* of a presupposition; how can the presupposition be certain if its meaning is uncertain? If "Thou shalt not steal" is a certain command of revelation, then "Thou shalt not embezzle"—an applicatory exegesis of that command—is no less

13. See Luke 1:4; cf. Acts 1:3; Rom. 5:2, 5; 8:16; 2 Tim. 1:12; 2 Peter 1:10; 1 John 2:3; 5:13.

certain. Both commands are the commands of God. And since, in one sense (see *(4)*, above), all knowledge can be seen as an application of our presuppositions, it is possible to say that all of our knowledge is certain.

We do not, however, always *feel* certain. Our sense of certainty rises and falls, for several reasons.

a. *Sin*

Because in this life we are not sinlessly perfect, we are not pure in our allegiance to our Lord. Thus our presupposition of the truth of God's Word competes in our minds with the contrary presupposition, and that creates doubt and wavering. Although the Heidelberg Catechism makes assurance a necessary element of faith (question 21), the Westminster Confession of Faith reminds us that "a true believer may wait long and conflict with many difficulties before he be partaker of" assurance (chapter XX). There is truth in both positions. Faith and assurance are inseparable because the very nature of faith is to accept God's Word as our supreme certainty. But in this life, faith itself is imperfect. Faith as a mustard seed, faith at its weakest, is sufficient for salvation, but a weak faith will be accompanied by many difficulties and doubts.

b. *Ignorance*

In addition to the problem of sinful doubt, there is an intellectual problem, too. Some Christians simply have not become conscious of the implications of their faith. They honestly confess Christ as their Lord and thus as their ultimate presupposition, but they have not thought through the implications of Christ's lordship for their intellectual lives. Thus the certainty of their faith is somewhat subconscious. They need to learn that faith means presupposing and that presupposing means certainty. A Christian may doubt, but in terms of his presupposition, he has no *right* to doubt, no *justification* for doubting.

c. *Limited Knowledge*

There is another kind of intellectual problem. We still do not understand much of the Bible as well as we would like to. Therefore many of our theological formulations are somewhat tentative, and the same is true for many of our ethical applications of Scripture. What does Scripture teach about nuclear disarmament, about the legitimacy of legislation against marijuana, and so forth? In many of these areas, we are uncertain because our knowledge is limited. Here it is important to remember that not *all* of our theology is tentative in this way. Most Christians do not regularly entertain doubts about the existence of God, the lordship of Christ, the resurrection, and salvation by grace, among other things. Progress in theology, then, involves extending the certainty we have about such "fundamental" doctrines to the whole teaching of Scripture.

Certainty, therefore, considered as a psychological state, rises and falls for various reasons. Christians, however, have a *right* to be certain. Scripture encourages Christians to be certain, and every Christian, merely by virtue of his faith, has achieved certainty in some measure. But does that emphasis on certainty mean that there is no role for probability in theology?[14] I think that there is such a role. As we have seen, because of the weakness of our faith, our certainty is not always perfect. To the degree that we lack certainty, all we have is probability. Furthermore, there are some matters that, in the nature of the case, are matters of probability. Even if our faith were perfect, there would still be some matters relevant to theology about which, because of our finitude, we could have only probable knowledge. For example, I doubt that even an unfallen Adam, living in the present, could know with absolute certainty the author of Hebrews. Nor could he know the future with absolute certainty, except to the extent that God specially revealed it.

Butler was right when he said that many of our decisions in life are based on probability rather than absolute certainty. And it is also true, as he said, that we have a moral obligation, when we do not have absolute certainty, to accept the most probable possibility. Scripture tells us to live according to wisdom, and such judgments are certainly part of wisdom. It would be very foolish, for example, for me to live in mortal terror that an earthquake would open up in front of my house and bury me alive. I cannot prove absolutely that such an earthquake *will not* occur, but the chances that it will are so remote that it would be irresponsible for me to let such a slight probability rule my life.

Where Butler went wrong was in saying that our belief in Jesus Christ for salvation is only a matter of probability and that that probability can be ascertained through "neutral" rational methods, apart from the presupposition of Scripture.

14. I remember one colleague who called me a disciple of Bishop Butler because I used the word "probability" in a theological argument.

(9) Hierarchies of Norms

a. *Nature and Scripture*

We have seen that in a sense all of creation is "normative." Scripture is normative; but its normativity is found not only in its explicit teachings, but also in its implications and applications. That means that we have normative revelation concerning a wide range of matters that are not explicitly discussed in the Bible, and that wide range is broad enough to cover all human actions and attitudes and all human knowledge (see *(4)* above). Furthermore, we know that God has revealed himself in nature and in ourselves as well. Thus the "facts" and the "self" have a normative dimension. And so it seems that everything is normative in one way or another. But if everything is normative, does that not mean that nothing is? And does that not mean that Scripture itself is just one norm among many? Have we not destroyed the unique authority of Scripture?

"Everything is normative" simply means that under God we are obligated to live in accordance with truth—all the truth in the universe. Thus we ought to respond appropriately to each and every fact in our experience. But how do we do that? Our faculties are fallible and our inclinations, apart from grace, are to sinfully repress the truth. But God has devised a way to intellectual blessing. Although "everything is normative," not every revelation is on equal footing, as far as God's way of blessing is concerned. Paul tells us in Romans 1 that though God has revealed himself clearly in nature, unregenerate mankind rejects that knowledge and exchanges it for a lie. Therefore there is no salvation through natural revelation alone. Salvation comes through another revelation—the gospel of Christ—which is not revealed through nature but by preachers (Rom. 10:9-15; cf. Acts 4:12). Because the purpose of that revelation is to save us from our errors, it must of necessity take precedence over our other notions, even when those notions have been derived from natural revelation. A simple illustration will illuminate the heart of the matter. A child tries and tries but for various reasons cannot get the answers right on his math homework. His father comes and gives him some answers—tells him some and explains how to get others. If the child accepts his father's help, he will allow his father's words to take precedence over his own ideas.

Scripture is well suited to that kind of corrective task, because it is a revelation *in word*, not only a revelation *of* the Word (for all revelation is that). God, like the father in our illustration, *tells* us the answers we need to have. But to accept His help is to accept the primacy of His words over our own ideas, even our ideas about the rest of revelation. Even in the Garden of Eden, Adam heard the spoken word of God (Gen. 1:28ff.; 2:16f.) and was obligated to obey it, to let it govern his use of natural revelation. It is not that Scripture is more authoritative than natural revelation. Everything that God says is equally authoritative. Nor do I wish to deny that an understanding of nature can sometimes lead us to correct our understanding of Scripture. That often happens. Nor do I want to deny that we can have certainty concerning the content of natural revelation. As we have seen, all of God's revelation gives us the right to certainty. I do want to say, however, that once we have reached assurance about the meaning of Scripture's teaching on a certain matter, that teaching must prevail over any ideas we may have gained from other sources. Here I am merely describing the faith of Abraham, who believed God's Word (Rom. 4) despite a great body of apparent evidence to the contrary. If we do not affirm this point, we can draw no distinction between walking by faith and walking by sight.[15]

b. *Priority Structures Within Scripture*

Even within the biblical canon, there are some norms that take precedence over others in particular situations. For example, Scripture commands us to be subject to the ruling authorities (Exod. 20:12; Rom. 13; 1 Peter 2:13ff.), but when those authorities command us to do something contrary to God's law, we must refuse (Exod. 1:15-22; Dan. 3; 6; Acts 5:29; cf. Matt. 10:35-37; Luke 14:26). Our submission to God takes precedence over our submission to human authority. Consider another example. Some rules that normally govern human life are suspended in cases of emergency (Matt. 12:3ff.). And Jesus taught that mercy is more important that sacrifice (Matt. 9:13; 23:23; cf. 5:24). Some matters of the law, then, are "more weighty" than others and so deserve more emphasis and attention.

c. *Priorities in Our Use of Scripture*

Because we are finite, we cannot keep all of God's commandments simultaneously. Often our inability to do this produces false guilt. One sermon tells us to spend hours in prayer, another to feed the hungry, another to study the Bible intensively, another to evangelize our neighborhoods, another to catechize our children, another to become politically active. All of these seem to be based on biblical norms, yet we often feel over-

15. For a longer discussion of this matter, see my "Rationality and Scripture," in *Rationality in the Calvinian Tradition*, ed. Hendrick Hart, Johan Vander Hoeven, and Nicholas Wolterstorff (Lanham, Md.: University Press of America, 1983), 293-301.

whelmed by such huge demands on us. There simply are not enough hours in the day to do all that we are exhorted to do.

It is helpful here to remember that when God commands us to pray, to evangelize, to help the poor, and so forth, He is speaking primarily to the church as a whole and only secondarily to each of us as individuals. These are works that the church must do. Each individual in the church must contribute toward their fulfillment. But *how* the individual contributes will depend on his gifts and calling. Not all of us are called to pray six hours a day or to ring doorbells in our neighborhoods or to start political movements. Each one of us, then, must prayerfully, under the guidance of Scripture, devise his own set of priorities among these communal norms. That sounds dangerous. How can there be "priorities" among ultimates? And how can a human being choose for himself what priorities he will give to God's laws? He can, because Scripture says that he can and must.

Many misunderstandings among Christians can be avoided if we keep these principles in mind. An evangelistic pastor looks at a canon-lawyer type (one who spends much energy trying to implement proper procedures in his session and presbytery) and perceives the canon lawyer as violating the Great Commission. But to the canon lawyer, the evangelist seems to be violating the biblical command to "do all things decently and in order" (1 Cor. 14:40). In this example, I believe that the evangelist is more nearly right than is the canon lawyer. Just as mercy is more important than sacrifice, evangelism is more important, in a scriptural perspective, than ecclesiastical procedure. But the canon lawyer is not entirely implausible when he replies that the Great Commission itself requires proper procedures: how often has disorganization hindered evangelistic efforts? So a study of priority structures in Scripture itself may not be sufficient to break through the impasse, but in such debates, it is often helpful for each party to consider (as, unfortunately, they rarely do) that the other is simply trying to follow priorities that are in part dictated by his own gifts and calling. If we were more aware of the need for such personal priority structures, it would help us to understand one another better, and it would help to foster church unity.[16]

16. For more on this topic, see my *Doctrine of the Christian Life*.

B. SITUATIONAL JUSTIFICATION

Under the normative perspective, we learned that our knowledge is justified by its adherence to God's laws for thought. Now we turn to the situational perspective where we will see that our knowledge is justified by its accord with the facts. Scripture is true because it agrees with reality, with truth, with "evidence."

(1) FACTS AND NORMS

Under the normative perspective, I argued that all facts are normative, so that the normative perspective embraces all reality.[17] It is also evident that all norms are facts: it is a fact that God has spoken to us. Thus the normative and situational perspectives are coextensive. Beliefs justified by Scripture will be the same beliefs as those justified by the facts. Scripture demands that we believe the truth, the facts—nothing more nor less.

Thus there are no "brute facts," facts that are devoid of interpretation. All facts are what they are by virtue of God's interpretation of them. And just as facts are inseparable from God's interpretation of them, so our understanding of facts is inseparable from *our* interpretation of them. Stating a fact and interpreting it are the same activity (see chapter 2, *D, (2), b* and Appendix D).

Non-Christian philosophy has always sought to separate facts from norms and to see them as somehow antithetical to one another. The form-matter dialectic of Plato and Aristotle, the rationalist-empiricist debate, Hume's arguments against deriving "ought" from "is" all manifest this tendency. On the one hand, the "norm" is the rationalist principle, the law of thought. It is isolated from the world so that it can be truly ultimate, a divine law *for* the world. It is changeless, but the world is changeable; it is perfect, but the world is imperfect; it is one, but the world is many. But once the norm is so defined, it is hard to find *any* meaningful relationship between it and the world. None of the norm's stipulations can be carried out in the world of change and imperfection. It is a principle without applications and therefore meaningless. On the other hand, the "facts" are conceived as "brutish," as something of which no values may be predicated. But as Aristotle and others recognized, such "facts" are scarcely distinguishable from "nothing."

17. See also Part One, Appendix D. Note also the clarification in Appendix J at the back of the book.

A Christian epistemology, on the contrary, will see facts as normative and norms as factual. Our knowledge of fact will differ only in "perspective" from our knowledge of norm. Facts are law-laden. They convey to us God's existence and His will for us (Rom. 1:20, 32).

There is a difference in perspective, emphasis, or focus: the normative perspective focuses on the role of Scripture, the situational on natural revelation; the normative focuses on law (imperative), the situational on fact (indicative). Nevertheless, the unity of the perspectives will always be evident, especially in the fact that even in the situational perspective, we must listen to Scripture. Scripture will tell us how to make use of natural revelation.

(2) Correspondence

When we spoke earlier (see chapter 2, *D*) about the coherence theory of truth, I mentioned that that theory was generally contrasted with the correspondence theory of truth. The correspondence theory, which defines truth as a correspondence between idea and reality, has generally been favored by empiricists, since it has often been thought that only sense-experience can provide the link between the ideas of the mind and the realities of the outside world. Rationalists and subjectivists generally deny the correspondence theory of truth because they deny the reliability of sense-experience. In their view, we do not know any reality independent of our own thoughts, whether those thoughts are understood as rational concepts (rationalism) or as our total stream of consciousness (subjectivism). Thus there is nothing for our thoughts to "correspond" to.

In a Christian epistemology, however, there is a place for correspondence, as there is a place for coherence. Either may be used as a definition of truth or as a test of truth (they are perspectivally related), as long as they operate within the framework of a biblical world view. Scripture teaches that through divine revelation, we *do* have access to the "real world." We discover the "real world" not only through sense-experience but also through rational concepts and subjective states and particularly through Scripture, our supreme criterion of reality.

Thus it is not surprising that when we seek the truth, our thought process is very much a kind of "comparison." We compare our present idea of the truth with that which God is leading us toward through Scripture and the various elements of our thought process. We never "get outside of" our own thoughts; the rationalists and subjectivists are right on that account. But God's revelation is able to penetrate our thoughts, so that even within our own subjectivity we are not without divine witness. Thus there is always a process of comparison between our thoughts and what God is showing us—a process of comparison that may be called a "search for correspondence."

(3) Evidence as Justification for Faith

Scripture teaches clearly that we can gain knowledge of God through the events of nature and history. In Psalms 8, 19, 29, 65, 104, 145, and 148 and in Acts 14:15-17; 17:17-28; Romans 1, and elsewhere we read of God's revelation in nature. Furthermore, God works great historical judgments "so that they may know that I am the Lord." These judgments include miracles (1 Kings 18, where there is a specific test made to determine who is the true God, is a good example), especially the resurrection of Christ (1 Cor. 15; Acts 17:31; Rom. 1:4), the fulfillment of prophecy (Deut. 18:21f.; Luke 24:25-32; Acts 2:16ff.; 26:22f.; etc.), and the full range of the apostles' experience of Christ (Acts 1:3; 1 John 1:1-3). From such events we learn about the reality of God—what He has done to save us. We also learn His law (Rom. 1:32), a fact that underscores the perspectival unity between situation and norm.

It is therefore entirely right and proper that apologists have appealed to such events as evidence for the truth of Christianity. The evidence is rich and powerful: through it God is "clearly seen" (Rom. 1:20). The evidence of nature alone is sufficient to leave sinners "without excuse" (Rom. 1:20). But God adds to the evidence of nature a great number of miracles and fulfilled prophecies and, of course, the self-attesting Scripture itself. So rich is the evidence that one never has the right or need to demand more (Luke 16:19-31). The evidence, then, is of such a high quality that it rightly *obligates* consent. A believing response to this revelation is not merely optional; it is required. Note the *demand* for repentance following Paul's apologetic for the faith as described in Acts 17 (v. 30; cf. John 20:27; Acts 2:38; Rom. 1:20).

Thus the evidential argument is *demonstrative*, not merely probable. The evidence compels assent; it leaves no loophole, no room for argument. This is a difficult point. We are talking about arguments of a generally empirical sort. Most philosophers hold that an empirical argument can never justify more than a probable confidence in its conclusion. Our senses deceive us, and even at their best, we are told, they don't warrant certainty.

That sort of criticism is strong when directed against traditional forms of empiricism (see chapter 2, C). It does not, however, threaten the certainty of the Christian evidential argument for the following reasons.

a. *Selected Facts*

One reason why empirical arguments are weak is that they deal only with a selection of facts. Since we are finite, usually we cannot appeal to *all* the facts of experience to prove our point. But the Christian argument, empirical though it is, includes *all* the facts of experience. God is revealed in *every* fact of creation. So we are not faced with a situation where some evidence favors our conclusion and other evidence counts against it. All the evidence leads to God. John Henry Newman spoke of an "illative sense"—a gradual accumulation of many probable arguments that yields a sense of certainty. If there is such a thing, then the sense of certainty produced by the totality of empirical evidence must be overwhelming.

b. *Probability and Theism*

The very concept of probability presupposes a theistic world view. What would it mean to say that one event is "more probable" than another in a world of chance?

c. *Evidence and the Holy Spirit*

The presentation of evidence is accompanied by the supernatural power of the Holy Spirit, who convicts of sin (John 16:8) and persuades of the truth (1 Thess. 1:5).

d. *Evidence and Presuppositions*

The Christian evidential argument is never *merely* evidential. The evidence is presented on Christian presuppositions, as part of a "broadly circular" argument (see chapter 2, *D*). That broadly circular argument is always fully cogent because its presuppositions are nothing less than the Word of God (hence section *(3)*, below).

Does that mean that there is no place for probability in theology, that all of our statements about God must be dogmatically certain? No. There are various reasons why our theological certainty rises and falls (see chapter 2, *D*). When we are not certain, the best we can do is to suggest what we think is most probable. (And when we do that, it is best to own up to it and not to pretend to have a greater degree of certainty than we really do.) But certainty is the goal and our right in dealing with God's revelation, and it is important that we acquire the spiritual and intellectual qualifications to achieve that certainty.

Our point here, however, is that the evidence for Christianity *warrants* certainty, whether we experience that certainty subjectively or not. Surrounded by His clear revelation, none of us should have any doubts about God's reality.

(4) EVIDENCE AND THE WORD

I have argued that evidence should be seen as one aspect of a broadly circular argument built on Christian, scriptural presuppositions. On this approach, there is a close, even inseparable, relationship between evidence and the Word of God. And that, indeed, is what we find in the Bible's own uses of evidence, as the following considerations will demonstrate.

a. *God's Word Accompanies His Works*

In the Garden, Adam both heard the voice of God and saw His creative handiwork. His task was to relate these to one another in obedient response. God never intended man to attend to natural revelation while ignoring His spoken word. Similarly, after the Fall, God's verbal revelation accompanied His mighty, "objective," redemptive deeds. The pattern of the relationship between God's saving works and revelatory words is that prophecy comes first, then the mighty, redemptive act, then further verbal revelation to interpret the act. In Jesus' ministry and in that of the apostles, we find again a verbal revelation that explains and interprets the miracles and redemptive deeds. Thus, for example, when Jesus appeared to Thomas, the evidence consisted not only of Jesus' wounded hands and side but also of Jesus' authoritative commands to Thomas: "Put your finger here; see my hands. Reach out your hand and put it into my side. Stop doubting and believe" (John 20:27). The *tekmeria*, the "infallible proofs" by which Jesus showed himself alive after His resurrection, were accompanied by forty days of verbal teaching (Acts 1:3).[18] And the great miracle of Pentecost, to cite another example, is interpreted by Peter's sermon (Acts 2:14-36).

18. See Thom Notaro, *Van Til and the Use of Evidence* (Phillipsburg, N.J.: Presbyterian and Reformed Pub. Co., 1980), 112ff.

b. *God's Works Presuppose a Scriptural Context of Interpretation*

God's works in nature are never presented in Scripture as events that are to be interpreted on some "neutral" or nonbiblical criterion of truth. The "nature Psalms" (e.g., Pss. 8, 19, 29, 65, 104) are utterances of God's redeemed people, expressing their faith. Furthermore, the Book of Psalms begins by speaking of the righteous man who "meditates on (God's) law day and night." As students of the Scriptures, the psalmists saw all of life, and indeed all of nature, in the light of God's statutes.[19]

Similarly, the miracles of Scripture are never presented as "brute facts," as sheer events from which somehow the entire edifice of Christian truth must be built up. Nor are they events that are presented on the basis of a "neutral" criterion. Rather, the miracles presuppose an already existing framework of interpretation. In most if not all cases, miracles are fulfillments of God's covenant promises. New Testament miracles fulfill Old Testament messianic expectations. They are persuasive not merely because of their unusual character (Satan can also do unusual things) but because they remind people of the Old Testament works and words of Jehovah God. Thus the resurrection of Jesus became credible to the disciples on the road to Emmaus when they came to see how all the Old Testament prophecies converged on Him (Luke 24:13-32). And in a similar way, the miracle of Pentecost and the other miracles in Acts were interpreted in the framework of Old Testament prophecy (Acts 2:1-41; 3:1—4:20; cf. also Acts 26:22f.).

Even Paul's addresses to the Gentiles at Lystra and Athens (the first arising out of a healing miracle, the second testifying to the great miracle of the Resurrection) contain Old Testament allusions (cf. Acts 14:15 with Exod. 20:11; Acts 17:24 with 1 Kings 8:27; Acts 17:25 with Ps. 50:9-12; Acts 17:26 with Deut. 32:8). The Athens address was, indeed, a continuation of Paul's disputation in the synagogue (see v. 17).[20] The Gentiles in these addresses are presented with facts they are assumed to know already—God's mercies in the rain and sunshine, their own ignorance, the divine immanence—which in their natural state they have failed to acknowledge. Far from affirming that natural state and its would-be autonomous criteria, Paul commands the Gentiles to repent of it. This is not "neutral" apologetics but gospel preaching (Acts 14:15). The conclusion warranted by this preaching is not mere probability but a certain proclamation of divine judgment and a command to repent (Acts 17:30f.).

19. I have been helped in this area by Stephen R. Spencer, particularly by his paper "Is Natural Theology Biblical?," so far unpublished.

20. For more on the Athens address, see chapter 11, *B*, *(3)*.

Even when the Old Testament reference is not prominent, the use of miraculous evidence presupposes an already revealed system of meaning. The Resurrection, for example, is not just an odd fact; it is the resurrection of the Son of God who died for our sins and rose for our justification. Doubting Thomas was not impressed by the sheer miracle of a man like Jesus appearing in the midst of a locked room (John 20:26). Even in his doubt, he realized more was needed than just a wonderful event. He would be convinced only when he saw evidence that this was the same Jesus who was crucified. And he received that evidence only when he gave heed to Jesus' *words*. The miracle itself, indeed, is a "sign" (20:30), a revelation of God's saving truth. And the author of the fourth Gospel goes further still, commending those who did not see the miracle but who believe on the basis of his authoritative account. The miracle, then, presupposes a certain revealed truth-content.

In Acts 2:14-36 and in Acts 26, the Resurrection is placed in the context of Old Testament theology: granted the nature and purposes of the God of the Old Testament, the resurrection of His Messiah-Son is entirely credible. The conclusion drawn is that the hearers bear responsibility for Jesus' death and that they must repent or face terrible divine judgment. As Notaro points out,[21] the Resurrection here serves as both evidence and presupposition, as part of a "broadly circular" argument.

In 1 Corinthians 15, the Resurrection is presented in a context of Old and New Testament theology; it is not presented merely by using "inductive evidence" apart from a theological framework of meaning. To be sure, Paul appeals to witnesses to establish the fact of the Resurrection (vv. 3-14), but even that is presented as part of Paul's authoritative apostolic instruction (v. 3). The point is not so much that the Corinthians could verify the Resurrection for themselves by consulting the witnesses, though that is true and though that fact does confirm what Paul says. Paul's point is rather that the testimony to the Resurrection was part of the apostolic preaching and is therefore to be accepted as part of that apostolic testimony. After making that point, Paul then gives an additional reason why the Resurrection ought to be believed: if it is denied, the whole doctrinal content of Christianity must also be denied (vv. 12-19). Paul then goes on to compare Christ with the Old Testament figure of Adam and Christ's redemption with the Old Testament description of man's sinful condition (vv. 20-22). Following that, Paul presents an even more theological discussion of the role that the Resurrection plays in the organism of revela-

21. Notaro, *Van Til*, 114ff.

tion. Clearly, then, the Resurrection is no "brute fact," and the grounds for believing it are not "purely empirical" or "purely inductive." Empirical considerations, such as witnesses, play a role, but the crucial point is that the Resurrection is central to the presuppositional revelation: we cannot consistently presuppose Christ if we deny the Resurrection.

Some have claimed that John 10:38 and 14:11 represent exceptions to this principle. In these passages, it is said, Jesus offers men the alternative of believing His works, even if they will not believe His Word. Thus the works are thought to be self-attesting, apart from any connection with the Word of God; they are seen as independent means of coming to faith. Such a conclusion, however, distorts the meaning of these texts. In John 10:37f. Jesus says, "Do not believe me unless I do what my Father does. But if I do it, even though you do not believe me, believe the miracles, that you may learn and understand that the Father is in me, and I in the Father." The issue here is whether Jesus does the things that God the Father does. The passage, therefore, presupposes a theological understanding: there is a God who has a certain character. Doubtless, that theological understanding comes from the Old Testament; Jesus is here talking to Jews. What Jesus asks them to do, therefore, is this: if they will not believe His words, they ought to compare His mighty works with what they know of the God of the Old Testament, comparing Jesus' works with God's revealed character. They are not being asked to accept mighty deeds as evidence in and of themselves but only in a context of already revealed truth about God.

John 14:11 is similar. Again, the Father's relation to Jesus is at issue, this time with a disciple rather than with Jesus' enemies. The miracles are evidence of Jesus' unity with the Father, and Philip was doubtless expected to judge that on the basis of the Old Testament revelation. Note also in verse 10 that the *words* of Jesus are listed among the works that the Father does in Him.[22]

The unity of word and deed is even more evident in the case of those (like us today) who have not seen the miracles first-hand but who hear testimony about them. In such cases, believing the miracle *is* believing the verbal revelation. The credibility of the miracle is the credibility of the verbal witness. Obviously, we are not in the position of Thomas. Even if his demand of Jesus could in some measure be justified, it is not a demand that modern people would be justified in making. We are not in a position

22. On this general subject, see Colin Brown, *Miracles and the Critical Mind* (Grand Rapids: Wm. B. Eerdmans Pub. Co., 1984).

to verify Jesus' resurrection by direct empirical evidence. We must believe on the basis of testimony—the Word—which according to Jesus is in any case the better way to go (John 20:29).

c. *God's Works Display the Meaning of His Word*

I have argued that *meaning* and *application* are near synonyms. If that is right, then in seeking the meaning of a text, it is important to see what its author *does* with it. The Word of God interprets His works, as we have seen, but the opposite is also true. Israel's redemption from Egypt displayed vividly what kind of a deliverer God is. The redemptive language of Scripture is constantly explained by reference to that great event. The work of Christ in His cross and resurrection illuminates, as nothing else could, the mysterious prophecies of Isaiah 53 and Psalm 22. Indeed, if the Resurrection had not occurred, says Paul, the Christian hope would be meaningless (1 Cor. 15:12-19).

d. *God's Works Prove the Truth of His Word*

Those who view the mighty works of God are obligated, on the basis of that experience, to believe in Him. And not only they but also those who hear or read the authoritative testimony of the witnesses to these events are expected to respond positively. Thus both the mighty work itself and the official testimony to God's mighty acts compel belief.

The argument, as we have seen, is circular, but not for that reason unpersuasive (see chapter 2, *D*). We are free, therefore, and encouraged to construct evidential arguments based on Christian presuppositions.

(5) EVIDENCE AND FAITH

What is a proper response to evidence for Christianity? Intellectual assent is never sufficient. We seek nothing less than true faith. But an argument by itself can never produce faith; that is the work of the Spirit. Nevertheless, it is proper to demand faith at the conclusion of an argument (see Acts 2:38), for though the argument does not *produce* faith, it *warrants and justifies* it.

One cannot respond properly to the evidence, then, unless he believes. Notice Jesus' words to Thomas: "Put your finger here; see my hands. Reach out your hand and put it into my side. Stop doubting and believe" (John 20:27). Jesus does not ask Thomas to make an unbiased, neutral judgment of the evidence. Rather, He calls him to look at the evidence in faith. Another way to put it is that we must look at the evidence with a believing presupposition.

C. EXISTENTIAL JUSTIFICATION

We learned in Part One that there is an "existential" dimension to knowledge in general, for knowledge always involves a subject, an object, and law. There is no knowledge without a knower! Thus whether a person has knowledge depends not only on the objects and the laws of thought but also on his personal capacity to be a knower. It may seem odd, however, especially within a Christian perspective, to relate this "existential dimension" to the *justification* of knowledge. Subjective capacities are important to knowledge, but how do they play a role in justification? And if they do, does not this fact introduce an element of subjectivism into the process of knowing? Despite these questions, I believe that there is such a thing as an "existential justification" of the knowledge of God (and indeed of the knowledge of everything). Consider the following points.

(1) Knowledge and Life: Pragmatic Truth

I suggested earlier (chapter 4, C) that epistemology could be understood as a subdivision of ethics. Knowing is knowing what we *ought* to believe. To justify our knowledge is to establish the presence of that ethical "ought." And once that "ought" is established, we must apply it to all the rest of life (the applications are the meaning!). All of our decisions should be reconciled with what we know to be true. We must live in truth, walk in truth, do the truth. Knowledge, therefore, is an ethically responsible orientation of the person to his experience. To know is to respond *rightly* to the evidence and norms available to us.

On the basis of this concept of knowledge, the unbeliever "knows nothing truly." In no area of life does he respond to God's revelation in ethical rightness. I argued in Part One that there is another kind of knowledge mentioned in Scripture that the unbeliever does have. It is parallel to Christian knowledge in some ways, and it renders the unbeliever responsible for his decisions before God. It may be called "knowledge" because of its external conformity (in some respects) to the divine law, but its radical ethical disorientation introduces severe distortion.

However that may be, it should be evident that when we seek to justify a belief, we are seeking to reconcile that belief with all aspects of our lives.

We are seeking, that is, a belief that we can *live* with. Francis Schaeffer describes John Cage, the composer, as a man whose philosophy says that all is chance—randomness—a philosophy that he seeks to express in his music. But as an amateur mushroom-grower, Cage does not abide by his philosophy of chance. Rather, he presupposes an order, a world of law. Some fungi are mushrooms, others toadstools, and it matters which ones you pick to eat! Thus Cage is unable to apply his philosophy of randomness to all of life; he cannot live with it. This fact casts doubt on whether he really believes it or not. I would say that he believes it, but not strongly or consistently; he also holds other beliefs inconsistent with this one (because he cannot escape God's revelation). Thus he is not able to apply his unbelief to all the areas of his life.[23]

These observations help us to see that the justification of knowledge does indeed have, after all, an "existential perspective," one in which the question of justification takes a distinctive form. Under the normative perspective we asked, Is this belief consistent with the laws of thought? Under the situational perspective the question was, Is my belief in accord with objective reality? Now we come to the existential perspective in which we ask, Can I live with this belief?

I have earlier referred to two of the classical "theories of truth," the coherence theory (see chapter 5, *A, (7)*) and the correspondence theory (see chapter 5, *B, (2)*). There has also been a third theory, formulated in different ways, but usually able to be summarized with a slogan such as "the truth is what works." We could call this the "pragmatic theory of truth." Some philosophers, like the Greek Sophists, have used this sort of principle in the defense of a radical subjectivism: there is no objective truth, only "truth for me"; whatever works for me, that I will believe.

Of course, a Christian epistemology will reject that kind of radical subjectivism. But there is some truth in the pragmatic concept of truth, nevertheless. Scripture does tell us that in the long run, only Christianity "works," that is, only Christianity brings the full, eternal blessing of God on those who believe. And, of course, what "works" is at the same time what is in accord with God's law. Note frequent correlations between obedience and blessing in Scripture (e.g., Ps. 1). And what "works" is also correlative with objective reality. We receive God's blessings when we recognize reality as God has made it and act on that recognition. Thus the prag-

23. Believers are inconsistent also, as I have said. The distinction is the same as in the doctrine of sanctification: believers are not under the *dominion* of sin (error); unbelievers are.

matic theory of truth becomes another "perspective" on a full Christian epistemology.

When a Christian asks, Can I live with this belief?, the life in view is the regenerate life in its fullest maturity. We are asking whether our beliefs are consistent with a fully sanctified Christian consciousness and experience. We are seeking to warrant our beliefs by showing that they are the legitimate products of a regenerate heart. Just as we justify ethical actions by showing that they arise from a proper motive, a motive of faith and love, so here we seek to justify our beliefs by showing that they are the outworkings of the new life within us, indeed that they are the "fruit of the Spirit."

(2) Persuasion and Proof

Another way of making the same point is to say that the justification of belief aims at *persuasion*. That is, we are not seeking merely to validate statements but to persuade people. Justification is a person-oriented activity. In trying to justify our beliefs, we often seek to persuade others and sometimes ourselves, but there is always some persuasion being attempted.

As George Mavrodes has pointed out,[24] it is possible to have an argument that is perfectly valid (the premises imply the conclusion) and perfectly sound (the premises, and therefore the conclusion, are true) that nevertheless fails to persuade. Consider his example.

> Nothing exists or God exists. Something exists. Therefore God exists.

The argument is valid, and Mavrodes believes it sound because he believes in God.[25] Evidently, however, there are many who would not be persuaded by this argument. In constructing arguments, therefore, it is important to give attention not only to their validity and soundness but also to their persuasive power. Our goal is not to establish propositions but to persuade people.

Therefore there is an existential element in justification. A proposition that is in accord with the laws of thought and with objective reality is, we might say, objectively justified. But I do not *have* a justification for believing it unless I have accepted those laws and realities into my own value system, unless they have become persuasive to me.

24. *Belief in God* (New York: Random House, 1970), 17-48.
25. If God exists, the first premise is true. A compound sentence connected by "or" is true if one of the two component clauses is true.

Mavrodes suggests that *proof* also should be defined in what he calls a "person-variable" way, so that an argument might be a proof to one person and not to another. His formulation for a proof is this: "We will have proved a statement to N if and only if we succeed in presenting N with an argument that is convincing for him."[26] If we ignore the element of persuasion or "convincingness," says Mavrodes, we may find ourselves constructing perfectly valid and sound "proofs" that are of no help to anyone.

(3) "Cognitive Rest"—A Godly Sense of Satisfaction

What is it that makes an argument persuasive to one person and not to another? It seems mysterious. When someone asks me why I am persuaded, I usually refer to norms and facts. What else is there? Yet two people can be presented with the same norms and facts, and one will be persuaded, the other not.

We see the difference as we observe our own processes of deliberation. Let us say that I am trying to decide between two incompatible conclusions, A and B. After completing my research, I am inclined toward position A. But I am uneasy. I mull it over. I re-examine the evidence that inclined me toward A. But as I think it over some more, that same evidence pushes me more and more towards B. It isn't necessarily that new arguments are put forth. Rather, it may be that arguments that used to seem sound now seem unsound or perhaps less weighty, and vice versa. After a while, I decide to adopt position B, and I find I am at rest. At an earlier point, I felt uneasy; I felt that more thinking had to be done. Now I feel no more need to rethink the problem.

What has happened to move me from position A to position B? The evidence has not changed; the arguments have not changed. In one sense, nothing new has been added. Is it that my final decision has been backed up simply by more time spent in thought? But sometimes I spend many years in thought without sensing that "cognitive rest." Other times it only takes a second or two. There doesn't seem to be any particular amount of thought-time that generates a sense of conviction.

The only way I can describe it will sound terribly subjectivistic to some readers, but I ask your indulgence. The "cognitive rest" seems to differ from my earlier states of mind because of the presence of something very much like a *feeling*. It is not like a feeling of hot or cold but like the sense of satisfaction that one experiences on the completion of a task. It is the

26. Ibid., 35.

sense that now one can commit himself to the belief, that he can "live" with it. Sometimes this feeling is hardly noticeable and rather commonplace, as when I commit myself to the belief that the morning mail has arrived. At other times it is exhilarating, as when I make a great, life-changing discovery, such as the truth of Christianity.

Coming to cognitive rest about Christianity is achieving a "godly sense of satisfaction" with the message of Scripture. There comes a time when we no longer struggle against the truth but accept it willingly. There are people who are "always learning but never able to acknowledge the truth" (2 Tim. 3:7). They struggle all their lives but never come to that godly sense of satisfaction in the Word of God. But when we do reach that satisfaction, sometimes the feeling is almost palpable, as with the disciples who met the risen Jesus on the road to Emmaus. "Were not our hearts burning within us," they said, "while he talked with us . . . ?" (Luke 24:32). Whether the feeling is intense or not, however, every Christian comes to the point where he can say, "Yes, this is for me; I can live with this."

(4) Knowledge, Regeneration, and Sanctification

Theologically, when we talk about the "cognitive rest," we are talking about noetic regeneration and sanctification, the "internal testimony of the Holy Spirit."[27] The Spirit accompanies His Word to produce conviction (John 3:3ff.; 1 Cor. 2:4, 5, 14; 1 Thess. 1:5; 1 John 2:20f., 27). Also, the "mind of Christ," His wisdom, is communicated to believers (Matt. 11:25ff.; Luke 24:45; 1 Cor. 1:24, 30; 2:16; Phil. 2:5; Col. 2:3). And to complete the Trinity, there are also passages that speak of God the Father as teacher of His people (Matt. 16:17; 23:8ff.; John 6:45). The cognitive rest, then, in which one commits himself to Christianity, comes by the grace of God, nothing less.[28] The cognitive rest is an element of salvation. Sin has kept us from true knowledge (Rom. 1; 8:7, 8; 1 Cor. 2:14; Eph. 1:19-2:6; 4:17-19), but the grace of God in Christ is sufficient to rescue us from this ignorance (Ezek. 36:25ff.; John 1:11ff.; 3:1-8; 6:44f., 65; 7:17; 11:40; Acts 16:14; 1 Cor. 8:1-4; 12:3; 2 Cor. 4:3-6; Eph. 1:17f.;

27. See John Murray, "The Attestation of Scripture," in P. Woolley and N. Stonehouse, eds., *The Infallible Word* (Grand Rapids: Wm. B. Eerdmans Pub. Co., 1946; reissued by Presbyterian and Reformed Pub. Co.); also my "The Spirit and the Scriptures," in D. A. Carson and J. Woodbridge, eds., *Hermeneutics, Authority, and Canon* (Grand Rapids: Zondervan Publishing House, 1986), 213-35.

28. Cf. the references to the "Word as God's presence" and the "Word through person-media" in my *Doctrine of the Word of God*, as yet unpublished.

2:1-10; 3:18f.; Col. 3:10; 1 Thess. 1:9f.; 1 Tim. 1:5-11; 1 John 2:3-6, 9-11, 20-27; 4:2f., 8, 13-17; 5:2f., 20).

Regeneration does not, however, immediately convey to the believer a sense of cognitive rest about all matters pertaining to the faith. Our basic presuppositional commitment to Christ begins at regeneration, but other commitments develop more gradually, or at least it takes a while for us to become conscious of them. Thus not only is there noetic regeneration, but there is also noetic sanctification (or, put differently, both definitive noetic sanctification and progressive noetic sanctification). There is a radical change when our relationship with Christ first begins and a gradual change thereafter.

Scripture teaches that this gradual change is inseparable from the overall process of sanctification; assurance on cognitive matters is inseparable from growth in obedience and holiness. It is sometimes said by theologians that "the Christian life is founded on Christian doctrine"; but it also works the other way around: our ability to discern doctrinal (and other) truth depends on the overall maturity of our Christian lives. In that regard, see John 7:17, and a group of passages that make an interesting use of *proof* (*dokimazein*). (a) In Romans 12:1f., Paul urges us, in view of God's mercies, to offer our bodies as living sacrifices, and that entails nonconformity to the world and transformation into holiness. This is the process of ethical renewal, and it is by this process, Paul says, that we will be able to "prove" what the will of God is. This is the opposite from what we usually hear, which (generally speaking) is that we should learn the will of God and then we will be able to become more holy. That advice is true enough, but it also works the other way around: be transformed, and then your renewed mind will be able to discern God's will. (b) Ephesians 5:8 describes starkly our fallen condition: you once *were* darkness. But now we *are* light! This light is defined as ethical transformation in verse 9. It is during the process of ethical transformation that we "prove" what pleases the Lord (v. 10). (c) In Philippians 1:9f., Paul prays that the Philippians' love will abound more and more in knowledge and depth of insight. Again, ethical renewal is the source of deeper knowledge. Then in verse 10, Paul says that it is that deeper knowledge that helps us to "prove" what is most excellent (perhaps what is the most fitting or proper thing to do on a particular occasion), and that in turn leads to more purity and blamelessness. Again, note the circular relationship between ethical sanctification and Christian understanding.

Hebrews 5:11-14 is a similar passage, though it does not use *dokimazein*. The author is impatient to begin his teaching on Melchizedek, but he knows his audience is not ready for such deep instruction. They are "slow to learn," ready only for "elementary" teaching. Their trouble is that they are babes, spiritually immature (v. 13), without "experience" of the word of righteousness. Maturity, in contrast, means that one's "faculties" have been "exercised by constant use to discern good and evil" (v. 14). Notice again, that theological maturity occurs together with ethical maturity. Ability to understand Melchizedek occurs as we learn to discern good and evil. And this ethical maturity does not occur primarily in the classroom but in the heat of Christian warfare; there is "exercise" (*gymnazein*) and "use" (*hexis*). The Christian life is a training process: the more experience we have making tough decisions in obedience to God, the better we will be able to do it in the future. The better we are able to make ethical decisions, the more equipped we will be to make theological decisions; the two are of a piece with one another.

Thus ability to come to cognitive rest concerning Christian teaching comes with sanctification, with growth in holiness. Many doctrinal misunderstandings in the church are doubtless due to this spiritual-ethical immaturity. We need to pay more attention to this fact when we get into theological disputes. Sometimes, we throw arguments back and forth, over and over again, desperately trying to convince one another. But often there is in one of the disputers—or both!—the kind of spiritual immaturity that prevents clear perception. We all know how it works in practice. Lacking sufficient love for one another, we seek to interpret the other person's views in the worst possible sense. (We forget the tremendous importance of love—even as an epistemological concept; cf. 1 Cor. 8:1-3; 1 Tim. 1:5ff.; 1 John 2:4f.; 3:18f.; 4:7ff.). Lacking sufficient humility, too, we overestimate the extent of our own knowledge. In such a case, with one or more immature debaters, it may be best not to seek immediate agreement in our controversy. Sometimes, we need to back off a bit, for a while. We need to go off and spend some time—months or years, perhaps—in constructive work for the Lord, fighting the Christian warfare, exercising our moral faculties. Then we can come back later to the doctrinal question and address it again from a more mature vantage point. Do you see how theological problems may sometimes, in effect, have practical solutions?

How many seminarians, I often wonder, have the spiritual maturity to warrant the theological decisions they are asked to make in preparation for licensure and ordination? In this context, Paul's words take on fresh importance: "Do not ordain a novice, or he may become conceited and fall under the same judgment as the devil" (1 Tim. 3:6).

(5) "SEEING AS"—EXISTENTIAL AND NORMATIVE PERSPECTIVES

This "cognitive rest," this "godly sense of satisfaction"—can anything more be said about it? Many questions arise at this point, for these ideas are rather vague and mysterious. In particular, some might be worried about the consistency of these concepts with the doctrine of the sufficiency of Scripture. Is this "satisfaction" a new revelation of the Spirit? Is it an addition to the canon? Is it an additional norm? If not, then what is it?

I strongly defend the Reformation doctrine of the sufficiency of Scripture.[29] But the Reformers saw no difficulty in affirming both the sufficiency of Scripture and the necessity of the Spirit's testimony. They made it clear (for even in their time there were misunderstandings in this area) that the Spirit's testimony was not a new revelation; rather, the Spirit's work was to illumine and confirm the revelation already given. In Scripture, the Spirit's testimony is to Christ (John 14:26; 15:26; 16:9f., 13ff.) and to the Word of God (1 Cor. 2:4; 1 Thess. 1:5). The Spirit witnesses that the Word is true, but the Word already has told us that!

Still, Scripture is not reluctant to describe this work as a work of revelation (Matt. 11:25f.; Eph. 1:17). It is revelation in the sense that through the Spirit's ministry, we are learning something of which we would otherwise be ignorant; we are learning the Word of God. Or, put differently, we are being "persuaded," "noetically regenerated and sanctified," "brought to cognitive rest." We are being given a "godly sense of satisfaction."

The Spirit's work also helps us to *use* and to *apply* the Word. Obviously, the Spirit cannot assure us of the truth of Scripture unless He also teaches us its meaning. And the meaning, as we have seen, includes the applications. We can see this in 2 Samuel 11 and 12 where David sinned against God by committing adultery with Bathsheba and by sending her husband, Uriah, to his death. Here, David, the "man after God's own heart," seemed trapped in a peculiar spiritual blindness. What happened to David? In one sense, he knew Scripture perfectly well; he meditated on God's law day and night. And he was not ignorant about the facts of the case. Yet he was not convicted of sin. But Nathan the prophet came to him and spoke God's Word. He did not immediately rebuke David directly; he told a parable—a story that made David angry at someone else. Then Nathan told David, "You are the man." At that point, David repented of his sin.

What had David learned at that point? He already knew God's law, and, in a sense, he already knew the facts. What he learned was an application—what the law said about *him*. Previously, he may have rationalized

29. See my *Doctrine of the Word of God*, as yet unpublished.

something like this: "Kings of the earth have a right to take whatever women they want; and the commander-in-chief has the right to decide who fights on the front line. Therefore my relation with Bathsheba was not *really* adultery, and my order to Uriah was not *really* murder." We all know how that works; we've done it ourselves. But what the Spirit did, through Nathan, was to take that rationalization away.

Thus David came to call his actions by their right names: sin, adultery, murder. He came to read his own life in terms of the biblical concepts. He came to see his "relationship" *as adultery* and his "executive order" *as murder*. He learned to "see as."

"Seeing as" is an interesting concept that a number of recent thinkers, notably Ludwig Wittgenstein, have explored. "Seeing as" is not the same as "seeing." One person, looking at a certain picture, will see it as a duck, another as a rabbit.

Fig. 3. The duck-rabbit.

In one sense, they see the same lines on the paper. But they see different patterns, different shapes, or *gestalts*. So it is with us when we seek to see our lives in the light of Scripture. One person will look at a sexual relationship as a "recreational dalliance"; another will see it as adultery. Sometimes the matter becomes more complicated when there seems to be more than one possible biblical interpretation of an event. Suppose that I feel anger. Is this the righteous anger that Jesus displayed with the money-changers in the temple, or is it the murderous anger that He forbids under all circumstances? Which biblical category does it fit under?

Those questions are not obviously questions about facts or norms. One usually doesn't answer them simply by giving information or a command. Rather, what is needed is exhortation that helps us to see things in a different way. Therefore, artistry and nuance play particular roles here. Nathan did not simply repeat the law; he told a story. That story had the effect of shaking David out of his rationalization, of helping him to make different patterns out of the facts, to call things by their right names. We need to be more sensitive to those circumstances and occasions when such methods are appropriate in theology.

Much of the Spirit's work in our lives is of this nature—assuring us that Scripture applies to our lives in particular ways. The Spirit does not add to the canon, but His work is really a work of teaching, of revelation. Without that revelation, we could make no use of Scripture at all; it would be a dead letter to us.

Thus in one sense, the Spirit adds nothing; in another sense, He adds everything. When we are asked to justify our Christian beliefs, we point not to the Spirit but to the Word, for it is the Word that *states* the justification. But apart from the Spirit, we would have no knowledge of that justification. And it often becomes important, in justifying beliefs, (1) to give evidence of our own spiritual maturity and thus to indicate our spiritual qualifications for making the statements we make, and (2) to state our justification in a properly artful way to help the other person to *see* the truth *as* we do.

(6) A Corporate Existential Perspective

Most of the preceding discussion has focused on the individual's knowledge of God that comes through his own private, inward awareness. I make no apology for that. God does care for each individual and relates to each of us individually. In some ways, all of us are different—with different heredity, life-histories, natural and spiritual gifts, and natural and spiritual weaknesses. God counts every hair and watches each sparrow fall; all the diversities of the creation are in His hand. He meets each individual's special needs with His saving grace. Scripture tells with love the stories of how God's love meets individuals. And it tells us that there is joy in heaven over one sinner who repents.

Yet, it may be argued, the emphasis of Scripture is different. That emphasis is not on the salvation of individuals but on the salvation of a *people*. Throughout history God has been concerned with families, nations, and, indeed, with a world. His goal is not merely the perfection of individuals but the perfection of the church, the body of Christ.

Ephesians is one of the most notable portions of Scripture in that regard. It also is a book that has much to say about the knowledge of God. We have cited Ephesians 1:17ff.; 3:14-19; and 5:8-21 in regard to the existential perspective. These texts show that knowledge of God is inseparable from the Spirit's revelatory and sanctifying witness. But "knowledge" in Ephesians seems not to be primarily the knowledge each of us has as an individual but the knowledge that the church shares as a body. It is ascribed to "you" (plural). It is a knowledge "together with all the saints" (3:18). The end result of that knowledge is

> Until we all reach unity in the faith and in the knowledge of the Son of God and become mature, attaining to the whole measure of the fullness of Christ. . . . We will in all things grow up into him who is the head, even Christ. From him the whole body, joined and held together by every supporting ligament, grows and builds itself up in love, as each part does its work (4:13, 15f.).

The "maturity" spoken of here is not the maturity of each individual, though that is implied, but the maturity of the corporate body as it grows up into Christ, its Head. It is best, then, to see the knowledge, also, as something shared by the whole body, though of course the knowledge of individuals is not irrelevant to that.

Thus it appears that there is a kind of "knowledge" possessed by the church, as well as a knowledge possessed by individuals. Like the individual's knowledge, the church's knowledge may be seen from three perspectives: it is based on scriptural norms, on the realities of creation and redemption, and also on the work of Christ and the Spirit in corporately sanctifying the body (Eph. 4:4f.; 5:22-33).

The "sociology of knowledge" has much to say about the effect of group loyalties on belief-commitments. Much has been written in this area from Marxist and Freudian viewpoints and from philosophers of science like Kuhn, Hanson, and Polanyi. Our presuppositions and our views of the objects in the world are profoundly affected by our various interpersonal relationships—family, nationality, religion, political party or ideology, economic status, educational background, occupation, professional association, and so forth. Groups tend to develop "group minds," which, without determining the thinking of individuals within the groups, do influence it deeply.

We tend to be suspicious of "groupthink," and in most cases rightly so. There are important intellectual benefits in cultivating independence of thought. But it is impossible to escape entirely from our associations with others, and such total independence is not really desirable. The ideal thing (a prefall situation) would be for the whole human race to work as a team, seeking out all the mysteries of the creation together, trusting one another, collaborating peacefully on a great edifice of learning, each contributing his bit to a body of knowledge far larger than any individual could comprehend.

Something like that is what God intends for His church. He wants us to grow together toward a knowledge of Him that is broader than any of us, which, marvellously, somehow matches that of its Head, Jesus Christ (cf. Eph. 4:15f.).

And of course the growth of corporate knowledge will enrich each individual. When the church reaches maturity, its individuals will "no longer be infants" (Eph. 4:14). Thus it is wise for us to listen to the church when it speaks through its elder-teachers and its judicial discipline (Matt. 18). The church and obviously the churches are not infallible, but they do have the authority to govern the teaching within their jurisdiction. Individuals in the churches need to cultivate a spirit of submission and humility, a recognition that in most cases the whole body of believers (especially the whole body throughout church history) knows more than any member does. If conscience forces me to go against the body, then I must take my stand, but even then I should not be hasty. Even the conscience is not infallible; it must be trained to discern properly, in accordance with Scripture.

And of course the church does more for us than merely to overrule our errors! Even if we never made errors, it would still be through the processes of discussing issues, loving one another (Eph. 4:16), bearing one another's burdens (Gal. 6:2), fighting the Christian warfare together, that we come to fullness of knowledge. God has given each of us as gifts to the others (Eph. 4:4-13).

Should this matter be discussed under the existential perspective, or (as in my syllabus, *Doctrine of the Christian Life*) under the situational? (There, the body of believers functioned as one aspect of our situation that our knowledge must take account of.) Well, since all the perspectives are interdependent, it doesn't much matter. The church also has a normative function—a derived authority from God, as we have seen. But Scripture seems to present corporate knowledge primarily as a kind of superindividual subjectivity that grows and develops as the individual does, to which the individual is related not primarily as subject to object but as member to body. Thus my subjectivity is part of the church's, and its subjectivity is the fullness of my own; a pain felt by the finger is fully experienced and understood only by the whole body.

(7) Autonomy Again?

In all of the above discussion, we have in effect conceded some truth to the subjectivist position: I cannot regard any belief as justified unless it accords with my subjective inclinations. "Cognitive rest," "sense of satisfaction," "seeing as"—what are these but subjective conditions? But have we not, then, opened the door to human autonomy?

The non-Christian subjectivist would say yes. He argues that whether you want to be a rationalist, empiricist, Kantian, Platonist, Buddhist, Marxist, or Christian, you can accept these viewpoints only by means of your own autonomous authority. If you accept rationalism, you accept it, finally, because it appeals to you. If you accept Platonism, you accept it because it feels right, because you can live with it. And the same is true for accepting Christianity, such non-Christian subjectivists would argue! Therefore whether we are rationalists, empiricists, Christians, or whatever, we are all essentially subjectivists at heart, the argument goes. Can this criticism be answered?

I think it can. Recall our earlier discussion of subjectivism (see chapter 4, *D*, *(3)*). Subjectivism is either self-refuting (claiming objective knowledge of the fact that there is no objective knowledge) or a renunciation of epistemological dialogue (in which case it has nothing to say to us). Furthermore, just as rationalism, empiricism, and other systems can be made to appear (as above) to reduce to subjectivism, the reverse is also true: subjectivism reduces to them! For the subjectivist must choose what element of his subjectivity will be "truth for him." He must choose his norm, his objects from many possibilities. He may choose as his norm reason, sense-experience, the Koran, or the Bible; but when he does, he will no longer be a subjectivist.

Our present concern, however, is whether under our existential perspective we have made any fatal compromises with subjectivism, so that our final position is autonomous, rather than the position of covenant servants. I think not. A little reflection will show us that, understood in a framework of Christian presuppositions, the existential perspective is really identical with the other two.

A Christian existential perspective does not urge people to follow their feelings uncritically, doing and thinking whatever, on first impression, feels good. We realize that what feels good initially may feel bad later on! And there are many *good* feelings that are not feelings of "cognitive rest." The cognitive rest we seek is a deep sense of satisfaction with our beliefs, which often requires much searching, analysis, and prayer. And it is not just any "deep sense of satisfaction." Rather, it is a sense of full conformity with God's revelation. We seek not just any feeling but *that* feeling. And we know how it comes, however elusive it may sometimes be: it comes through testing all of our ideas by the criterion of Scripture, by applying that criterion to the whole body of our experience. For a Christian, no other criterion yields that kind of assurance, that "godly sense of satisfaction."

Thus the godly sense of satisfaction may be defined in terms of Scripture. What satisfies me is what I believe Scripture warrants. Or it may be defined situationally as a feeling that I have understood the facts. The three perspectives are one! The Spirit of sanctification will not lead us anywhere else than to God's Word and to a true understanding of His creation.

D. WHICH PERSPECTIVE IS ULTIMATE?

Rationalists, empiricists, and subjectivists down through the years have tried each to do justice to the concerns of the others. Yet they have usually argued that one of these approaches must be given primacy. Rationalists agree that we must give attention to sense-experience and feelings to help us through life, but they insist that in case of any conflict, the final, decisive vote must go to reason. Reason, after all, must decide what use of sense and subjectivity is reasonable! Where else can we turn?

The empiricist would reply that what we think is "reasonable" depends on habits of thought developed over the course of our experience. Any claim to rationality must be tested by looking at the facts. All theories must be judged by the facts, not vice versa.

The subjectivist, then, will point out that what we call "reasonable" and "factual" depends very much on what we want to believe, and ultimately such arguments persuade us only if we want to believe them.

But the empiricist and the rationalist will reply to the subjectivist: you *ought* not to feel rest until you know what is really true. And how do you know when you have found rest? How can you identify that feeling, if you have no criterion and no knowledge of facts?

So we go around and around in a circle. And Christians sometimes raise the same questions, in effect, about our three perspectives. They ask which is "prior" or "ultimate." Commonly, Christians want the normative perspective to be primary because of the supreme authority of Scripture. Others (perhaps more sophisticated) take note that the Bible, though inspired and infallible, is an account of something else—creation, fall, redemption. Those events, they say, are more ultimate, more fundamental than the scriptural account of them. Thus we must look *through* the Bible to those events described therein. Still a third group of Christians, though agreeing with the others on scriptural authority and the importance of the events described therein, find the center of Christianity in the new life, the transformed heart, by which alone Scripture and its history can be appropriated. Then the first group replies that the heart is transformed only by the obedient hearing of the Word, and so on, and so on.

Well, do we really need to choose? Can we not agree with all of these groups and say that there is a *mutual* dependence (ultimately an identity) among the three perspectives? Of course Scripture is authoritative. Of course we read it, not for its own sake, but for the sake of its teaching. Of course we cannot appropriate the Book or the teaching without renewed hearts. Of course we cannot get renewed hearts without appropriating the Book and its teaching.

The strongest objection against such mutual, reciprocal priorities among the three perspectives is that which comes from the "normativists"—the normative perspective absolutely must be prior because Scripture is prior. It is, after all, our supreme authority. This objection, however, fails to recognize that there is a difference between the Bible and the "normative perspective." The two are not the same. The normative perspective is not the Bible; it is my *understanding* of the Bible in its relations to me and all creation. Under the normative perspective, I examine all of my knowledge, *focusing* on Scripture (but also on other forms of God's normative revelation). Under the normative perspective, I look at all of my knowledge as "application of Scripture" (see this chapter, A, *(4)*). So understood, the normative perspective is certainly important, but it is not the Bible, and the primacy of Scripture does not of itself entail the primacy of the normative perspective. Especially is this the case since the other two perspectives also deal with Scripture: the situational looks at it as the central "fact" in the authority structure, the existential as the most authoritative subjective datum. Ultimately, the three perspectives differ only in *emphasis* or *focus*. Each includes the other two, and so the three all cover the same territory; they have the same content.

Thus I maintain that the three perspectives are equally ultimate, equally important. Each depends on the others, so that without the others, it could not be intelligible.

E. JUSTIFICATION IN APOLOGETICS

All well and good for theology, one might say. But what if you are trying to present the truth to an unbeliever? It is fine among believers to seek the truth by examining the world according to the criterion of Scripture until we reach cognitive rest. But how can we expect an unbeliever to accept such a procedure? He won't accept the criterion of Scripture, and therefore he won't accept the same facts that we do, and he won't agree with us as to when he should find cognitive rest.

So goes the objection. But, I reply, what alternative is there? To reason on some *other* authority? But that would be idolatrous and would lead the unbeliever *away* from the truth. Should we avoid any authority at all, reasoning neutrally? But there is no neutrality.

So we reason the only way God intended us to reason. We reason in the only way that will lead us into the truth. On the one hand, if the non-Christian rejects this, he rejects his only hope. But that is his own fault; "deep in his heart," he knows better. On the other hand, if he accepts our witness, he accepts it by grace.

There is no special method of justification in apologetics besides that which we use in theology and, indeed, in all the rest of knowledge. There is only one truth and only one way to find it. Those who don't like that way are like the paranoid in our earlier illustration (see this chapter, A, *(6)*, *e*). We can pray for them, witness to them, even reason with them (our way, not theirs), but we may not compromise with their unbelieving presuppositions. Rather, we seek to bring every thought captive to Christ (2 Cor. 10:5).

PART THREE

THE METHODS OF KNOWLEDGE

We now move to the subject of method. Here the question is *How* do we obtain knowledge? In this part of our study, we will be focusing somewhat more narrowly than before on the specific concerns of theology and apologetics. We have seen, of course, that there is no sharp line between theological knowledge and all the other kinds of knowledge—"all knowing is theologizing." To consider all forms of knowledge in detail, however, would be an unrealistic project for a book of this size. Thus we will be thinking about theology in a somewhat narrow sense, trusting, of course, that what we learn here about theology will in some measure (and in an important way) be applicable to other disciplines as well.

In one sense, this part of the book will focus on the "existential perspective," since we are asking what the *subject* must do to obtain the knowledge he seeks. As we have seen, however, the three perspectives regularly overlap and intersect. Thus also in the area of method, there are normative, situational, and existential aspects.[1] Here, the normative perspective will deal with our use of Scripture (not forgetting that Scripture

1. If one wants to multiply technical categories, he can consider this part as dealing with existential-normative, existential-situational, and existential-existential perspectives. And of course, these can be still further subdivided into existential-normative-normative, existential-normative-situational, and so forth, *ad infinitum*. I do not, however, believe in multiplying a technical apparatus beyond its anticipated usefulness, and so I will not use such a detailed structure.

must be understood in the context of God's revelation in nature and in the self). The situational perspective will deal with the use of extrabiblical facts and "tools" (such as the sciences) for discovering those facts (not forgetting that Scripture itself is the criterion of factual knowledge and that facts are not understood apart from a personal interpretative framework). The existential perspective will deal with the knower's capacities, skills, faculties, and attitudes relevant to his knowledge (not forgetting that those matters must be understood through Scripture and applied to our circumstances).

This part, therefore, will have four sections. Chapters 6 through 10 will deal with theological method under the three perspectives, and chapter 11 will discuss matters of specific interest to apologetics.

There is, of course, no such thing as a "theological method" in the sense of a series of definite steps by which all theological problems can be solved. As we will see, theology is in many ways more like an art than like a science (though science itself is more like art than is often acknowledged). There are always many factors to be weighed, many dangers to be avoided, many procedures for resolving questions. Each problem is in some ways different from all others. Still, there are general points that have some usefulness over a wide range of issues, some of which I seek to describe in what follows.

CHAPTER SIX

The Normative Perspective—The Use of Scripture

When we discuss the use of Scripture in theology, we are, of course, entering the area of biblical hermeneutics. Experts in hermeneutics generally have expertise in linguistics or in Old Testament or New Testament studies or in Heideggerian philosophy—none of which is among my areas of specialization. I am therefore reluctant to enter the hermeneutical discussion as such. I feel compelled, however, to discuss some issues that have not been extensively covered in the hermeneutical literature but that nevertheless have important bearing on our theological use of Scripture.

A. ANTI-ABSTRACTIONISM

One common concern of exegesis and theology has been that Scripture be read "in context." At the simplest level that means that when you try to understand John 3:16, you ought to relate that verse to John 3:1-15 and 17-21, the verses that come before and after it. But there are, of course, many levels of "context." It is often useful to relate a verse not only to what immediately comes before and after it but also to the larger concerns of the book in which it is found. Another context might be the place of the verse in the corpus of a particular author's writings (in our illustration, the Johannine writings). Or, one might ask how a passage relates to other passages with similar vocabulary or concerns or with others of the same literary *genre* or with others of common purpose. Or one might ask the function of the verse in the overall context of the New Testament or even of the entire Bible. A New Testament passage might be related to its Old Testament "background" or an Old Testament text to its New Testament "fulfillment." Or one might ask about the *extra*biblical "context" of the verse. How does it relate to the life of the early church, to the general culture of the time, to our situation today? What is its relation to the various realities described in Scripture—to God himself, to Christ, to redemption? And if the text teaches a particular doctrine, it is always useful to see how it is related to other doctrines, to its "doctrinal context." Since that particular kind of context is especially important for theology, I would like to look at it in more detail.

Theologians have always tried to present their doctrines "in relation to" one another. They have rarely been content merely to formulate a doctrine such as the doctrine of creation *ex nihilo*, for example. Rather, they have sought also to describe the relationships between that doctrine and other doctrines, such as divine sovereignty, the power of the Word of God, regeneration, and cosmic renovation. It is that sort of concern (coupled, of course, with a desire to achieve some measure of comprehensiveness) that has led many to write "systems" of theology.

In the modern period, however, the concern for context and relation has become a pervasive, perhaps even fundamental, concern of theologians, even theologians who are opposed to the very idea of a theological system, as the following quotations illustrate.

> God's Word is not a thing to be described, nor is it a concept to be defined. It is neither a content nor an idea. It is not "a truth," not even the very highest truth. It is the truth because it is God's person speaking, *Dei loquentis persona*. It is not something objective. It is the objective, because it is the subjective, namely, God's subjective. Certainly God's Word is not the formal possibility of divine speech, but its fulfilled reality. It always has a perfectly definite, objective content. God always utters a *concretissimum*. But this divine *concretissimum* can as such neither be anticipated nor repeated. What God utters is never in any way known and true in abstraction from God Himself. It is known and true for no other reason than that He Himself says it, that He in person is in and accompanies what is said by him. . . . we must regard it in its identity with God Himself. God's revelation is Jesus Christ, God's Son.[1]

1. Karl Barth, *Church Dogmatics* (New York: Charles Scribner's Sons, 1936), I, 1, 155.

Note how the distinction between "concrete" and "abstract" pervades that quotation. The Word of God, says Barth, is never to be abstracted from God himself. Nor is the Word "known" or "true" in abstraction from God himself. God is in the Word and is the Word. Therefore its relation to Him is its most important characteristic and must, in Barth's view, determine everything else we say about the Word. Furthermore, the content of the Word, what it says, is always "perfectly concrete" (*concretissimum*).

The quotation from Barth is a good example of what I call "anti-abstractionism" in modern theology. It emphasizes the importance of seeing certain things "in the context of" or "in relation to" other things (in the above quotation, seeing God's Word in relation to God himself). To see something in its proper context is to see it "concretely." When we fail to see it that way, we are seeing it "abstractly." Some common synonyms (more or less) for "in abstraction from" are "in isolation from," "separate from," "apart from," and "independent of." "Concretely" can be expanded to indicate the specific context of the concreteness: "in relation to x," "in connection with x," "in its identity with x" (recall this terminology in the Barth quotation). Sometimes, however, "concrete" and "abstract" are used absolutely, as it were (I am tempted to say "abstractly"), without a particular relationship in view. The abstraction is not an abstraction *from* anything in particular, and the concreteness is not a particular relationship *to* something. The "*concretissimum*" in the above quotation is used in that way. Barth tells us that God always utters a *concretissimum*, but he doesn't seem at this point to mean that the utterance is in relation to a particular something.

That kind of argumentation is very common in Barth but also in many other recent theologians. Here are some other examples.

> All abstraction has been taken away from [our thinking] when in the light of the concrete Word of God we see the place from which, without rashness, we are to listen to the revelation which is for us and for our children.[2]

> What, then, do we know of *Thou*? Just everything. For we know nothing isolated about it any more. . . . In the beginning is relation.[3]

2. G. C. Berkouwer, *Divine Election* (Grand Rapids: Wm. B. Eerdmans Pub. Co., 1960), 25. Berkouwer is the "high priest of anti-abstractionism." This type of argument permeates all of his writings.

3. Martin Buber, *I and Thou* (New York: Charles Scribner's Sons, 1958), 11, 18.

> The authors of the Scriptures never abstract, they never theologize, not even Paul.[4]

> By "word" we do not mean the single word. This word, as a unit of language, is an abstraction over against the original conception of word as containing an encounter.[5]

> . . . God was not a proposition completing a syllogism, or an abstract idea accepted by the mind, but the reality which gave meaning to their lives.[6]

> With this dynamic view of revelation as an ongoing process (for God is not dead but is the Lord of history) we are not bound by fixed words or by historic formulations of the faith. The important factor in education is *relationships*. The language by which we communicate the truth of God at work in history and in the lives of men is the language of relationships.[7]

> We shall make no progress on the common grace problem with the help of abstractions.[8]

Thus we see that writers from many theological positions—conservative as well as liberal—from different philosophical orientations and from different interests all sing the praises of concreteness, relationships, and so forth, and they denounce abstraction, separation, and isolation. Thus we may well ask, how did abstraction get such a bad name among recent theologians?

It's a long story, and I cannot shorten it very much, but I'll try to be as concise as I can be. Philosophers have always been seeking what might be called the "ideal context" for thought. According to later writers, Thales, usually regarded as the first Greek philosopher, taught that "all is water." We may, perhaps, construe this as the assertion that water is the most fundamental reality and that other things can best be understood by considering their relationship to water. Other philosophers disagreed with Thales and sought other sorts of "master contexts," most of them far more complex.

4. A. De Graaff, in A. De Graaff and C. Seerveld, *Understanding the Scriptures* (Hamilton, Ont.: The Association for the Advancement of Christian Scholarship, 1968), 2; cf. 9, 11.

5. G. Ebeling, *The Nature of Faith* (Philadelphia: Fortress Press, 1961), 185.

6. John Hick, *Philosophy of Religion* (Englewood Cliffs, N.J.: Prentice-Hall, 1963), 61.

7. Randolph C. Miller, *Education for Christian Living* (Englewood Cliffs, N.J.: Prentice-Hall, 1956).

8. C. Van Til, *Common Grace* (Nutley, N.J.: Presbyterian and Reformed Pub. Co., 1972), 74; cf. 34, 68, passim.

We may describe the search for a "master context" as a search for "concreteness" in our theological sense—a search to discover the most significant relationships in this world. Ironically, however, as it seems from our modern perspective, the Greeks saw abstraction as an indispensable and valuable tool in the search for concreteness. Thales, after all, had to think very abstractly indeed to conclude that water was the essence of everything. Water, to him, became "being," the highest abstraction.

The atomist philosophers (Democritus, Epicurus, and later the Latin poet Lucretius) seemed to be something of an exception to this general pattern among the Greek thinkers. They viewed the universe not as abstract "water" or abstract "being" (Parmenides) but as a collection of tiny, indestructible objects. Those tiny "atoms" certainly appear, to our minds' eye, as concrete realities. But the atomists reached this world view by abstract reasoning. No one had ever seen an atom; it was not an element of anyone's experience. The atomists, furthermore, postulated the existence of atoms as something common to all beings, stripped of all those qualities that distinguish one being from another. In these respects, the atoms were as abstract as Thales' "water" or as Parmenides' "being."

It certainly seemed, therefore, that abstraction was the royal road to knowledge, even knowledge of concrete realities. In abstraction we seek, in one way or another, to think of what various things have in common, apart from the "specifics" that distinguish them from each another. We think of Coby, Misty, Muffy, Midge, Bonnie, Pebbles, and Rusty, and we group them under the general ("abstract") term *Welsh corgi*. Then we think of Welsh corgis, collies, cocker spaniels, weimaraners, poodles, and so forth, and we group them under the abstract term *dog*. Then, perhaps, we will want to move on to higher levels of abstraction: mammal, animal, life-form, creature, and (the highest) being.[9]

It is understandable that for many thinkers such abstraction was considered the best road to knowledge. After all, education may be understood as the process by which we learn to see higher and higher levels of likenesses between things. It is an achievement in learning when we note, for example, what all corgis have in common so that we may use the abstract term *corgi* to refer to that commonness. Advances in intellectual development (at some levels and of some sorts) can be measured by the per-

9. Thus to "think abstractly" is to think of generalities. Perhaps we should note, however, that in the modern theological discussion it is possible to "think abstractly" even about a particular individual. We "think abstractly" about Coby, for example, when we consider him "separately from," "in isolation from," "in abstraction from" his "context" from Misty, Muffy, et al., for example.

son's increasing ability to use abstract terms and concepts. Thus it was plausible to assume that the best thinkers were the ones who thought most abstractly. After all, someone who knew about "being," the highest abstraction, knew something about everything! And it was the abstract thinker, so it seemed, who knew the most, even about concreteness. For the person who knows "corgi-ness" is the one who knows the relationships (likenesses) among Coby, Misty, et al. The one who knows about dogs-in-general is the one who knows the different relationships between corgis, collies, and so forth, and therefore among Coby, Misty, and the rest. At least that line of reasoning seemed like a promising epistemological program.

But there were problems in relating abstractness to concreteness. As it turned out, focusing on higher and higher abstractions was not the road to perfect knowledge. It was, in fact, a path that had many disadvantages. The man who spends his time thinking about "being-in-general," ignoring specific features of individual things, will not, it turns out, know very much at all. Someone who thinks a lot about "dogness," without learning anything about individual dogs, will be ignorant in certain significant respects. Abstract terms do add generality to our knowledge, but they subtract specificity. In one sense, the higher you go on the abstraction ladder, the less you know about specific things. "Coby" denotes a specific dog; "Welsh corgi" does not. "Welsh corgi" denotes certain specific properties of a certain kind of dog; "dog" does not. Thus, when a philosopher seeks knowledge by reaching into the higher levels of abstraction, he often fails to say anything important about the world in which we all live, the world of specific realities.

This discussion may be related to the discussions of "irrationalism" and "rationalism" in Part One. Through abstract knowledge, a rationalist may seek to gain an exhaustive, certain knowledge of reality. But the higher he moves on the abstraction ladder, in one sense, the less he knows. "Being," the highest abstraction, refers to everything, but it denotes nothing specific about anything. "All things are beings" tells us nothing about everything! As Hegel pointed out, it is impossible even to distinguish meaningfully between "being" as a generality and "nonbeing" (close your eyes, and try to picture the difference between them). Or think of it this way: "All things are beings" is a statement without specific applications and is therefore meaningless, according to our earlier discussions of *meaning*. Thus the rationalist, who holds that the only true knowledge is the knowledge of the highest abstractions, is no better off than the irrationalist. The irrationalist knows nothing; the rationalist knows nothing about everything.[10]

Philosophers came to see, then, that something more than abstraction was needed. The Greek Sophists and skeptics saw that the abstractionist project was leading nowhere. This suspicion of abstract thought was picked up by medieval nominalists and modern empiricists. Even rationalists sought some kind of anchorage in particulars, especially knowledge of the self as Socrates' statement "Know thyself" and as Descartes's "I think, therefore I am" illustrate. Aristotle and Aquinas sought a role for sense experience in knowledge and made a knowledge of individual things ("substances") the focus of all understanding. But for them, still, knowledge in the truest sense was knowledge of the *form* of a thing, of its abstract properties. What distinguished one dog from another was "matter," something that was strictly unknowable, indeed was in the strict sense nonbeing, unreality. Thus they remained "abstractionists"; they never solved the problems of abstractionism.

Theology, too, chafed under the constraints of abstractionist methodology. After all, Scripture means above all to tell us something very specific, not general truths about being-as-such but about the Lord, the living God, about specific historical events in which God saved us from sin, about our own character, decisions, actions, attitudes, and so forth. Theistic proofs that concluded the existence of "a first cause" or "an unmoved mover" did not seem to say what needed to be said. Thus Christians generally have had difficulties with abstraction as a preeminent theological method.

Therefore there developed among thinkers a desire to find a new way of knowing, a way that was less dependent on abstract thinking and more helpful in increasing our knowledge of concrete realities. Immanuel Kant (d. 1804) suggested a "transcendental" method. He argued that human thought (abstract thought included) was incapable of knowing the "real" world—"things in themselves," "the noumenal world," things as they really are. We can, however, achieve a dependable knowledge of our own experiences (of "appearances" or "phenomena") by asking the question, What are the conditions that make thought possible? Kant's proposal was a move toward "concreteness," an emphasis on knowledge as knowledge of our own experience and of the nature of our own reasoning capacity.

10. Van Til refers to this as the "problem of the one and the many." On the one hand, abstraction gives us "unity" among many particulars but puts us out of touch with the *differences* among these particulars, their *pluralities*. On the other hand, a focus on pluralities can put us out of touch with the unities of experience.

G. W. F. Hegel, the next great philosopher after Kant, thought that contrary to Kant, we could indeed know the "real world" if we went about knowing it in the right way. He granted Kant's point that the human mind gets snarled up in contradictions when it seeks knowledge beyond its immediate experience. But in Hegel's view, these contradictions are only apparent, and, if we are clever enough, we can use them as clues to the nature of ultimate reality. The contradictions show that the real world, the "concrete" world, is a mixture of positive and negative features. Each state of affairs negates itself as it moves ahead to the next state of affairs. Situations generate their opposites, which, at the same time, complete and fulfill the original situations. Similarly, human thought moves from one idea to its opposite until it arrives at a consummated "absolute" knowledge. This absolute knowledge was knowledge of an absolute reality—a "concrete universal," as Hegel called it. He hoped and believed that he had discovered a program for attaining completeness of knowledge without losing concreteness.

Others, however, disputed Hegel's claim. Soren Kierkegaard, for example, argued that Hegel's system was unable to account for human individuality. No system, Kierkegaard thought, was capable of that. True self-knowledge transcends all rational systems and can be achieved only through something like a decision of faith (cf. our discussion in Part Two of "cognitive rest," or "godly sense of satisfaction" under the "existential perspective"). Later, "phenomenologist" and "existentialist" philosophers sought to describe further Kierkegaard's way to concrete knowledge—either in Kierkegaard's own Christian framework or in a secularized form. They distinguished between the "abstract," "objective" knowledge discovered by the sciences and the concrete knowledge of pretheoretical or nontheoretical experience.

Meanwhile, in Britain and America philosophers of language analysis came to discover important differences between what could be learned from abstract systems and what could only be determined through attention to the experiences of ordinary life, as described in "ordinary language."

At the same time, the alleged objectivity of science itself was called in question (see my discussion in Part Two). Sociologists of knowledge, modern linguists, Marxists, Freudians, Kuhnites and others, as well as phenomenologist philosophers, argued that science itself starts with presuppositions derived from our "concrete," nonscientific experience.

Anti-abstractionism, therefore, has been pervasive in the modern philosophical climate. Both rationalists like Hegel and (more or less) irrationalists like the existentialists have seen value in it. Modern rationalism avoids abstraction so that it can seek exhaustive knowledge of all particulars; modern irrationalism seeks to avoid the constraints of a system of abstract rationality.

The philosophical climate inevitably influences theological mentalities. Christians have, as we indicated earlier, their own reasons to be suspicious of abstraction. And liberal theologians have added their own distinctive reasons, especially a dislike for "propositional revelation," "revealed doctrine." Since propositions and doctrines are formulated in terms that are abstract in some ways and degrees, liberal theologians found it convenient to argue that God, and perhaps mankind also, could not be known or experienced by way of abstractions. Both "transcendence" and "immanence" motifs (see Part One) have been used to remove God from the reach of abstractions. On the one hand, the (non-Christian) transcendence doctrine argues that God is unique and therefore cannot adequately be described by any abstract concept (recall that every abstract concept refers to more than one being; the argument is that there is no other being with whom God can be joined under a common abstract label). On the other hand, the (non-Christian) immanence doctrine seeks to avoid any formulations that "isolate" or "separate" or "abstract" God from the world.

Anti-abstractionist rhetoric, however, is used not only of the God-man or God-world relation but also of relations within creation—the relation of the Bible to history, of believers to the church, of believers to unbelievers, of Christianity to culture, and so on. Theology, too, we are told, must always be done "in relation to" certain realities, biblical concepts, theological categories. Thus we have had an era of "theologies of" this and that: theologies of hope, liberation, personal encounter, Word of God, crisis, reconciliation, covenant, feeling, history, kingdom of God, existential self-understanding, and so forth.

Thus Schleiermacher, the father of modern liberal theology, argued that no doctrine can be accepted "unless it is connected with [Christ's] redeeming causality and can be traced to the original impression made by his existence."[11] Note the somewhat vague use of "connected with," typical of the anti-abstractionist vocabulary. Ritschl sought to avoid speculation by taking his readers back to the concrete historical situation in which Christianity first appeared. Barth, as we have seen, makes extensive use of the abstract-concrete contrast. Brunner, Buber, and other "encounter"

11. F. Schleiermacher, *The Christian Faith* (Edinburgh: T. and T. Clark, 1928), 125.

theologians evacuate revelation of all content, save the sheer relation between God and human persons. Bultmann follows the existentialist approach, presenting a gospel that he thinks is totally removed from objective or abstract concepts. Pannenberg follows Hegel, seeking to achieve a "concrete" rationality, one in which it becomes difficult to distinguish God from the historical process. Modern liberationists and process theologians seek a God who is "not separate from" the world, though the God they claim to have found is scarcely distinguishable from it.

Anti-abstractionism, then, is a mentality that pervades contemporary theology—conservative, liberal, Roman Catholic, Protestant, Reformed, Arminian. It enters into nearly every subject of theological discussion. I believe, for example, that the major *theological* argument of liberal theologians against the orthodox doctrine of biblical authority is of the anti-abstractionist type. Liberals argue that the orthodox view "abstracts" Scripture from God himself, from Christ, history, personal encounter, socio-economic "praxis," and so forth. There are also, of course, arguments about whether science, archaeology, or biblical criticism have demonstrated errors in Scripture. These arguments, like all arguments, are theological in a sense, but their theological character is not apparent until one identifies the presuppositions underlying the various positions. Of the arguments that are *explicitly* theological, all of them, in my view, are of the anti-abstractionist type. Furthermore, many other theological issues similarly turn on this kind of debate. Thus it is important that we develop an analytical and critical perspective on anti-abstractionism. And so consider in that regard the following observations.

a. *The Meanings of "Abstract" and "Concrete"*

The meanings of *abstract* and *concrete* are not always as clear as they might seem. (i) I have already mentioned the ambiguity between the absolute and relative uses of these terms: something may be described either as "abstract from" something else (e.g., a view of the Bible in abstraction from Jesus Christ) or as "abstract" pure and simple (e.g., "*being* is an abstract term"). The first may be described as a "relative" use of *abstract*, the second as an "absolute" use. (ii) *Abstract* and *concrete* may apply to different kinds of subjects. One may speak of abstract or concrete terms, concepts, realities, propositions, discussions, methods, even attitudes (see below!). (iii) In the "absolute" sense, these terms are generally applied to words, concepts, and realities (things, persons). In the "relative" sense, they are applied to all the different types of subjects listed under *(ii)*. When they are applied to words, concepts, and things in a relative sense, the focus of attention is usually on a discussion or method employing those words, concepts, and things or an attitude toward them. For example, someone will urge us to see grace "concretely" in a context of justice, for example. That point is really a point about our formulation, method, or attitude, rather than about the intrinsic nature of grace as a term, concept, or reality (though it is often emphasized that a proper formulation, method, or attitude is needed if we are to understand the nature of grace). Therefore I shall discuss the "absolute" use of these terms as it applies to words, concepts, and realities and the "relative" use as it applies to discussions, methods, attitudes.

b. *The Absolute Sense of "Abstract" and "Concrete"*

Let us first, then, look at "abstractness" and "concreteness" in the absolute sense as they apply to words, concepts, and realities. Words, concepts, and realities, of course, are not entirely similar, and they don't all have the same kinds of "concreteness" and "abstractness." Nevertheless, the problems raised at these three levels are similar. (i) Note some absolute uses of our terms: "*Being* is an abstract term," "Justice is an abstract concept," "That tree is a concrete reality." This "absolute" use is, in some respects, not absolute at all, for it permits differences of degree. There are many *degrees* of abstraction in this sense (Coby, Welsh corgi, dog, mammal, life-form, creature, being). It is not always clear in the anti-abstractionist literature what degree of abstraction is permissible and what degree is forbidden.

(ii) Not only are there different degrees of abstraction and concreteness, there are also differences in *kind*. Modern theologians use "abstract" and "concrete" not only to refer to levels on the traditional abstraction ladder but also to refer to various kinds of "separations" between things. Thus we read about "revelation in abstraction from God." We might speak, then, of "the chalk in abstraction from the blackboard." But of course, there are many different kinds of relations between chalk and blackboard, revelation and God, and therefore many ways in which "separations" can occur. Nonidentity between objects (or, similarly, nonsynonymy between terms) can be one kind of separation (recall the quotation from Barth in which he insisted on an *identity* between God and the Word, regarding any lesser relation as "abstract"). But chalk and blackboard can also be separated by distance (there are, of course, many degrees of separation by distance) or by their different functions or by having different colors or shapes or textures or material constituents. They may be "together" in one relationship, "separated" in another. Similarly, God and the Word are related in a wide variety of ways. God speaks the Word; in an orthodox view He writes it on paper; the Word bears His wisdom, and so forth. If I affirm these but deny Barth's alleged relation between God and the Word, am I thereby thinking abstractly? Not obviously so.

(iii) If someone replies that *no* degree or kind of abstraction is permitted, then we must question the intelligibility of the demand. It is doubtful whether any word, concept, or thing can be *purely* abstract or *purely* concrete. Even "Coby," some have argued, may be seen as an abstraction from our varied experiences of this particular dog—the feel of a fuzzy ear, the sound of a bark, and so forth. And "sound of a bark" is itself an abstract concept, formed as a generalization from many particular barks and distinguished ("isolated") from other kinds of noises. What is the concrete reality (the *perfectly* concrete reality) from which the abstract concept is, supposedly, ultimately derived? Some philosophers ("logical atomists") have argued that our experience of dogs, barks, and so forth is made up of certain ultimate constituent experiences of "atomic facts"—momentary experiences of blueness, loudness, or what have you. But what is a "momentary experience of a blue patch"? Can any of us remember such an experience? Or is that concept itself precisely an abstraction? Doesn't our concept of a "momentary blue patch" arise by abstraction from our nonmomentary experiences of, say, looking at the sky? Thus there is no perfect concreteness; whenever we seek it, we are back to abstraction again. That is my reply to Barth's talk (see the first quotation earlier in this discussion) about God always revealing a *concretissimum*. The search for a perfectly concrete mode of human knowledge is an apostate search, an attempt to obtain what only God has. (A perfectly concrete knowledge would be a knowledge of every detail of creation—the exhaustive knowledge unique to God.) When anyone seeks it, his "concrete" knowledge vanishes in the shades of abstraction.

(iv) Similarly, there is no "pure abstractness." Although *being* is the most abstract term there is, there are some senses in which even it is concrete. (A) It refers to the world of our experience. (B) Although *being* covers all reality in one sense, in another sense it does not. For *being* must be distinguished from *beings*. I am a being; I am not being-in-general or being-in-the-abstract. Thus *being* designates one (concrete, specific!) aspect of the world (the abstract aspect!) that may and should be distinguished from others. (One way of describing the difficulty of the Greek philosophers is to say that in one sense their abstract "being" covered everything in the universe, but in another important sense it only covered the abstract aspect of the universe, leaving out everything of concrete interest to us.)

(v) Since no word, concept, or thing is perfectly abstract or perfectly concrete, we must say that each is both concrete and abstract in some degree or way. It is not surprising, then, that concreteness is often in the eye of the beholder. Imagine a well-decorated room with a fine painting over the fireplace. An interior decorator might say: "Think concretely. You must see the painting in the context of the room. Apart from its environment, the painting is an abstraction." But an art critic might look at it differently: "We must think not abstractly of the room in general but concretely of the painting in and of itself." Who is thinking abstractly, the interior decorator or the art critic? Is the painting one of the concrete realities out of which the room is composed, or is the room the concrete reality from which we abstract its various aspects and parts? Which is concrete, the part or the whole? Well, both, in different respects. The art critic thinks concretely in the "absolute" sense, thinking of the painting as a palpable object. The interior decorator thinks concretely in the "relative" sense, seeking to relate the painting to what he thinks is its appropriate "context." And here is another way to look at it. The art critic is most interested in the painting; that is the "focus" of his thought. The decorator is interested in the room as a whole. Thus, for the critic, the painting is the concrete object; for the decorator, the room is. Smaller or larger units might also be taken as "concrete." To an expert on paint, the molecules on the canvas might be the concrete units. To an architect, the room itself might be only an "abstraction" from the total building, which is the really concrete (perhaps literally!) unit. What is "abstract" or "concrete" to us depends on our interests, our values, our points of view. When we understand the person-relativity of the concept of abstraction, we can see how difficult it is to make a case that someone else is "thinking abstractly."

c. *The Relative Sense of "Abstract" and "Concrete"*

Let us now consider what we earlier (*a*, above) called the "relative" uses of *abstract* and *concrete* as they apply to discussions, methods, and attitudes. Sometimes, on this understanding, an "abstract" discussion is one that deals with a number of abstract words, concepts, or realities. We have already, in effect, discussed some issues surrounding this type of discussion. Second, though, an "abstract" discussion can also be a discussion in which the proper relationships between things are not adequately dealt with. In the first sense, an "abstract" discussion may be desirable; in the second sense, to call a discussion "abstract" is always a reproach. It is possible to confuse these two senses of *abstract* to our theological detriment.

Let us now think about discussions that are abstract in the second sense. What does it mean to describe them as "abstract"? Let us try to interpret the phrase "We should not see x in abstraction from y."

In my judgment, this kind of language is highly ambiguous. Let us consider some things that it might mean. (i) My first impression, when I hear such admonitions, is that the writer wants me to have a particular mental image. To "see revelation in relation to God" would be to have a mental picture or diagram of "revelation" (as somehow) in close physical proximity to God. (Since the "seeing" is evidently not physical, we think, it must be some kind of *mental* "sight"—a mental image.) Obviously, that is not what these writers mean, but I think the apparent clarity of their proposals is linked to the ease with which we construct such mental pictures. Once we start asking what *else* might be meant by these admonitions, their apparent clarity vanishes.

(ii) Sometimes, something like an "emphasis" seems to be in view. To "see x in relation to y" is to emphasize y whenever we speak of x. Thus "see revelation in relation to God" means that we must emphasize God whenever we speak of revelation. But problems arise here as well. (A) Emphasis is a matter of degree. *How much* must we emphasize God in order to "see revelation in relation to" Him? How would we calculate that? (This sort of question underscores the oddness of the demand being made.) Is it necessary to *talk* about God a certain percentage of the time when we talk about revelation? How much? Surely that cannot be the point. (B) Is it really plausible to say that theology must be done with one "emphasis" rather than another? Although it is true that Scripture has a "central message," a message that ought to be the chief concern of our theological work, it seems to me that valuable theological work can be done on areas that are relatively "minor" or distantly related to the "central message" of Scripture. For example, someone might write an article on the veiling of women in 1 Corinthians 11. Is that article illegitimate because it pays relatively little attention to the "central message" of Scripture? Must we disparage that article because it doesn't have a proper "emphasis"? (C) It is impossible for theology to have precisely the same "emphasis" as Scripture does. To do that, theology would have to simply *repeat* Scripture from Genesis to Revelation. But the task of theology, as we have seen, is not to repeat Scripture but to apply it. Thus theology not only may but ought to have a different emphasis from Scripture itself. (D) If a theologian requires of us an emphasis that is *not* the emphasis of Scripture, where does that theologian's emphasis come from? I know of no source other than Scripture by which a "normative emphasis" might be established. (E) Granted, theological discussions are sometimes weak because of *perverse* emphases—emphases that mislead the reader concerning the truth or that generate unclarity, detract from the cogency of the author's case, and so forth. (In such cases, indeed, we use Scripture as our criterion for judging the emphasis to be faulty, without requiring the theologian in question to reproduce the emphasis of Scripture itself.) But in those cases, the problem can more clearly be analyzed not as a problem of "emphasis" but as a problem of truth or clarity or cogency. The problem is not with the emphasis as such but that in this particular case the emphasis misleads.

(iii) Often, I think, when theologians ask us not to abstract God from revelation, for example, what they really want to say is that we should hold certain *views* about God and certain *views* of revelation. Fair enough. But the anti-abstractionist language tends to obscure the nature of the debate between opposing positions. Both Gordon Kaufman and Herman Ridderbos, for example, say that "revelation must never be abstracted from history." For Kaufman, that statement entails that revelation must be subject to the canons of secular historiography, but for Ridderbos it entails the opposite—historiographers must recognize the presence of divine revelation in history and submit themselves to it. The fact is that most anti-abstractionist slogans can be accepted—enthusiastically—by almost *all* professedly Christian theologians. But they are so ambiguous that the same slogan will have contradictory doctrinal entailments in the systems of different thinkers. Thus the slogan suggests a kind of common ground that does not actually exist. I can agree with Barth, for example, that revelation should be seen "in relation to God," but my idea of that relation is very different from his. For me to affirm that statement does not draw me one bit closer to him than I was before. I must say, therefore, that the use of such slogans is often, perhaps usually, either ignorant or dishonest. It is ignorant if the theologian uses such slogans without an awareness of their ambiguity. It is dishonest if he is aware of their ambiguity yet uses them to deceive readers into imagining a false common ground. (For consideration of some actual views thought to be necessitated by anti-abstractionist principles, see *d* below.)

(iv) The most defensible use of the anti-abstractionist language, in my opinion, is to reinforce the traditional theological concern for contextual exegesis. In the narrow sense, this means that we are called to let Scripture interpret Scripture, to read every part of the Bible in the light of the rest. In a somewhat broader sense, it refers to our concern as theologians to have a consistent or "systematic" theology in which each doctrine is understood in a way that is consistent with the others. Stating this concern is not to demand of the theologian any particular mental images or emphases or theological conclusions.

It is especially important for us to show the relations that each text and each doctrine sustain to Christ and His redemptive work. He is the key to the Scriptures (see Luke 24:13-35; John 5:39-47). We have not understood what is most important about a biblical passage until we have seen how that passage preaches Christ.[12]

Even at this simple, obvious, and valid level of anti-abstractionism, however, some warnings are in order. (A) Remember what I said earlier (first paragraph of this section, A): each verse has *many* contexts that are relevant to its interpretation—contexts both within and outside of Scripture. There is no single context that must always be in the foreground, in all situations where we teach the passage, for all audiences. This is to repeat the point made earlier in my definition of theology (Part One)—that the task of theology is not to reorganize Scripture into some kind of ideally perfect order for *all* occasions but to *apply* Scripture, arranging its presentation to meet the needs of a *particular* audience. Theology is free to use various contexts of interpretation, as long as it does not distort the teaching of Scripture in the process.

(B) There are too many contexts for us to do justice to all of them simultaneously. Therefore some relationships and contexts, important in themselves, must be overlooked in any particular theological discussion. We ought not to be embarrassed about this; it is simply a consequence of our finitude. Scripture itself often sets forth doctrines without exploring all the significant relationships between them and other doctrines. James presents his teaching on faith and works without doing adequate justice to the Pauline teaching on justification. Hebrews 6 presents a view of apostasy that does not begin to answer our questions about perseverance. The Song of Solomon speaks of human love, without addressing the reader's questions about how that love, precisely, is related to God or to Christ. (I said earlier that Christ is the key to the Scriptures and that the most important thing about any text or doctrine is its relation to Christ. I would not say, however, that every time that we study the text, Christ, the most important context, must be in the foreground. Sometimes it is legitimate to consider aspects of a text or doctrine that are "less important." It is not wrong to

12. See E. Clowney, *Preaching and Biblical Theology* (Grand Rapids: Wm. B. Eerdmans Pub. Co., 1961; reissued by Presbyterian and Reformed) for a strong argument to this effect. Christ fulfills law and prophecy. He is the antitype of all Old Testament types. He is the perfect prophet, priest, and king. He is the chief concern of the New Testament gospel (1 Cor. 2:2).

write an article seeking to identify the practice of the veiling of women in 1 Corinthians 11, even though that practice is, in general, less important than the passage's bearing on the overall gospel of salvation.)

(C) As important as it is to stress relationships among texts, doctrines, and theological realities, there is also value in "isolating" these in a certain way. John 3:16, for example, has a meaning of its own that is distinct from the meaning of verses 1-15 and verses 17-21. Although its meaning in some ways depends on its context, that meaning is not *reducible to* the meaning of its context. It is important at some stage in the inquiry to ask, What does verse 16, specifically, *add* to the overall context? If that is a form of "isolation" or "abstraction," then so be it.

(D) The idea that there is one "master context" in Scripture that must always have some kind of supreme prominence in any theological discussion is dangerous. It suggests that we need some "bedrock of truth," some "ultimate starting point" other than the *whole* of Scripture (Matt. 4:4).

(E) The points about exegeting Scripture in context and understanding all doctrines in the light of all the others can be made much more clearly and effectively without the use of the anti-abstractionist rhetoric.

d. *What Are Anti-Astractionists Trying to Prove?*

Having explored the various ambiguities in the *meaning* of the anti-abstractionist language, let us now ask what theologians seek to *prove* by using arguments of an anti-abstractionist type. When we hear slogans like "revelation must not be abstracted from God himself," what *conclusions* are we expected to draw? The fact that this rhetoric can be used to recommend many different kinds of conclusions will help us to see even more clearly the intrinsic ambiguity of this language. Let us return to the quotations mentioned at the beginning of this section to see something of the variety of conclusions (and types of conclusions) that the anti-abstractionists urge on us.

(i) In the quotation from Barth, the author seems to want us to posit a metaphysical or ontological identity between God and the Word. Anything less than that he would consider an improper "abstraction" of one from the other. But that, interestingly enough, is the kind of concreteness demanded by Hegel (whose thought in other respects is *anathema* to Barth, as it was to Kierkegaard)—the ultimate ontological identity between the mind and its objects. Something similar seems to be going on also in the

Buber quotation, but that is harder to say.[13] Yet, surely, the anti-abstractionist language does not *usually* entail ontological identity. When someone says, "Napoleon must not be understood in abstraction from the economic situation of his time," he is certainly not asserting any ontological identity between Napoleon and "the economic situation." And the same holds true in the other theological examples, such as "We must not see the doctrine of election in abstraction from redemptive history." The point here, too, is certainly not an ontological identity. And clearly, if Barth wishes to establish an ontological identity between God and the Word, he will not, therefore, be able to establish it on the basis of his anti-abstractionism alone. Granted our reluctance to "abstract the Word from God himself," it clearly does not follow that the Word *is* God himself; nor is it clear that the anti-abstractionist language lends any plausibility at all to Barth's case, except by adding to it some rhetorical flourish.

(ii) Some of the other expressions in the Barth quote indicate *epistemological* relationships between the terms of the nonabstractable relation. The Word is true and knowable because of its relationship to God himself. But surely that could be said by many non-Barthians also. An orthodox Protestant, for example, could say that the Word is true and knowable because God has spoken it in a way that makes it true and knowable. It is not clear what the anti-abstractionist rhetoric adds to this assertion.

(iii) Sometimes the anti-abstractionist language seems to be a way of expressing dislike for intellectualism, the reduction of God's reality or His redemptive actions to a set of intellectual concepts. The quotations from Berkouwer, De Graaff, and Hick seem to have that sort of thrust. But, again, it is not clear how the anti-abstractionist vocabulary really helps them to make this kind of point. Evidently, Berkouwer wants to say that when we are savingly impressed by the Word of God, we tend to forget about our bright, clever theological theories and face the Lord with awe, wonder, repentance, and faith. True enough. But in what sense is "abstraction taken away" from us in that sort of experience? Are we forbidden to use abstract terms in addressing our Lord? Nonsense. Does the sense of separation between Creator and creature disappear in such a confrontation? Surely not; quite the contrary is true (cf. Isa. 6). Is the anti-abstractionist rhetoric here, perhaps, just an unclear way of expressing the inadequacy of theoretical thought? Probably so, but not, I think, in a very clear or effective way. Similarly, the quotation from De Graaff, if taken lit-

13. Buber seems to be asserting an ontological primacy to relationships themselves (whatever that may mean), rather than an ontological identity between the things being related.

erally, is nonsense; the biblical writers do abstract. De Graaff is probably thinking not of abstraction in any literal sense but of theoretical thought (probably in the technical Dooyeweerdian sense of that phrase). His language on any interpretation is unclear, and it is not clear, either, what the anti-abstractionism adds to a polemic against intellectualism. In the quotation from Hick, the contrast is between God as an "abstract idea" and God as a "reality." God is, of course, in Christian thought, a concrete individual rather than an abstract form of some kind; but that seems obvious and hardly relevant. How many of Hick's readers are tempted to think of God as a Platonic form? Rather, here, as in the quotations from Berkouwer and De Graaff, the anti-abstractionist language seems only to be a kind of rhetorical flourish in a denunciation of intellectualism.

(iv) The Miller quotation (and I think some of this may lie behind Buber's language also) draws together the dynamic-static contrast with the abstract-concrete ("relation") contrast. Here the point is that interpersonal relationships are the most important thing—relations between ourselves and God, ourselves and one another. However, (A) it is not clear to me why God's lordship over history entails that "we are not bound by fixed words" or why the latter conclusion makes relationships more important than they would otherwise be. Imagine what it would be like if God *did* reveal himself by "fixed words," empowering and applying those words to us ever anew by His Spirit, as on the orthodox conception. Would our relationship to Him then be any less important than on Miller's construction? (B) Miller seems to be making an almost unconscious transition between an epistemological point and a pastoral point. If we may read between the lines of his argument, revelation, on his view, consists not of "fixed" (= "abstract"?) truths but of a kind of truth that is in constant change as circumstances change, and that therefore is "in relation" to the changing world. Therefore since revelation is "in relation" to circumstances, education must be carried on through interpersonal relationships. But that argument is clearly a *non sequitur*. (C) Miller ignores the crucial question of content. Granted that God's education of Israel was an education in and by a relationship and that our education of one another must be similar, what is it that we are going to teach by means of the relationship? Are there "fixed words," or is there some other form of communication? The emphasis on relationship really doesn't answer that question at all. Within a relationship, many kinds of content can be taught, including the content of "fixed words." Thus it is simply wrong to say that "teaching in relationship" excludes (or that it is an intelligible alternative to) teaching by "fixed words." (D) But my main purpose here is to note another element of unclarity in the anti-abstractionist vocabulary: its emphasis on epistemological relations often gets transmuted into an emphasis on interpersonal relations, without any clear logical justification.

(v) The quotation from Van Til (in context, and following the pattern of his reasoning elsewhere)[14] equates abstract thinking with a human lust for autonomy. This, too, is an epistemological point (though somewhat different from the others); but most importantly, it is a religious point: abstraction is a defect in piety, a defect in one's devotion to God. Certainly, it is true that a desire for autonomous knowledge is rebellion against God. And the desire for autonomy certainly lies behind the method of the Greek philosophers—to seek exhaustive knowledge through abstraction—as we have seen. Thus autonomy and abstraction are indeed related. Still, it is easy to exaggerate this point. The fact that abstraction was part of the idolatrous Greek epistemology does not mean that *all* abstraction comes from idolatrous motives. Why should we think that it does? Perhaps lying behind this idea is the thought that since God is unique, He may not be placed with other beings under a common label, which always happens in the use of abstract terms. Thus to speak abstractly about Him would seem to reduce God to the level of other things or to raise those other things to His level. As we have seen, however, no terms are entirely devoid of abstraction. If we avoided abstract language entirely, we could not speak of God or of anything else at all! Most theologians, including Van Til, employ some doctrine of analogy or other principle to indicate that even when God is grouped with other realities under a common label, He is nevertheless uniquely different from all of them. Thus the anti-abstractionist rhetoric is unnecessary.

(vi) The quotations from Berkouwer, De Graaff, and Hick suggest other senses in which abstraction may be a defect in piety. (A) This point is related to *(iii)* above: abstract thinking (= "intellectualism"?) sets up a kind of barrier between God and ourselves. The thought is understandable. Often, normally pious persons feel some decrease in their closeness to God when they are thinking "abstractly" about Him. But it is not evident that this always happens or necessarily happens or that it is a function of abstract thinking as such rather than of the thinker's own weakness. Nor is it even evident that when we lose the *feeling* of closeness to God we are necessarily committing any kind of sin. It is not evident that God always intends His people to *feel* close to Him. (B) And one wonders, in reading these theologians, whether *abstract* sometimes *means* "thinking without a

14. Ironically, this is also an emphasis in Barth's writings.

proper 'relationship' to God." I am tempted to think that in some writers (not Van Til, but perhaps Berkouwer) this may be the case. But surely this kind of talk is based (as *(iv)*) on a confusion between different kinds of "relationships." (C) While we are thinking about the God-man relationship, it is important to point out that despite all that can be said about the importance of a "relationship" or even a "closeness" between the believer and God, it is equally important to stress the *distinction*, indeed the *distance*, between the Creator and the creature. Perhaps "abstract" thinking, if it somehow increases our sense of distance, may be of *positive* devotional value! (D) Theologians of all types (not only conservatives) have a tendency to question the piety of those who disagree with their views. This is not surprising, and it is not always wrong. Sometimes false ideas do result from and manifest impiety. Theologians, however, are often reluctant to say this explicitly. It is easier for them to say "So-and-so is impious because he reasons abstractly" than to say "So-and-so is impious because he disagrees with my view of revelation." It may be, however, that the two ways of speaking boil down to the same thing.

e. *A General Philosophical Observation About Anti-Abstractionism*

We saw earlier in our too rapid historical survey that problems with abstraction as a general method of knowledge led philosophers and theologians to replace abstractness with concreteness as a general goal of knowledge. Abstraction led to emptiness, to a loss of specifics. By abstractionist methods, rationalism led to ignorance. But now we should be able to see that concreteness as a general goal of knowledge is just as problematic as was abstraction. (i) A "pure concreteness" is just as unimaginable as is "pure abstractness." As we have seen, no term is perfectly abstract or perfectly concrete. And no human act of knowledge is able to account perfectly for all the specific characteristics of its objects. To seek that kind of concreteness is as rationalistic as to seek perfect abstractness. It is to seek a knowledge available only to God. (ii) And just as abstractionist rationalism leads to ignorance and irrationalism, so does anti-abstractionist rationalism. When we are unsatisfied with anything short of perfect concreteness, we will never achieve our goal. Thus we will end up knowing nothing, except those things we learn inadvertently in ways that are contrary to our own methods. Thus anti-abstractionist thinkers tend to seek knowledge, not by any definite methods at all, but by leaps of faith, mystical experiences, and the like. Now there is a place for faith in knowledge, and there is something mystical, we might say, about the "cognitive rest" that we discussed earlier. But there are normative revelations from God telling us how to achieve that cognitive rest. Modern anti-abstractionist thinkers (unless their thinking is strongly tempered by a normative perspective, as is Van Til's) deny the existence of such normative revelation, thinking the very idea of normative revelation is too abstract. Thus they really have no criterion of truth, no way of knowing when they have achieved their goal. (iii) This is, of course, the reason why the Greeks sought knowledge in the abstract realm. When they looked toward their apparently concrete experience, all they found was bewildering movement and change. Nothing, they found, could be identified or named without abstract terminology. Modern thought, being frustrated by the world of abstractions, has now turned back to the "flux" of here-and-now experience. But modern thinkers have been no more successful than the Greeks at rationalizing the world of flux. They have sought nonabstract ways of understanding it and have found nothing. (iv) Finally, is it not self-contradictory—not only *prima facie* but in the final analysis—to seek concreteness in general, concreteness in the abstract? Does this contradiction not show the impossibility of a purely concrete knowledge at the human level?

Thus we have seen a great many problems with anti-abstractionism. It is ambiguous in many ways. There have been a great many different kinds of criticisms of abstraction made in modern theological literature, with a wide variety of different intents. The anti-abstractionist vocabulary can be used to argue a particular kind of relationship (such as ontological identity), to make epistemological points, to oppose intellectualism, to recommend an emphasis on "personal relationships," to oppose autonomy, or to denounce certain kinds of impiety. In all of these cases, either the anti-abstractionist language is too unclear to be useful in making the point or else the point itself is invalid. And we have seen that the very desire for a "perfectly concrete" knowledge of God and the world is a sinful one and therefore one that God will not honor. It is a search for a knowledge identical to God's or for some infallible reference point outside of His inspired Scriptures. For those reasons, I avoid the use of anti-abstractionist language. (Occasionally, I may use it as a rhetorical flourish on a point made elsewhere in clearer fashion, having made clear that my own epistemology is radically different from the prevailing autonomous anti-abstractionism.) I advise students and other theologians to do the same. The "abstractness" of a term, concept, proposition, discussion, or method is never a sufficient reason either for accepting or rejecting it.

A biblical epistemology sets us free to reason abstractly (recognizing the limitations of abstractions) and to seek (relative) concreteness (realizing that we will never escape entirely the abstract nature of finite thought). It reminds us never to seek our ultimate epistemological security in either the abstraction or the concreteness of our own thinking but to seek it in the infallible certainty of God's own Word. Sinful thought-patterns always tempt us to think that we need something more secure than that or at least something in our own thought that provides us with an infallible access to the infallible Word. In that respect, the theologians most opposed to the idea of infallibility are, ironically, often most eager, in effect, to find that elusive, infallible something. (Their real problem, of course, is not with the idea of infallibility as such but with their tendency to seek infallibility in themselves, rather than in God.) But God calls us to walk by faith. He has given us a sure Word of truth that He expects us to obey. We can know it, understand it. We do not need to have some utterly abstract or concrete knowledge; we need to be faithful, obedient. And faithfulness often means being satisfied with something less than the knowledge we would like to have. Walking by faith often means walking without sight, looking through a glass darkly. And that in turn may mean accepting either more or less abstraction than that which would make us fully comfortable. God gives us cognitive rest, but He often withholds total cognitive comfort.

B. PERSPECTIVALISM

I discussed "perspectival" relationships earlier in this book. There we saw that law, object, and subject, as aspects of human knowledge, are perspectively related. That means, for example, that when we come to know the law, inevitably we also come to know the object and the subject at the same time (and similarly for the other two perspectives). The law, then, is not merely one *part* of human knowledge; it is the *whole* of human knowledge as seen from a particular "perspective."[15] One may not ask, then, whether knowledge of law "precedes" or "follows" knowledge of the object or the subject. It is not meaningful to ask about "priority" here. Because we learn about law, object, and subject at the same time, there is no temporal priority. Because knowledge of each perspective is equally dependent on the other two, there is no priority of dependence.

Within theology there are a great many relationships of that sort. I believe that the perspectival approach to knowledge is fruitful in helping us to understand the divine attributes, the persons of the Trinity, the aspects of human personality, the commandments of the Decalogue, the order of

15. See also Appendix A at the end of Part One.

the divine decrees, the offices of Christ, and perhaps other matters as well.[16] Understanding these matters perspectivally helps us to avoid the rather fruitless arguments about "priority" that have taken place in theology over many years. Is intellect "prior to" will in human nature? Is God's decree to elect a people "prior to" His decree to create them? Is God's benevolence "prior to" His justice? As we will see later, although *prior* in theology is highly ambiguous, it has played a large role in the history of theology because, in my opinion, theologians have neglected the option of seeing relationships perspectivally.

God's Word tends to present relationships perspectivally because it reflects the nature of God himself, I would surmise. God is one God in three persons; He is many attributes in one Godhead—the eternal one-and-many. None of the persons is "prior to" the others; all are equally eternal, ultimate, absolute, glorious. None of the attributes is "prior to" any of the others; each is equally divine, inalienable, and necessary to God's deity.

In this section my interest is to set forth the perspectival nature of theology as such. My suggestion here is that the various doctrines of Scripture are perspectivally related, as are other elements or aspects of Scripture.

Our discussion of anti-abstractionism (A, above) points us in this direction. In that discussion I stressed that though it is legitimate to seek a "contextual exegesis" of Scripture, we must beware of assuming that there is one single "master context" that must always be in view. There is, to be sure, a focus to Scripture. There is a "central message." Scripture is written so that people will believe in Christ (John 20:31) and so that believers might be built up in godliness (2 Tim. 3:16f.). Christ is the center of the Scriptures (Luke 24:13-35; John 5:39-47). But of course not every part of Scripture is equally important in the light of those purposes. (As John W. Montgomery once observed, we often give out the Gospel of John to people on the streets; we rarely give out copies of 2 Chronicles.) Thus in one sense, Christ's redemptive work is the "central" context of the Scriptures. Consider, however, the following qualifications. (1) To understand the full scope of Christ's redemptive work, we need the *whole* biblical canon. Otherwise, God would not have given us such a large document! (2) Thus the central message of the Scriptures, even though it is found more prominently in some passages than in others, is defined by the whole Bible. (3) Therefore there is a "perspectival" reciprocity between the central message of Scripture and its detailed, particular messages. The central message

16. I hope to expound these relationships in future writings.

is defined by the particular messages, and the particular messages must be understood in the light of the central message.

(4) The redemptive work of Christ may be described in many different ways: covenant, sacrifice, atonement, resurrection, purification, new creation, obedience-righteousness, kingdom-conquest, liberation, reconciliation, redemption, propitiation, revelation, judgment, courtship, adoption, giving faith, hope, love, joy, peace, and so forth. These, too, are perspectivally related. Each summarizes the whole gospel from a particular point of view. As I mentioned earlier, in the modern period there have been many "theologies of this and that"—theologies of the Word of God, of liberation, hope, encounter, crisis (judgment), and so forth. Each of those theologies has advanced cogent arguments to show why it expresses the "central message" of Scripture. Well, one can agree with all of them, up to a point! Almost all of these theologies have some genuine insight into Scripture. Each has discovered a concept or doctrine that can be used to summarize the whole gospel. Each has discovered a "central doctrine." That means that Christianity has *many* "centers," or, to put it another way, Christianity has one center (Christ) that can be expounded in many ways.

(5) Although we may agree with these theologians in their affirmation that hope, liberation, Word of God, or whatever, is "central" to Scripture, we must disagree with them over their attempt to *exclude* rival "centers." If these concepts are perspectivally related, then they do not exclude one another; we do not have to choose among them. Rather, we can find in each an aspect of the precious diversity, the precious richness that God has written into His Word.

The idea that there is one and only one "central concept" that permeates the whole canon to the exclusion of others is initially implausible. My colleague Allen Mawhinney reminds me of the relevance, for example, of the "occasional" character of Paul's writings. They simply do not look like the work of a man who is developing a tight system centered around one particular idea. Rather, Paul uses a wide variety of resources to deal with whatever problem is at hand. Different ideas are prominent, depending on the nature of the gospel to be sure, but also depending on the problems currently at issue.

(6) To say that Christ is the center is not to say that a theology must always be talking about Him or "emphasizing" Him. As I mentioned earlier, there is no reason why a theologian might not write an article on the veiling of women in 1 Corinthians 11, without mentioning Christ at all

(though his long-range motive ought to be to glorify the name of Christ through his theological work). The same is true of the various "subcenters" of theologies (e.g., hope, liberation).

(7) When a theologian says that we must "see everything in relation to x (a 'central doctrine')" or that we must "never theologize in abstraction from x," he is using highly ambiguous expressions, and he is in danger of making a great many methodological errors (as discussed above in section A). He is also in theological danger—the danger of adopting something less than the *whole* Scripture as his final authority.

(8) Not all "perspectives" are equally prominent in Scripture or equally useful to the theologian. It is quite right for a theologian to prefer one perspective to another. He errs only when he gives to that perspective the kind of authority due only to the biblical canon as a whole or when he seeks to exclude other perspectives that also have some validity.

(9) This sort of talk sometimes sounds like relativism. Actually, though, it is far from that, and the motive behind it is quite the opposite. The main point of my arguments for perspectivalism is to defend the absolute authority of Scripture as a whole over against all the pretensions of theologians. It is Scripture that is our authority, not this or that "theology of" something or other. It is the whole Scripture that is our authority, not this or that "context" within Scripture. Yes, to "absolutize" Scripture we must somewhat "relativize" theology. I make no apologies for that. Theology is a fallible, human work (though it has a kind of certainty, too; see Part Two).[17]

C. CONTEXTUAL EXEGESIS

In the preceding sections, I have endorsed (in general terms) the traditional concern for "contextual exegesis," in particular the concern to relate all of Scripture to Christ and His redemptive work. I have also, however, indicated some dangers in talking about "contexts," as well as some senses in which it is good to "isolate" a text from its context (see earlier under A). A few more observations on these subjects, however, are in order.

17. In this section I am indebted to some unpublished writings of Vern S. Poythress (as he has also been indebted to me for some of his formulations!).

(1) Sentence-Level Exegesis

First of all, "contextual exegesis" means that words are to be interpreted in the contexts of the sentences of which they are a part. That sounds like a fairly obvious point, but it is a principle that many theologians have violated. The biblical scholar James Barr first made his reputation by telling this story.[18] As he explains it, theologians who had abandoned the concept of "propositional revelation" needed some source of theological truth in the Bible other than biblical propositions. Therefore they sought to develop their theology out of *word studies*, hoping that they could find theological truth in the Bible's theological terms and in the concepts underlying those terms, rather than in the sentences of the Bible. But in analyzing the meanings of biblical words, theologians often came to depend on etymologies and fanciful theories about lexical stock (e.g., that the Hebrews thought more "dynamically" and less "abstractly" than the Greeks because of the supposed prominence of action-terms in the Hebrew language). Barr pointed out that such theories were largely fallacious and that the appeal to etymology was wrong. The etymological meanings of words are often very different from what those words actually meant when they were used at the time that the Scripture in question was written. Instead of depending on word studies to determine the meaning of words, Barr argued that we should derive the meaning of words from their use in sentences, paragraphs, and larger literary units.

Evangelical Christians have no problem with propositional revelation and therefore should have no difficulty in following Barr's program (though Barr himself is very critical of evangelicalism). Evangelical theology ought to be built on biblical sentences, paragraphs, and books, not on words "in the abstract." But evangelicals, too, sometimes err in this area. It is, after all, almost too easy to use concordances and dictionaries of Bible terms to try to determine the meaning of words. These tools can be useful in illuminating biblical *sentences*, but beware of depending too heavily on word-study materials as a source of theology. Some of the most famous word-study books (like Kittel's *Theological Dictionary of the New Testament*) have at times fallen into the methodological errors cited by Barr.

Related problems sometimes crop up in systematic theology. A theologian will sometimes accuse another of error because the second theologian uses terminology that has been used in the past for unwholesome purposes.

18. See his *The Semantics of Biblical Language* (London: Oxford University Press, 1961) and *Old and New in Interpretation* (London: SCM Press, 1966).

In the volume *Jerusalem and Athens*,[19] Robert D. Knudsen finds fault with Cornelius Van Til because the latter uses *analytical* in reference to God's self-knowledge. Knudsen argues that *analytical* has been used in the past in the interests of philosophical rationalism, and he charges Van Til with compromising Christianity with rationalism. Knudsen, however, apparently has not paid significant attention to the actual sentences in which Van Til uses *analytical*. In those sentences Van Til explains precisely what he means (namely that God does not need to gain knowledge from outside of himself), clearly distancing himself from philosophical rationalism. Should I never use *transcendence* because it has been used incorrectly by some theologians? Nonsense! G. C. Berkouwer often reproaches other theologians because they use this or that term, or this or that image, or because they "speak of" this or that. In my view, a theologian may "speak of" anything he likes. He may be criticized only when he says something wrong about it! If we were allowed to use only those terms that had been used only by perfectly orthodox thinkers, then we could not use any terms at all! I'm afraid that here I see a kind of linguistic perfectionism.

The etymological problem we just discussed is also related to anti-abstractionism. The anti-abstractionist tends to see all theological problems in terms of *spatial* metaphors. The anti-abstractionist often phrases questions about revelation, for example, like this: "How close is revelation to Christ?"—as if we could measure the truth of a theological view by determining the "distance" between revelation and Christ. The anti-abstractionist tends to think of theological issues in terms of "proximity of concepts" or "proximity of terms," rather than asking what is actually being *said* by the user of those terms. Such a use of spatial imagery encourages a theology that is centered on terms, instead of on propositional content. Ironically, theologians like Berkouwer who are quite anti-abstractionist are the ones who tend most readily to look at terms, words, and concepts "in abstraction from" the sentences in which they are used!

(2) Multiple Contexts

I would also like to reiterate here what was said at the beginning of section A. When we speak of "contextual exegesis," there are *many* levels of context to be dealt with, many significant relations between language units, and between language units and extralinguistic realities.

19. Edited by E. R. Geehan. Nutley, N.J.: Presbyterian and Reformed Pub. Co., 1971.

(3) Proof Texts

"Proof-texting" has become almost a term of reproach today, but that was not always the case. After it completed its Confession and Catechisms, the Westminster Assembly was asked to add proof-texts to those documents to indicate the scriptural basis of the assembly's teaching. And many other respected people in the history of doctrine have supplied proof-texts for their theological assertions.

A proof-text is simply a Scripture reference that is intended to show the basis for a particular theological assertion. The danger in proof-texting is well known: proof-texts are sometimes misused and their contextual meaning distorted in an attempt to use them to support teachings they do not really support. But it has never been shown that texts are *always* or *necessarily* misinterpreted when they are used as proofs for doctrines. And after all has been said, theology really cannot do without proof-texts. Any theology that seeks accord with Scripture (that is, any theology worthy of the name) has an obligation to show where it gets its scriptural warrant. It may not simply claim to be based on "general scriptural principles"; it must show *where* Scripture teaches the doctrine in question. In some cases, the theologian will display this warrant by presenting his own contextual exegesis of the relevant passages. But often an extended exegetical treatment is unnecessary and would be counterproductive. The relationship of doctrine to text might be an obvious one once the text is cited (e.g., Gen. 1:1 as proof of the creation of the earth), or it may simply require too much space to go over the exegetical issues in detail. In such cases the mere citation of a Scripture reference, with no extended exegetical discussion, may be helpful to the reader. To forbid proof-texts would be to forbid an obviously useful form of theological shorthand. I can see no argument against this procedure, except one that comes from an extremely rigid and fanatical anti-abstractionism. Furthermore, the Bible itself uses proof-texts as I have defined them, and that should settle the matter.

Obviously, we should not cite proof-texts unless we have a pretty good idea of what they mean in their context. We do not, however, have an obligation always to cite that context with the text, and far less do we have an obligation always to present an exegetical argument supporting our usage of the text. Scripture can, and often does, speak without the help of the exegete.[20]

20. Recall, too, what I said in section A. Although it is important to see each text "in relation to its context," it is often also important, in another sense, to see the text "apart from" its context—that is, to ask what, specifically, this text contributes *to* its context.

(4) Exemplarism

There has been much discussion recently[21] over the use of biblical characters as examples for our lives. On the one hand, not everything a biblical character (even a good one) does is normative for us. (Joshua was called to kill the Canaanites; we are not called to kill off the unbelievers in our land.) On the other hand, the New Testament does use Old Testament figures as examples (e.g., Rom. 4; Heb. 11). The basic point is that when we use examples of biblical characters (as in other situations, e.g., when we seek to make use of the Old Testament law), we should be aware of differences as well as similarities between their situations and ours, and we should also be aware of whether or not Scripture approves of their actions. If Scripture does approve of their actions, and if their situations are like ours in relevant respects, then it is not wrong to use such examples in preaching.

(5) The Richness of Scripture's Meaning

The traditional concern for contextual exegesis must be qualified somewhat by some implications from our principle (expounded in Part One) that meaning is application and application is meaning. The meaning of a text is any use to which it may legitimately be put. That means that in one sense the meaning of any text is indefinite. We do not know all the uses to which that text may be put in the future, nor can we rigidly define that meaning in one sentence or two.

Thus we find that Scripture itself sometimes uses Scripture in surprising ways. "Do not muzzle the ox while it treads the corn" (Deut. 25:4) is used in 1 Corinthians 9:9 as the proof-text for a paid ministry. The story of Hagar and Sarah (Gen. 21) is used in Galatians 4 as an allegory of the relationship between Judaism and the Christian church. We would be perplexed by these uses of the Old Testament if we followed the principle of asking, What did the text mean to the original (human) author or audience? That question is important and useful, but it doesn't always tell us what we need to know. Most likely, Paul's use of Deuteronomy 25:4 did not (consciously) occur to Moses, nor did Paul's use of Genesis 21. At least we could not use any hermeneutical method of which I am aware to *determine* that such ideas occurred to Moses. Thus, unless we wish to accuse Paul of misusing the Old Testament at those points, we must find some other principle at work.

21. E.g., Sidney Greidanus, *Sola Scriptura* (Toronto: Wedge, 1970).

The relevant principle, I think, is simply this. The Old Testament texts that Paul used are capable of being used in the ways he used them. Whether or not Moses conceived of Genesis 21 as an allegory, it happens that the text is *suited* to being used that way. Since it is suited to such a use, we know that this usage was in the mind of the divine author, even if it was not consciously intended by the human author. God knows and predetermines all the uses that are proper for His inspired Word. And surely the unique double-authorship of Scripture must influence our interpretation of it. The principle, then, is that we may use Scripture in any way that it is suited to be used. And the meaning of any text, then, is the *set* of uses to which it is suited.

This sort of approach opens the doors of our creativity! It encourages us to make allegories out of other passages too! That is well and good; there is nothing wrong with that. But our governing principle must be to present the gospel clearly and cogently. If an allegorical illustration helps to that end, then no one may forbid it. But obviously we are not warranted to turn theology into an allegorical flight of fancy as did Origen. (Origen's mistake was not that he allegorized Scripture but that he misused his allegorical interpretations to try to prove substantive theological propositions. That is *not* what Paul is doing in Galatians 4, where he uses his allegory only as an *illustration* of, not as the basis for, his theological point. Paul's basis for his argument, he makes clear, was his own private revelation from God—Gal. 1:1, 11f.)

(6) Text and *Telos*

But if the meaning of a text includes all its legitimate applications, and if this fact makes the meaning indeterminate, then what must be said about the *purpose* (*telos*) of a text? Is that purpose, then, vague, indefinite?

On the one hand, the concept of "purpose" corresponds with "meaning." Like the meaning of a text, the purpose of a text is constituted by its legitimate uses. God gives us the text so that we may use it in these ways. Therefore if there is a sense in which meaning is indefinite, there is also a sense in which the text's purpose is indefinite. We cannot now predict all the uses to which the text may legitimately be put.

On the other hand, there is another sense in which the purpose is definite. We can determine exegetically what the authors (divine and human) intended the text to do in its original setting. Thus in a sermon where we are trying to explain the original meaning of the text that original purpose must play a central role. We want to tell our audience what the biblical writer was telling his audience. If our audience does not know that, they are missing something important. And naturally, we will want to bring to the attention of our audience any parallels between the ancient and modern situations so that the text might have the same effect in the lives of our audience that its author intended it to have in the lives of its original audience. And that is what the standard "expository sermon" seeks to do. It seeks to present the original intent of the original author and to reproduce that intent in the modern setting. As long as we claim to present such sermons, they ought to include those elements. Are expository sermons the only kind of sermons that are biblically warranted? Must the original use or purpose of a scriptural passage always govern the way we use that text today? I think not on both counts, but perhaps the specialists in practical theology are better equipped than I to answer those questions.

D. USES OF SCRIPTURE

Mention of the richness of Scripture's meaning and purpose leads us to consider other varieties in Scripture's content and purpose that encourage corresponding varieties in theology.

(1) Varieties of Biblical Language

What *in* Scripture is authoritative? What is it *about* Scripture that makes it authoritative for us? Theologies differ on this question. In our discussion of James Barr (C, *(1)*, above), I noted that some theologians have sought to avoid the authority of biblical *propositions*, seeking to derive their theology from biblical *words* or *concepts*. (I also indicated, following Barr, the fallaciousness of that procedure.) Others, such as Austin Farrer, have tried to locate biblical authority neither in propositions nor in concepts but in the *images* of Scripture.[22]

Orthodox Christians are tempted to say that Scripture is authoritative in its *propositional* content, in the information it conveys, in its doctrines. On that basis, "authority" would be equivalent to inerrancy; to say that Scripture is authoritative is to say that its propositions are inerrant. No doubt, God has revealed doctrines to us, and these are authoritative; we are obligated to believe them. But Scripture contains forms of language other than propositions. It contains commands, questions, exclamations,

22. See his *The Glass of Vision* (Westminster: Dacre Press, 1948).

promises, vows, threats, and curses. A command, for example, is not a proposition. A command is an imperative; a proposition is an indicative. A proposition states a fact; a command gives an order. A proposition seeks change in our beliefs; a command may seek change in many other aspects of our behavior.

Scripture, therefore, conveys propositional revelation, but it also conveys revelation of many other types. And it is authoritative not only in its propositions but in *everything* that it says (Matt. 4:4). "Authority," then, is a broader concept than "inerrancy." To say that Scripture is authoritative is not only to say that its propositions are true, it is also to say that its commands are binding, its questions demand answers of us ("Shall we sin that grace may abound?"), its exclamations should become the shouts of our hearts ("O, the depth of the riches, both of the wisdom and the knowledge of God!"), its promises must be relied upon, and so forth.[23]

These authoritative aspects of Scripture are perspectivally related. One can divide up the sentences of the Bible into propositions, commands, questions, and so forth, so that propositions form one part of Scripture, commands another part, and so on. But it is also possible to see each of these as a "perspective." In one sense, *all* Scripture is propositional; to know the doctrinal content of God's Word, one must look not only at the explicitly propositional sentences in Scripture but also at everything else. The whole Bible, not merely the propositional "part," is the doctrinal basis of our theology. Similarly, to properly understand what God commands of us, what questions God asks of us, or what promises God makes to us, we must look at the whole Bible. Therefore the propositional content of Scripture coincides, in one sense, with its commands, questions, and so forth. "Propositional truth" is both a part or aspect of Scripture and a perspective on all of Scripture. All Scripture is propositional in that it seeks to convey to us the truth of God. But all Scripture is also command; it aims to change our behavior in every aspect of life. And all Scripture is question, promise, and exclamation (shout of joy).

Thus we can understand why orthodox people have often wanted to equate Scripture with "propositional revelation." In one sense, all Scripture *is* propositional revelation. But we can also see why this conclusion has been unsatisfying to others. The proper conclusion is that all Scripture is propositional revelation, but it is also much more.

23. At one time, I thought I had an original idea here! Then I ran across chapter XIV, section 2 of *The Westminster Confession of Faith*. That's the way it is in theology: most of our best ideas are old—as, of course, are many of our worst.

Theology ought to reflect this variety in the authoritative aspects of Scripture. The work of theology is not merely to state biblical doctrines in propositional form but also to question us, command us, and exclaim the greatness of God. Theology should seek to apply all of those different aspects of Scripture—a task that can best be done, most likely, by adopting new forms of expression. There is no reason why theology must be done only in the form of academic scholarship. It should also take other forms, more calculated to open the reader to the fullness of Scripture's meaning.

(2) Literary Forms

Thus it is important for us to think about another sort of variety in Scripture, the variety of its own *literary forms*, a variety that can guide us toward a similar variety in the forms that theology takes. In the following explanations, we will find that Scripture's literary variety has "perspectival" characteristics.

Scripture contains narrative, law, poetry, wisdom, prophecy, apocalypse, treaty,[24] parable, epistle, and various other, more specific categories. Theologians have debated whether the focus of biblical authority is to be found in the biblical *narrative* (since, for some, Scripture's most basic intent is to narrate the history of redemption), in biblical *poetry* (since Scripture is essentially a collection of religious symbols (according to Tillich, Farrer, and others), or in *apocalypse* (since on some views Jesus' message is "consistently eschatological").

On an orthodox, biblical epistemology, all Scripture, regardless of its literary form, is God's Word. Therefore history and law, poetry and wisdom, apocalypse and epistle—all literary forms within the canonical documents are equally authoritative.

Therefore when someone says that Scripture is "basically narrative" or "basically poetry" or that its authority is limited to one or more of those forms, he is wrong. But that sort of idea is sometimes plausible. It is true that all Scripture is narrative, in a sense, for all Scripture sets forth the history of redemption. To understand the history of redemption, we need the whole canon. But the same argument can be made with regard to wisdom. The wisdom of God is found throughout Scripture. The same may also be said for law and for seeing all of Scripture as poetry: Scripture supplies us with images, memorable words, and rhythms that reverberate throughout

24. See M. G. Kline, *Treaty of the Great King* (Grand Rapids: Wm. B. Eerdmans Pub. Co., 1963).

the soul. In other words, each of those literary forms can be seen in two ways: (i) as a characteristic of *some* parts of Scripture and (ii) as a perspective on *all* of Scripture.

Literary forms, like the grammatical differences noted in *(1)*, determine various forms of biblical authority. Scripture's narrative is authoritative; we must believe it. But canonical poetry is also authoritative. What is "authoritative poetry"? To us that phrase may seem singularly inappropriate, but it would not have been at all inappropriate during the biblical period, a time when poetry was used for the most serious of documents. In those days, much serious material was put into poetry so that it could more easily be committed to memory. Authoritative poetry is poetry to be learned, to be written on the heart—songs to be sung with all our being.

And therefore these literary forms provide us with possibilities for theological models. Why shouldn't theology take the form of poetry? Poetry is an effective means of "application," one found even in Scripture itself.[25]

(3) Speech Acts

"Ordinary language" philosophers in our century have done much study of "speech acts." A speech act is a human act that is connected with speech in a certain way. First, there is the act of speaking itself, the *locution* or *locutionary* act. Then there are those acts that we perform *in* speaking, which are known as *illocutionary* acts. Finally, there are those acts performed *by* speaking, which are called *perlocutionary* acts. Examples of illocutions include asserting, questioning, commanding, praising, joking, promising, threatening, accusing, avowing, expressing emotion, and announcing policy. Examples of perlocutions include persuading, instructing, encouraging, irritating, deceiving, frightening, amusing, inspiring, impressing, distracting, embarrassing, boring, and exciting. Note that a perlocutionary act always has an effect on someone; an illocutionary act may or may not have such an effect. Joking is illocutionary, amusing is perlocutionary. Joking has the purpose of amusing, but one may tell a joke without amusing anyone.[26]

25. I do not believe that theology is limited to those forms found explicitly in Scripture. As I said earlier, theology has a mandate to place the truth in a *different* form from that of Scripture itself so that it may be applied to people's needs. But certainly theology ought to use *at least* the variety of forms found in Scripture itself, as long as they serve to communicate to current audiences.

26. For more on these distinctions, see J. L. Austin, *How to Do Things With Words* (Cambridge, Mass.: Harvard University Press, 1962).

Now Scripture contains a wide variety of speech acts, some of which (asserting, questioning, commanding, and so forth) I have already discussed. Enumerating these can be helpful in reminding us, again, of the wide variety of ways in which Scripture teaches us and of the ways that we, as theologians, may seek to teach others the Word of God. Each speech act is a form of biblical authority; Scripture exercises its authority over us by the speech acts it performs. It calls us to believe God's assertions, to obey His commands, to sympathize with His joy and grief, to laugh at His jokes!

Those speech acts can also be seen in perspectival relation to one another. All Scripture asserts, questions, praises, promises, expresses God's attitudes, and so forth.[27] Thus we see the incredible richness of each passage of Scripture, the rich potential in every text for sermons and theology. As I said before, the meaning of each text is so rich that it can scarcely be described!

(4) Pictures, Windows, and Mirrors

Richard Pratt, in an interesting short article,[28] mentions another sort of variety in our use of Scripture. He suggests that we look at Scripture in three different ways that correspond to the metaphors of Scripture as "picture," "window," and "mirror." (i) Scripture may be seen as *canon*, as an object of interest in itself because of its unique character as the Word of God. As such, it is the object of literary analysis. We analyze its character as a literary object, just as an art critic analyzes the characteristics of a painting—hence the metaphor Scripture-as-"picture." (ii) Scripture may also be seen as a means of showing us God's mighty acts in history for our salvation. As such, it is of interest not only for its own sake but as a means of showing us something else, namely the divine activity described by the canonical text. As such, Pratt represents Scripture as a "window," something we look *through* to see something else. Corresponding to the "literary analysis" of Scripture-as-picture, Scripture-as-window is the object of historical analysis. (iii) Finally, we may look at Scripture as a means of meeting our own needs, answering our own questions, addressing our interests—topics of concern to us. To do this is to engage in thematic or topical analysis, and the appropriate metaphor at this point is Scripture-as-mirror.

27. Yes, Scripture is also a joke. The gospel is foolishness to the world, and one day it will be manifested as a great, cosmic joke of which the wicked are the butt. See Psalm 2:7.

28. "Pictures, Windows and Mirrors in Old Testament Exegesis," *WTJ* 45 (1983): 156-67.

Pratt's triad corresponds with my own group of triads fairly easily. His picture is my normative perspective, his window my situational perspective, and his mirror my existential perspective. Thus we can see that Pratt's three hermeneutical metaphors are perspectivally related. The picture is of no interest to us unless it speaks of God's redemptive deeds and thus meets the needs of our hearts. The window gives a clear view only if it is also a divinely painted "picture," a normative revelation; and it is of interest only insofar as it mirrors our own lives. The mirror offers us help only insofar as it mirrors our relation to God in history as He has normatively revealed that relation to us. All three forms of analysis, therefore, are of importance.

(5) Areas of Application

And, as we have said in other contexts, there is also a great variety in the areas of human life to which Scripture may be applied. Scripture wants us to apply it to business, politics, music, the arts, economics, and science, as well as to preaching, worship, evangelism, and so forth.

Even in its application to theology, Scripture plays many different roles. David Kelsey points out[29] that although most professedly Christian theologians claim to do theology "in accord with Scripture," they differ greatly among themselves as to what that means. They appeal to different aspects of Scripture (propositions, images, agent-description), and they also differ as to the role that the biblical material plays in theological arguments. Is it merely *data* to be analyzed and evaluated according to the theologian's autonomous criteria? Or does Scripture, in some way or other, also provide "warrants" and "backing"—the criteria *governing* our use of theological argumentation?[30]

For the orthodox Christian, *sola scriptura* is the rule in all these matters. Scripture has the final word, though the sufficiency of Scripture does not rule out, but rather requires, the use of extrascriptural data in theology and in other fields of thought.

But my major concern here is again to impress you with the richness of God's written Word and to encourage you to reflect that richness in your own theological work.

29. *The Uses of Scripture in Recent Theology* (Philadelphia: Fortress Press, 1975). See my review in *WTJ* 39 (1977): 328-53.

30. Kelsey explains that "warrants" are the principles on the basis of which we derive conclusions from premises. "Backing" is the evidence by which the warrants are established.

E. TRADITIONAL THEOLOGICAL PROGRAMS

We now must look at some of the traditional forms of theology: exegetical, biblical, systematic, practical. These have sometimes been described as "divisions" or "departments" of theology, but I find that that language tends to isolate (!) these disciplines from one another too much. That language suggests that they are distinguished by having different subject matters. On the contrary, I tend to see them as related perspectivally—each embracing the whole of theology and therefore embracing the others. Therefore I prefer to describe them as different "programs," "methods," "strategies," or "agendas." They are, that is to say, different ways of doing the same thing, not sciences with different subject matters. They differ from one another in focus and emphasis and in the way they organize their material, but each is permitted (and obligated) to use the methods characteristic of the others, as we will now see.

(1) Exegetical Theology

In exegetical theology, the focus is on *particular passages* of Scripture. The exegetical theologian is expected to apply[31] the teaching of particular texts. Yet this focus is not a constricting one. An exegetical theologian may deal with texts of any length: one verse, a paragraph, a book, a testament, the whole Bible. Exegetical theology is distinctive because the theologian must go through the text word by word or phrase by phrase, seeking the meaning of each sentence in its context.[32]

Referring again to Pratt's metaphors (above, *D, 4*), in exegetical theology, the technique of literary analysis ("Scripture-as-picture") predominates. We are concerned to focus on Scripture as canon, according to its literary characteristics, phrase by phrase, sentence by sentence, and to interpret its words, concepts, and so forth according to the author's intention, the literary structure, and the reception of the text by the original audience.

Exegetical theology may deal with the whole Bible, and therefore it deals with all of God's truth. Exegetical theology is not merely a *part* of theology; it is the *whole* seen from a particular perspective; it is one way of doing theology. All exegesis is theology, and all theology (because all the-

31. Let me remind you that *all* theology is application.

32. There is a rough synonomy between "biblical studies" and "exegetical theology" and, correspondingly, between "Old Testament studies" and "New Testament studies" and "exegetical theology."

ology ascertains the meaning of Scripture texts) is exegesis. Thus it is misleading to use the name "exegetical theology" exclusively for this particular discipline.

(2) Biblical Theology

Biblical theology studies the *history* of God's dealings with creation. As a theological discipline, it is the application of that history to human need. It is sometimes called "the history of redemption" or, more broadly (to include the preredemptive and consummation periods), "the history of the covenant."

Biblical theology is an exciting discipline. Seminary students often find it a fascinating surprise. As developed by Reformed biblical scholars like Geerhardus Vos, H. N. Ridderbos, Richard B. Gaffin, and Meredith G. Kline, biblical theology opens the Scriptures to many students in a fresh, new way. The surprise comes about this way: though most seminarians have had some exposure to exegetical theology (through the use of commentaries and through hearing expository sermons) and to systematic theology (through catechetical studies) before coming to seminary, most have not been exposed to biblical theology.[33]

Biblical theology traces the outworking of God's plan for creation from the historical perspective of God's people. It traces the history of the covenant, showing us at each point in history what God has done for the redemption of His people. In Pratt's schematism, biblical theology focuses

33. Those readers interested in exploring biblical theology should note especially the following titles, which are representative and important works of biblical theology from within the tradition of Protestant orthodoxy. (Of course, there are also many biblical-theological works written from outside of that tradition.) Early and seminal works in the field include Geerhardus Vos's writings, especially *Biblical Theology* (Grand Rapids: Wm. B. Eerdmans Pub. Co., 1959); *The Pauline Eschatology* (Grand Rapids: Wm. B. Eerdmans Pub. Co., 1972; reissued by Presbyterian and Reformed, 1986); *Redemptive History and Biblical Interpretation* (Phillipsburg, N.J.: Presbyterian and Reformed Pub. Co., 1980). Herman N. Ridderbos, *The Coming of the Kingdom* (Philadelphia: Presbyterian and Reformed Pub. Co., 1973) and *Paul: An Outline of His Theology* (Grand Rapids: Wm. B. Eerdmans Pub. Co., 1975) are virtually encyclopedic. A simple, but profound, introduction to the importance of biblical theology for preaching is Edmund P. Clowney, *Preaching and Biblical Theology*. Another simple and useful introduction is S. G. Degraaf, *Promise and Deliverance* (St. Catherines, Ont.: Paideia Press, 1977), a four-volume survey of Scripture designed to help its readers teach the Bible to children. Some valuable recent studies include Richard B. Gaffin, *Resurrection and Redemption*, formerly *The Centrality of the Resurrection* (Grand Rapids: Baker Book House, 1978; reissued by Presbyterian and Reformed, 1987) and his *Perspectives on Pentecost* (Phillipsburg, N.J.: Presbyterian and Reformed Pub. Co., 1979). Some of the most creative work in the field is being done by Meredith G. Kline, as in his *Images of the Spirit* (Grand Rapids: Baker Book House, 1980).

on Scripture-as-window and stresses the method of historical analysis. However, if biblical theology is truly theology (= application), then it cannot be divorced from the other perspectives and methods of analysis. It studies the history of redemption as a normative revelation from God and as a history that is addressed to our deepest needs. At each point in redemptive history, we are enabled to put ourselves into the stories, to imagine what it must have been like to have lived as a believer in the time of Abraham, or Moses, or Paul, for example. We learn to think the way David, Isaiah, and Amos must have thought about God's dealings, thinking in their terms, in their language. We thereby come both to recognize the depth of God's revelation to them and to appreciate the limitations of that revelation in comparison with the completed canon.

At its best, biblical theology shows us in a wonderful way how the diverse aspects of Scripture fit together into a single, coherent whole. It reveals the diverse viewpoints of the different gospel writers, the differences between Old and New Testaments, between Kings and Chronicles, and so forth. But amidst all the diversity of Scripture, biblical theology traces the historical development of God's plan, which with the necessity of a well-crafted drama culminates in Christ, especially in His atonement, resurrection, ascension, and sending of the Spirit at Pentecost. Thus the student of biblical theology experiences something of what the disciples must have felt (in Luke 24:13-35) when Jesus expounded to them "in all the Scriptures the things concerning himself" (v. 27). And sometimes the hearts of students of biblical theology may even burn with excitement, much as did the hearts of Jesus' disciples when He explained the Scriptures to them on the road to Emmaus (Luke 24:32)! Biblical theology at its best does not, however, allegorize every Scripture into arbitrary Christ-symbolism; it is a serious, scholarly discipline, and that makes the discovery of the Christ-centeredness of the Scriptures all the more wonderful. In that kind of biblical theology, the reader is assured that the applications of Scripture to Christ are neither a human invention nor a fanciful imposition on the text but something that is necessitated by the scriptural text.

Thus biblical theology leads us to see the Old Testament not only as law and judgment but also as gospel. It is the story of how God chose a people to redeem them from sin and of how God's grace persevered with them despite their rebellion and hatred of Him. Thus every divine act, every deliverance, every judgment, every ceremonial law, every prophet, priest, and king in the Old Testament foreshadows Christ, because He is the one in whom God's redemptive activity culminates.[34]

Together with the excitement of growth in the knowledge of God's Word, biblical theology often engenders the somewhat more worldly excitement of learning a new jargon. Biblical theologians talk a lot about "covenant," "the already and not-yet," "the semi-eschatological," "culture and cult," and so forth, and students (especially younger ones) often seem to enjoy being able to use such esoteric terminology, which uninitiated people cannot understand. At best, as in most disciplines, such technical vocabulary is a useful shorthand; in most cases it is a harmless game. The danger, however, is that jargon can become a source of pride among those "in the know," leading them to an attitude of contempt for those outside the favored group.

That danger is not entirely imaginary. I have seen seminary students develop an attitude toward biblical theology that is scarcely to be distinguished from cultic fanaticism, and for that reason, I must now discuss some of biblical theology's *limitations*. I do not wish to dampen anyone's excitement. Even at my age, I am still thrilled about biblical theology.[35] I only wish the reader to see biblical theology in its proper *perspective*.

(i) Scripture is a redemptive history but not *only* that. It does not belong exclusively to the historical *genre*. (A) It includes a law code, a song book, a collection of proverbs, a set of letters (and these not merely as historical sources). (B) The content of Scripture is intended not only to give us historical information but also to govern our lives here and now (Rom. 15:4; 2 Tim. 3:16f.; etc.). This is not the usual purpose of a historical text. (C) As is often pointed out, the Gospels are not biographies of Jesus; they are *Gospels*. Their purpose is not merely to inform but to elicit faith. Most histories do not have this purpose.

It would, of course, be possible to define "history" so broadly as to include all those functions, speaking even of the Psalms and Proverbs as in some sense "interpretations" of redemptive history. But such a definition would be so far removed from normal language as to be misleading. "Interpretation" in the usual sense is not the *chief* purpose of Psalms and Proverbs. I am therefore willing to say that Scripture is a redemptive history, but I am reluctant to say that this is the only way or the most important way of characterizing Scripture. At the very least, we would have to mod-

34. Clowney's summary of this is excellent in *Preaching and Biblical Theology*, cited earlier.

35. Recall my emphasis in Part One on covenant lordship; that was biblical theology. The biblical theological method is prominent in my *Doctrine of the Word of God* and *Doctrine of God*, both as yet unpublished.

ify the phrase "redemptive history" to say that Scripture, unlike any other history, is *normative* redemptive history—history intended not only to inform but also to *rule* the reader (2 Tim. 3:16f.). But to say that Scripture is *normative* history is to say that Scripture is not only history but also *law* and that "history" and "law" are at least equally ultimate ways of characterizing Scripture.[36]

And I would argue that there are still other important ways of characterizing Scripture. Scripture is not only history and law, it is also *gospel*. Its purpose is to elicit faith in Christ. And it is promise, wisdom, comfort, admonition, and much else besides.

Does this "perspectival" approach compromise the centrality of Christ in His death, resurrection, and ascension? No! Christ is not only central to history, He is central also as the eternal lawgiver (Word), as the wisdom of God, as prophet, priest, and king. It could be argued, therefore, that a more flexible approach to theologizing does *more* justice to the centrality of Christ than does a narrowly redemptive-historical approach. Furthermore, the death, resurrection, and ascension of Christ and the pentecostal outpouring of the Spirit are important not merely as historical happenings (though over against the skepticism of modern thought, it is vitally important to affirm them as historical happenings) but also for their present impact on us, not least in their normative function (Rom. 12:1ff.; Eph. 4:1ff.).

(ii) Since Scripture, then, is not merely or primarily a "history," I would resist the view of some who argue that theology ought to be "controlled" by redemptive history. (A) Theology ought to be controlled by *everything* Scripture says. That includes not only its statements of historical fact and its interpretations of history but also its commands, poetry, and so forth. (B) Theology, therefore, must *take account* of redemptive history but not of redemptive history only. It must also be concerned to do justice to Scripture as law, poetry, wisdom, gospel—all the authoritative aspects of the Word of God. Theology is not, therefore, to be controlled exclusively by redemptive history, in opposition to other aspects or perspectives.

(iii) People often get excited about biblical theology (as opposed, particularly, to systematics) because it seems to them to be close to the biblical text. It uses more of the actual biblical vocabulary than does systematics, and it goes through the Scriptures in roughly historical order, rather than topically, as systematics does. I enjoy these features of biblical theology,

36. Such correlativity between "history" and "law" is to be expected if, as Kline believes, Scripture is a "suzerainty treaty." See his *Treaty of the Great King*.

but I would caution the reader from concluding on the basis of the reasons just mentioned that biblical theology is "more biblical" than systematic theology. As we have indicated earlier, the work of theology is not to mimic the scriptural vocabulary or its order and structure but to *apply* the Bible. And to do this, theology may (indeed must) *depart* somewhat from the structure of Scripture itself, for otherwise it could only repeat the exact words of Scripture, from Genesis to Revelation. Thus a theological discipline that departs a great deal from the structure of Scripture is not necessarily less adequate, less biblical, than one that departs to a lesser extent. Furthermore, the resemblance between Scripture and the biblical theologies is sometimes overstated. There is a great deal of difference between Vos's *Biblical Theology* and the Pauline Epistles, for example! For that reason, I consider the term "biblical theology" a misnomer and would prefer to call this discipline the "history of the covenant." Force of habit, however, and the desire for brevity being what they are will dictate otherwise.

(iv) Those who "major" in biblical theology risk the danger of doing injustice to those aspects of Scripture other than the narrowly historical.

(v) Students who become "fanatical" about biblical theology sometimes lose a proper sense of the goals of theology and preaching. I once heard a student say that a sermon should never seek to apply Scripture but should only narrate redemptive history, letting the congregation draw its own applications. But that idea is quite wrong for these reasons. (A) Biblical theology itself is application. There is no difference between finding meaning and finding applications (see Part One). (B) The purpose of preaching must be nothing less than the purpose of Scripture itself, which is not merely to narrate historical facts but rather to incite people to faith and good works (John 20:31; Rom. 15:4; 2 Tim. 3:16f.).

(vi) Unbalanced attachment to any theological "perspective" can be a source of ungodly pride that can result in contempt for those who do not share this attachment and in division in the church.

(vii) Unbalanced advocacy of biblical theology is often defended by anti-abstractionist argument such as: "We must never abstract revelation from redemptive history." On the ambiguities and fallacies of that kind of argument, however, see above under *A*.

(viii) Edmund Clowney's wise words[37] on the importance of biblical theology to preaching must be balanced by similar observations that could be made about exegetical and systematic theology. I believe that anyone writing a textual sermon ought to be aware of the redemptive-historical con-

37. *Preaching and Biblical Theology*.

text of his text. He need not, however, always make that context prominent in the sermon itself. There are other contexts, other relationships that are also important. The choice of what will be prominent in a particular sermon will depend on the preacher's gifts and on his concerns and judgments about the needs of the congregation.

(3) Systematic Theology

Systematic theology seeks to apply Scripture *as a whole*. While exegetical theology focuses on specific passages and biblical theology focuses on the historical features of Scripture, systematic theology seeks to bring all the aspects of Scripture together, to synthesize them. Systematics asks, What does it all add up to? In investigating faith, for instance, the systematic theologian looks at what the exegetical commentators say about Romans 4, Ephesians 2:8, and other passages in the Bible where this topic is presented. He also listens to what the biblical theologians say about faith in the life of Abraham, of Moses, of David, of Paul. But then the systematic theologian asks, What does the *whole* Bible teach about faith?—or about anything else. It could be a topic mentioned in Scripture itself, like faith, or it could be a topic taken from our own experience—What does the whole Bible teach about abortion, about nuclear disarmament, about socialism?

Since theology is application, that question can also be put this way: What does the Bible say *to us* about faith? After we learn what faith meant to Abraham, Moses, David, and Paul, we want to know what *we* are to confess. Thus there is something very "existential" about systematic theology, something that is rarely noted. In Pratt's schematism, systematic theology focuses on thematic or topical analysis and therefore on Scripture's function as "mirror." It is precisely when we do systematic theology that the specific question of application is *explicitly* raised (though that question is posed implicitly by all the theological disciplines).

On the one hand (as is often noted), systematic theology depends on exegetical and biblical theology. To develop applications, the systematic theologian must know what each passage says and the mighty historical acts of God that are described therein. It is especially important for systematic theologians today to be aware of the developments in biblical theology, a discipline in which new discoveries are being made almost daily. Too frequently, systematic theologians (including this one!) lag far behind biblical theologians in the sophistication of their exegesis.

On the other hand (and this point is less often noted), the reverse is also true: exegetical and biblical theology also depend on systematics. One can surely exegete the parts of Scripture better if he is sensitive to the overall teaching of Scripture as discovered by systematics. And one can understand better the history of redemption if he has a systematic perspective. Thus the three forms of theology—exegetical, biblical, systematic—are mutually dependent and correlative; they involve one another. They are "perspectives" on the task of theology, not independent disciplines.

What does the word "systematic" mean in the phrase "systematic theology"? At first glance, we might guess that it refers to logical consistency or orderly structure. But clearly, not only systematics but all forms of theology ought to seek such consistency and structure. Another possibility might be that systematic theology seeks a particular object, the "system of truth" of the Scriptures. But what is that "system"? Is it the Scripture itself? If so, then to refer to it here is not helpful. Is it something *in* Scripture or *behind* Scripture? To move in that direction is dangerous. Earlier, in Part One, I criticized the notion that there is something called "the meaning" or "the system" that stands between the theologian and his Bible. There is always danger that this "system" will be given (in practice, if not in theory) more authority than Scripture itself, if only as a kind of screen or grid through which scriptural data must be fed. And that, of course, is the chief danger in systematic theology. For those reasons, I cannot make any positive use of the term "system" in the phrase "systematic theology," and this means that the three terms—"exegetical theology," "biblical theology," and "systematic theology"—are all misnomers!

Nevertheless, I cannot stop without expressing my own excitement over the potential of systematic theology in our day. If systematic theology were merely an attempt to tidy up past systems like those of Calvin, Hodge, and Murray or an attempt to develop another system after their model, it could be seen as a boring discipline indeed. And, I'm afraid, students often look at it that way today, preferring their newfound thrills in biblical theology to what they perceive as the drabness of systematics. Thus there seem to be few good systematic theologians in the world today. But if students would only see systematics for what it is—the attempt to answer whole-Bible questions, applying the sum-total of biblical truth to life—then systematics could again be seen as something exciting, as something worthy of a lifetime commitment. Systematics is really a wide-open discipline. There are so many tasks waiting to be done, so many questions being asked today that have never been dealt with seriously by orthodox systematic theologians—the nature of history, the nature of religious language, the crisis of meaning in modern life, the theology of economic liberation, and on and on. And systematics is wide-open also in regard to its form. According to my definition, systematic theology does not need to take the form of an academic treatise or to imitate the conventions of philosophical systems. It can take the form of poetry, drama, music, dialogue, exhortation, preaching, or any other appropriate form. But there are few people doing this work; we need more strong arms to pull the oars.

(4) Practical Theology

At first glance, we might think that the work of exegetical, biblical, and systematic theologies was to find the meaning of Scripture and that practical theology was charged with the task of finding its application. But as I have argued, meaning and application are two ways of looking at and of talking about the same thing. Exegetical, biblical, and systematic theologies are already engaged in application, and in that sense they are practical.

Then what is left for practical theology to do? I would define practical theology as the science of *communicating* the Word of God. This definition seems to accord well with the typical concerns of practical theologians: preaching, teaching, counselling, missions, evangelism, worship. As such, practical theology would be a division of systematics. It asks a particular kind of "whole-Bible" question: What does the whole Bible teach about how best to communicate the Word of God?

Thus "practical theology," like "exegetical," "biblical," and "systematic" theology, is a misnomer. *All* theology is practical—at least *good* theology is!

CHAPTER SEVEN

The Situational Perspective—Language as a Tool of Theology

As we have seen, the three perspectives—normative, situational, existential—overlap, interpenetrate, and include one another. Therefore as we discuss the situational perspective, we are not really leaving the normative behind. We are still talking about the uses of Scripture because theology *is*, after all, the use of Scripture. And Scripture is as important to the situational perspective as it is to the normative. Scripture is that central fact on the basis of which all other facts are to be interpreted.

Nevertheless, theology also makes use of extrabiblical data of various kinds. That is inevitable if theology is not just to repeat the language of Scripture but to apply and relate that language to the world of our experience. Theology uses extrabiblical data to link the Scriptures with our situation. Under the "situational perspective," we will be considering that process.

Extrabiblical data relevant to theology comes from many sources: language, logic, history, science, philosophy, modern culture. Sciences analyzing such data serve as "tools of theology." We shall now look at a number of these tools.

One of the chief tools of theology is the theologian's understanding of language. Language is important, especially because the Bible itself is language. Knowledge of the original languages of Scripture and of linguistic, exegetical, and hermeneutical principles—all of these are extremely valuable to the theologian. Language is also important because theology itself is, for the most part (not forgetting the importance of "theology by example"), a body of language. The theologian begins with the language of Scripture and seeks to communicate that content to others in language of his own.

Contrary to David H. Kelsey,[1] there is no sharp distinction between the translation of Scripture and theology. Both are attempts to apply the scriptural text to people other than the original audience. Both require skills in the linguistic sciences, knowledge of the target culture, and so forth. Both depart somewhat from the form of the original text, though a translation is generally closer in form to the text than a theological discussion would be. The difference is only a difference in degree. What we say here, then, bears on translation and exegesis as much as on theology.

We have already discussed several issues that bear on the use of language in theology: the issue of whether all language about God must be figurative (chapter 1, *B, (1), b*), the question of the "oddness" of religious language (chapter 5, *A, (3)*), the relation between meaning and application (chapter 3, Appendix C), the vagueness of anti-abstractionist rhetoric (chapter 6, *A*), context and perspective in exegesis (chapter 6, *A* and *B*), and the varieties of biblical language (chapter 6, *D, (1)*). In this section I would like to address the general issue of vagueness in theological language, with particular reference to technical terms, theological distinctions, and analogies. In much of what follows, I am indebted to unpublished writings and utterances of Vern S. Poythress, Professor of New Testament at Westminster Theological Seminary in Philadelphia, but I take full responsibility for inadequacies in the discussion.

A. VAGUENESS IN LANGUAGE

Human language is not an instrument of absolute precision. Only God knows, and can state precisely, all the facts in the universe. This is not to deny the power of human language to state truth. Human language does state truth. God's Word in human language, for instance, is absolute, inerrant truth. But there is a difference between truth and precision. Although evangelicals have always insisted that Scripture is true, they have generally agreed that Scripture is not necessarily, never completely, precise. Human

1. *The Uses of Scripture in Recent Theology* (Philadelphia: Fortress Press, 1975); reviewed by me in *WTJ* 39 (1977): 328-53.

language may be used to state truth, but it does not speak with absolute precision. Vagueness in language and in our understanding of it has a number of sources.

(i) *Cutting the pie in different ways*. First, there are many possible ways to refer to the world by means of language, as evidenced by the large number of actual languages in the world. Languages differ from one another not only in using different words to designate the same thing (*window* in English, *fenetre* in French) but also in the "things" that the language is able to distinguish. Different languages, for example, divide up the color spectrum differently. In one language there may be eight basic color-terms, in another, five. Therefore *red* in the first language may have no precise equivalent in the second. Or a word like *red* in the second language might include the colors designated by both *red* and *purple* in the first. Speakers of the first language may think that speakers of the second are confusing *red* and *purple*. Speakers of the second language may think that speakers of the first are illegitimately separating (abstracting!?) two forms of *red*. Who is correct? Well, no language is able to capture *all* of the differences among shades on the color spectrum, of which there is an indefinite number. Nor is any language able to note all the analogies among shades (e.g., between red and purple). The first language, we might say, distinguishes more shades by distinct color-nouns (though the second may be able to make the same distinctions by other means, e.g., by distinguishing subtypes within its major categories). By making purple, in effect, a shade of red, the second language reflects in its lexical stock an analogy or likeness that the first language lacks. (The first language, of course, might also be able to make that analogy by other means.) Reality has often been compared to a pie that is cut up into different shapes by different languages. Many different arrangements are possible and useful, and frequently we cannot say that one is right and another wrong. If we say, "Yes, but what is red *really* like, apart from the various different conceptions of it in different languages?" we will not receive any precise answer.

(ii) *Natural kinds*. We can understand that kind of imprecision in a word like *red* because, after all, redness (it seems) is somewhat "subjective," relative to the "eye of the beholder." But what of words like *fish*? *Fish* designates a "natural kind." Surely, it might be supposed, every language must have separate nouns for *fish* and *mammal*. But consider the following. (A)

Fish is not all that different from *red*. *Red* is not merely a description of a subjective state; it is a real quality of things. There is a subjective factor in our decision of how to cut up the "pie" of the color spectrum, but there are similar decisions to be made even with regard to animals. Should *fish* include or exclude the whale? That depends on whether we want to stress the analogies between whales and fish or the analogies between whales and land-mammals. And that question (like the question, Should *red* include *purple*?) will be answered in part by determining what is most useful or convenient to us, and that might be called a "subjective" factor. Or consider the question, Is the tomato a fruit or a vegetable? Biologists tend to answer this question one way, chefs another. Who is correct? The answer is not clear. We must make a choice of what "context" to stress—the context of biological relations or the context of foods that "go together." (B) We are fallible in identifying natural kinds. Biologists have sometimes had to revise their judgments about which animals constitute distinct species. (C) Imprecisions in the applications of terms often occur, even with respect to natural kinds. *Tiger* and *lion* denote natural kinds. But when a tiger and lion mate, producing offspring, what term should be applied to the young? Are they tigers? Lions? A third category? Here it is clear that even a term like *tiger* has "fuzzy boundaries." It is not always perfectly clear when it applies and when it does not. *Rain* may seem like a perfectly clear concept. We know what it is, we think, and we know when it is raining and when it is not. But what of a heavy mist? Do we call that rain or not? Or do we call it rain under some conditions but not others? Clearly, there is no rule in our language that automatically answers such questions. We may invent one, of course, but we may not claim that our invented rule sets forth "the meaning" of *rain*. (D) Even once we have defined a natural kind, the words of the definition will not be perfectly precise, and that fact may cause further problems.

(iii) *Family resemblances*. Often (some would say always) it is impossible to specify one set of conditions that is always present when a term is properly used. Ludwig Wittgenstein[2] noted that *game* is used in a wide variety of ways. Some games are games of amusement, some involve winning and losing, some are games of skill, and others games of luck, but no one of those features is found in every activity that we call a game. *Game*, therefore,

2. *Philosophical Investigations* (New York: Blackwell, 1958), 31f.

does not designate a specific group of qualities that is always present in every game. Rather, it is used for a group of activities that have "overlapping and criss-crossing" resemblances to one another. Wittgenstein called these "family resemblances." At a family reunion of the Blodgetts, one will have the Blodgett nose, another the Blodgett dimple, another the Blodgett forehead, and so forth. Quite possibly no one member will have *every* "typical Blodgett feature." And the same is true for *game*. Some games are games of amusement, some involve winning and losing, and some are games of skill, but no one game may have all of those typical game features. For that reason, too, there are "fuzzy boundaries" in the way *game* is used. How many game characteristics must an activity have to be called a game? There is no way to establish a figure for all times and cases, and so it is difficult to define *game* precisely, to state its "essence," to tell what it "really is."

(iv) *Meaning and use*. And there are other words that seem even more mysterious. Take *time*. Augustine said, "What is time? If nobody asks me, I know; but if someone asks me, I don't know."[3] We all know what "time" is. When someone asks us the time or tells us that there is no more time for the exam or tells us to be ready on time, we know what is meant. But if someone asks us "What *is* time?"—if someone asks for its "essence" or its definition—we shrug our shoulders. Thus we are in the paradoxical position of thinking we understand a word but not being able to *say* what it means. Wittgenstein's answer to this riddle is to say that to understand a word is to be able to *use* it, not to be able to define it. There are many words, when we come to think of it, that we understand pretty well that we are not able to define, and that is especially true of children.

When children learn to speak, definitions play a very small role. "Defining terms" is a process most children do not learn until they have been to school for several years. Our earliest language learning proceeds more informally as we seek to *imitate* the usage of our parents and others. It is a process of trial and error. Our "imitation" is sometimes more, sometimes less successful. It never results in any absolute precision in the use of terms. Sometimes, to be sure, "ostensive definition" plays a role: a child may learn *chair* as his parent points to the chair and says the word. That process would seem to lead to greater precision. But does it? There is, after all,

3. Ibid., 42.

plenty of room for error and misunderstanding in the process of "ostensive definition." Even assuming that the child has a general understanding of the meaning of the pointing gesture, how does he know through that gesture that the parent is defining *chair* in terms of the object as a whole, instead of in terms of its color or shape? How does he know that the parent is using *chair* as a general term for all such objects, rather than as a proper name for the particular object he is pointing to? The pointing gesture itself is too vague to make such distinctions. The child must simply do the best he can, by trial and error, eventually getting the "hang" of his new language. He learns, ultimately, not through the pointing gesture but through the whole range of activities that give meanings both to words and to gestures. The meaning is the use, the application; and as the child learns the use, he learns the meaning, whether or not he can supply a definition.

A "use" is difficult to describe in words, and even when it can be so described, the words used to do so must themselves be learned through use. And this is another reason for the vagueness of language: it is difficult to say what any term means since meaning is basically a result of use, not definition.

I am an advocate of clarity in theology, and often clarity requires us to define terms. But now I must make a seemingly opposite kind of point: demands for definitions are not always legitimate. Sometimes, someone will suggest that I cannot really understand or use a term unless I can define it. That idea is clearly wrong. Learning to use a word, in most cases, precedes our ability to define it. We all know how to use *time*, but few of us—possibly none of us—could come up with an adequate definition of that concept. And that is often the case with theological language. *Substance*, *person*, *eternity*, *eternal fatherhood*, and *covenant*, for example, are difficult to define, perhaps impossible. They are, perhaps, "logical primitives," undefinable terms that we use to define other terms.

(v) *Language changes*. Another reason for vagueness is that language is constantly changing. Definitions are often inadequate because they do not reflect the current state of the language or the usage of the actual speakers under consideration.

(vi) *Abstraction*. Abstract terms are vague for another reason. On the one hand, they designate general things or qualities, leaving out, to some extent, reference to particularities. On the other hand, as we saw in our discussion of anti-abstractionism, all language is abstract to some extent. Even if there could be a perfectly concrete language, a language devoid of abstraction, that language could not be known by human beings, and so in an important sense such a language would be vague.[4]

(vii) *Intentional vagueness*. Furthermore, much language is intentionally vague. Consider another illustration from Wittgenstein. A photographer tells a model, "Stand roughly there." He says exactly what he means. His command is not a sloppy way of saying, for example, "Stand exactly 2.8976 feet from the wall." The photographer is not *intending* to be as precise as that. If you ask my age and I give it down to the minute and second, I am (in most cases) being silly and defeating the purpose of our communication. Thus in most cases I will intentionally avoid that level of precision. We habitually use round numbers, metaphors, and other vague expressions as linguistic shortcuts.

B. VAGUENESS IN SCRIPTURE

It is clear that God's Word in Scripture is not an exception where vagueness is concerned. Like all language, Scripture, too, is vague in certain ways. *Vague* here should not be taken as a term of reproach but merely as the opposite of *precise*. Evangelicals have always been quick to emphasize that though Scripture is true and though it says exactly what God wants to say through it, it is not "absolutely precise." It contains round numbers, imprecise quotations, nonchronological narration, and so forth. And Scripture contains all the other kinds of vagueness that we have seen in language generally. Does that imply that there are errors in Scripture? No! As evangelicals maintain, Scripture does exactly what it claims to do: it tells the truth, though not necessarily according to the standards of precise modern science or historiography. But why does God allow vagueness in His inerrant Word? Because vagueness is often both necessary and desirable for communication (see above, *A, vi*), and God's purpose in Scripture is to *communicate*, not to state the truth in the most precise form possible.

4. As I argued earlier, a "perfectly concrete" language would be one that expressed exhaustively every truth about its subject matter. Only God can speak in that kind of language.

C. TECHNICAL TERMS

Theologians have traditionally sought to minimize vagueness by the use of technical terms. A technical term may either be a term that has specially been invented for purposes of theoretical analysis or a term from ordinary language that has been given a definition different from its ordinary use (also for theoretical purposes). Thus theologians have given technical meanings to *inspiration*, *substance*, *person*, *miracle*, *covenant*, *calling*, *regeneration*, *faith*, and *justification*, for example. Several points should be noted about such technical terms.

(i) Some of these terms (e.g., *substance* and *person*) have extrabiblical origins. That fact, however, does not represent a violation of *sola scriptura*. The Bible does not say explicitly that God is one substance and three persons, but it clearly teaches that God is one in one respect and three in another respect. *Substance* and *person* are merely terms taken from our philosophical heritage to facilitate discussing these "respects." As I have said frequently, we must use extrascriptural knowledge to apply Scripture to human questions, and this is one way of doing that. People sometimes object to using technical terms in theology that have had significant usage in non-Christian thought. In my view, however, such objections are not warranted. (A) Such objections fail to understand the importance of using terms that non-Christians can understand. (B) Such objections seem to presuppose that content is communicated at the word-level, rather than at the sentence-level (see chapter 6, C). On the contrary, the crucial thing is not what words are used but what they are used to say. (C) Words taken from non-Christian philosophy can be redefined and used in ways that convey biblical content. I am not aware of any distortions of the biblical message that have come through the use of *substance* and *person* in the trinitarian discussion, though this is sometimes alleged. (D) If we are prohibited from using any terms with significant non-Christian histories, there is scarcely *any* term that we will be able to use. Even biblical terms have been used by heretics and unbelievers.

(ii) Most of the technical terms in the list above are biblical terms that have been given special technical definitions. It should be noted that in these cases, the technical theological definition is never equivalent to the biblical usage, because (as I indicated earlier) the biblical usage is not generally intended for purposes of technical precision. Biblical language is "full of" connotation and nuance, and these are sacrificed for the sake of greater precision when biblical terms are technically defined for theological purposes. And sometimes biblical terms have different meanings in different books and in different contexts, differences that are lost when the terms are defined technically.

(iii) Now that fact does not imply that technical definitions are always wrong. The technical definition of *regeneration* as the absolute initiation of spiritual life probably does not coincide with every use of *regeneration* in the New Testament, but from a biblical point of view it is important to say that there *is* such an initiation and that that initiation comes by sovereign grace. Some term is needed to refer to that initiation, and it would be hard to find a better one than *regeneration*.

(iv) But we must be on our guard lest we confuse the technical theological definitions of biblical terms with the ways those terms are used by the biblical writers. It would be wrong to assume that whenever *covenant* is found in Scripture, the Westminster Confession's "covenant of grace" is meant. It would certainly be wrong to assume that a full saving faith is in view whenever Scripture speaks of someone "believing" (cf., e.g., John 8:31 with v. 37-47) or that whenever someone is "called" in Scripture that effectual calling is meant.

(v) Clearly, then, when we adopt a technical definition, we have no right to claim that we have found the "real meaning" or the "deeper meaning" that is only obscurely expressed by the biblical terms. Technical theology does not represent anything deeper or more authoritative than the biblical canon itself. On the contrary, technical theology always *sacrifices* some biblical meaning to make some biblical points more vivid to the reader. That sacrifice is not wrong. We must sacrifice something in our teaching, since we cannot say everything at once. But we must never assume that a theological system will teach us anything more than Scripture itself. Theology is application, not discovery of some new teaching.

(vi) Nor do we have any right to say that there is only one proper set of technical terms and definitions to use in theology. In theology, as well as in all other areas of human life, there are many ways of cutting the cake. One theologian might define faith as assent and then later show that true assent involves a commitment of the whole person. Another person might define faith as trust and later point out that intellectual assent is a necessary aspect of trust. Here are two different definitions of faith but no indication of any substantive difference between the two views of faith generated by the definition. (See my discussion in Part One of the definition of theology. There is no one "right" definition, but there are some things that need to be said). But frequently the fact that two theologians cut the cake differently will lead to misunderstandings and even to hostility between them. In such cases, loving counsel and careful analysis are needed.

I think that that kind of misunderstanding lies behind some of the important theological controversies in church history: the supralapsarian-infralapsarian dispute, the common grace debate, the creationism-traducianism controversy. And such linguistic confusion also has hindered communication in other disputes where there has been more than merely linguistic disagreement: the debates over the incomprehensibility of God, the relation of works to justification, the continuance of tongues and prophecy, the doctrine of guidance, and theonomy.[5]

(vii) Sometimes technical definitions can actually mislead us, as when Hodge defines a miracle as an "immediate act of God" or when Hume defines it as a "violation of natural law." Although neither of those definitions is required by biblical references to miracles, that fact is not in itself ground for objection. One might adopt those definitions and then say on the basis of Scripture that miracles, so defined, do not occur! (But then one would have to find some term[s] other than *miracle* to translate the biblical terms such as *dunamis*, *semeion*, *teras*.) But when *miracle* is defined in that sort of way and the biblical texts are assimilated to such definitions (or when someone like Hume uses such a definition to reject the biblical teaching), then the use of such technical definitions must be rejected.

(viii) One particularly dangerous manifestation of that type of problem is in modern liberal theology where biblical teachings about God's character and actions are frequently wrenched out of their contexts, stripped of all their biblical qualifications, and turned into metaphysical principles. (A) In liberal theology, for example, the biblical picture of Jesus' love is rendered technically by the phrase "man for others" and then used as a way of reconstructing the whole biblical doctrine of God: God attracts no praise to himself, has no eternal nature, and so forth. (B) In Barth's theology, the notion of divine sovereignty becomes the technical concept "freedom of God," which implies that God can revoke His Word, change into His opposite, and so on. (C) In liberation theology, the concept of salvation is reduced to the technical term "liberation," which in turn is equated with social and economic liberation of all sorts, even that based

5. On supra- and infralapsarianism, see B. B. Warfield, *The Plan of Salvation* (Grand Rapids: Wm. B. Eerdmans Pub. Co., 1942) and my discussion in chapter 8 of this book. On common grace, see C. Van Til, *Common Grace and the Gospel* (Nutley, N.J.: Presbyterian and Reformed Pub. Co., 1972). On the continuance of tongues and prophecy, Richard B. Gaffin, *Perspectives on Pentecost* (Phillipsburg, N.J.: Presbyterian and Reformed Pub. Co., 1979) is a useful source. On the other matters, see standard systematic theological works such as Charles Hodge, *Systematic Theology* (Grand Rapids: Wm. B. Eerdmans Pub. Co., 1952) and John Murray, *Collected Writings* (Edinburgh: Banner of Truth Trust, 1977), especially volume 1.

on antiscriptural Marxist ideology. (D) In Tillich's teaching, the divine name Yahweh is invoked to justify saying that God is "being-itself," in a sense that for Tillich has pantheistic overtones.

(ix) I mentioned the danger of confusing technical meanings of terms with the meanings of those terms in biblical texts. There is also the danger of confusing such technical definitions with "ordinary language usage," whether within or outside of Scripture—an error frequently found in Dooyeweerdian philosophical circles.[6] Poythress thinks that much of the persuasive power of Dooyeweerd's thought rests on a systematic confusion between the ordinary meanings of certain terms and Dooyeweerd's technical definitions of them. I have also noticed that when the followers of Dooyeweerd criticize those outside of his school, they sometimes assume (totally against all reason) that their opponents are using terms in Dooyeweerdian technical senses![7]

(x) Technical terms, though invoked to increase precision, are never themselves wholly free from vagueness, as can be seen from the general observations under A, above. Sometimes, too, technical terms can actually increase vagueness, as often happens, for example, when metaphorical terms are made to do the work of technical terms.[8]

(xi) If, as I implied earlier, Scripture itself contains intentional vagueness, then we must beware of trying too hard to eliminate vagueness from theology. We do not want to be *less* precise than Scripture is, but (and this point ought to be better appreciated in orthodox circles) we don't want to be *more* precise than Scripture, either. I'm afraid that theologians sometimes seek maximum precision in theology, contrary to the intent of Scripture itself. Thus they multiply technical terms far beyond their usefulness, a practice that has occurred in much writing on the "order of the decrees," trichotomy, and so forth.

(xii) Similarly, we should not seek to impose on church officers a form of creedal subscription intended to be maximally precise. We are often tempted to think that heresy in the church could be avoided if only the form of subscription were sufficiently precise. Thus in some circles there is the desire to require officers (sometimes even members) to subscribe to every proposition in the church's confession. After all, it might be asked,

6. See Vern S. Poythress, *Philosophy, Science and the Sovereignty of God* (Nutley, N.J.: Presbyterian and Reformed Pub. Co., 1976).

7. See my "Rationality and Scripture," in *Rationality in the Calvinian Tradition*, ed. Hendrick Hart, Johan Vander Hoeven, and Nicholas Wolterstorff (Lanham, Md.: University Press of America, 1983), 315 n. 55.

8. See John Frame, *The Amsterdam Philosophy: A Preliminary Critique* (Phillipsburg, N.J.: Harmony Press, 1972), 12f., 16f., 23; also see *D*, below.

why have a confession if it is not to be binding? But that kind of "strict" subscription has its problems, too. If dissent against any proposition in the confession destroys the dissenter's good standing in the church, then the confession becomes irreformable, unamendable, and, for all practical purposes, canonical. And when a confession becomes canonical, the authority of the Bible is threatened, not protected.

In churches with looser subscription formulas than that described above, there is often pressure to define the church's beliefs more precisely. Where officers subscribe to the confession "as containing the system of doctrine taught in the Scriptures," there are sometimes demands made that that "system of doctrine" be defined precisely. What belongs to the system of doctrine and what does not? It seems that we must know this before we can use the confession as an instrument of discipline. But once again, if the church adopts a list of doctrines that constitute the system, and if that list becomes a test of orthodoxy, then the list becomes irreformable, unamendable, and canonical. It will not then be possible to challenge that list on the basis of the Word of God. Thus those who seek a much stronger form of subscription are, in effect, ironically asking for a weakening of Scripture's authority in the church.

The fact is that Scripture, not some form of "precise" theology, is our standard. And Scripture, for God's good reasons, is often vague. Therefore there is no way of escaping vagueness in theology, creed, or subscription without setting Scripture aside as our ultimate criterion. Theology does not dare to try to improve the preciseness of Scripture. Its only role is to apply what Scripture teaches. Let us be satisfied with that modest task, for it is glorious.

D. METAPHORS, ANALOGIES, MODELS

Another source of vagueness in Scripture and theology is their frequent use of figurative language. In Part One, I argued that not *all* of our language about God is figurative. I would not deny, however, that much biblical language is figurative or that such language is a useful way of conveying truth. Therefore it is entirely proper that theology also make use of such language.

Sometimes, indeed, metaphors come to our *rescue* in theology and play roles that are quite central. Even extrabiblical metaphors often take on profound importance. Think, for example, of the "federal headship" over mankind exercised by Adam and by Christ. In Scripture, the relations between Adam and the human race (and, similarly, those between Christ and His people) are hard to construe. They are, after all, unique: the only parallel relation to Adam's federal headship is that of Christ, and there are differences between the two of them (Rom. 5:12ff.). Theologians, then, have labored to find some way to explain it all. Is Adam a Platonic form of humanity, so that humanity-in-general can be said to have sinned in him? Is Adam merely a symbol of each of us in our sinful nature? Is it sufficient to say that we are guilty of Adam's sin because we were, in a biological sense, "in his loins"? None of those formulations has seemed fully satisfying to the Reformed tradition. But here a metaphor comes to the rescue. Reformed theologians have suggested that we think of Adam as our "representative." Now that suggestion has many perils, especially today, considering how we now use the term "representative." To call Adam our representative today might suggest that he was elected by secret ballot and that our disapproval of his behavior entitles us to remove him from office! Furthermore, as we think of political representation today, the constituents of a congressman, for example, are not held guilty for the congressman's sins. Thus the concept "representative" must be trimmed, qualified, modified to fit the biblical teachings. We must make clear how Adam is *not* like our congressman. And once we finish making all the qualifications, it might even seem as though the illustration is counter productive. But the exercise has been useful. The metaphor provides us with a way of structuring the discussion—a way of gathering together all the strange biblical descriptions of this relationship and tying them in, both by comparison and by contrast, with something familiar to the reader.

That kind of metaphor—a "master" metaphor around which a theological doctrine is organized—might be called a "theological model." There are other examples of such models, such as the use of *substance* and *person* in the doctrine of the Trinity (a model derived from philosophy) and the use of *redemption* to describe salvation (an economic model). (Salvation itself is described by many models in Scripture: revelation-teaching, rescue-deliverance, new creation, new birth, renewal of the divine image, cleansing, reconstitution of virginity, courtship, reconciliation, sacrifice, propitiation, victory, resurrection, justification, adoption, sanctification, glorification, even a sharing of the divine nature [2 Peter 1:4—remember, that is only a metaphor!].) In general, those models are perspectivally related.

In that and in many other ways, then, metaphors are helpful to theology. There is no reason to have any general theological preference for literal language over figurative or to assume that every metaphor must be literally explained in precise academic terms. Scripture does not do that. Often, in fact, figurative language says more, and says it more clearly, than corresponding literal language would do. Think of Psalm 23:1, "The Lord is my shepherd. . . ." We could paraphrase that in more literal theological terms by saying that the Lord is the author of providence and redemption. But is that really *clearer* than Psalm 23:1? Does it improve on Psalm 23:1 in any way? For anyone? I doubt it. Sometimes, indeed, we need literal language to clarify the meanings of metaphors, but sometimes the opposite is also true. For many people, "The Lord is my shepherd" helps to clarify the more abstract concepts of providence and redemption.

Nevertheless, there are some dangers in the theological use of metaphor. Consider the following.

(1) Use of a metaphor may be helpful in one context, misleading in another. Consider the contention of J. M. Spier that "law is the boundary between God and the cosmos."[9] "Boundary" is a good metaphor for expressing the *authority* of God's law. God's law is like a boundary in that we may not "transgress" it or "trespass" into forbidden territory. It is not, however, a good way to describe the metaphysical structure of the universe, particularly the relation between Creator and creature. In that sort of context, the term "boundary" raises the question as to whether law is some kind of reality intermediate between Creator and creature, neither fully divine nor created. (It is this sort of thinking that lay behind the ancient heresies of Gnosticism and Arianism.) Questions then arise about whether God is *ex lex*, outside all law, arbitrary in His actions and decisions. My conclusion is that it is best not to use that particular metaphor unless its purpose and reference can be clearly limited and specified in context.

(2) On the one hand, we have said that metaphors in theology are useful and that they do not always need to be "unpacked," that is, explained in more literal language. On the other hand, metaphors ought not to be asked to do work for which they are unsuited. Theologians and philosophers of religion often use metaphors in contexts where more literal language is needed. Spier, again, seeks to define the relation between pretheoretical and theoretical thought by saying, "In science we maintain a certain distance between ourselves and the object of our investigation."[10] Dooyeweerd says, on the same subject, that science tries to "grasp" its ob-

9. *An Introduction to Christian Philosophy* (Philadelphia: Presbyterian and Reformed Pub. Co., 1954), 32.

10. Ibid., 2.

jects, which in turn "offer resistance" to it.[11] Theoretical thought "sets things apart,"[12] while naive experience sees them in the "continuous bond of their coherence."[13] In naive experience, "our logical function remains completely immerged in the continuity of the temporal coherence between the different aspects."[14] Not only "immerged" but even "embedded."[15] Naive experience "distinguishes" subjects and objects, but theoretical thought "opposes" them, breaking asunder that experience that the naive mind perceives in "unbreakable coherence."[16] Now Dooyeweerd and Spier do offer somewhat more technical descriptions of the relations between naive and theoretical thought, but the technical descriptions are always explained in terms of these metaphors: distance, grasping, resistance, continuity, coherence, bond, immerged, embedded, opposition, unbreakable—all of which are metaphorical when used in this kind of epistemological context. My problem is not that Dooyeweerd and Spier *use* metaphors or even that they fail to interpret them. Rather, my difficulty is that they use these metaphors to do a job suited only to more literal terms, namely to make a technical epistemological distinction between two forms of experience that, in their view, must be precisely related and never confused with one another. That distinction, indeed, is fundamental to their epistemology. But their use of uninterpreted metaphors obfuscates their doctrine. Nevertheless, they use that distinction as if, indeed, they had succeeded in clearly defining it, and they berate other thinkers who, in their view, have confused it. But how can Spier and Dooyeweerd require other thinkers to maintain a sharp distinction here, when they have not defined it with any precision? The moral is that we should use metaphors but that we should not expect an uninterpreted metaphor (or even a group of them) to do the job of a precisely defined technical term.

(3) The quotations from Dooyeweerd and Spier suggest a kind of kinship between misuse of metaphor and anti-abstractionist rhetoric. Much anti-abstractionism, I think, gains its plausibility from the metaphor of "togetherness." Christians have a sense that certain things "belong together"—revelation and Christ, faith and history, ethics and redemption, and so forth. From this rather vaguely formulated sense of togetherness, anti-abstractionism is born. To say that faith and history "must not be ab-

11. H. Dooyeweerd, *In the Twilight of Western Thought* (Nutley, N.J.: Presbyterian and Reformed Pub. Co., 1968), 8, 126.
12. Ibid., 11.
13. Ibid., 12, cf. 16.
14. Ibid., 13.
15. Ibid., 14.
16. Ibid., 17.

stracted from one another" is to say that they "belong together." Much of the vagueness of anti-abstractionism, however, is due to the vagueness of the togetherness metaphor. We can understand what it means, in general, for man and wife, love and marriage, or bread and butter to be "together." It is not so clear what it means for revelation and Christ or faith and history or ethics and redemption to be "together." There are, as we have seen, *many* relations between revelation and Christ, for example. Thus to say that they "belong together" or "must not be abstracted" is to say nothing intelligible, unless much further explanation accompanies the remark.

(4) Analogies and disanalogies between God and creation deserve special attention. I argued earlier (Part One) that not all human language about God is figurative; it is possible for us to speak literally of Him. Nevertheless, analogy between creatures and God pervades our language. Everything in creation bears some analogy to God. All the world has been made with God's stamp on it, revealing Him. Creation is His temple, heaven His throne, earth His footstool. Thus Scripture finds analogies to God in every area of creation: inanimate objects (God the "rock of Israel," Christ the "door of the sheep," the Spirit as "wind," "breath," "fire"), plant life (God's strength like the "cedars of Lebanon," Christ the "bread of life"), animals (Christ the "Lion of Judah," the "Lamb of God"), human beings (God as king, landowner, lover; Christ as prophet, priest, king, servant, son, friend), abstract ideas (God as spirit, love, light; Christ as way, word, truth, life, wisdom, righteousness, sanctification, redemption). Even wicked people reveal their likeness to God, with, of course, much irony—see Luke 18:1-8. These analogies presuppose our Lord's covenant presence in the world He has made.

But for every analogy there is also disanalogy. God is *not* an inanimate object—not a mere rock or door; He is *not* a plant, animal, human being, or abstract idea. To *identify* God with any of those things is idolatry. Disanalogy represents God's transcendence, His control and authority over His creation.

And there are different degrees and kinds of analogy. God is analogous to wicked men, as we have seen, but not in the way in which He is analogous to good people (or, better, the way in which they are analogous to Him). That corresponds to the degrees and forms of God's covenant presence: God is present everywhere, says the Old Testament, but He is present in a special way in Israel. And within Israel, He is present in an even more special way in the holy city, Jerusalem, and even more in the temple, and even more in the Holy of Holies, and even more in the ark of the covenant. Some places, things, and people become special vehicles of God's presence and thus peculiarly analogous to Him.

Thus we should be wary of pressing analogies too far or of denying their legitimacy altogether. Some writers take the presence of God in the believer in an almost pantheistic sense (e.g., mysticism, some "higher life" teaching, Barth's assertions about the ontological impossibility of sin since all are in Christ); others draw no distinction between God's presence in the church and in the world in general (e.g., liberation theology, process theology); still others deny any image of God to the lost (e.g., some Lutherans, some who deny common grace). All of these at best, I think, miss the complexity of the biblical picture of God's presence and of the analogies and disanalogies between God and the world. At worst, they fall into the grip of what I called in Part One the "non-Christian concepts of transcendence and immanence."

(5) Another kind of mistake is made by people who think that we need special technical terms to refer to God's transcendence. They think that biblical language is insufficiently "literal." In Part One, I referred to Jim Halsey, who, in criticizing an article of mine, suggested that only a term like "qualitative difference" is adequate to define the difference between God's knowledge and man's. Theologians have often invented special terms of that kind: *omniscience*, *omnipresence*, *omnipotence* are not found in Scripture (though the ideas are there), but they have been thought necessary for drawing a *clear* distinction, or disanalogy, between God's attributes and man's. Interestingly, however, Scripture rarely, if ever, takes that option. There are few, if any, biblical terms referring to God that do not also refer sometimes to creation. *Lord*, *king*, *savior*—all sometimes refer to humans. Even *elohim*, "God," refers to human judges in Psalm 82:1, 6. Yet Scripture does manage to describe God's transcendence, using phrases, sentences, and so forth, without recourse to specific "transcendence terms."

(6) Therefore it is wrong to criticize a theologian simply because he uses a certain metaphor. So often we read in theology that Professor so-and-so is wrong because he "compares x to y." Professor so-and-so may have compared the Reformed view of the Lord's Supper to the Roman Catholic view or God's love to the love of a bird for her chicks, or predestination to philosophical determinism. Professor so-and-so is rebuked by being told that x and y are not at all comparable or that they have no relation to one another or that they have nothing to do with one another. That sort of argument is the opposite of anti-abstractionism: it is antirelationism with a vengeance! Certain points need to be made about such arguments. (A) In

God's world, everything is, after all, comparable to everything else. Granted, we tend to wince a bit when something we love or admire is compared to what we consider an unworthy object. But remember, Scripture even compares God to an unjust judge. Everything is related to everything else. There is nothing that "has nothing to do with" anything else. The strength of anti-abstractionism is that it recognizes that fact. (B) To criticize a metaphor as such is to engage in criticism at the word-level, rather than the sentence-level, which is an illegitimate practice, as we have seen. If someone compares God to a watermelon, for example, that fact is of little interest. What is of interest is what that metaphor is used to *say* about God. (If someone uses it to say that God's attributes, like the seeds of the watermelon, can be removed from Him, he is telling a lie about God. If he uses it to describe the "sweetness" of our fellowship with God, he is telling the truth.) Metaphors are not important in themselves; sentences containing metaphors can be important. Those sentences are, of course, open to criticism; but such criticism will deal with the truth of the sentence, rather than with the metaphor itself. (C) Nevertheless, some metaphors have often been used in misleading ways by theologians, and those ought to be pointed out—such as the analogy between God and "being" (e.g., in Tillich) and that between common grace and special grace (e.g., in liberation theology).

E. NEGATION IN THEOLOGY

Another source of unclarity in theology is the use of negative expressions. Negation is, of course, very important in theology, as in all other forms of knowledge. We understand the meaning of a term, in part, by being able to *contrast* that term with others, by showing what it does *not* mean. Scripture, though its fundamental message is a positive one, also often speaks negatively, contrasting the truth with error and sin, speaking God's judgments against unbelief, warning believers against false teaching.

The history of doctrine, too, has progressed very largely by negation. Most classic formulations of doctrine have been set forth by way of contrast to some heresy: creation *ex nihilo* against Gnosticism, the doctrine of scriptural canonicity against Marcion, the Nicene doctrine of the Trinity against Sabellianism and Arianism, the Chalcedonian Christology against Eutychian and Nestorian positions, the Reformation confessions against Romanism and sectarianism.

It can even be argued that some doctrines have very little meaning except for their negative function of excluding heresy. I think this is the case with creation *ex nihilo*, creation out of nothing. "Nothingness" is, of course, impossible to conceive, since every human thought is a thought of "something." And it is difficult to find anything in the Bible that specifically teaches that the world was created out of nothing, however that term be construed.[17] The doctrine does, however, clearly *exclude* two heresies: the pantheistic idea that the world is part of the divine nature and the Platonic picture of the world being created out of a preexisting eternal substance. I would say that denial of those two heresies constitutes the *meaning* of the doctrine of creation out of nothing. The doctrine does not seek to tell us *how* God made the world, except to tell us that He *didn't* do it in either of those two ways. Construed negatively, the doctrine can be proved from Scripture. For Scripture excludes pantheism, and it also denies that there is anything uncreated, except for God himself (e.g., Col. 1:16).

And the same is true for the use of *substance* and *person* in the doctrine of the Trinity. It does not seem to me that these terms have any precise meaning that uniquely qualifies them to describe the oneness and plurality of God. *Ousia* and *hypostasis*, which in Greek respectively designate the oneness and the plurality of God, might have been reversed, so far as their meaning potential is concerned. *Hypostasis* might have designated the oneness of God (as, in fact, did the similar Latin term *substantia*), and *ousia* might have designated the plurality of persons. Thus the use of those terms doesn't give us much positive information on the divine nature. They don't seek to solve the great mystery here but only to exclude certain illegitimate attempts to solve it. What those terms do for us is to exclude the heresies of Sabellianism and Arianism. Thus when we seek to prove the doctrine of the Trinity, we should not go looking through the Bible to find some specific justification for the use of those technical terms, rather, we should simply ask whether Scripture teaches Sabellianism or Arianism. If Scripture excludes those teachings, then that fact is sufficient proof of the orthodox doctrine.

Negation, therefore, is a useful tool of theology. But there are problems that arise from its misuse. Consider the following.

(1) John Woodbridge, in criticizing the Rogers and McKim volume *The Authority and Interpretation of the Bible*, accuses those authors of a kind of mistake that I believe is common in much theological writing.

17. I hope to discuss this issue in more detail in my forthcoming *Doctrine of God*.

> In their study Rogers and McKim work with a whole series of what we might coin "historical disjunctions." They assume that certain correct assertions about an individual's thought logically disallow other ones from being true. Their assumption is sometimes accurate, if the thoughts being compared directly contradict each other. However in their historical disjunctions the authors create disjunctions between propositions that are not mutually exclusive. . . .
>
> A partial listing of the authors' more important "historical disjunctions" would include these: because a thinker believes the central purpose of Scripture is to reveal salvation history, it is assumed that he or she does not endorse complete biblical infallibility; because a thinker speaks of God accommodating Himself to us in the words of Scripture, it is assumed that he or she does not believe in complete biblical infallibility. . . .

Woodbridge lists a number of other "historical disjunctions." These are a subdivision of a larger category that might be called "false disjunctions." It is all too common in theology for writers to present two things as contradictory that really are not. Such arguments look like those sound negative arguments that we have claimed to be important and valuable in the history of doctrine. It is certainly true, for example, that if one affirms creation from a preexisting substance, he must logically deny creation *ex nihilo*. But in a false disjunction, such arguments are constructed on the basis of relations between statements that are not truly contradictory.

(2) We saw earlier that theologians sometimes misuse negation in a way that is parallel but opposite to anti-abstractionism. That happens when they overstate distinctions, alleging that something has "nothing to do with" or is "not a matter of" something else, denying all analogy between one thing and another, and so forth (cf. *D*, *(6)*, above).

Of course, in God's world everything is related to everything else. Everything is "a matter of" everything else. Everything has "something to do with" everything else. To be sure, there are differences in degree here. Some relations are more important than others. But theologians often seem to turn these differences of degree into sharp distinctions. (That error is at the opposite extreme from anti-abstractionism, but it is dependent on similar kinds of confusion.)

Often, I think, that type of problem could be avoided if theologians would make use of the word "merely." They tend to use the word "not" when they should say "not merely" or "not only." Reflecting on God's love, the older liberal theologians concluded that God was not a righteous judge. The proper conclusion would have been that God is not *merely* a judge but is also a God of mercy. Reflecting on God's immanence, modern process theologians conclude that God is not supratemporal. The proper conclusion, rather, is that God is not *merely* supratemporal but also is involved in the temporal world. Think again of Woodbridge's "disjunctions." It would be true to say that Scripture is "not merely" infallible and inerrant, since it is also accommodated to our human condition and since it also has the purpose of conveying salvation history; but accommodation and redemptive-historical purpose do not entail any lack of infallibility.

Multiperspectivalism in theology often helps restore the proper balance, because it helps us to see that some doctrines that are apparently opposed are actually equivalent, presenting the same truth from various vantage points. Thus we are able to avoid futile oppositions between theologies of this and that, between partisans of the normative and partisans of the existential perspective (as I have called them), between those who favor this or that divine attribute as "central" and those who favor another.

(3) An error opposite to the last one discussed is the tendency among some theologians to attack "dualisms" in a general way. This is a form of anti-abstractionism (see chapter 6, *A*). Perhaps the most extreme example of an undisciplined attack on dualism is John Vander Stelt, *Philosophy and Scripture*.[18] In this book, Vander Stelt seems to charge almost every twofold distinction with "dualism," not only the distinctions between body and soul and between intellect and emotion but even the distinction between Creator and creature. Yet (maddeningly!) he is willing to advocate his own set of (Dooyeweerdian) twofold distinctions (naive/theoretical thought, heart/human functions). Apparently, then, he does not believe that *every* twofold distinction is a dualism. (Petrus Ramus can rest in peace!) But his criteria for determining what distinctions fall under this criticism are totally obscure. He just seems to have some distaste for twofold distinctions, a distaste that he expresses with mysterious selectivity but with no cogency whatsoever.

Doubtless, theologians have sometimes drawn too sharp oppositions between things. But much more needs to be said to determine when a distinction, separation, or "dichotomy" becomes improper. Without such explanations, the "dualism" critique often becomes, like other forms of criticism, a word-level, rather than a sentence-level, critique. When an author is criticized, for example, for contrasting *body* and *soul*, with no further explanation of his alleged error, then the criticism amounts to a criticism of his vocabulary, not a criticism of any of his actual positions. Let me repeat:

18. Marlton, N.J.: Mack Pub. Co., 1978.

theological criticism ought not to be a critique of someone's vocabulary; it ought to be a critique of what he *says* with that vocabulary. We ought not to criticize a theologian's words but his sentences and paragraphs.[19]

We ought to keep in mind that just as everything is analogous to everything else (above, *D, (6), (A)*), so everything is distinct from everything else. (No two things are identical; if they were, they would not be two but one!) Therefore any two things may be "distinguished" from one another. And if any two things may be distinguished, they may be "isolated" (in the sense of considering alone the features of the one thing that distinguish it from the other); they may be "opposed" (stressing the features that one "has," as opposed to what the other "has not"); they may be "separated" in some senses. (The common phrase "distinguish but not separate" is usually unclear when "separate" is used in a figurative sense, i.e., for something other than physical separation. In such a context, "separate" usually means the same thing as "distinguish," "isolate," "oppose," but perhaps to a greater degree.)

F. CONTRAST, VARIATION, DISTRIBUTION

Some Christian linguists, such as Kenneth Pike and Vern S. Poythress, emphasize the distinction between contrast, variation, and distribution as aspects of meaning in language. Contrast identifies the meaning of a term by its differences from other terms; variation indicates the changes (plurals, verb-endings, different pronunciations, different uses) an expression can undergo while remaining essentially the same expression; distribution identifies the contexts in which the expression typically functions. These are sometimes identified as static, dynamic, and relational perspectives, respectively, and are related to the physical concepts of particle, wave, and field. Poythress correlates the idea of contrast with our normative perspective, variation with our existential, and distribution with our situational.

We have seen that vagueness in each of those three areas can lead to misunderstandings in theology. Contrast has been stressed in our discussion of negation (*E*), distribution in our discussion of anti-abstractionism (chapter 6, *A*), and variation in our general discussion of

19. Vander Stelt once criticized a lecture of mine on the basis of the subtitles alone! The lecture was about Scripture, and the subtitles were "Scripture and God," "Scripture and History," "Scripture and Us," or something similar. Vander Stelt announced that he could tell from these subtitles alone that I was infected with dualistic tendencies. I did not find his criticism devastating.

vagueness and ambiguity (chapter 7, A and B). The perspectival relations between those three ways of understanding meaning will suggest to some readers ways in which those problems may be interrelated. I will not, however, seek to systematize such interrelations here.

G. SYSTEMATIC AMBIGUITY IN NON-ORTHODOX POSITIONS

Another source of vagueness can be seen in the rectangular diagram that I explained in Part One, which contrasts Christian and non-Christian viewpoints on transcendence and immanence and on irrationalism and rationalism. If that analysis is correct, then the non-Christian positions are ambiguous, not only for the reasons noted above but also for reasons deriving from the nature of non-Christian thought. Consider the following.

(1) Non-Christian transcendence is supposed to stand in contrast with non-Christian immanence, but in fact the two positions depend on one another and are reducible to one another. Thus there is this unclarity: to what extent is transcendence-irrationalism opposed to immanence-rationalism? To what extent and in what way are the two identical? The very meaning of the two positions fades from view under such scrutiny.

(2) Non-Christian transcendence maintains its plausibility by rhetorical confusion between it and Christian transcendence. Thus there is in non-Christian thinking a *need* for ambiguity.

(3) Liberal theological positions present an even more bewildering combination of Christian and non-Christian motifs, deceiving, if it were possible, even the elect. Hence the bent in liberal theology toward arguments of the anti-abstractionist type.

H. LABELS

One hears many objections to "labelling" in theology, and it is easy to understand why labelling is resented. On the one hand, when my thought is dismissed by being stuck in some category ("fundamentalist," "presuppositionalist," or whatever), I rarely feel that justice has been done, even if the label is appropriate. We all prefer, and we are all entitled, to think of ourselves as in some way unique, not as mere exemplifications of a trend or school of thought.

On the other hand, labels are important to learning. One could argue that education is the process of learning labels for things. If we were not allowed to use labels (i.e., descriptive nouns), we could say very little indeed. There are such things as "trends" and "schools of thought." There are general truths about groups of things and people, and it is important to be able to speak about these, as well as to speak about individual distinctives.

Generalized opposition to labels (an anti-abstractionist position, or is it antirelationist?), then, is untenable. On the one hand, there are times when it is justifiable to identify a thinker merely by his party affiliation or some other label. We don't always have time to list the unique qualities of every thinker we refer to; labels are an important kind of theological shorthand. On the other hand, while using labels we ought to recognize their inadequacies. Certainly, there is something rather unhelpful about books and articles that merely put various philosophers or theologians into categories without telling us anything important about their unique ideas.[20] Such writing is unjustifiably vague.

I. MORALS ON VAGUENESS

Vagueness in theology cannot be entirely avoided, and it is not even desirable to avoid it completely, lest we seek to be more precise than Scripture. Yet in many cases, for the sake of better communication, it is desirable to minimize ambiguity or at least to make clear to our audience where the ambiguity lies.

Theologians often use vague expressions without recognizing how vague their expressions are. Thus they may treat their terminology as if it were perfectly clear, as if it had one clear meaning. Some terms often used that way include "author of evil," "free will," "qualitative difference" (see discussion of this in Part One). In such cases, the reader may have a certain *feeling* about a term. Some terms just don't feel right, such as "author of evil" applied to God or "free will" in a Calvinist context. Thus we may think that we have a clear idea of the meaning of the term, when all we really have is a feeling. In such cases, misunderstandings arise because we make judgments based on the "sound" or "feel" of someone's words, rather than on the basis of what he actually says.

Thus sometimes it is useful, even necessary, to analyze in detail the meanings of theological terms, phrases, and sentences. It is often impor-

20. An example of a book that is weak in this sort of way is Francis N. Lee, *A Christian Introduction to the History of Philosophy* (Nutley, N.J.: Craig Press, 1969).

tant to show our readers how ambiguous certain expressions are. Here are some ways of doing that.

(1) Make lists. Simply write down all the possible things that might be meant by an expression. Determine how each of those interpretations might affect the theological point being made. Try to decide what is the most likely meaning of the author you are seeking to interpret. Try to determine what interpretation of his language would make his argument strongest, weakest. I used this technique in Part One. Recall the lists of possible interpretations of divine incomprehensibility and of the unbeliever's knowledge of God.

(2) Point out intermediate cases, fuzzy boundaries, areas where it is unclear precisely how a word applies. Show your audience that language is not a rigid, cut-and-dried system where each word always has a perfectly plain meaning and each sentence is obviously true or false. Be hesitant to pass judgment on theological issues until you have diligently sought out ambiguities in the formulations.

J. LANGUAGE AND REALITY

Virtually all schools of philosophy in our time are preoccupied with the study of language. This is true of phenomenologists, existentialists, the various schools of language analysis, the philosophers of hermeneutics, and the developments in structuralist linguistics towards a comprehensive philosophy. (Marxists may be something of an exception to this trend, but many Marxists are also influenced by the other philosophical currents listed.)

Why the "linguistic turn" in recent philosophy? It is partly a result of a weariness with the perennial problems of philosophy. Philosophers today discuss essentially the same problems that were discussed among the ancient Greeks. It seems that philosophy is a discipline in which little, if any, progress takes place. Thus modern philosophers are asking if some or most of the lack of progress is due to misunderstanding, lack of communication, or lack of clarity—hence the turn toward the examination of language.

Another reason for the linguistic turn has been that many philosophers have come to believe that the study of language provides a sort of key to the nature of reality. Philosophers of the past have sought such a key. Some have tried to investigate metaphysics per se. Others have investigated human knowledge and reason as a gateway to metaphysics, assuming that "the real is the rational and the rational is the real" (Hegel). We must presuppose that the world is rational, they said, if we are to try to know it at all, and thus its basic structure must reflect the processes of human thought. Others have sought such a key in ethical or aesthetic values. These approaches have not led to any consensus, and in fact their failure has led to general skepticism about metaphysics.

In our century, however, an alternative has emerged. To describe it, we might modify Hegel's slogan to read "The real is the sayable, and the sayable is the real." The idea is that study of language can reveal what can be spoken of; thus study of language reveals the basic nature of the world.

This kind of philosophical quest has led to some errors, such as the theory of the early Wittgenstein and of Bertrand Russell that a perfect language would be a kind of "picture" of the world.[21] Yet it does seem to me that we can say at least this much: learning language involves learning the world. Language is a set of tools by which we accomplish tasks in the world. On the one hand, you cannot "understand" language or know its "meaning" unless you know some things about the world. On the other hand, without language it is impossible to have a knowledge of the world that is worthy of our human status. Thus learning language and learning about the world are simultaneous and correlative processes, perhaps perspectivally related. Learning what a tree is and learning the meaning of the word *tree* are essentially the same process.

Language, then, is a kind of gateway to reality, to metaphysics. But other gateways are equally important: epistemology, value theory, and metaphysics proper.

K. LANGUAGE AND HUMANITY

Language is, I maintain, an indispensable element of the image of God in which we are created. (1) It likens us to God, who does all things by His powerful Word and who is identical with His word (John 1:1ff.). (2) It distinguishes us from the animals, giving us a powerful tool of dominion. (3) It is central to human life. Man's first experience recorded in Scripture was the experience of hearing God's word (Gen. 1:28ff.), and his first task was the task of "naming" the animals (Gen. 2:19ff.). James, building on Proverbs, teaches us that if a man can control his tongue, he can control his whole body (3:1-12). Sins of the tongue take prominence in biblical lists of

21. For an exposition and critique of this idea, see J. O. Urmson, *Philosophical Analysis* (London: Oxford University Press, 1956). See also my Appendix D (after Part One) on the referential theory of meaning, which was associated with this approach.

sins, such as Romans 3:10-18. Redemption is often presented as a cleansing of the lips (Isa. 6:5-7) or of language (Ps. 12; Zeph. 3:9-13).

The points I have been making, then, about the responsible use of theological language, are not merely of academic interest. Speaking truthfully, for edification (rather than speaking lies, blasphemies, and foolishness), is a crucial part of our responsibility before God (1 Cor. 14:3, 12, 17, 26; Eph. 4:29).

CHAPTER EIGHT

The Situational Perspective— Logic as a Tool of Theology

The second "tool of theology" we shall discuss is logic. Reformed theology was once famous for its rigorously logical character. Even critics of Calvinism often grudgingly admired the Reformed use of logic. At the same time, however, these critics expressed their suspicions that Calvinists were more interested in being logical than in being scriptural. Reformed theologians were seen as building a system by working out logical implications from a few ideas (like the sovereignty of God), rather than by letting Scripture control their reasoning in a comprehensive way. In my view, these criticisms, though containing a small amount of truth, were never really justified.

Today, however, it is hard to imagine Calvinists being accused of overconfidence in logic. Except in the writings of Gordon H. Clark, John H. Gerstner, and some of their disciples, it is difficult now, in fact, to find any positive words about logic in Reformed theology and easy to find warnings against its misuse. Berkouwer frequently warns us against developing doctrines by drawing deductive inferences. Van Til, while not denying the legitimacy of logical inference, is more concerned with the dangers of overreliance on logic than he is with the dangers of neglecting it. The followers of Dooyeweerd, too, are more concerned with the danger of "absolutizing the logical aspect" than they are over the danger of being illogical.

I am not sure where this suspicion of logic comes from. In Calvin's thought there is no embarrassment about being logical, but there is a polemic against intellectualism. Calvin emphasized that intellectual arguments could not save in the absence of the Spirit's work. He noted the inadequacy of knowledge that merely "flits about in the brain," rather than taking root in the heart. Perhaps this polemic against intellectualism somehow evolved into the antilogicism of later writers, though this later attitude is certainly different from Calvin's.

However that may be, the result of this development is that many Reformed people are confused and uncertain about the role that logic should play in their theology. I hope in this section to offer some clarifications on that subject. Logic has its limitations, but logic is a tool of great value to theology, one that we ought to use without shame. It is certainly no more dangerous, as a tool, than is language or history, and it is no less indispensable to theology than these.

Some persons, such as those in the Clark group, will be pleased to hear this encouragement toward the use of logic. These prologic thinkers, however, may be disappointed that I am giving to logic such a subordinate role in the outline of this book. Logic, they might note, is generally placed among the "laws of thought," rather than among the "facts of experience." Thus, they might argue, consideration of logic properly belongs under the "justification of knowledge" (Part Two, above), rather than as a mere "method." And if logic is a method, they might say, then surely it belongs under the normative perspective, rather than merely under the situational!

Well, there is some validity in the view that logic is a "law of thought." But (the reader will recall) our three perspectives are mutually inclusive, so that all norms are facts and all facts are norms (i.e., they govern thought). Thus everything we consider under the situational perspective may be regarded as a norm of sorts. What to consider under what perspective is to some extent a matter of choice, a choice made on pedagogical grounds.

My current pedagogical purpose is to demystify logic, as much as possible, to discourage both irrational fear and inappropriate adulation of it. Logic is a law of thought, if you will, but as such is subordinate to Scripture, which is our ultimate law of thought. It is Scripture that warrants our use of logic, not the other way around. As such, logic is in a position similar to linguistics and history—a discipline that gives us information that is useful in the application of Scripture, information that ought, indeed, to *govern* our thinking about Scripture but information that itself is subject to biblical criteria.[1] The logician is no less fallible than are the linguist and

1. The circularity here, of course, is unavoidable, as with all the other tools of theology.

the historian; he has no priestly authority over the believer. I shall elaborate this position in what follows.

A. WHAT IS LOGIC?

(1) The Science of Argument

Basically, logic analyzes and evaluates the human activity known as argument. *Argument*, in ordinary language, sometimes suggests a hostile confrontation of some kind, but no such thing is suggested by the technical meaning of the term. In its technical sense, in fact, an argument need not even be *between* two or more people. In the technical sense, an argument is simply a conclusion, supported by grounds or reasons expressed in sentences called "premises." In the traditional example, "All men are mortal; Socrates is a man; therefore Socrates is mortal," there are two premises and one conclusion. When an argument is stated in formal terms (as is the argument about Socrates), it is called a "syllogism."

Argument is something that people do all the time, something that they have been doing since the beginning of our historical record. People argued before the science of logic was ever invented, and they argue today, whether or not they have studied logic. We all try, in other words, to set forth reasons for the things we believe and do. Parents do this with their children and teachers with their students (and vice versa!). Pastors do this in many situations. Every sermon is an argument or a group of arguments; it is an attempt to persuade people to change their beliefs or behavior in some way, and it offers reasons for making those changes. Every speech on the floor of a presbytery, synod, or convention, similarly—not to mention the various articles and papers on various subjects that ministers are often called upon to write—contains arguments. Logic, then, is a practical science. It helps us with our everyday lives.

Logicians, then, did not invent argument any more than the art critics invented art or the sports writers invented baseball. What logicians do is to *study* argument, to analyze it critically, to show us what makes arguments succeed and what makes them fail.

In evaluating arguments, logicians are concerned particularly with two concepts that are central to their inquiry. The first is called *implication*, *entailment*, or *inference*. In a valid argument, the premises are said to *imply* or *entail* the conclusion. Or, looking at it from the other direction, the conclusion is said to be *inferred from* the premises. This means that *if* the premises are true, the conclusion cannot fail to be true. That "if" can be a big "if." Take the argument "All Westminster Seminary students are communists; Ronald Reagan is a Westminster Seminary student; therefore Ronald Reagan is a communist." Now that argument is as false as it can be: two false premises and a false conclusion. It is "unsound," as some logicians put it. But the premises do *imply* the conclusion. That means, *if the premises were true* the conclusion would also be true. In fact the premises are not true; but *if they were*, the conclusion would be also.

Valid is a technical term for an argument in which the premises imply the conclusion, whether or not the premises and/or conclusion are true. Thus the argument above, concluding that Reagan is a communist, is a valid argument, strange as it may sound to call it that. It is not, however, "sound." Soundness involves not only logical validity but also the truth of the premises and conclusion.

Implication is something that pervades our experience. In all sorts of situations we notice premises entailing or implying conclusions. Often people notice implications and act on them without consciously formulating any argument at all. In a football game, a quarterback notices a telltale motion in the opponents' backfield. He concludes that his opponents are executing a particular defensive strategy, and he adjusts his offense accordingly. Doubtless, the quarterback in this situation does not set forth this implication as a formal argument; if he did, it would be too late, and he would be crushed by the oncoming defensive players. Rather, he reacts almost subconsciously, instinctively, instantaneously. But he has noticed an implication, nonetheless.

A woman whose husband has gone to war has not heard from him in several months. She sees a military car pull up in front of the house. Two officers get out of the car, wearing somber expressions. They walk toward her door. At that point, she knows that there is bad news. Doubtless, she has not formulated any explicit argument; yet she has recognized some facts together with their implications and has reacted accordingly.

Such implications occur to us each day, virtually every moment. The alarm rings, we "deduce" that it is time to get up. We smell coffee, we "deduce" that someone is fixing breakfast. And on and on.

Logic maps some of those kinds of implication, showing what makes them work, translating them into a formal symbolism, evaluating alleged implications of those types. It gives us some useful quasi-mathematical[2] ways of evaluating purported implications. These techniques focus on the

2. Logicians have argued over whether mathematics and logic are one science or two.

use of certain key terms in the argument, such as "all," "some," "if . . . then." These terms have been thoroughly examined as to their "logical force," so that arguments (like the ones earlier about Socrates and Reagan) that turn on the use of these terms may be properly evaluated.

There are, however, many kinds of implication that have not been so formalized by the science of logic (among them, I think, the cases of the quarterback and the military wife above). Often we draw implications without formulating verbal arguments at all or without, at least, formulating arguments based on the use of *all*, *some*, and so forth. Many times, indeed, we just get a "feeling" or a "sense" that one thing implies another (a sense that, to be sure, sometimes misleads us). The science of logic sharpens that sense, just as physics sharpens our ability to perceive relations among physical objects. But the science has not (in either logic or physics) made the sense superfluous. In fact, even our acceptance of logical principles depends on our ability to "sense" that they are true (cf. my doctrine of "cognitive rest").

The second central concept in logic as the science of argument is the concept of *consistency*. Two propositions are consistent if and only if they can both be true at the same time—a concept that we use in everyday life. A legislator says that he believes in law and order, but he votes against all appropriations for law enforcement. Certainly, some editorial will appear and charge him with inconsistency. Of course, the inconsistency, the contradiction, may only be apparent. There are ways of refuting charges of inconsistency, and we sometimes are mistaken in making such charges. Yet we do make judgments of that sort all the time, whether we have studied logic or not. As with implication, we have a sort of "sense" that warns us of inconsistency.

Logic, then, seeks to formalize and refine that sensitivity. It helps us to translate statements into terms that make their consistency or inconsistency more evident. It gives us quasi-mathematical techniques for determining which statements are consistent and which are not. Thus the "law of noncontradiction," which is often regarded as the most fundamental principle of logic, states: Nothing can be both A and not-A at the same time and in the same respect. For example, "Bill is a butcher" and "Bill is not a butcher" cannot both be true at the same time and in the same respect. (Another formulation, more suited to the modern logic of propositions, is "No proposition can be both true and false at the same time and in the same respect.") We must, of course, take note of the qualifiers. The two statements about Bill could both be true at *different times*; Bill could be a nonbutcher in 1975 but become a butcher by 1982. And the statements could both be true in *different respects*, for example if *butcher* is used figuratively in one of the sentences. But if there is no relevant difference of time or respect, we know that the two sentences cannot both be true.

(2) A Hermeneutical Tool

Because logic is the science of argument, it is also a valuable tool in the interpretation of language. In theology it helps us to understand the Bible.

In the syllogistic argument about Socrates, the conclusion unpacks *meaning* implicit in the premises. In one sense, the conclusion adds nothing new to the premises. If you know that all men are mortal, and that Socrates is a man, you know that Socrates is mortal. That does not seem like a new piece of knowledge. Implication does not add anything new; it merely rearranges information contained in the premises. It takes what is implicit in the premises and states it explicitly. Thus when we learn logical implications of sentences, we are learning more and more of what those sentences *mean*. The conclusion represents part of the meaning of the premises.

So in theology, logical deductions set forth the meaning of Scripture. "Stealing is wrong; embezzling is stealing; therefore embezzling is wrong." That is a kind of "moral syllogism," common to ethical reasoning. Deriving this conclusion is a kind of "application," and we have argued that the applications of Scripture are its meaning. If someone says he believes stealing is wrong but he believes embezzlement is permitted, then he has not understood the *meaning* of the eighth commandment. Another example: "Whosoever believes on Christ has eternal life (John 3:16); Bill believes on Christ; therefore Bill has eternal life." That argument, too, sets forth part of the meaning of the biblical text. Thus logical deduction is important even in the vital area of assurance of salvation.

When it is used rightly, logical deduction adds nothing to Scripture. It merely sets forth what is there. Thus we need not fear any violation of *sola scriptura* as long as we use logic *responsibly*. Logic sets forth the *meaning* of Scripture.

(3) A Science of Commitment

There is a peculiar "necessity" about logical inference. We feel that when you accept the premises of an argument, you "must" accept the conclusion. What is the force of that "must"? In what sense "must" we accept logical inferences?

The necessity is obviously not physical. No one is pulling strings on our vocal cords, physically compelling us to assert the conclusion of a valid argument. The compulsion can be resisted and often is; many people refuse assent to sound arguments despite the "must," the necessity, of logical inference. Nor is the necessity pragmatic, in any obvious way. That is to say, we do not accept logical conclusions merely because doing that makes life more pleasant for us or serves our self-interest in some obvious way. Often, accepting a logical conclusion makes life harder; thus many flee from the reality represented by the conclusion of a sound argument.

In my view, the necessity is of two sorts. First, it is an *analytic* necessity. That is to say, if someone believes a premise, then in one sense he *already* believes the implications of that premise. He may not admit that he believes them, but at some level of his consciousness, he does. And that is like the teaching of Romans 1 about the unbeliever: he may resist God, but at some level he does believe in Him. Thus to say that someone "must" accept the conclusion of an argument means, in part, that he already *does* believe it. He may also hold other beliefs, contradictory to the conclusion in question. We have seen that people do hold contradictory beliefs sometimes. But the fact that someone believes "not-p" is no proof that he does not also believe "p." The law of noncontradiction says that he *ought* not to believe contradictory propositions, but it does not prevent him from doing so.

But there is a second sort of necessity. The logical "must" indicates a *moral* necessity. To say that someone "must" accept a conclusion is to say that he *ought* to accept it, that he has an *obligation* to accept it. The obligation is to believe in the fullest sense—to accept it as authority, to bring all the rest of life into conformity to that belief. Why should we urge such a moral obligation to believe upon people who in one sense believe already? Because, as Romans 1 teaches with respect to the knowledge of God, people often "suppress" their knowledge of a logical conclusion; or they believe it but refuse to admit it; or they believe it, but refuse to act accordingly; or they believe it, but also believe other things inconsistent with it that compete for their loyalty.

Thus we can see that logical implication is not a religiously neutral something. It is dependent on ethical values, which ultimately are religious values. Logical necessity can be understood as a form of ethical necessity, which is ultimately a religious necessity. Logic, therefore, can be viewed as a brand of ethics. But the only true ethical values are those revealed to us by God. Therefore, logic presupposes Christianity.

B. THE CERTAINTY OF LOGIC

Compared with the principles of other sciences like physics and history, the laws of logic seem to have a peculiar certainty about them; and in this respect, they are similar to the laws of mathematics.[3] We may well doubt a historian's assertion that the Treaty of Versailles brought about the Second World War. But we cannot doubt, it seems, that $2 + 2 = 4$. If someone added two pieces of chalk to two others and the total came out five, we would assume that someone had played a trick. We would not (or would we?) under any circumstances question the truth that $2 + 2 = 4$. Nor, apparently, can we doubt that if all men are mortal, and Socrates is a man, that Socrates is mortal. That syllogism seems to carry with it a certainty that transcends all sense-experience, that takes precedence over all nonlogical and nonmathematical claims.

What makes logic so certain? A number of theories have been proposed, the following among them.

(i) *Innate ideas*. Some have said that logic is certain because of its origin: we do not learn it through sense-experience but through innate ideas of some sort. However, it is very difficult to prove that any particular idea is an "innate" idea. Most philosophers, I think, postulate innate ideas by process of elimination; it seems to them the only way of solving the sort of problem we are discussing. But unless there is some independent evidence of such innate ideas, the proposed solution is not very credible. Furthermore, it is not clear why the innateness of an idea makes it certain. Might we not have some innate ideas that are false? Indeed, it could be argued that at least some of the data of sense experience is just as certain as the laws of logic. I am now looking at my hand, and I think I am just as certain of the existence of my hand as I am of any law of logic.

(ii) *Convention*. Others have argued that logic is certain because it is "true by convention." The certainty of logic, on this view, is like the certainty of the sentence "All bachelors are unmarried." Isn't it amazing that we know infallibly that all bachelors are unmarried?! We could take a Gallup poll of all the bachelors in California, and we wouldn't find a single one who is married! We could even poll all the bachelors in the universe and get the same result! We know that infallibly. Why? Where does this marvellous knowledge come from? Well, some would say that there is no

3. Again, on some views, logic and mathematics are a single science.

mystery about it at all. We know that all bachelors are unmarried simply because we have agreed to define *bachelor* that way. Similarly, some have said that logic and mathematics consist of *definitions* and the implications of those definitions. Some would go beyond this view and say that for this reason logic and mathematics don't tell us anything about the world, only about the definitions of our language. Another way of putting it is to say that the laws of logic and mathematics are "analytic," rather than "synthetic." The predicate is included in the definition of the subject.

The distinction between "analytic" and "synthetic," however, has been subject to much discussion in recent years. To many writers it no longer seems possible to distinguish sharply between these or between "truths by definition" and other kinds of truth.[4] For one cannot sharply distinguish language from reality, the truth of definitions from the truth of other statements. Language is part of reality; it is a tool by which we find our way in the world. We do not define terms arbitrarily, but we seek to define them in a system that helps us to carry out our tasks in creation.

As we saw earlier in our discussion of language (chapter 7, *1*), the meaning of every term has fuzzy boundaries; no definitions are absolutely precise. What would we say about a bachelor living with a woman without formal wedding ceremony, which relationship in some states (but not in others) would be described as a common law marriage? Would he be a married bachelor? Well, the definition of the term doesn't settle the question; reality might cause us to stretch our definitions a bit, and that's how language develops.

The truths of logic and mathematics may consist to some extent of definitions, but the truths they express were not invented by us. If these particular definitions did not reflect the nature of the world, we would not use them. The existential perspective, here as always, presupposes the normative and the situational. The equation "2 + 2 = 4" is a fact about the world. It really is the case that two objects added to two others yields four. That would be the case even if we chose arbitrarily a system of definitions that made that equation (or an equivalent equation, using different terms) false.

(iii) *Triperspectivalism*. The approach I consider most adequate is (what else?!) threefold. (A) The Situational Perspective. Logic and mathematics describe very "obvious" truths about the world, plus the (often not so ob-

4. A seminal work in this discussion is W. V. Quine, "Two Dogmas of Empiricism," in Quine, *From a Logical Point of View* (New York: Harper and Row, 1961), 20-46. Other essays in that volume are also relevant.

vious) implications of those truths. They are certain because of that obviousness. At this level, there is little difference between "2 + 2 = 4" and "My hand is now in front of my face." (B) The Normative Perspective. Since Scripture teaches us to live wisely, in accordance with truth, in effect it commands us to observe these obvious facts. Thus these facts, like all facts, become normative. We are *obligated* to honor them. And since they are more obvious, less controversial, than many other facts, they take precedence over most other claims to knowledge. (This is not *always* the case. Sometimes observance of facts will lead us to modify our system of logic in some way.) Thus (in a somewhat qualified way) the laws of logic may be described as "laws of thought." (C) The Existential Perspective. We must, indeed, make a choice of whether or not to recognize these law-facts. If we do, then we seek to reflect them in our definitions and in our thinking in general. This is, as we saw earlier, an ethico-religious decision. To accept logic presupposes (even for the unbeliever) the law-fact structure of the universe that was created as such by God. For most people, it is true to say that they cannot "live without" logic. For most of us, to assume that 2 + 2 = 5 would throw our lives into chaos. Thus logic has a subjective and practical necessity, as well as situational and normative necessities.

C. BIBLICAL WARRANT FOR USING LOGIC IN THEOLOGY

One may do theology without logic in one sense but not in another. One may theologize without having studied logic and without making any explicit use of logical rules or symbolism. One may not, however, do theology or anything else in human life without taking account of those truths that form the basis of the science of logic. We cannot do theology if we are going to feel free to contradict ourselves or to reject the implications of what we say. Anything that we say must observe the law of noncontradiction in the sense that it must say what it says and not the opposite. Thus many have said that logic is necessary to all human thought and action. In general, this is true. We shall have to note some qualifications of this principle in the next section, but for now my purpose is to indicate the positive importance of logic for theology.

When we see what logic is, we can see that it is involved in many biblical teachings and injunctions. (i) It is involved in any *communication* of the Word of God. To communicate the Word is to communicate the Word as opposed to what contradicts it (1 Tim. 1:3ff.; 2 Tim. 4:2f.). Thus the biblical concepts of wisdom, teaching, preaching, and discernment presuppose the law of noncontradiction.

(ii) It is involved in any proper *response* to the Word. To the extent that we don't know the implications of Scripture, we do not understand the meaning of Scripture. To the extent that we disobey the applications of Scripture, we disobey Scripture itself. God told Adam not to eat the forbidden fruit. Imagine Adam replying, "Lord, you told me not to eat it, but you didn't tell me not to chew and swallow!" God would certainly have replied that Adam had the logical skill to deduce "You shall not chew and swallow" from "You shall not eat." In such a way, the biblical concepts of understanding, obeying, and loving presuppose the necessity of logic.

(iii) Logic is involved in the important matter of assurance of salvation. Scripture teaches that we may *know* that we have eternal life (1 John 5:13). The Spirit's witness (Rom. 8:16ff.) plays a major role in this assurance; but that witness does not come as a new revelation, supplementing the canon, as it were.[5] So where does the information that I am a child of God come from—information to which the Spirit bears witness? It comes from the only possible authoritative source, the canonical Scriptures. But how can that be, since my name is not found in the biblical text? It comes by *application* of Scripture, a process that involves logic. God says that whosoever believes in Christ shall be saved (John 3:16). I believe in Christ. Therefore I am saved. Saved by a syllogism? Well, in a sense, yes. If that syllogism were not sound, we would be without hope. (Of course, the syllogism is only God's means of telling us the good news!) Without logic, then, there is no assurance of salvation.

(iv) Scripture warrants many specific types of logical argument. The Pauline Epistles, for instance, are full of "therefores." *Therefore* indicates a logical conclusion. In Romans 12:1 Paul beseeches us, "Therefore, by the mercies of God." The mercies of God are the saving mercies that Paul has described in Romans 1-11. Those mercies furnish us with grounds, reasons, premises for the kind of behavior described in chapters 12-16. Notice that Paul is not merely telling us in Romans 12 to behave in a certain way. He is telling us to behave in that way *for particular reasons*. If we claim to obey but reject those particular reasons for obeying, we are to that extent being disobedient. Therefore Paul is requiring our acceptance not only of a pat-

5. See my article, "The Spirit and the Scriptures," in D. A. Carson and John Woodbridge, eds., *Hermeneutics, Authority, and Canon* (Grand Rapids: Zondervan Publishing House, 1986). Also see John Murray, "The Attestation of Scripture," in N. Stonehouse and P. Woolley, eds., *The Infallible Word* (Grand Rapids: Wm. B. Eerdmans Pub. Co., 1946; reissued by Presbyterian and Reformed), 1-52.

tern of behavior but also of a particular logical argument. The same thing happens whenever a biblical writer presents grounds for what he says. Not only his conclusion but also his logic is normative for us. If, then, we reject the use of logical reasoning in theology, we are disobeying Scripture itself.

An interesting task might be to see if a complete system of logic might be developed out of the normative argument-forms found in Scripture. I am told that some people are busy doing that, though I have not seen their work in writing. If that task were to be successful, the results would be useful to us in showing more clearly the biblical basis for logic. But logic can be defended from Scripture even without such data. And such a "biblical system" would, if found, not exhaust the argument forms permitted to the Christian, anymore than the tools of gospel-communication found in Scripture exhaust the permissible means of communicating the gospel today.

(v) Scripture teaches that God himself is logical. In the first place, His Word is truth (John 17:17), and *truth* means nothing if it is not opposed to *falsehood*. Therefore His Word is noncontradictory. Furthermore, God does not break His promises (2 Cor. 1:20); He does not deny himself (2 Tim. 2:13); He does not lie (Heb. 6:18; Tit. 1:2). At the very least, those expressions mean that God does not do, say, or believe the contradictory of what He says to us. The same conclusion follows from the biblical teaching concerning the *holiness* of God. Holiness means that there is nothing in God that *contradicts* His perfection (including His truth). Does God, then, observe the law of noncontradiction? Not in the sense that this law is somehow higher than God himself. Rather, God *is* himself noncontradictory and is therefore himself the criterion of logical consistency and implication. Logic is an attribute of God, as are justice, mercy, wisdom, knowledge. As such, God is a model for us. We, as His image, are to imitate His truth, His promise-keeping. Thus we too are to be noncontradictory.

Therefore the Westminster Confession of Faith is correct when it says (I, vi) that the whole counsel of God is found not only in what Scripture explicitly teaches but also among those things that "by good and necessary consequence may be deduced from Scripture." This statement has been attacked[6] even by professing disciples of Calvin, but it is quite unavoidable. If we deny the implications of Scripture, we are denying Scripture.

6. E.g., recently by Charles Partee, "Calvin, Calvinism and Rationality," in *Rationality in the Calvinian Tradition*, ed. Hendrick Hart, Johan Vander Hoeven, and Nicholas Wolterstorff (Lanham, Md.: University Press of America, 1983), 15 n. 13.

Of course, our logical deductions are not infallible, as I shall stress in the next section. But we must see that fact in perspective. We are fallible in our use of *all* the tools of theology, including language, archeology, and history, as well as logic. Yet all of these, including logic, are means for us to discover God's infallible truth.

I would therefore recommend that theological students study logic, just as they study other tools of exegesis. There is great need of logical thinking among ministers and theologians today. Invalid and unsound arguments abound in sermons and theological literature. It often seems to me that the standards of logical cogency are much lower today in theology than in any other discipline. And logic is not a difficult subject. Anyone with a high school diploma and some elementary knowledge of mathematics can buy or borrow a text like I. M. Copi, *Introduction to Logic*[7] and go through it on his own. If, for some reason, you cannot handle the complications of formal logic, you can do the next best thing: become more self-critical; *anticipate objections*. As you think and write, keep asking how someone might find fault with what you say. This simple process—really only an outworking of Christian humility—will help you to avoid invalid arguments and inconsistencies.

Most people in the pews have not studied logic, and they will not be able to subject their pastors' sermons to formal logical scrutiny. Yet all rational people, I think, have what we earlier called a "sense" of implication and consistency. They may not recognize in every case when they are being given an invalid argument or an inconsistent position. But when logical fallacies are prominent in a sermon, many in the congregation will feel uneasy about it. They will not find it adequately persuasive. Even if they cannot pin down what the problem is, they will sense that a problem exists. Thus, for their sake, and indeed for the sake of the truth itself—God's noncontradictory truth—we must make much greater efforts than are now common among theologians to be logical.

D. THE LIMITATIONS OF LOGIC

I trust that the preceding discussion will assure the reader that I am neither an irrationalist nor against logic in any meaningful sense. Nevertheless, a balanced picture will have to reveal not only the values of logic but also its limitations. Logic is important, but there are some things it cannot

7. New York: Macmillan, 1961.

do. We must be warned against placing unjustifiable demands on our logical tools. The limitations of logic are such, moreover, as to make us hesitate in drawing some apparently justified logical conclusions.

Some writers seem to think that if logic is necessary for the very intelligibility of human thought, we dare not say anything negative about it at all. To claim any limitations to logic, they seem to say, would be to attack the intelligibility of thought itself. The limitations I have in mind, however, are limitations that we can live with. They do not call into question the fabric of human thought as such, only some particular operations of it. We can live with inadequacies in our understanding of language and history; and similarly, we can live with inadequacies in our human logic. Specifically, I have in mind the following kinds of inadequacies.

(i) *Fallibility*. Human logic is fallible, even though God's logic is infallible. That's just the way it is with all human thinking, except when God intervenes, as in the inspiration of Scripture. Now I do think that some logical principles are taught in Scripture itself (C, above), including the law of noncontradiction. Therefore it could be said that we know these principles infallibly, in the same way that we have infallible knowledge of justification by faith, for example. (I said earlier that we can make mistakes even about biblical doctrines, but some of these doctrines are so pervasive in Scripture and obvious to the reader that they function as presuppositions, and thus as certainties, for our thinking. The law of noncontradiction would certainly (!) be one of these. See chapter 5, *A*, *(8)*.) But to know infallibly, in that sense, the law of noncontradiction does not entail infallible knowledge of any particular *system* of logic.

Logic, after all, cannot do its business with the law of noncontradiction alone. From the law of noncontradiction itself, nothing can be deduced. Even if you add some empirical premises to the law of noncontradiction, nothing can be deduced. The whole work of logic requires not only that basic law but many other principles, argument forms, symbolisms, and calculation rules as well.

There have been many systems of logic throughout history. Aristotle practically invented the science of logic (though, of course, people were thinking logically before he invented it)—a remarkable achievement—and his system has been the most influential down through the years. But others have added to it—the medieval logicians, Leibniz, Mill, and others. Early in this century, Bertrand Russell maintained that Aristotle's system would lead to some contradictions except as amended by Russell. Others have defended Aristotle on that point. Nevertheless, it should be clear to all that logic as a human science is no different from physics, chemistry, sociology, or psychology; it changes over the years. What is accepted in one century may not be accepted in another, and vice versa. These are fallible systems, human systems. They may not be equated with the mind of God. God's logic is divine; human logic is not.[8]

(ii) *Incompleteness*. Present systems of formal logic are incomplete in important ways. I said earlier that logic seeks to chart the instances of implication and consistency that we recognize in all areas of life but that it has so far only charted those arguments (and possibly only some of them) that turn on certain logical constants like "all," "some," "if . . . then." Thus there is a great deal more work to be done. And we can expect much change in logical systems in the future to accommodate new developments.[9]

(iii) *Proofs not enough*. George Mavrodes argues that we cannot learn all that we know from logical proofs. He comments:

> Argumentation then, as a method of proof, is not a substitute for knowledge any more than a hammer is a substitute for lumber or a needle is a substitute for cloth. Like these other tools, the techniques of valid argument are useful only if we are already in possession of something else besides these tools. If we also have lumber, a hammer may be useful in constructing a house but without lumber it is useless. Similarly, if we already have some knowledge, an argument may help us to know something further but if we know nothing to begin with then argument cannot help us.[10]

Mavrodes does admit that "all things can be learned from proofs," if certain kinds of circular arguments are permitted. (That fact, I think, is more significant than he recognizes in context.) But his basic point is a cogent one: logic won't help you if you don't have premises, and the premises are not given by logic alone. Thus, in one sense, the conclusions of logic are dependent on our sense-experience, divine revelation, subjective

8. For a survey of some controversial areas in mathematics, see Vern Poythress, "A Biblical View of Mathematics," in *Foundations of Christian Scholarship*, ed. Gary North (Vallecito, Calif.: Ross House, 1976), 159-88. This article makes it clear that the sciences of mathematics and logic do not consist *entirely* of truisms, however "obvious" their fundamental propositions may be.

9. In this connection, see Gilbert Ryle, "Formal and Informal Logic," in Ryle, *Dilemmas* (London: Cambridge University Press, 1954), 111-29; also see Stephen Toulmin, *The Uses of Argument* (London: Cambridge University Press, 1958).

10. George Mavrodes, *Belief in God* (New York: Random House, 1970), 42.

sensitivities, and all the other forms of knowledge. No conclusion of a logical argument may claim more certainty than those. Thus in the most important sense—at the level of application—logic has no more authority than sensation.

There are other reasons, too, why we "cannot learn all we know from proofs." (A) The famous theorems of Kurt Godel indicate, for example, that the consistency of formal systems that are elaborate enough to include number theory cannot be demonstrated within those systems and that such systems contain propositions the truth of which is undecidable within those systems. Formal systems, then, depend on knowledge that we gain by other means. (B) Philosophers have long despaired of being able to give a fully satisfactory theoretical justification of induction (the principle that the future will resemble the past), and yet many arguments rely on induction for their logical force. (C) As we saw earlier, logic presupposes ethical and religious values. If we have no such values, we can do nothing with logic. Logic presupposes a rational God, a rational world, a rational human mind. Those who doubt any of these have no right to insist on the certainty of logic. But knowledge of those things does not come from logic alone. (D) Use of logic also presupposes that we have some criterion for truth and falsity. But such a criterion is essentially presuppositional and religious, as we have seen, and may not be derived from logic alone.

(iv) *Apparent contradictions*. While it is true that reality is noncontradictory and therefore that the presence of a real contradiction in a proposition is adequate to refute it, *apparent* contradictions are something else. When we are studying someone's position and we find an apparent contradiction in it, we do not—indeed we ought not—reject that position for that reason. We know that many things that appear contradictory to us turn out on closer inspection not to be contradictory at all. Therefore when we run into apparent contradictions, we ought not automatically to reject the view under consideration. Rather, we should take the apparent contradiction as a problem to be resolved. Perhaps on further investigation we shall find the view consistent. Or perhaps we will still find it inconsistent and reject it on that account. Or perhaps (and this is an important option) we shall be unable to resolve the apparent contradiction, yet we shall still have such strong reasons otherwise for accepting the view that we will leave the logical problem in abeyance, hoping for a resolution at some time in the future.

That is, of course, what we do when people find apparent contradictions in Scripture. We believe that Scripture is logically consistent, but we realize that for many reasons (our finitude, our sin, the inadequacies of our logical systems, the inadequacy of our premises, our understanding of the terms of the argument, etc.) Scripture may *appear* contradictory. But we do not abandon our faith because of apparent contradiction. Like Abraham, we persevere in faith despite the problems, even when those problems are problems of logic. Thus our human logic is never a final test of truth.[11]

Note therefore that when you seek to refute someone's position, it is never sufficient merely so set forth arguments for an alternative (and incompatible) view. Many modern theologians, for example, argue against the orthodox view of Scripture by presenting arguments for various liberal constructions, without even considering the biblical evidence that motivated the orthodox view in the first place. Many pro-abortionists talk on and on about women's rights, the tragedy of rape, and so forth, without giving any serious attention to the nature of the fetus, the most crucial datum in the anti-abortion case. A prolifer might be unable to refute the pro-abortion arguments, but he will not on that account abandon his position. He may rightly suspect that something *may* be wrong in the abortionist's case, for he is so certain of the arguments that produced his own view. In such situations it is best, then, not only to argue an alternative view but also to refute the arguments that produced the view you are seeking to overthrow.[12] Even then, of course, an opponent convinced of the rightness of his cause may take refuge in the possibility of your being wrong. But the more you cast doubt on those considerations that weigh most heavily with your opponent, the more adequate your argument will be.

(v) *Limitations of the principle of noncontradiction.* The qualifications on the law of noncontradiction noted earlier must also be reckoned with. "Nothing can be both A and not-A *at the same time and in the same respect.*" Those limitations indicate that logic can examine consistency and implication only in relatively changeless situations, that is, when relevant meanings and referents of terms remain the same over the course of the analysis. But as we know, the real world is changing all the time. Therefore logical analysis often can only approximate; it can deal adequately only

11. See my article, "The Problem of Theological Paradox," in *Foundations of Christian Scholarship*, 295-330, also published as a pamphlet, *Van Til the Theologian* (Phillipsburg, N.J.: Pilgrim Publishing, 1976).

12. This may be part of "answering the fool according to his folly" (Prov. 26:5).

with those aspects of reality that do not change—a rather small subset of our experience.

(vi) *Technical terminology*. Logic, in its present form, requires us to translate propositions and arguments that we wish to evaluate into a technical terminology. It is a bit like using a computer. To get the computer to process information, you have to translate that information into a language that the computer understands. Often, however, the meaning of an argument changes somewhat when it is translated into technical language. That is to say, the technical language is not quite equivalent to the language of the original argument. The most obvious case is that of "if . . . then," a very fundamental expression in logic. Many arguments turn on the use of this expression. Its technical meaning, however, is quite different from its meaning in ordinary language. "If p, then q" is equivalent in the technical language of logic to "not p or q." "If you push the button, the bell will sound," then, can be paraphrased, "either you do not push the button, or else the bell will sound." No actual *causal* relation is asserted, as is usually the case in ordinary language.

(vii) *Law of excluded middle*. Like the law of noncontradiction, the "law of the excluded middle" is another basic principle of logic. It says that "Everything is either A or not-A," or "Every proposition is either true or false." This principle simplifies logic by making possible a two-value calculus. But it has been challenged on technical grounds. Three-value and n-value logics have been proposed. From a nontechnical standpoint, we should keep in mind that the principle sometimes distracts our attention from the "fuzzy boundaries" of language. Thinking in terms of the law of the excluded middle, we are inclined to say "either it is raining or it is not raining." There is, it seems, no third possibility, no "middle." What, then, do we say about a heavy mist?[13] Is that rain, or is it nonrain? It should be one or the other, it seems, but neither alternative is comfortable. Either, it seems, we must stretch our normal concept of rain, or we must stretch our normal concept of nonrain. A three-value system in this instance would seem to fit our instincts better. Mist can be treated as "rain" or as "nonrain" equally well and with equal awkwardness. It can be done; we can deal with mist in terms of two values of rain. But to do it that way

13. I owe this illustration to Vern S. Poythress.

somewhat distorts the patterns of ordinary language (as in *(vi)*, above) and presents a somewhat misleading picture of what mist is.

In all these ways, then, logic is limited: it is fallible, is dependent on other disciplines and tools, is incomplete, sometimes distorts the concepts it employs, and does not always speak the decisive word. Therefore it is not unreasonable, sometimes, to be suspicious of *apparently* sound logical reasoning. When someone says that God's goodness is logically inconsistent with the existence of evil or that the oneness of God is inconsistent with His threeness, we may not be able to refute his argument, but we do know now (I trust) that sometimes things *do* go wrong in logic, that an *apparently* sound argument is not always sound after all. Thus, though we ought not to ignore that kind of argument, we need not be intimidated by it, either. Even if we cannot reply, we know that our God has an answer and that He will, in His time, rebuke the foolish (no matter how formidable) objections of men.

E. LOGICAL ORDER

In theology one hears much about the need to put things in logical order or to observe "logical priorities." We may recall Charles Hodge's comment (see Part One) about how theology puts the scriptural teaching into its "proper order." Battles have been fought in theology over such matters as whether God's decree to create "precedes" His decree to elect, or vice versa, whether God's love or His justice has priority over the other, whether or not regeneration "precedes" faith, whether our intellect has "primacy" over our other human faculties, whether the doctrine of predestination ought to be discussed under the doctrine of God or under the application of redemption, whether doctrine is prior to life, or vice versa.

Words like *priority* and *order* are normally used of temporal relations. When we speak of something coming "before" something else, we usually, in the most literal sense, refer to temporal precedence. Most often, however, when theologians talk of priorities, they deny that they have a temporal priority in mind. The order of the divine decrees, for instance, is clearly not a temporal order, for the decrees are all eternal. And a theologian who says that regeneration is prior to faith does not necessarily hold that one can be regenerate *before* believing.

But if the priority is not temporal, what is it? Clearly, at least (and we should remind ourselves of this fact from time to time), *order* and *priority* are used metaphorically and so are subject to all the limitations of metaphors that I discussed in chapter 7, *D*, above.

But in *what* metaphorical sense are those terms being used? Here, matters get confusing. Theologians tend to describe themselves as speaking "not of a temporal but of a *logical* order." But "logical order" is not a clear concept. (Wittgenstein remarked, "Where our language suggests a body and there is none: there, we should like to say, is a *spirit*."[14] Here I am tempted to paraphrase him: when our language suggests temporal order, and there is none: there, we should like to say, is a *logical order*.) A great many relations may be described by *logical order*. Here are some examples.

(i) *Different kinds of order*. In the science of logic itself, there are many kinds of order. There is, first, the priority of premise to conclusion in the *writing* of a syllogism. The premise is generally presented before the conclusion, though there is no absolute necessity for doing it that way.

(ii) *Premise as ground of conclusion*. The premise also "precedes" the conclusion in the more metaphorical sense of being the *reason* or *ground* on the basis of which the conclusion is argued. Remember, however, that this sort of priority can sometimes be reversed. Consider the following two syllogisms.

> (A) If Bill's hair is shorter today than yesterday, it was cut today. His hair is shorter today than yesterday. Therefore it was cut today.
> (B) If Bill's hair was cut today, it is shorter than yesterday. It was cut today. Therefore his hair is shorter today than yesterday.

Notice that in the first syllogism "His hair is shorter . . ." is a premise and "It was cut today" is the conclusion. In the second syllogism, these are reversed. Often, such is the case in logic. A sentence that is "prior to" another (in the sense under discussion) in one argument can be "posterior to" the same sentence in another argument. Thus we cannot speak of the one sentence as being "prior to" the other sentence except in the context of a particular argument. It makes no sense to ask in relation to the above syllogisms if the sentence about the shortness of Bill's hair is "prior to" the sentence about its being cut.

(iii) *Necessary conditionality*. Another kind of "priority" in logic is *necessary conditionality*. "P is a necessary condition of q" means that if q is true,

14. Ludwig Wittgenstein, *Philosophical Investigations* (New York: Macmillan, 1958), 18, no. 36.

p is also true, "p" and "q" being variables representing propositions. It is sometimes described by the phrases, "If q then p," or "q only if p." This means that the truth of p is *necessary* to the truth of q. In valid syllogisms such as those quoted under *(ii)*, the conclusion is a necessary condition for the conjunction of the premises; that is, only if the conclusion is true can all the premises be true.

(iv) *Sufficient conditionality*. Then there is also *sufficient conditionality*, which is in one sense the reverse of the above. "P is a sufficient condition of q" means that if p is true, q is also true. This is symbolized, "If p then q" or "p only if q." Here, the truth of p is *sufficient* to the truth of q. In valid syllogisms, the truth of the premises (all of them) is a sufficient condition of the truth of the conclusion. Notice that if p is "prior to" q in the sense of being the necessary condition of q, then q is "prior to" p in the sense of being the sufficient condition of p.

(v) *Both types of conditionality*. Sometimes a condition may be *both necessary and sufficient*. In these cases, we say "p if and only if q." Here, p is prior to q and q is prior to p, and each priority exists both in sense *(iii)* and in sense *(iv)*.

There are other kinds of priority noted in logic texts, but those above are the ones most likely to be noticed by theologians. But notice that none of them gives us grounds for saying that one doctrine or divine attribute or divine decree is in some general sense "prior" to another. Propositions that are "prior" as necessary conditions are "posterior" as sufficient conditions. Propositions that are "prior" in one argument may be "posterior" in another. So it makes little sense to ask in general whether a particular proposition is prior or posterior to another.

We should, however, consider some other forms of "priority" that do not emerge from the science of logic itself but that are sometimes described as "logical" priorities.

(vi) *Causal priority*. First, there is *causal* priority. A is prior to B if A is the cause of B.

(vii) *The part-whole relation*. Some philosophers find "priority" in the *part-whole relation*. To some, the parts of something, being more "basic," being the things out of which the whole is made, are "prior to" the whole. Others, however, perceive that relation inversely. The whole is more important than any part and therefore is "prior." (Hence the differences, for example, between atomists and idealists.)

(viii) *Teleological priorities*. There are also *teleological* priorities. A is prior to B if A is the purpose for which B exists. Note that this form of priority often leads to opposite results from that of *(vi)*. When A is causally prior to B, B is often teleologically prior to A, since the cause is often for the sake of the effect.

(ix) *Anticipated causality*. There are also priorities of *anticipated causality, teleology, temporality*. A divine plan, for instance, may be understood as organized according to God's anticipations of its outworkings in history. Decree A may be prior to decree B because the event decreed by A has causal, teleological, or temporal precedence over that decreed by B. It is not that decree A actually causes (etc.) decree B but that the historical events ordained by them have such relations.

(x) *Moral or legal causality*. There is also a priority of *moral or legal causality*. Here, A is prior to B because A provides the moral or legal justification for B. These priorities are, of course, important in biblical soteriology.

(xi) *Presuppositional priority*. One may also speak of a *presuppositional* priority—the priority of a presupposition to what presupposes it. One may speak in such a way of authorities, criteria, laws, norms.

(xii) *Instrumental priority*. Also, there is *instrumental* priority, the priority of an instrument to its purpose. This is not quite the same as causality, nor is it quite the reverse of teleology, but the theological distinctions here become quite imprecise. "Instrument" is used metaphorically, since theology does not use literal hammers, saws, and so forth. But its metaphorical character tends to obscure its meaning.

(xiii) *Pedagogical priority*. Finally, I think that often when theologians talk about "logical priority," what they are really talking about is *pedagogical* priority. A good teacher begins with what his students know and proceeds to what they don't know. The students' past knowledge and capacities (plus other factors, such as the teacher's abilities and interests) dictate a certain order of presentation. A pedagogical order can never be engraved in stone; it may change with each audience. But one can often specify roughly where it is best to start in the teaching of a certain doctrine.[15]

Now as one studies the various theological controversies about "logical order," one should be impressed with the fact that theologians are not at all clear about what kind of logical order they are talking about. Consider the classic controversy about the "order of the divine decrees." Supralapsarians and infralapsarians produced two different concepts of how God's eternal decrees were ordered. Since the decrees were eternal, these theologians emphasized that they were not talking about temporal orders, but about logical orders. Here are the two lists of decrees.

Supralapsarianism	*Infralapsarianism*
1. Decree to bless the elect.	1. Decree to create.
2. Decree to create.	2. Decree to permit the Fall.
3. Decree to permit the Fall.	3. Decree to elect.
4. Decree to send Christ.	4. Decree to send Christ.
5. Decree to send the Spirit.	5. Decree to send the Spirit.
6. Decree to glorify the elect.	6. Decree to glorify the elect.

Note that decrees 4-6 are the same on both lists, the only difference being that decree *1* on the supra list becomes, in effect, *3* on the infra list. Now on neither list is there any consistent principle of "order."[16] The supra list begins with a decree that is prior to the others in a teleological sense. It designates the overall purpose that the other decrees bring into effect. Clearly, however, *2* and *3* on the supra list are *not* related teleologically nor are any other two decrees on either list. The relation between *2* and *3* on the supra list may be understood either as anticipated temporal or as presuppositional priority. The rest may be seen the same way, though it is perhaps best to see 4 as providing the moral and legal basis for 5 and 6. The infra list follows mainly a pattern of anticipated temporality, though the place of *3* represents a departure from that pattern, and, again, the relation of 4 to the others is better construed as moral-legal causality.

The whole project, then, seems rather confused, and to our modern eyes, highly speculative. (How can we dare to read the divine mind in this way?) What were these theologians trying to do, anyway? Most likely, in

15. A complete list of "logical priorities" would have to include a great many more, such as the "propositional relations" discussed by modern linguists. See, for example, Robert A. Traina, *Methodical Bible Study* (Wilmore, Ky.: Asbury Theological Seminary, 1952).

16. One could, perhaps, interpret both lists as organized according to necessary conditions, *1* being the necessary condition of *2*, etc. If we interpret them that way, however, the whole dispute appears pointless. The decree to elect and the decree to create could both be necessary conditions of one another. There would then be no need to oppose the two systems.

my view, they were engaging in a kind of primitive anti-abstractionism. The supras were saying, in effect, "See everything in the context of God's electing love." The infras were saying, "See everything in the context of God's unfolding, historically ordered drama." (The infras were the "biblical" theologians of their day.) When we look at it that way, we can see some of the validity of the discussion that generally eludes our modern perception, and we can also see more clearly the nature of its confusion. It is unclarity of the same sort that plagues modern anti-abstractionists. The anti-abstractionist thinks there is some special "relation" between two things that must somehow always be kept in view. But he rarely states clearly what that relation is or distinguishes it from other possible relations. In effect, what the supras and infras had were two *pedagogical* orders that they pitted against one another without recognizing their actual compatibility. They thought they had something *more* than a pedagogical order, but they were misled. (That is a common problem in theology. When we develop a system or strategy that is useful in communicating the truth, we often get puffed up with pride and think that system is really the reflection of some deep, hitherto undiscovered truth about something hidden in the divine nature. I keep having to remind myself of that problem when I meditate on my triperspectivalism, which, sometimes, *seems* to me to reflect something very deep in God's trinitarian nature.)

Similar things can be said about the *ordo salutis*, the order of the events that bring about individual salvation: calling, regeneration, faith, justification, adoption, sanctification, perseverance, glorification. Here, straightforward causal priorities are found, for example, between calling and regeneration and between regeneration and faith. But the relation between faith and justification is *not* causal but "instrumental" in Protestant theology, though the meaning of *instrumental* here has never been clarified to my satisfaction. Justification, furthermore, is neither the efficient cause nor the instrumental cause of adoption or sanctification. Here, something like "legal causality" is in view. But sanctification is not the legal ground of perseverance and glorification. Rather, here, the order seems to follow a pattern of anticipated temporality.

Thus questions about the order of the decrees and the *ordo salutis* are often not clear questions. Similarly, questions about priorities among the divine attributes, the faculties of man, theology and life, and so forth are often not clear. Often these confusions could have been averted if the theologians had been more open to the possibility of *reciprocal* or *perspectival* relations between these realities. The church has, to a large extent, overcome subordinationism within the Trinity and among the divine attributes by, in effect, seeing them perspectivally—each person of the Trinity involving the other two, each attribute involving all the rest. (Such, at least, has been the orthodox understanding of these doctrines. Subordinationism, along with difficulties over "priority," has appeared again in the modern period.) Now such an approach could be of obvious help in discussions of the order of the decrees. When God decrees the creation, of course His decree takes into account His plan to elect and redeem. But the reverse is also true. Each of God's decrees takes account of all the others. Each advances the purposes of all the others.

With the *ordo salutis*, however, it is probably best not to use a perspectival model.[17] There are problems in making justification equivalent to sanctification, for example, at least in the technical theological senses of these terms. (The biblical language, though, suggests broader possibilities. God's holiness and justice, after all, are as inseparable on earth as they are in God's own nature.) And there do seem to be some irreversible priorities in this *ordo*. It would be difficult to find any sense in which, on the Reformed view, faith is prior to regeneration or sanctification to regeneration, for example. But if the *ordo salutis* is not a straightforward order based on a single principle of order and if it is not a group of perspectives, then perhaps it is no longer useful as a central focus of theological discussion. Individual relations among the different doctrines (e.g., the causal priority of regeneration to faith, John 3:3) are still important, but I question the value of putting all these doctrines into a single "logical" chain. The *ordo* may have been a useful *pedagogical* tool at one time, but I believe that as such it has probably outlived its usefulness. But again, we are tempted to mistake pedagogical tools, sanctified by tradition, for doctrinal necessities. Let us have the courage to change our pedagogy when the need arises—becoming all things to all men that we may gain some.

I have a similar reaction to the more recent attempts to make a certain order of topics normative for theology. We recall (see the discussion in Part One) Hodge's claim that theology puts biblical doctrines in their "proper order." Even in our own century, some theologians have argued, for example, that it is wrong to discuss predestination in terms of the doctrine of God. Rather it is necessary, they argue, to discuss it under the ap-

17. Of course, our *knowledge* of these doctrines is clearly perspectival. We cannot understand sanctification fully until we have understood justification—and vice versa. We understand all doctrines simultaneously, as it were.

plication of redemption.[18] There are some advantages in certain pedagogical orders, but these advantages are subtle, and they vary greatly, depending on the audience. Although there is value in discussing predestination, for example, as a source of assurance of salvation, there is nothing wrong with presenting it as an eternal act of God which, of course, it is. There is no order that is normative for all audiences and situations, unless that order be the order of Scripture itself, an order from which every theology, in the nature of the case, departs to some degree. To claim some normative order for theology is either to misunderstand the nature of theology (as an imitation of Scripture rather than an application of it) or to find fault with Scripture's own form.

Such claims are, moreover, anti-abstractionist in character, demanding that we "see x in the context of y rather than in the context of z." As such, they fall prey to all the theological and linguistic confusions characteristic of anti-abstractionism.

Again, let us recognize a pedagogical order for what it is, not seeking to turn it into some metaphysical or epistemological necessity. It is a tool to use with a particular audience to make a specific point from the Scriptures. Let us not try to give it extra dignity by calling it a "logical" order. Those who can be the most help to us here are not logicians but educators.

F. MUTUAL IMPLICATIONS AMONG DOCTRINES

As theologians ponder the truths of Scripture, they come to see more and more relations between them, to see them more and more systematically. God's Word is a wondrous organism, and as we read it in faith, we come to see new ways in which the parts are interrelated, testifying to its divine authorship.

Thus each doctrine reveals intimate connections with all the others. This happens to such an extent that each doctrine becomes a perspective on the whole biblical message. Full understanding of the doctrine of God, for example, requires an understanding of the doctrines of Scripture, man, sin, Christ, salvation, and eschatology. Thus, in a sense, the doctrine of God includes or implies all the others, and they also include and imply the doctrine of God.

18. See Brian Armstrong, *Calvinism and the Amyraut Heresy* (Milwaukee, Wisc.: University of Wisconsin Press, 1969), reviewed by me in *WTJ* 34 (1972): 186-92. Also see my Appendix A, "On Theological Encyclopedia," following Part One above.

And so it often comes as an exciting discovery that doctrines that seem at first glance to be opposed are actually complementary, if not actually dependent one on another. For Calvinists, for example, divine sovereignty and human freedom are examples of that sort of dependence and complementarity. Although at first glance those doctrines *appear* to be opposed to one another, a closer look shows that without divine sovereignty there would be no meaning in human life and therefore no meaningful form of freedom. And if our concern for freedom is essentially a concern to maintain human ethical responsibility, we should observe that divine sovereignty is the source of human responsibility. Because the *sovereign* Lord is the cause of and authority over human responsibility, we can say that God's sovereignty—His absolute lordship—*establishes human responsibility*. Thus Scripture often places the two doctrines side by side, with no embarrassment or sense of impropriety whatsoever (cf. Acts 2:23; 4:27f.; Phil. 2:12f.). Human responsibility exists not "in spite of" but "because of" God's sovereignty. Not only are the two compatible; they require each other.[19]

For the reasons we just discussed—the connectivity and complementarity of doctrines—theological doctrines have a tendency to become analytic as opposed to synthetic. Recall this distinction from our earlier discussions: an "analytic" statement is a statement that is true by virtue of the meanings of its terms, such as "Bachelors are unmarried." All other statements are synthetic. Now I mentioned earlier that this distinction is not a sharp one since meanings are often fuzzy and changeable. If, for example, we include "spotted" in our definition of a Dalmatian, "The Dalmatian is spotted" will be analytic; otherwise the same sentence would be synthetic.

Now "God is good" sounds like a synthetic statement. One can imagine some "gods" that are not good. But the more we study Christian theology, the more we learn that God's attributes are inseparable from Him—inseparable to the extent that He would not be God at all if He were not, for example, good. Thus *good* becomes part of the definition of *God*, part of its meaning. "God is good," then, becomes analytic. Even a historical statement like "Jesus was born of a virgin" can be taken analytically. Evangelicals often speak in this manner: "The only Jesus we know is the Jesus who is virgin-born; any other Jesus is not the Bible's Jesus, not our Jesus at all." Thus it is that *virgin-born* becomes part of the definition of *Jesus*, an attrib-

19. For more on these matters, see my "The Problem of Theological Paradox," cited earlier.

ute defining Him, inseparable from Him. And thus it is that everything in Scripture becomes in our minds inseparable from the "central message" of Scripture.

In Part One, I argued that there is a very close relation in Scripture between understanding God's truth and believing it. It is, of course, possible for unbelievers to know God after a fashion, to have some understanding of the truth. But, as we have seen, that understanding is seriously defective, even from an "intellectual" perspective. For Scripture teaches that it is *stupid* to know God's revelation and to refuse to obey it. Those who understand the truth in the most profound sense will inevitably believe and obey. Our discussion here of analyticity confirms that conclusion. Since the teachings of Scripture are analytically included in its concepts, one cannot adequately understand the concepts without understanding the teachings. And this process ordinarily presupposes not only understanding but belief. Someone, for example, who is certain that a virgin birth is impossible will have to conclude that the biblical concept, the biblical definition of Christ, is incoherent. Thus, because of unbelief, he will fail to understand the very meaning of *Christ*.

The analytical nature of theological statements is correlative to and illustrative of the peculiar certainty that (as we have seen) attaches to propositions that articulate our fundamental presuppositions. Analytic statements like "Bachelors are unmarried" and "Dalmatians are spotted" are generally considered to be statements of the highest degree of certainty (though see the qualifications on this point made above under *B*). Similarly, the analytical nature of "God is good" helps us to sense the kind of certainty that this sort of statement has for the Christian. I would not want to say that such statements are certain *because* they are analytic; the reasons for our certainty are deeper than that. But the analytical nature of those statements is an index of the quality of certainty that we have. Studying interrelations among doctrines, then, is an apologetic tool, a means of challenging unbelief and of strengthening our faith.

Exploring those relations of meaning and logical interdependence among doctrines is particularly the work of systematic theology. Such explorations give to the believer a sense of the unity of the Scriptures and of the wisdom of God. These must be balanced, of course, with an appreciation for the transcendence of God's wisdom. Often because of our finitude or sin or both, we are not able to *see* those interconnections. Often, indeed, doctrines appear to contradict one another.[20] But we must keep

20. This matter, also, is discussed above.

trying to see what we can see, what God has revealed to us. And often the interdependences are wonderful to behold.

G. BURDEN OF PROOF

Frequently in a theological argument, it is important to establish where the burden of proof lies. Here are some examples.

(1) Baptism

An obvious example is the question of infant baptism. Because the New Testament is relatively silent on this question, we are faced with two alternative approaches. We can assume continuity with the Old Testament principle of administering the sign of the covenant to children, unless New Testament evidence directs us otherwise, and this is the paedobaptist approach. Or we can assume that only adult believers are to be baptized, unless there is New Testament evidence to the contrary, and this is the antipaedobaptist (= "baptist") approach. On the first approach, the burden of proof is on the baptist to show New Testament evidence against infant baptism. On the second approach, the burden of proof is on the paedobaptist to show New Testament evidence for it. In this case, determining the burden of proof pretty much decides the question, since there is little explicit New Testament evidence on either side and since the two parties are pretty much agreed on the Old Testament data. It seems to me that the first approach is correct: the church of the New Testament is essentially the same as the church of the Old. When first-century Jews heard Peter say "The promise is to you and to your children" (Acts 2:39) and when people were baptized by households, surely, it seems to me, they would have taken these words as indications of continuity with Old Testament covenant thinking. A man upon conversion brings his family with him, and the sign of the covenant is administered to all. It is possible that this system may have changed with the transition to the New Covenant, but if such a change has taken place, baptists must demonstrate this.

(2) Abortion

Another example concerns abortion. Must we assume that the unborn child is a person in the absence of evidence to the contrary, or must we demand proof of his personhood before according him the rights of a human being? Here we are not faced with an argument from total silence. Scripture does speak of the unborn child in personal terms (e.g., Ps. 139), and there is Old Testament legislation that, on the best interpretation, protects the interests of the unborn (Exod. 21:22-25). Still, the case for the personhood of the child is not, in my view, watertight. Ought we, then, to "hang loose" on the issue until we hear a clinching argument, or should we treat the child as a person until its personhood is disproved? I believe the latter course is the right one. At the very least, we can make a highly probable case that the child is a human being, protected by the sixth commandment. Scripture warns us against even the accidental killing of a human being (Deut. 19:4-7; cf. Matt. 5:21-26). Therefore even "probable" cases of murder are to be avoided. We are to give the benefit of the doubt in life-and-death issues.

Burden of proof, then, must not be assigned arbitrarily. To determine who has the burden of proof, a theological argument based on Scripture is required. Often, however, this important matter is not discussed, and contending parties simply make their own assumptions in this area, frequently without stating them. Thus communication is obscured. But the issue of burden of proof is often a very important matter that must be decided before the relevance of the other evidence can be ascertained.

H. SOME ARGUMENT TYPES

Obviously, it will not be possible to include a full course in logic in this book. The student of theology, however, ought to be aware of some types of logical reasoning, both good and bad, that are relevant to his discipline, and that is the purpose of this section and the next. In this section I will examine several general types of arguments of interest to us, and in the next section I will discuss fallacies. The argument types are as follows.

(1) DEDUCTION

Logicians have traditionally divided arguments into the categories of deduction and induction. A deductive argument claims that its premises imply the conclusion. That is, if the premises are true, the conclusion cannot fail to be true. In a "valid" deductive argument, that is the case; the premises necessitate the truth of the conclusion. In a "sound" deductive argument, not only is the logic valid but the premises are true, yielding therefore a true conclusion. There are many deductive arguments in theology, such as "God's Word is true; the Bible is God's Word; therefore the Bible is true." I have defended earlier the propriety of such arguments, having also noted above (C and D) some of the limitations of logical deduction.

(2) INDUCTION

An inductive argument is an argument that does not make the claim of a deductive argument. An inductive argument claims not that the premises render the conclusion certain but only that the premises render the conclusion *probable*. Usually an inductive argument will begin with particular facts and reason to the probability of a general conclusion. Experimental methods in science yield inductive arguments. An experiment repeated a few hundred times is evidence for a general conclusion, a conclusion that the whole universe behaves in accordance with a certain law. Obviously, if we are seeking *deductive* proof, a few hundred experiments do not prove anything about the whole universe. But in some cases they may constitute a sufficient statistical sample for making generalizations, thus warranting an inductively legitimate conclusion.

There are inductive arguments in theology. For example, "Scripture in x number of cases refers to unborn children using personal terms (personal pronouns, etc.) and never refers to them in any way that suggests they lack personhood. Therefore it regards unborn children as persons." That argument, I think, has considerable force, granted the burden of proof argued earlier (G) on this matter. But it has less force, I think, than an explicit statement in Scripture of the conclusion or than a deductive argument might have.

Another example: "Scriptural teachings have proved true over and over again against the assaults of unbelieving science; therefore Scripture is God's Word." True enough, I think, but it doesn't exhaust all the relevant data. Not *every* conflict between Scripture and science has been decisively resolved in the Bible's favor; "problems" remain. This argument is not, therefore, as strong as the deductive argument: "God's Word is true; Scripture is God's Word; therefore Scripture is true."[21]

21. Stephen Toulmin, in *The Uses of Argument* (cited earlier), objects to the classification of all arguments as "deductive" and "inductive," believing that this twofold division obscures other important distinctions. His point has some force, but his alternative distinctions, I think, would make this discussion much more technical, without providing more help in the theological context.

Still, there is a place for inductive arguments in theology to confirm the deductive arguments and our exegetical formulations. On the questions of probability and certainty, see chapter 5, *A, (8)* and *B* in this chapter.

(3) *REDUCTIO AD ABSURDUM*

The categories "deduction" and "induction" exhaust, I believe, all logical arguments, but there are other ways of "dividing the pie." There are certain *kinds* of deductive and inductive arguments that deserve reflection. One kind of deductive argument that plays a large role in theology is the *reductio ad absurdum*, the reduction of an opposing position to absurdity. In logic, this phrase refers not to mere ridicule but to a logical process. The opposing position is assumed to be true "for the sake of argument." From that position, as a premise, there is deduced an absurdity. The fact that an absurdity is deduced from the premise proves (or such is the claim) that the premise is false. A *reductio* is like an indirect proof in geometry.

Thus theologians often seek to refute one another by showing what they take to be the "logical consequences" of the other's view. Arminians argue that the Calvinistic view of divine sovereignty reduces men to the status of robots. Van Til claims that traditional apologetics implicitly denies the Creator-creature distinction. Process theologians argue that if God is supratemporal, He cannot answer prayer. Theonomists (who maintain that the penalties for crimes listed in the Mosaic law are still in effect) claim that those who disagree with them are at least "incipiently" or "latently" antinomian (i.e., denying our obligation to obey any divine commands). In Van Til's apologetics, the *reductio* plays a central role. The apologist presupposes the unbeliever's position "for the sake of argument" and on the basis of the unbeliever's own premises seeks to show that the unbeliever's position reduces to sheer chaos, incoherence. (More on that in chapter 11.) Sometimes, such arguments are cogent, sometimes not. Careful analysis is needed.

A *reductio* may be invalidated by ambiguity, logical fallacy, or errors in the premises. Also, the concept of "absurdity" may lead us astray. What is absurd to one person may not be to another. Subjective judgments are involved here, and the theologian must always subject his judgment to the Word of God and must listen carefully to others who don't share his aversion to a particular "absurd" conclusion. What is absurd often depends on the overall structure of a particular theological system. Thomas Kuhn indicates that in scientific disputes what is self-evident to one school of thought may seem absurd to another. To geocentric astronomers, for example, the thought of the earth "moving" was absurd, because to them the earth was the reference point from which all other motions were calculated. But in a heliocentric view, a moveable earth is not only a meaningful concept, it is taken to be an obvious truth and not at all difficult to prove. To Einsteinian scientists, the notion of "curved space" seems reasonable, but that concept may seem absurd to the average lay person.

Now in theology, something similar often happens. Before the Reformation, it would have sounded absurd, to many, to talk about "justification apart from works." Isn't this notion a blatant contradiction to James 2:24? And doesn't it contradict the overall biblical teaching that justified persons will do good works? But during the Reformation, new distinctions were made, particularly a technical distinction between justification and sanctification, and a distinction between the basis of justification and the accompaniments of it. Granted those distinctions, talk of "justification apart from works" (carefully guarded against misunderstanding) could be seen as an obvious, biblical truth.

A true and valid *reductio* must be distinguished from its fallacious imitators, one of which is the "slippery slope" argument. A slippery slope argument goes like this. "If you take position A, you run the risk of taking position B; position B is wrong, therefore A is also wrong." Thus it is sometimes said that once one abandons belief in a pretribulational rapture, he runs the risk of denying the bodily return of Christ altogether, thus opening himself up to a thoroughgoing liberalism. Or it is sometimes argued that if one accepts the textual criticism of Westcott and Hort, he runs the risk of denying biblical authority altogether. Thus the slippery slope argument appeals to fear—to our fear of taking undue risks and to our fear of being linked with people (such as liberals), disapproved of in our circles, lest we incur guilt by association.

Often slippery slope arguments are buttressed by historical examples. Such-and-such a theologian began by denying, say, total abstinence from alcoholic beverages, and five years later he abandoned the Christian faith. Or such-and-such a denomination rejected the exclusive use of Psalms as hymns in worship, and twenty-five years later it capitulated to liberalism. On the use of such historical references in theological arguments, see chapter 9. In general, they prove nothing. Usually, they do not rest on a sufficient statistical sample to establish even probable conclusions. And they ignore the complexities of historical causation. A denomination becomes liberal for *many* reasons, never just one. On the one hand, it may well be that rejection of exclusive Psalmody is in some cases at least a *symptom* of advancing liberalism. (I say that as an opponent of exclusive

Psalmody, who nevertheless recognizes that people sometimes reject exclusive Psalmody for very bad reasons.) On the other hand, the denomination may be rejecting exclusive Psalmody for good reasons. This development may be quite independent of any trend toward liberalism, or it may bear a paradoxical relation to that trend. For example, the liberal trend may, for a time, help the church to break free of unbiblical traditions—God's bringing a good result out of an overall evil development. (It could be argued that development toward liberalism in the Presbyterian Church U.S., for example, enabled that denomination to take a strong stand against dispensationalism, a stand that to many nonliberals was a good thing.) Thus not very much can be deduced from historical examples. They ought to make us think twice about what we are doing. They suggest possibilities, but they are never normative in themselves.

The fact, then, that seminaries and denominations that deny total biblical inerrancy often come to reject other Christian doctrines does not, in itself, *prove* that inerrancy is true. In this case, however, I think the historical generalization—the correlation between denying inerrancy and denying other biblical doctrines—is a sound and cautionary one that can be supported with many historical examples and that makes intuitive sense. When people deny the fundamental authority for Christian doctrine, one may expect that sooner or later they will reject some of those doctrines themselves. But there is no *logical necessity* for that happening. James Orr, for example, denied inerrancy in the sense that Warfield affirmed it, but Orr remained orthodox all his life in other areas of doctrine. Thank God for human inconsistency!

(4) Dilemma

A dilemma is a kind of double *reductio* that seeks to show that an opposing view leads to either of *two* undesirable consequences. Paul Tillich, for example, often sought to show that those who opposed his views were forced into a choice between two bad alternatives. He said that unless one adopted his view of "theonomy" (very different from the kind of theonomy referred to in the last section!), he would be forced to choose between "autonomy" (man as his own law) or "heteronomy" (bondage to some less-than-ultimate authority). "Theonomy," he explained, was "autonomous reason united with its own depth" that escapes the inadequacies of the other two approaches.[22]

22. Tillich, *Systematic Theology* (Chicago: University of Chicago Press, 1951), I, 83-86.

Van Til also makes frequent use of the dilemma. He seeks to show that non-Christian thought must choose between rationalism and irrationalism or some (necessarily unstable) combination of the two (cf. earlier discussions in this book). He also charges that less-than-Reformed types of theology either deify the creation or reduce God to the level of creation, thus invalidating the Creator-creature distinction.

Dilemmas can be sound logical arguments, but unsound examples abound in theology. Tillich's are often good examples of the latter. Frequently, he presents his view as if it were the only alternative to the undesirable positions he mentions, when in fact there are other possibilities. Furthermore, he suggests that anyone who denies his view must hold one of the undesirable ones, a suggestion that is often simply untrue. Orthodox Calvinists, in my view, are neither "autonomists" nor "heteronomists" in Tillich's sense. (Tillich would probably charge them with heteronomy; but their submission to the Word of God is *not* submission to something finite; it is submission to God himself.) Tillich, in other words, "stacks the deck" in his favor by listing only certain possible positions out of many—two obviously undesirable views and his own. Thus he makes his own view appear inevitable—true by process of elimination. All this is understandable enough, and Tillich is not being consciously dishonest. To him, his own view *is* inevitable and the only viable alternative, for he has presupposed a structure in which that is the case. But the rest of us cannot and ought not to accept Tillich's structure uncritically.

(5) *A Fortiori*

An *a fortiori* argument is one "from the lesser to the greater." It occurs in Scripture. The author to the Hebrews argues, for example, that if the Old Testament law was binding and transgressions against it punished, then certainly (an implicit "all the more") rebellion against the New Covenant will be punished (Heb. 2:3f.; cf. Rom. 5:15, "For if the many died by the trespass of the one man, how much more did God's grace and the gift that came by the grace of the one man, Jesus Christ, overflow to the many!" cf. v. 17). One hears this type of argument also in theology. For example, "If children received the sign of the covenant in the Old Testament, is it not all the more likely that they would receive it in the New Testament as a result of the greater grace of the New Covenant?"

Obviously, however, not all *a fortiori* arguments are sound. Consider this one. "Since the poor are entitled to free medical care, certainly the rich ought to be given the same." Or consider this one. "If God worked miracles prior to the closing of the canon, certainly He should do so even more afterwards to testify to the completion of His revelatory work." And here is another: "If getting baptized once is a means of grace, getting baptized many times is an even greater means of grace." You can see that this type of argument is not always cogent.

To avoid the pitfalls of *a fortiori* arguments, we need to remember the following. (A) "Greatness" can mean different things that presuppose different kinds of value judgments. (B) To make an *a fortiori* argument work, the greatness must be of a type that is relevant to the particular argument. (C) Even relevant forms of greatness do not justify corresponding increases in all other variables. "Getting baptized many times" is numerically greater than "getting baptized once," but the former is not accompanied by an increase of grace parallel to its numerical superiority.

(6) THROWAWAY ARGUMENTS

What I call "throwaway arguments" are those that carry little weight, but that—at least for those who already accept the conclusion—have some confirmatory value. For instance, orthodox writers on scriptural authority sometimes point out that the phrase "Thus says the Lord" is found hundreds of times on the pages of Scripture, indicating its claim to being the Word of God. This argument carries little weight with liberals, for they can easily account for the phrase as the utterances of prophets, not about the written canon but about their own prophecies. Furthermore, even if this phrase did deal with the canon of Scripture, a liberal would feel free in terms of his system to declare that utterance in error. Thus the argument in question presupposes the conclusion it seeks to establish and is therefore somewhat "narrowly circular" (that phrase recalling our earlier discussion in chapter 5, A, (6)) and so is relatively unpersuasive to those who reject that conclusion.

At the same time, the argument is not entirely worthless. "Thus says the Lord" clearly does apply to those portions of Scripture that are of prophetic origin. And there are reasons for saying that all Scripture is *prophecy* in that sense. Thus granted at least a few orthodox assumptions (and of course there is no such thing as an apologetic argument without assumptions), the argument has some force for those who are already convinced. Thus this sort of argument ought not to be the "centerpiece," at least, of a presentation to the unpersuaded.

(7) OTHERS . . .

For anti-abstractionist arguments, see chapter 6, *A* and later (passim). For arguments based on analogy, metaphor, and models (what Arthur Holmes calls "adduction"), see chapter 7, *D*. For the argumentative use of parables and other unusual theological devices to motivate "seeing as," see chapter 5, C, *(5)*. For arguments using historical, scientific, and philosophical information, see below.

I. FALLACIES

In this section I will point out some ways in which theological arguments can (and do) fail. Although it is not possible to enumerate all of them or even to approach the completeness of a full text in logic, the student should be aware of at least some of the more common reasons that arguments fail—arguments in general and theological arguments in particular.

We also should note—something we do not usually do—that even fallacious arguments generally have some value. Many fallacious arguments do prove something or at least yield some confirmation, presumption, or probability. The main problem with fallacious arguments is that their usefulness is misconstrued by their authors, their audience, or both. I shall try to point out the positive values and the limitations of these arguments.

Some forms of fallacious reasoning have already been discussed. For circularity, see chapter 5, *A*, *(6)*—noticing again both the limitations and the value (indeed the necessity) of circular argument and the different kinds of circularity. For anti-abstractionism, see chapter 6, *A*; for problems of ambiguity, see chapter 7—especially references to technical terms, word-level versus sentence-level arguments, misuses of metaphors, and negation. Also see "the limitations of logic" in chapter 8, *D* and "logical order" in section *E* of that same chapter (a section that exposes ambiguities in the concept of "logical priority"). For mistakes in assessing burden of proof, see section G in this chapter. For "slippery slope" arguments, see the immediately previous section (section *H*) under heading *(3) reductio*. Note also the other discussions in section *H* that show how otherwise legitimate argument forms can lead to false conclusions.

We will now discuss the following fallacies.[23]

(1) Irrelevant Conclusion

Irrelevant conclusion (also known as *ignoratio elenchi*) refers to using an argument for one conclusion, irrelevantly, to prove a different one. For example, in a debate over Dooyeweerd's distinction between naive experience and theoretical thought, a speaker defended Dooyeweerd by saying that theoretical thinkers ought not to look down their noses at common people. He argued well against intellectual snobbery but said nothing relevant to Dooyeweerd's specific distinction. Or note the tendency of politicians to speak in generalities about our need to "have compassion for the poor" or our need for "a strong defense"—generalities that are usually accepted by all parties, ideologies, and candidates but that have little clear relevance to the specific problems at issue. Another theological example is this. In an argument over infant baptism, a Baptist might argue that it is wrong to give children a false assurance of salvation. A paedobaptist will reply that infant baptism does not do this, since the fact of baptism does not guarantee the salvation of the individual. To the paedobaptist, the Baptist's argument is irrelevant.

Related to this fallacy is the tendency for theologians to counter a theological assertion with another that is not clearly contradictory to it. See the earlier discussion of "false disjunctions" in chapter 7, *E*.

We should seek to make our arguments relevant to our conclusions, and we should also remember that relevance is a relative matter. As I indicated in the discussion of anti-abstractionism, everything is, after all, related to everything else. Someone might be charged with irrelevance for including an exposition of Isaiah 26:19 in a lecture on "Paul's Doctrine of the Resurrection." After all, Isaiah is not Paul! But the lecturer might reply that the reference is relevant because both Isaiah and Paul are inspired writers, and whatever Paul's view is, he will not disagree with Isaiah. Thus an exposition of Isaiah 26 at least tells us something that Paul would not disagree with! Well, yes, there is *some* relevance in that argument, though perhaps not enough.

Similarly, the speakers in our earlier examples might claim *some* relevance to their arguments. The Dooyeweerdian's distinction between naive experience and theoretical thought indicates a real fear (perhaps a serious

23. Many of the illustrations and much of the general structure of what follows come from Irving M. Copi, *Introduction to Logic*. The theological illustrations and observations are my own.

motivation behind Dooyeweerd's own thinking at this point) that without some such distinction our everyday thinking would be nothing more than a defective version of theoretical thought. In effect, the Dooyeweerdian is challenging the non-Dooyeweerdian to provide an alternative means of avoiding this danger. To one who accepts the unstated premise that only Dooyeweerd's philosophy escapes this problem, the argument in question is cogent. The politician who advocates "compassion for the poor" is generally convinced (on other grounds, presently unstated) that only a certain political program is really able to help the poor. Thus, he believes, that anyone who opposes that program either lacks compassion or is unintentionally hindering the implementation of compassion. Assuming an audience that agrees with those assumptions, the argument is not entirely irrelevant, though even with such an audience it is usually best to be more specific. The baptist really believes that people grow up in paedobaptist churches with a false assurance, no matter what the official theology of the church may say. That is a matter of deep concern to him, so much that it may be a major factor in motivating him to adopt his particular view (though it is not properly a *reason* for such a view). To some, the perceived ability of baptist theology (and the inability of paedobaptist theology) to deal with this question is the most weighty consideration in the argument.

Thus there are *degrees* and *kinds* of relevance. And an "irrelevant" argument, as our examples reveal, is often an argument that has unexpressed premises that a particular audience would prefer to have expressed. This, too, is a relative issue. No argument expresses *all* of its premises. Expressing all the premises of an argument would require one to express all his presuppositions: metaphysical, epistemological, and ethical. It would also require him to construct arguments for each of the premises of the argument under consideration and to state each of *those* premises explicitly. No argument does that. Thus one must try to use good judgment in deciding *how many* premises of a particular argument he will explicitly state. And that judgment will depend, at least in part, on what audience is being addressed. If one makes a wrong judgment for a particular audience, the argument may be perceived as irrelevant.

The question of relevance also has *theological* ramifications. What is relevant often depends on one's theological presuppositions. To some biblical scholars, sayings of Jesus recorded in the Gospels that agree significantly with the thought of the postresurrection church as expressed in Acts and the Epistles are suspected of being nonauthentic. To evangelicals, that argument is quite irrelevant. Agreement of Jesus with the apostolic church is not cause for suspicion; rather it is the expected thing. Thus relevance is not only a pretheological or metatheological issue; it is often a theological issue as such.

(2) THREAT OF FORCE

Threat of force (also known as *ad baculum*) is a specific form of the fallacy of irrelevance described above and of the argument *ad hominem*, which we will discuss next. It has a specific thrust that deserves to be discussed separately. This sort of argument says, "Accept this conclusion, or else something bad will happen to you." In politics it often takes the form, "Vote for this legislation, or my group won't support you for re-election." In orthodox theology, the equivalent threat is that of church discipline. It might seem that this type of argument is rare in liberal circles, but that is not the case. In liberal theological circles the threat of academic ostracization is strong. Those who stray from fashionable liberalism often find themselves denied teaching positions, tenure, and opportunities to publish. When Bultmann declared that modern men "cannot" believe in the miraculous, he was expressing his version of the rules of the liberal theological game. Those who break those rules do not find peer approval. It is important to recognize that. Often it is claimed that people become liberal out of "intellectual honesty," out of a desire to formulate their honest convictions apart from the heavy pressures of tradition and discipline. But that claim must be questioned. The traditions of the liberal academic establishment are every bit as narrow and coercive as is church discipline within orthodoxy.

An "argument" based on the threat of force is not a sound one. The fact that one will be punished for believing "p" doesn't make "p" false. At the same time the threat of force is not *entirely* irrelevant to the conclusion under discussion. As Thomas Kuhn points out, theories and other important beliefs are based on "paradigms"—presuppositions of a sort—that are accepted by a whole community, not merely by individuals. That is certainly the case with theology. And every community has the right to determine its membership. Every theological community must decide how much deviation from the group's presuppositions is consistent with community "membership in good standing."

In the Christian church, discipline has been ordained by God. If I maintain a disputed view and someone points out that this view has been deemed heretical by my church, I must take that seriously. I have taken solemn vows to accept the discipline of my "fathers and brothers" in Christ. I respect the teachers of my church, otherwise I would not be a part of it. Not that the church is infallible. But its judgment is generally better than that of any individual, including myself. This is especially the case with doctrines like the Trinity, which have been officially defined for hundreds of years. Although it is theoretically possible for the church to be wrong that long, it is most unlikely.

Thus the argument *ad baculum* reminds me to respect legitimate authority. Also, the threat itself is not irrelevant to me. Obviously, I do not *want* to undergo discipline. That is not necessarily a selfish desire. I do not want to be cut off from my brothers in Christ—for my sake, but also for theirs, and for the sake of the unity of the body, which is precious to God. If in conscience I must separate, then I must. In the final analysis, we must obey God rather than men (Acts 5:29), but I must seek to avoid such a break, even at high cost.

The argument *ad baculum* is also helpful in revealing the structure of a system. Often when such a threat is made (though frequently this is not true in theology!), it is made about something very central to the system—a basic presupposition. We can sometimes learn what is most important to a thinker when we learn those propositions for which he is willing to fight.

(3) Comparative *Ad Hominem* Argument

Ad hominem means "to the man." Thus an *ad hominem* argument is an argument directed against a person, rather than against a conclusion. As such, it is a form of "irrelevant conclusion argument." This form of *ad hominem* argument, which I call "comparative," is sometimes called "abusive." In this argument, one attacks a conclusion by attacking the people who hold it. This sort of argument is common in theology. For example, someone might argue that "Van Til shouldn't believe in a concrete universal, because Hegel held that view, and Hegel taught many errors." The argument can also be used in reverse to recommend a conclusion by praising the people who believe that conclusion. For example, "You should believe in predestination because Calvin did, and Calvin was a great man."

Now it is not very hard to show that those kinds of arguments are invalid. Often, theological "bad guys" are right, and often "good guys" are wrong. The invalidity of this type of argument is especially clear in the following example. "We must not believe in one God, for Arminius believed in one God, and he taught many errors." Also, ambiguity often plays a role. In the earlier example, Van Til's concept of the "concrete universal" is very different from Hegel's.

The *comparative ad hominem argument* is even more obviously wrong when it is based on *terms*, rather than on sentences.[24] Often a theological view will be condemned simply by associating it with a despised label or term, as in "This is a *dogmatic* view." Or as in "Professor X holds a *static*, rather than a dynamic, view of revelation." Or "Orthodoxy thinks *abstractly* about Scripture" (see chapter 6, A). Most often, too, the term in question is undefined and used as a nasty name, rather than as a serious description.

Another direction this type of argument takes among theologians is to condemn a position merely because it originated during a period of church history that they do not highly regard. (This type of argument also may be seen as a species of the genetic fallacy. See below, *(11)*.) Those who oppose biblical inerrancy often contend that it began in twentieth-century fundamentalism, in seventeenth-century orthodoxy, in medieval scholasticism, in postapostolic legalism, or in intertestamental Judaism. These theologians propose alternative views that they trace to more favored periods: the modern age ("the newest is the truest"), the Reformation, Augustine, Paul (perhaps!), Jesus.

That sort of reasoning not only is found in discussions of inspiration but is common in theological debates on all subjects. Thus theological discussions (especially, but not only, in liberal theology) are often terribly predictable. Substitute almost any doctrine for "x" in the following schema; it will sound familiar to those well read in contemporary theology!

> We should believe doctrine x. Though x was taught by Jesus and Paul, later New Testament writers, influenced by legalism, de-emphasized it, as did the Apostolic Fathers. Glimmerings of this truth are found in Ignatius, Irenaeus, and Tertullian but not in Clement or Origen. Augustine rediscovered it, but taught it inconsistently, whereupon it was neglected during the dark ages. Luther and Calvin made it the center (!) of their thought, but it was ignored by their seventeenth-century successors (except for glimmerings in the Westminster Confession and in the writings of some of the Puritans). There it languished until rediscovered by Professor A in 19xx.

On the general question of resolving theological issues by appeals to church history, see chapter 9. Here I would note that such arguments are unsound for the following reasons. First, there is no reason why a good doctrine cannot originate in a "bad" period, or vice versa. Second, these critics radically differ among themselves as to *which* "bad" period marked the

24. See the critique of word-level versus sentence-level arguments in chapter 6, C, *(1)*.

beginning, for example, of the orthodox view of inspiration. Their differences on this matter (and many others) are so great that their views virtually cancel one another out. It is hard to avoid the suspicion that arguments like those are usually arbitrary concoctions to present the doctrine in question in the most favorable light (a little bit like using the testimony of celebrities to advertise soap), rather than the results of serious historical study. Third, the idea of a "bad" period of church history is terribly unclear and generally hard to prove. And the thinkers in question almost never assume the burden of proof.[25]

Nevertheless, even the comparative *ad hominem* argument has some value. As I indicated earlier in *(2)* above, theologians are members of communities, and the very nature of communities is that they have communal heroes and villains—communal loyalties and communal enmities. These loyalties and enmities are not necessarily wrong. One often joins a community precisely because he admires the same theologians, the same confessional tradition that that community admires, and he agrees also with the community's dislikes. Association of a doctrine with a community hero does not prove the truth of that doctrine, but it does rightly give us a favorable predisposition to it. Calvin, for example, was not right about everything; but he was on target so often, and his divine gift of theological perception is so evident, that we disagree with him at considerable peril.

Similarly, if I am told that my doctrine was held by, say, the Gnostics or the Pelagians, I should rightly worry a bit, and perhaps rethink or even reconsider it. The errors of heretics are often interrelated, and so my proud doctrinal discovery may be at best a "backdoor" route to heresy. If we do use an idea from Arius or Pelagius, we should exercise special care to separate the idea from their errors. If someone is notoriously confused, we ought at least to be wary of agreeing with him.

(4) Positive Circumstantial *ad Hominem* Argument

The positive circumstantial *ad hominem* argument urges the hearer to believe a proposition because of his special circumstances. For example, "You're a democrat; therefore, you should be voting for bigger welfare programs." Or "Because you are wealthy, you should support repeal of the graduated tax." Or "Because you are a woman, you should have voted for Geraldine Ferraro." Or "Since you are a Presbyterian, you should never support independent mission boards." Or "Since you are a modern man,

25. See my review of Brian Armstrong, *Calvinism and the Amyraut Heresy*.

you ought not to believe in angels and demons" (Bultmann). Or "Believe in process theology, for it enables us to support such fashionable modern goals as the liberation of women, blacks, and the third world" (a kind of argument found often throughout John Cobb and D. R. Griffin, *Process Theology* [Philadelphia: Westminster Press, 1976]).

On the one hand, like the other fallacies, the positive circumstantial *ad hominem* does not prove its conclusion. The fact that one is a woman, for example, does not prove that she has any obligation to vote for Geraldine Ferraro. In some ways, this type of argument is degrading because it views the audience as members of a group who vote or believe blindly, according to what the group believes. It is "groupthink" in its worst sense. And even as a plea to consider group self-interest, it is often very superficial. There are great differences among women, among the rich, among blacks, among Presbyterians, and among "modern men."

On the other hand, this kind of *ad hominem* argument, like the other arguments considered here, has some value. As we indicated earlier, we are members of communities, we do have group loyalties, and we do have common interests. At times it is important for us to be reminded of these. "You're an Orthodox Presbyterian! I'm so surprised to hear you arguing for believer's baptism," someone might say. Such an argument is, in effect, an accusation of inconsistency that can force you to rethink your positions. Of course, even if I do agree that I have been inconsistent, that does not resolve the question. I must still decide which of the two inconsistent positions, if either, to hold. Do I renounce believer's baptism, or do I renounce my allegiance to the Orthodox Presbyterian standards? Still, the rethinking generated by the *ad hominem* argument may be beneficial.

Van Til's apologetics makes much use of circumstantial *ad hominem* arguments. He seeks to show the unbeliever that *on his premises*, he ought to believe in a universe of chaos—a universe that is meaningless and unintelligible. The unbeliever may not want to be consistent in that way, but at least he is brought face to face with his inconsistency. That is entirely appropriate. Apologetics is by its very nature *ad hominem*. Its goal is not to produce arguments, even sound arguments, but to persuade people. (The same is true, of course, of preaching and teaching.) Apologetics directs its arguments toward a particular person or audience, urging them to rethink their own personal commitments at the most basic level. And the *ad hominem* argument is appropriate, considering the impossibility of debate on common presuppositions—presuppositions joyfully honored by both parties. Since we cannot reason from such "common ground," we must look at both Christian and non-Christian presuppositions "for the sake of argument" (see chapter 11) and investigate one another's consistency from within our respective presuppositional frameworks.

Scripture contains much *ad hominem* argument. Jesus' teaching is almost maddeningly *ad hominem*. He frequently refuses to answer the questions of His antagonists directly, rather giving them an answer that challenges their personal relation with God (see Matt. 21:23-27; 22:15-33; John 3:1-14; 8:19-29).

(5) NEGATIVE CIRCUMSTANTIAL *AD HOMINEM* ARGUMENT

The negative circumstantial *ad hominem* argument says that someone's view is false (or at least that he has no right to hold it) because of his special circumstances. Some of Jesus' contemporaries argued that His teaching was false because He came from Nazareth, and everyone knew that nothing good came from Nazareth (John 1:46)! Or someone might argue that because I am an Orthodox Presbyterian, I have no right to criticize the evangelistic practices of other denominations, since my denomination has not been outstandingly evangelistic. The "*tu quoque*" ("you too") argument fits under this heading: "You may not criticize me, because you are just as bad as I am."

The negative circumstantial *ad hominem*, too, is fallacious. It attacks the person, rather than his views. But there is some value in it, nonetheless. Scripture tells us to "take the plank out of [our] own eye" before we criticize someone else (Matt. 7:5). Therefore when we consider a theological argument, we have an obligation to look not only at the validity and soundness of the argument but also at ourselves (see 1 Tim. 4:16; also see chapter 10). There are times when we ought to forbear making judgment, knowing that we ourselves will be judged by the same standard (Matt. 7:1-6).

Unbelievers, too, must be challenged to look at themselves and not only at the arguments for Christianity. If they do not see the relation of the argument to *them*, they will never be persuaded. Francis Schaeffer has very effectively used *ad hominem* arguments that challenge the unbeliever's right to speak (and especially to live) as he does. He tells us, for example, about the composer John Cage, who believes that the universe is pure chance and who seeks to express this in his music. But Cage is also a mushroom grower who once said, "I became aware that if I approached mushrooms in the spirit of my chance operations, I would die shortly. So I decided that I would not approach them in this way."[26] Schaeffer comments, "In other words, here is a man who is trying to teach the world what the universe intrinsically is and what the real philosophy of life is, and yet he cannot even apply it to picking mushrooms." Cage's philosophy of chance is not disproved merely because Cage is unable to apply it consistently. Still, this argument has a great deal of force. First, it shows *something* wrong in Cage's life—something that needs to be changed in one way or another. Second, it lessens the attractiveness of Cage's position. Most of us want a philosophy that we can live with, but if even Cage himself cannot live by his philosophy, there is little reason to believe that others will be able to. Third, it suggests problems in Cage's thought of a deeper sort—the rationalist-irrationalist dialectic as described by Van Til.

(6) Argument From Silence or Ignorance

An argument from silence or ignorance (also known as *ad ignorantiam*) alleges that something is true because it has not been proved false, or vice versa.

Whether this form of argument is a fallacy depends on whether a burden of proof has been established (see G, above). In the argument over infant baptism, for instance, one might determine that the Old Testament covenantal pattern must be followed unless there is explicit New Testament direction to change that pattern. That principle establishes the burden of proof. Anyone who wants to prove a change in pattern must prove it from the New Testament. Since the New Testament is (relatively) silent in this area, the Old Testament practice stands intact. Thus the silence of the New Testament may be used to prove something, once the burden of proof is established. And, indeed, if the burden were reversed, one could derive from the New Testament silence the opposite conclusion.

The argument from silence is never sound, in my opinion, when it operates on the word level, rather than the sentence level. The fact that Scripture does not use a particular word or that it does not use one word in contrast with another is never adequate grounds for rejecting such word-usage. The lexical stock of Scripture is not normative for theology; if it were, we would have to write theology in Hebrew and Greek.

26. Francis Schaeffer, *The God Who Is There* (Chicago: Inter-Varsity Press, 1968), 73f.

(7) Appeal to Pity

The appeal to pity is also known as *ad misericordiam*. Among other things, Clarence Darrow is famous for his emotional appeals to juries to have pity on a defendant—a defendant who had little hope except for mercy. Often in church courts, the same thing happens. Christian charity is invoked as a ground for leniency in church discipline. Often those seeking through discipline to purify the body are accused of being unloving. This is the opposite fallacy to the argument *ad baculum*.

Now as with the other fallacies, we can see more clearly what is wrong with the appeal to pity when we see its strength. On the one hand, Scripture does indeed exhort us to be loving and charitable, to be understanding of others, not to keep a list of wrongs. Indeed, there are some questions that Scripture *forbids* us to strive over (1 Tim. 1:3ff.)—"foolish controversies." People who find themselves entering every battle in the church ought to ask themselves whether they are honoring this principle.

On the other hand, Scripture also urges us to contend vigorously against false teaching, heresy that denies the gospel. Scripture warrants excommunication for those who will not hear the church's rebuke (Matt. 18:15ff.; 1 Cor. 5:1-5). Such discipline does not arise out of hatred but, indeed, out of love (1 Cor. 5:5) and for the good of the sinful brother. Therefore an appeal to love and pity should not be ignored. When a body is considering discipline that exceeds the gravity of the offense, that appeal ought to be heard and acted upon. But in other cases, the appeal is not proper.

In any case, the appeal to pity is never sufficient to demonstrate the truth of a proposition. We can never establish the truth of a doctrine by urging pity toward those who hold it.

(8) Appeal to Emotion

The appeal to emotion (also known as *ad populum*) is a fallacy that is somewhat broader than the last and that includes it. Here the appeal is not to pity alone but to a wide variety of other emotions as well. It is *ad populum* ("to the people"), because speakers facing large crowds often try to sway them with emotional appeals.

Thus if one has a new idea, he uses emotively positive words to describe it, words such as "progress," "creativity," and "fresh," calling his opponents "reactionary" or "static." If he has an old idea, he may speak of "the wisdom of the past," the "tried and true," of "American values," and so forth, and attack "radical" or "revolutionary" ideas.

Much theological language has more emotive than cognitive content. A good theology (whatever your viewpoint) is one that is "dynamic," "relevant," "concrete." It is "Christ-centered," "a theology of grace"; it "takes history seriously" and promotes "freedom" and "unity." It makes "distinctions," while rival views make "dichotomies" or "dualisms." (Generally, *dualism* is used to refer to a distinction that a person doesn't particularly like.) If someone accuses me of a having a "static" theology, my first response is to show how "dynamic" mine is and to show how his is actually much more "static" than mine. (Of course, this is always much easier if neither party defines *static* or *dynamic*.)

I think that much of the theology that I have criticized as being "antiabstractionist" and as using "word-level" arguments derives its force and persuasiveness from such emotive connotation language. Indeed, modern theology uses much orthodox terminology, rejecting its traditional meaning but trading on the emotive value such language has to those influenced by Christianity. Tillich, for example, speaks of "the cross of Christ," referring not to the historical crucifixion of Jesus but to a cosmic process of dialectical self-negation. Yet many readers are reassured of Tillich's Christian commitment when they read words like those in his writings. The connotations, at least, seem to be present, hovering over the words, as it were, even though the orthodox denotations are absent.

Sometimes to make an emotional appeal, it is enough merely to use a certain tone of voice or facial expression. I recall one theologian who for some reason did not approve of sermon titles. I do not remember his argument, but I do remember him letting out a huge sigh and saying slowly, with a tone of tragic sadness, the words "sermon titles." It was as if he expected his audience, along with him, to register the same sadness, the same disgust. I confess I did not share it. I was waiting for a cogent argument, which never came.

Examples of the appeal-to-emotion (*ad populum*) fallacy are many and amusing, but the point is made. Clearly, you cannot prove a conclusion merely by registering a particular emotional response toward that conclusion. Nevertheless, emotion is not entirely irrelevant to theological discussion (see chapter 10). Emotion does convey content, often important content. It may convey how important a proposition is in someone's thinking. It may communicate an idea so vividly that it would be impossible to convey the same idea through "detached academic" prose. It may communicate a thinker's presuppositions, his bias concerning a matter (and of course no one is without such bias).

We are, after all, human beings. Theology is one of the most human of disciplines. We seek to communicate the deepest convictions of our hearts. Trying to do this without emotion is like trying to do it standing on one leg; it is pointless and detracts from the task. Trying to state these convictions without emotion is, in most cases, impossible. And if it were possible, it would actually distort the content of the conviction in view.

(9) Appeal to Authority

The appeal to authority also is known as *ad verecundiam*. In general, appeal to authority is a fallacy in the sense that it does not *necessitate* the conclusion being argued for. As a matter of fact, however, in our everyday reasoning, appeals to authority are indispensable. We believe many propositions important to our thinking that we have not personally verified. Most of our knowledge of history, science, and indeed of theology we have learned from others more knowledgeable than we, and we have accepted it on their authority.

There are numerous appeals to authority in theology. There are appeals to Scripture, of course, but also to creeds and confessions, to philosophers (Aquinas's citations of Aristotle, Bultmann's attitude toward Heidegger), and to other theologians and theological traditions. Sometimes, even famous athletes take on the role of religious authorities, seeking to win people to Christ just as they might otherwise be selling cereal or beer.

Scripture's authority alone is decisive. An appeal to Scripture's authority is not fallacious but is the most fundamental argument of orthodox theology, an argument that underlies all others. In other types of thought, other presuppositions are thought to have a similar authoritative status. So the argument *ad verecundiam* is unavoidable at a very basic level. Like circularity, appeal to authority is inevitable at the presuppositional level, and it indirectly influences every argument, since it supplies the most fundamental criterion of truth in any system. But it need not always be explicit. And of course, appeals to less-than-ultimate authorities are always fallible and often avoidable.

(10) False Cause

The next group of fallacies involves the concept of causality. The first of these, which is merely a mistake in assessing the cause of something—*non causa pro causa*—often results from a confusion between temporal relations and causal relations. Doubtless, you've heard the story about the rooster who thought that his crowing caused the sun to rise, since every day the sun rose after he crowed. Such confusion is technically called *post hoc ergo propter hoc* ("after this, therefore because of this"). Or consider this example. When the sun goes into eclipse, members of a certain tribe are said to beat their drums furiously. They believe that such drum-beating brings the sun back, for ir the past the sun has always returned following their rhythmic entreaties. Modern medicine, too, faces this sort of question. Often, a patient will feel better, or even experience healing, after taking a drug, even when that drug has no physiological effect on his illness. Such psychological healing is called the "placebo effect." But this placebo effect makes it more difficult to assess when a drug is actually effective and when it is not. Careful sampling, where the effect of the proposed drug is *compared* with the psychological effect of a placebo, must be done so that scientists can learn which drugs actually *cause* healing and which merely, on occasion, precede it.

In politics we find many examples of this type of fallacy. For example, "Reagan was elected, and the nation went into recession." Was that *propter hoc* or only *post hoc*? Reagan replies, "The recession was the result of Carter administration policies." Is that a proper reply or merely another example of the same fallacy? Is it not possible that neither administration is to blame but that the Federal Reserve Board, Congress, or even the American people are? Is it possible that there was *multiple* causation, that *many* people and institutions were at fault?

In theology, too, there are many examples. Theologians blame many of the world's ills on theological views with which they disagree. Arminians say that lethargy among the Reformed concerning missions is due to the Calvinists' belief in predestination. The "slippery slope" argument discussed earlier (*H, (3)*, above) assumes, for example, that when a denomination goes into decline, that decline is traceable, in large measure, to one crucial doctrinal decision. Sometimes, arguments like that are cogent, but we must remember that God's world—and His plan for history—are generally more complicated than we imagine them to be. We should not be as quick as we often are to assess causation—that is, to assign blame.

(11) Genetic Fallacy

The genetic fallacy is another problem with causation. It assumes a close similarity between the present state of something and its earlier (or original) state. One type of example would be Bible word studies in which the etymological meaning of a term is assumed to be the same as its biblical usage.

Philosophers have sometimes argued that the state originated as an instrument of class coercion and therefore must have the same function today. Or biologists argue that since mankind evolved from some species of higher ape, we are still "essentially" apes. Christians ought to question the premises of both of those arguments, but they also should recognize the faulty logic by which the conclusions are established.[27]

There is also a reverse form of the genetic fallacy that assumes that because something is now such and such, therefore it must already have been such and such at an earlier stage. This is the fallacy of scientific uniformitarianism, which insists that all laws presently operative must have been operative for the duration of the existence of the universe.

(12) Ambiguities of Causality

Causality has also meant a number of different things. Aristotle identified four types of causes. The *efficient* cause is that which makes something happen, and this is the most usual concept of cause. The *final* cause is the purpose for which something happens. The *formal* cause is the most essential quality of something that makes it what it *is*, and the *material* cause is that out of which something is made.

Others have also distinguished *instrumental* causality (a tool or assisting means by which something is accomplished—for example, faith as an "instrument" of justification), *judicial* or *moral* causality (the legal or moral basis upon which something takes place—for example, the righteousness of Christ as the ground of justification), *necessary and sufficient conditionality* (see *E*, above), *material implication* (the logical "if . . . then"—see *D*, above), and so forth.

Like the concept of "priority" (see *E*, above), the concept of "cause," or of "causality," can be ambiguous. And in fact, the two concepts are often interchangeable.

The concept of causality is important in theology, because theology is concerned about creation (the cause of the world), the divine decrees (the causes of events in the world), the causes of salvation (e.g., election, intertrinitarian counsel, Incarnation, the active obedience of Christ, the

27. My editor reminds me of another common example: "Because Christmas trees were originally used by pagans, they have a pagan meaning, and so we should not use them."

Atonement, the Resurrection, the application of redemption by the Spirit). Often, theological disputes will center on the concept of causality. Roman Catholics and Protestants disagree on the sorts of causal efficacy to be ascribed to good works, sacraments, faith, and the righteousness of Christ in regard to salvation, for example.

The word *necessary* functions as an adjective to qualify many of the kinds of causality we have just examined. Several years ago, a godly professor at a leading seminary proposed that good works were "necessary" for justification. Opponents of this view argued that the professor was thereby putting works in the place reserved for faith or even replacing with works the righteousness of Christ as the ground of salvation. He denied any such intent, argued that he thought of works only as a necessary *accompaniment* to justification (as in James 2:14-26) and as necessary *evidence* for justification. In my opinion, this discussion was marred by a mutual unwillingness (on the part of people who should have known better) to analyze the ambiguities in the term "necessary." That misunderstanding led to the dismissal of the professor from the seminary faculty and to a great deal of ugly polarization and division among brethren.

Perhaps you are beginning to see what a practical science logic is or at least should be! *Love* for our brethren requires careful thought. Unfortunately, we often leap recklessly to conclusions precisely on those matters that are most important, matters that require the most careful analysis. We jump to conclusions on those matters because we are passionate about them. The passion may be appropriate, but it ought to be channeled in a healthier direction. Our passion ought to give us a greater zeal for *truth* and for the means of attaining truth.

(13) Confusions Between Multiple and Single Causation

Often an event has many causes, and it is difficult to single out one of them as having pre-eminence over the others. What made the United States a powerful nation? Natural resources? Economic liberty? Relatively free immigration? Religious freedom? Christian roots (however presently eclipsed)? A few years ago, a commercial for a restaurant chain posed this question: "Who is the most important employee of the restaurant?" The manager? The chef? They concluded that the clean-up crew was most important, since that crew created the fresh, clean atmosphere that made dining at the restaurant such a pleasure. Well, the crew *was* important, even necessary. And its importance was rightly stressed in a commercial that emphasized the cleanliness of the place. But this importance and necessity did not make the crew any *more* necessary than the chef, waiters, or manager, who were also important and necessary.

Sometimes in theology a cause, perhaps a necessary condition, for example, is singled out from all the others as *the* cause of something. Since, for example, liberation of the poor is one necessary element of the biblical gospel, some theologians have sought to make it the *essence* of Christianity. But there are other elements that are equally necessary, equally important. Others will argue that Presbyterian procedures ("All things decently and in order") are necessary to the work of the church and thus will waste countless hours of session and presbytery time on the perfection of minutes, procedural debates, and so forth. These people do not realize that even if they are right, even if such procedures are "necessary" in some way, they are not thereby of *first* importance. Other things may be (and are, in my view) equally or more important.

The age-old controversy over the "relation of doctrine to life" also comes up appropriately at this point. Some will say, "Doctrine is important and necessary to the very life of the church," and they will want to spend every moment of time in church, session, and presbytery trying to achieve perfect agreement in every detail of theology. And since the church's theology is never perfect, such people begrudge any time devoted to any other subject. Others will say, "Evangelism is important and necessary to the life of the church," and they will want to spend all the church's time formulating strategies for mission. Others are concerned in a similar way about prayer, social justice, Christian politics, or economics. These "priority differences" often cause division in the church and make unions between denominations difficult. The Orthodox Presbyterian Church and the Presbyterian Church in America have the same doctrinal standards and are both committed to scriptural authority, but many resist union of the two denominations because of perceived priority differences.

In the interest of unity, it is important to emphasize a logical point. *All* the matters mentioned above are important and necessary to the life of the church. But none of them is thereby more important than any of the others. Therefore we dare not spend all of our time, for example, in a vain pursuit of present doctrinal perfection, for if we do we will neglect other matters that are equal in importance. Indeed, if we pursue doctrinal purity to the neglect of missions, our doctrine itself will thereby be rendered impure, for the Great Commission is also a doctrine! Note how all these necessary matters are perspectivally related. Thinking of them that way can be a help in achieving balance. There are, of course, some matters in Scripture that are more important than others. Jesus speaks of the "weightier matters of the law" (Matt. 23:23). It is also the case that when we *apply* the Scriptures to practical situations, we must often make the judgment that one principle rather than another deserves our attention at a particular time. See the earlier discussion of "Hierarchies of Norms" in chapter 5, A, (9). Such judgments, however, ought to be based on careful reflection, not on mere tradition or on our "gut" feelings. Here I simply want to make the logical point that to say that a doctrine of Scripture is "important" or "necessary" is not to prove that it is always more important than some other doctrine or that it always deserves a greater emphasis.

(14) Complex Question

We now leave the concept of causality and look at fallacies associated with *questions*. The "complex question" fallacy treats two questions that ought to be answered separately as one question. The most famous example is the question "Have you stopped beating your wife?," or, more broadly, "Have you given up your evil ways?" Whether you answer Yes or No, you incriminate yourself. The problem is that "Have you stopped beating your wife?" is in one sense really two questions: (A) "Have you been beating your wife?" and (B) "If you have been, have you now stopped?" Of course, if the answer to *(A)* is No, then *(B)* is not even applicable. But "Have you stopped beating your wife?" *presupposes* an affirmative answer to *(A)*. To escape the question, we must show what it presupposes and deny that presupposition by saying something like this: "My good man, you are *assuming* that I have been beating my wife. Since that is not the case, your question is inappropriate."

Here are some other examples. "Will you be good and go to bed?" "Is he one of those unthinking Fundamentalists?" Note that there are many questions that cannot be answered Yes or No. These are additional examples in which the law of the excluded middle can mislead us (see *D*, above). For this and other reasons, in parliaments and presbyteries members often ask to "divide" a question, to vote separately on each constituent part.

In theology, complex questions are often posed because theologians simply are not clear about which of many possible questions they are asking. A good example is the following from G. C. Berkouwer (in whose writings one can find many examples of this fallacy).

> Miracles are not proofs addressed to the intellect that thereby man should be convinced. They do not make faith superfluous. On the contrary, they summon us to believe. The witness character of miracles puts before man the decision which he must make as to Christ. .

> . . Miracles are inscrutable acts of God, which can be accepted as acts of God only through faith.[28]

What question is Berkouwer addressing in that paragraph? I can isolate a number of them. (A) Are miracles proofs? (B) Are miracles addressed to the intellect, as opposed to other human faculties? (C) Are miracles given for the purpose of convincing us? (D) Do miracles make faith superfluous? (E) Do miracles merely *propose* a decision, as opposed to *requiring* a particular decision? (F) Are miracles inscrutable? I would guess that Berkouwer believes these questions are all interrelated, so that the right answer to one determines right answers to all the others. Not all persons, however, will accept that presupposition. I, for one, would answer Yes to *(C)* and *(F)* and No to the others. Berkouwer, I gather, would answer Yes to *(E)* and *(F)* and No to the others. But the discussion is confusing. It would have been much more helpful if Berkouwer had distinguished those questions and argued each one separately.

For other examples, see the "false distinctions" noted earlier in chapter 7, *E*. As I noted there, Woodbridge seeks to distinguish certain questions that he believes are confused by Rogers and McKim, for example the question of whether Scripture is accommodated to human understanding and the question of whether Scripture is infallible. Here, too, as in the question "Have you stopped beating your wife?" the tying together of questions is based upon certain presuppositions, in this case the presupposition that anyone who believes that Scripture is inerrant cannot possibly believe that Scripture is accommodated to human understanding. Here, as elsewhere in theology, it is important to expose the presuppositions behind what is said and critically to evaluate those presuppositions in the light of Scripture.

Of course, many theological questions *are* "tied together," as we have seen, but they are "tied together" in a wide variety of ways that require careful analysis. One almost needs to discuss each one separately to show *how* it is "tied to" the rest.

(15) Equivocation

I will now mention three fallacies that involve ambiguity (cf. chapter 7 and *D*, *(5)* above). The reader will recall that in a valid implication the relevant terms must be used in the same sense throughout the argument.

28. G. C. Berkouwer, *The Providence of God* (Grand Rapids: Wm. B. Eerdmans Pub. Co., 1952), 215. In other respects, Berkouwer's discussion of miracles is very helpful.

When they are not, there is a fallacy of equivocation. Consider these examples. (A) "Some dogs have fuzzy ears; my dog has fuzzy ears; therefore my dog is some dog." (B) "Modern theologians deny the inerrancy of Scripture; Cornelius Van Til is a modern theologian; therefore Cornelius Van Til denies the inerrancy of Scripture." (C) "If Scripture is infallible, then God's Word can be possessed; God's Word cannot be possessed; therefore Scripture is not infallible." (D) "Christians do not sin (1 John 3:6); Bill commits sin (1 John 1:8-10); therefore Bill is not a Christian." (E) "The unbeliever can know nothing truly; 'the book is on the table' is a true statement; therefore the unbeliever cannot know that the book is on the table." (F) "Either we are justified apart from works (Rom. 3:28) or the moon is made of green cheese; we are not justified apart from works (James 2:24); therefore the moon is made of green cheese."

(16) Amphiboly

This is a type of ambiguity that arises from grammar. Often, amphiboly produces jokes—double entendres such as, "Save soap and waste paper." Or "Anthropology: the science of man embracing woman." In the first example, "waste," intended as an adjective, may be misconstrued as a verb. In the second example, "embracing," intended to modify "science," may be misconstrued as modifying "man." I have found it difficult to locate theological examples of this type of fallacy. One, however, may be familiar: "We can know God only in His revelation." The statement is true, I think, if "only in His revelation" modifies "know." That would mean that our knowledge of God is limited to what He has revealed. If, however, "only in His revelation" modifies "God," then I think it is false because we know some facts about God as He existed by himself, before He created anything or revealed anything to anyone. (There is, perhaps, some residual ambiguity in this illustration.)

(17) Accent

This is an ambiguity of stress that depends on the tone of voice with which we speak. The meaning of the statement "Woman without her man would be lost" is fairly clear in print. But that sentence would have a different meaning if it were punctuated in this way: "Woman—without her, man would be lost." In oral communication, some unclarity might arise if the punctuation is not clearly indicated by vocal inflection.

"We should not speak ill of our friends" has a distinctive meaning if the word *friends* is emphasized. From that stress, one could deduce that we may speak ill of our enemies; otherwise, we could not draw that implication. (This is one of those bits of "informal" logic that is not reducible to formal symbolism—see *D*, above. Logicians have not yet learned how to deal with arguments that turn on a change in one's tone of voice.)

Note this quote from E. J. Young, "The Bible is not written for the sake of style, but to convey information to the reader."[29] On the one hand, one could interpret Young's statement as suggesting that the whole purpose of Scripture is propositional: to convey information. Interpreted that way, Young would be denying (or at least ignoring) the variety of other kinds of language in Scripture. On the other hand, though Young was probably not sophisticated in distinguishing the functions of speech acts in language, he probably would not have opposed a view that was broader than his own. The contrast in the quotation is not between information and, say, questions, commands, promises, and so forth, but between information and *style*. Young's intent is not to contrast informatory speech acts with others but to contrast style with substance. In the context of present-day discussions, *content* would have been a clearer term than *information*. We must remember not to read this quote with a tone of voice that puts a stress on *information* that Young himself probably would not have used.

Much is said these days about the need to reproduce in our theology the "emphasis" of Scripture. I think that in most cases this demand is confused and illegitimate (see chapter 6, *A*).

(18) Composition

In this fallacy, what is true of a part is asserted of the whole, or what is true of an individual is predicated of a collection of individuals. Here, one might argue that because each part of a jet plane is light, the plane itself must be light; or because each member of a soccer team is great, the team must also be a great team.

Some predicates attach to every member of a class, but some attach only to the class itself. "Men are mortal" ascribes mortality to human beings as individuals. "Men are numerous," however, applies "numerousness" to the whole race, not to every man.

29. E. J. Young, *Thy Word Is Truth* (Grand Rapids: Wm. B. Eerdmans Pub. Co., 1957), 115.

Theological examples of this fallacy include the following. (A) "Joe is adulterous, therefore his congregation is adulterous." People sometimes actually reason that way! (B) "Pastor A holds a heretical view; he is a member of denomination X; therefore denomination X holds a heretical view."

(19) DIVISION

This is the reverse of the last fallacy. Here one argues that what is true of the whole (or the collection) is also true of the parts (or members). Thus one might argue that since a car is heavy, it must have a heavy cigarette lighter. Or because a grove is thick, each tree in that grove must be thick. One might mistake predicates of a class for predicates of individuals, as in this specious argument: "American Indians are disappearing; Joe is an American Indian; therefore Joe is disappearing."

Theological examples include these. (A) "Christ commands His church to evangelize the whole world; I am a member of the church; therefore Christ commands me to evangelize the whole world." Much grief is wrought by pastors who take commands in the Bible that are intended for the church as a whole and impose them on individuals, as if each individual had to do the whole job himself. Thus individuals are led to think that they must pray all day, evangelize their neighborhoods, become experts in Scripture, Christianize the institutions of society, feed all the poor in the world, and so forth. No! Those commands are for the church as a *whole*, and individuals contribute to these purposes in accordance with their particular gifts (Rom. 12; 1 Cor. 12-14). (B) "The Old Testament testifies of Christ; 1 Chronicles 26:18 is in the Old Testament; therefore 1 Chronicles 26:18 testifies of Christ." In a sense that is true but not in the sense that one could preach Christ from that verse alone, ignoring all others. This sort of mistake leads preachers to read into a text all sorts of invalid typological meanings. (C) Process Theology (as in Whitehead, Hartshorne, Cobb) is, one might say, *based on* the fallacy of division. For its central argument seems to be that since nature and human life are "in process," in constant change, therefore the smallest components of the world (the "actual occasions") must also be in constant change—a sort of change, furthermore, that reflects the characteristics of those changes that we experience in ordinary life. I fail to see any necessity at all in this reasoning.

Often, the parts do have qualities that are also shared by the whole. Arguments like those in *(19)* and in *(18)* help us to see that. But that is not *al-*

ways the case. Therefore this type of argument cannot be depended on to produce a valid and sound conclusion.

(20) Denying the Antecedent

Finally, we must glance at a couple of fallacies that are usually dealt with under the rubric of *formal* logic. So far, we have been dealing with *informal* fallacies—fallacies that arise from the misuse of ordinary language. Only a few kinds of fallacies have actually been reduced to logical symbolism, two of which are "denying the antecedent" and "affirming the consequent." The fallacy of "denying the antecedent" has the following form: "If p then q; not-p; therefore not-q." "P" and "q" are "propositional variables." Therefore any proposition may be substituted for "p," any other proposition for "q." For example, "If Bill is a Presbyterian, he believes in election; Bill is not a Presbyterian; therefore he does not believe in election." You should be able to see intuitively that this argument fails. Even if the premises are true, the conclusion may be false.

(21) Affirming the Consequent

This argument has the following form: "If p, then q; q; therefore p." For example, "If it rains, the picnic is cancelled; the picnic is cancelled; therefore it is raining." We can see that this argument is invalid. The cancellation of the picnic may have occurred for reasons other than rain. Sometimes this fallacy and *(20)* can be very plausible. Take, for instance, this example: "If Ruth believes, then she is regenerate; she is regenerate; therefore she believes." That example seems more persuasive than our example of the rain and the picnic, but it is the same fallacy. The reason the second example seems more plausible is that regeneration and faith are mutually implicatory. If you have either, you have the other (not here taking into account the complications of regeneration in infants). Thus it is also true that if Ruth is regenerate, Ruth believes. And from that premise the conclusion in question does follow. The quoted argument, therefore, seems plausible because it closely resembles another one that is valid.

To summarize, here are some of my thoughts about logical fallacies. (A) In general, of course, they ought to be avoided. God calls us to think according to truth, and that entails that we should not present an argument as cogent when it really is not, since doing so is a form of deception. (B) Still, fallacies are not entirely worthless. (1) They sometimes have a valid purpose, as we saw earlier under *ad hominem*, for example. (2) They sometimes amount to incomplete arguments—arguments that would be sound if additional premises were added. We ought to try, therefore, to "read between the lines" of theological arguments to see if apparently invalid arguments can be improved so as to yield truth. (3) And invalid arguments, like the argument *ad baculum*, for example, teach us something about the systems of thought—and the adherents of those systems—that produce the arguments. They help us to see what is presupposed.

CHAPTER NINE

The Situational Perspective—History, Science, and Philosophy as Tools of Theology

A. HISTORY

Christianity is a religion of historical fact. It is, among other things, a message about events that took place in time and space; and in this respect, Christianity is unique among the world's religions. Other religions seek only to communicate eternal truths, doctrines, and ethical principles that are true apart from the occurrence or nonoccurrence of any historical event. Christianity also teaches some eternal truths (the existence of God, His attributes, His trinitarian nature, etc.), but it is focused on the historical events of Jesus' incarnation, death, resurrection, and ascension and the coming of the Spirit at Pentecost. Inevitably, therefore, Christianity is involved with history. It makes historical claims, seeks historical verification, and attempts to repel the criticisms of anti-Christian historians. Miracle stories are an embarrassment to sophisticated Buddhists, but miracle is the lifeblood of Christianity. Indeed, its central message is about a miracle, the miraculous life, death, and resurrection of Jesus Christ.

The church, too, is historical—a living organism that exists throughout the centuries. Its "growth" is not only the growth of the individuals that make it up; it develops also by a principle of corporate growth, above and beyond its individual members (see chapter 5, C, (6)). God has prompted that growth through historical events—periods of persecution, periods of prosperity, doctrinal enrichment and decline, and the rise and fall of worship, evangelism, and social conscience. He has given teachers to the church to whom she must give heed, though many are no longer living. For those reasons, it is important for the church to refresh its corporate memory—to hear its teachers, to build on its successes, to profit from its mistakes. Doing that involves historical study.

Thus three kinds of history are especially important for Christians: the history recorded in Scripture itself, the history of the ancient world in which the events of redemption took place, and the history of the church. The first of these was discussed earlier (see chapter 6, *E*, *(2)*). The other two will occupy our attention here.

(1) Ancient History—Archaeology

I am not a specialist in either of these areas, and there are many articles and books on these subjects by people who are. Therefore I shall be brief. Ancient history and archaeology are important disciplines that help us to understand the meaning of the Bible and to verify its reliability. In that second function of those disciplines, historical data becomes part of a "broad circle" that confirms the presuppositions of the Christian faith. Those Christian presuppositions, in turn, serve as the historian's ultimate criterion of truth. They warrant his historical judgments about the selection and evaluation of evidence. The Christian historian can never take a religiously neutral position, no matter how many philosophers of history tell him that neutrality is inevitable for modern men.

In its task as a hermeneutical tool, ancient history studies the use of biblical terms, of phrases and sentences inside and outside of the Scriptures, and the parallels to these expressions in other languages. It studies ancient customs, extrabiblical historical events, and extracanonical writings as a "context" in which to understand the biblical material (cf. the earlier discussions of context in chapter 6, *A* and *C*). This discipline, too, is obligated to operate on Christian presuppositions, and if it does, we have no cause to fear it. Sometimes we rightly worry that a scholar is using not Scripture but his understanding of ancient cultures as his norm. We sometimes worry also that such a scholar may be making too much of extrabiblical patterns in his exegesis—forcing the Bible to say what the Babylonian or Egyptian or Ugaritic or Hittite documents say. This is a real danger, of course, and it sometimes happens. But the answer to this danger is not to forbid the use of such material in biblical scholarship, for we cannot, after all, do without it. To ignore the extrabiblical historical context of Scripture is to deny the historical character of the redemptive events themselves. The answer is rather to demand theological accountability of biblical scholars, not only orthodoxy in terms of adherence to the church creeds but an ongoing subjection to Scripture in areas not covered by those creeds—historical epistemology, presuppositions, and method.

(2) Church History—Historical Theology

The second type of history with which I shall deal is the history of the postcanonical church. In this connection, we must investigate the roles of tradition and creed in theology.

a. *Tradition*

Tradition, of course, is not the ultimate norm for Protestants, but it is important. It includes all the teaching and activity of the church down to the present day. On the one hand, as I indicated earlier, the Christian has an obligation to hear the teachers that God has given the church over the hundreds of years of its existence. They must be heard critically; we wish to profit from their mistakes, as well as from their achievements. On the other hand, it would be foolish for us to try to build our theology from the ground up, as it were, seeking to ignore all tradition. Descartes tried that in philosophy, but his successors have recognized that we can never begin to think without some preconceptions. Although those preconceptions can be critically purified, we cannot do without them altogether. Therefore when we seek to escape the bonds of tradition, we merely substitute one set of preconceptions for another. Indeed, what we do then is to substitute our own half-baked, ill-conceived preconceptions for the mature thought of godly teachers. To try to start totally afresh ("just me and my Bible"), as many cultists have tried to do, is an act of disobedience and pride. The work of theology is not the work of one individual seeking to gain a complete knowledge of God on his own but the corporate work of the church in which Christians together seek a common mind on the things of God (cf. chapter 5, C, *(6)*).

b. *Creeds*

If we have the Bible, why do we need a creed? That's a good question! Why can't we just be Christians, rather than Presbyterians, Baptists, Methodists, and Episcopalians? Well, I wish we could be. When people ask what I am, I would like to say, quite simply, "Christian." Indeed, I often do. And when they ask what I believe, I would like to say with equal simplicity "the Bible." Unfortunately, however, that is not enough to meet the current need. The trouble is that many people who call themselves Christians don't deserve the name, and many of them claim to believe the Bible.

So when people ask what, for example, Westminster Seminary teaches, it is not enough to say "Scripture." True as that answer is, it does not distinguish Westminster Seminary from schools of the Jehovah's Witnesses, Mormons, or other cults, to say nothing of the other branches of mainline Christianity—Baptists, Methodists, and so forth. We must *tell* people what we believe. Once we do that, we have a creed.

Indeed, a creed is quite inescapable, though some people talk as if they could have "only the Bible" or "no creed but Christ." As we have seen, "believing the Bible" involves applying it. If you cannot put the Bible into your own words (and actions), your knowledge of it is no better than a parrot's. But once you do put it into your own words (and it is immaterial whether those words be written or spoken), you have a creed.

There is, of course, always the danger of confusing your creed with Scripture, but that is the same danger that we face in any attempt to do theology—distinguishing our work from God's. That is a danger that must be faced, not avoided by a deceptive "no creed but Christ" slogan. Not to face it is not to accept our responsibility as ambassadors for Christ.

c. *Orthodoxy and Heresy*

If we must have a creed, we may reason, then let's find a *perfect* one; let's find one that perfectly expresses biblical orthodoxy. Unfortunately, that search will be in vain. There is no perfect creed, and there never will be. A perfect creed would of necessity have the same authority as Scripture, and that can never be. In fact, Scripture itself is the only perfect creed. So if we ask for a creed in words that are different from Scripture and if we demand perfection in that creed, then we are, in effect, seeking to improve on Scripture. Similarly, no definitive criteria for orthodoxy can be laid down once and for all. If such criteria were definitive, then they would be on a par with Scripture. Rather, criteria of this sort are always *applications* of Scripture to various situations; and situations change.

Thus the criteria of orthodoxy change too. In the time of Justin Martyr (second century), some trinitarian formulations were permitted that would have been considered heretical after the Council of Constantinople in A.D. 381. Of course in Justin's day, few people had a really clear concept of the Trinity. God taught His church bit by bit, as we so teach our children, and as God teaches individuals. But by A.D. 381, enough study had been carried on, indeed, enough struggling had taken place, so that the church had a clear idea of what the Bible taught about the doctrine of the Trinity. Even so, much remained to be learned in other areas. There were few if any clear statements of justification by faith, for example, until A.D. 1517. That means that the criteria of orthodoxy in A.D. 381 were properly more detailed than those of A.D. 80 or A.D. 150 and that those of A.D. 1648 were even more detailed. It sounds strange to talk about the criteria of orthodoxy changing, but they do, and they should. Such changes are indices of the church's maturity, of what God has taught His people.

This teaching process generally proceeds by a pattern of challenge and response, to echo historian Arnold Toynbee. The great creeds are responses to heresy. Properly speaking, a heretic is not a Christian who makes a doctrinal or practical mistake—people who make such mistakes are treated very gently by Jesus (John 4) and Paul (Rom. 14; 1 Cor. 8-10)—but a person who challenges the gospel at its core (Gal. 1:6-9; 1 John 4:2f.), seeking to win the rest of the church to his position. The church must respond and has responded to such challenges. It responded to Arianism with the Nicene and Constantinopolitan Creeds, to the Eutychians and Nestorians with the Chalcedonian Declaration, to the Arminians, sectarians, and Roman Catholics with the Reformation confessions.

There is a need for new creeds today, for Christians to confess their faith anew against *modern* heresies. There are new heresies in theology (which, of course, are only old ones in new terminology, with new slants) and also in those branches of theology (!) known as politics, economics, philosophy, and science. And the Reformed churches have learned much theology since the Reformation confessions. They have learned much about covenants, biblical inerrancy, redemptive history, Christian epistemology, apologetics, personal ethics, and social issues.

Perhaps, however, it is impossible to write any serious creeds today. The major obstacle, in my view, is the disunity of the church. A proper creed represents a broad consensus of Christians, and such a consensus does not seem to be attainable now. That, then, is another reason why church union is such an urgent priority (cf. chapter 5, C, (6)). And if church union must precede the writing of significant creeds, it would perhaps be better to abstain from creed-writing for the present. For in the present context, new creeds are *obstacles* to union and therefore, ironically, obstacles to really significant creedal work.

d. *Progress in Theology*

I mentioned above that the Reformed churches have continued since the Reformation to learn new things from God's Word. Therefore there is such a thing as "theological progress" or "progress of doctrine." The concept of theological progress can be misunderstood from both liberal and conservative directions. Liberals, on the one hand, typically understand progress as an increasing vagueness in commitment, coupled with ready acceptance of fashionable thinking in philosophy and science. Conservatives, on the other hand, typically understand theological progress (if they accept the idea at all) as a march toward increasingly more precise statements of doctrine or as progress toward an objective truth that is free from subjective influence. A biblical position, I believe, repudiates both of those concepts of theological progress. The liberal concept represents a denial of biblical teaching, the conservative (at best) a misunderstanding of it. Scripture does not demand absolute precision of us, a precision impossible for creatures (see chapter 7). Indeed, Scripture recognizes that for the sake of communication, vagueness is often preferable to precision. Furthermore, the sort of conservatism under discussion often seeks to be more precise than Scripture itself, thus adding to God's Word and creating a modern form of Pharisaism. Nor is theology an attempt to state truth without any subjective influence on the formulation. Such "objectivity," like "absolute precision," is impossible and would not be desirable if it could be achieved (cf. chapter 3).

Our concept of theology as application will help us form a better view of theological progress. Theology progresses as it learns to apply God's Word to each situation it encounters, and we have seen evidence of that throughout church history. The great strides in theological understanding come about when the church creatively and faithfully responds to difficult situations on the basis of Scripture.

The Reformed faith is especially well equipped to make theological progress. In the Reformed faith, the concept of application is not a threat to *sola scriptura*, because Calvinists believe in a comprehensive revelation of God in Scripture, the world, and the self. Everything reveals Him, for everything is under His control, authority, presence. Nor ought Calvinists to be burdened with any demand for absolute precision or objectivity. The Reformed faith has a clear view of the Creator-creature distinction; only God has perfectly precise and perfectly objective knowledge (though even for Him, such knowledge is not devoid of subjectivity).

Therefore of all the forms of Protestantism, Reformed theology has been one of the most successfully "contextualized." Reformed theology has sunk deep roots in many places: Switzerland, Germany, France (before it was brutally persecuted there), Italy (many of the successors of Calvin were of Italian background), the Netherlands, the English-speaking countries, Hungary, and Korea. Contextualization applies Scripture to the experience of a particular culture to make its message better understood there. Like apologetics, contextualization faces the danger of distorting the faith to make it more acceptable to those it seeks to reach, but that need not be the case, especially given Reformed presuppositions. Rather, the progress theology makes is precisely a progress in contextualizing its message.

Reformed theology has also made exceptional progress in the more common sense of learning new things from Scripture. These discoveries too, however, are applications or contextualizations, answers to current questions. Lutheran theology has not changed very much since the seventeenth century, nor has Arminian theology. But Calvinism has developed new understandings of the covenants, of redemptive history, of biblical inerrancy, of apologetics, of theological encyclopedia, and of the relationships of Christianity to politics, economics, education, the arts, literature, history, science, and law. That progress has come about because belief in the sovereignty of God sets the Calvinist free to explore the fullness of God's revelation in Scripture and creation.

e. *Subscription*

That concept of theological progress raises anew the question of how closely we ought to be tied to our past. Granted, creeds and confessions are necessary, but what sort of allegiance do we owe to them, given our desire to move beyond them toward new applications?

Clearly, an extrascriptural creed is not infallible, except insofar as it accurately applies the Scriptures. But we have no way of infallibly determining when it does that. Nevertheless, a creed must have some authority, for otherwise it cannot do its job of representing the convictions of a body of believers. Thus our attitude toward our creeds should not be one of indifference. Neither, however, should it be an attitude of subscribing to a creed's every jot and tittle, an attitude that binds us to endorse every proposition taught in a confession. Why? Because if we are required to have that attitude towards creeds and confessions, they could never be amended; anyone who advocated change would automatically be a vowbreaker and subject to discipline. To keep them from usurping the role and authority of Scripture as the church's *ultimate* standard, creeds and confessions *must* be amendable.

Presbyterian churches have addressed this issue by using ministerial vows that do not speak of any jot-and-tittle subscription but of subscription to the "system of doctrine" taught in the Westminster Confession of Faith and its Catechisms. "System of doctrine" is a vague expression that has given rise to many debates about what properly belongs to the system.[1] The unclarity in this concept has led some to urge the church to define (precisely!) once-and-for-all what belongs to the system and what does not. Rightly, the church has consistently refused to do that. For if it ever did define the "system" precisely, once-and-for-all, it would then be setting forth that system as an *absolute, unamendable* authority. And to do so would, in effect, require "jot-and-tittle subscription," albeit to a somewhat abbreviated creed. Thus it seems that here, as elsewhere in theology, we must be satisfied with vagueness.

The "system of doctrine" is not, however, a totally unworkable concept. Requiring subscription to the "system" means that he who takes the vow must accept the confession as his own confession, by and large, with some minor reservations, if necessary. Whether his reservations are minor or major (that is, whether they transgress the "system") is ultimately for the church courts to decide. The "system," then, is redefined for every specific case. The "system" means what a particular session, presbytery, or general assembly says that it means. As long as those courts stand under the authority of God's Word and therefore under the guidance of His Spirit, they probably will not err too greatly. There are no guarantees of perfect judgment here, but that is the nature of life in a finite and sinful world.[2]

f. *Confession and Theology*

Some have tried to draw a sharp distinction between confession and theology, especially those who are under the influence of Dooyeweerd's distinction between pretheoretical and theoretical thought.[3] As with the latter distinction, the distinction between confession and theology is unclear to me. Apparently, "confession" is considered to be pretheoretical knowledge of some sort and "theology" a kind of theory. The distinction is usually invoked in favor of a claim to academic freedom, as in "We are bound on 'confessional' issues but free on 'theological' matters." Several

1. See chapter 6, *E, (3)* for more on the concept of "system."

2. Even with "jot-and-tittle" subscription, the church courts would have to make (fallible) judgments as to whether someone was correctly interpreting the jots and tittles to which he has subscribed. It is not clear, then, that "strict" subscription would give us any greater objectivity of judgment than "system-of-doctrine" subscription.

3. See my *The Amsterdam Philosophy* (Phillipsburg, N.J.: Harmony Press, 1972).

points, however, need to be made. (A) There is, of course, a legitimate distinction between matters on which a confession does and does not take a stand. The church's formal discipline, in my judgment, is properly limited to the former category, and that only in terms of the "vagueness" described in *e*, above. (B) All confessions and creeds, however, are examples of theology, and all theology represents the personal confession of the theologian. The "pretheoretical-theoretical" distinction is not sharp.[4] (C) Theology is bound (with the qualifications noted in *e*) to its confessional standards; its "theoretical" character, whatever that may be, does not absolve it from that responsibility.

g. *Church History and Historical Theology*

The church historian seeks not only to tell "what happened" in the church's past but also to interpret, analyze, and evaluate those events, those facts. Conscious analysis, evaluation, and interpretation are necessary because there are no "brute facts," facts that somehow "speak for themselves." All facts that we speak about are, by definition, interpreted to a greater or lesser extent.

The church historian is concerned both with the events of church history and with the history of doctrine (i.e., "historical theology"), the ideas of theologians (and heretics), the formulations of creeds and confessions, and the development of theological consensus on various matters, whether or not expressed confessionally. Here, as in redemptive history, words and events go together. God has raised up teachers for the church over many years, but their teachings cannot be fully understood "in word only." The meanings of words are found in their applications, in what people *do* with them. Therefore it is important to know not only what our teachers say but also what they do with their convictions. Church history illuminates theology by recounting the words of teachers in their life-contexts. It shows us how the teachers of the church behaved under pressure, how their lives were or were not consistent with their teaching. It shows how the gospel teaching took root (or failed to take root) in the lives of rulers, farmers, tradesmen, soldiers, the poor, and the homeless.

As such, historical theology is properly a form of theology. It is an application of the Word of God, for that Word is the historian's criterion of evaluation. It applies the Word to the church's past for the sake of the church's present edification, and thus it also applies Scripture to the church of the present. And in so applying the Word, it reveals its meaning

4. Ibid.

in new and exciting ways, as we see how our ancestors applied Scripture to a broad variety of situations.

h. *Dogmatics*

Dogmatics is a synonym for *systematic theology*. In many contexts, the two terms are interchangeable. Theologians of European (especially Continental) background tend to use *dogmatics*; *systematic theology* is more common among American writers. (There are exceptions here, however: Wilhelm Herrmann and Paul Tillich wrote "systematic theologies," but W. G. T. Shedd wrote a *Dogmatic Theology*).

Though the two terms are fairly synonymous, there is sometimes, at least, a difference of nuance between them, a difference that will reveal the reason why I discuss the matter at this point. *Dogmatics* sometimes conveys the thought that theology is a conversation between the theologian and church tradition—especially between the theologian and the church creeds (dogmas). *Systematic theology* sometimes tends to connote a dialogue between the theologian and Scripture itself—not that either nuance excludes the other. Dogmatics is (or ought to be) based on Scripture as its ultimate authority; systematic theology is (or ought to be) responsible to the confessions of the church. The two nuances, however, represent different emphases, or perhaps different images, different models of the work of theology. Ultimately, if done correctly, the two concepts will coincide as "perspectival" views on a single discipline; but there will be differences in method, in presentation, in language, and in the thought processes by which that single discipline is practiced.

The model of "dogmatics"—theology in dialogue with its tradition—is valuable in a number of ways. Chiefly, it presents a warning against individualism and pride, against the notion that we can build up theology from the ground floor, just the theologian and his Bible. While seeking to preserve the values of this model, however, I tend to prefer the other one (despite the fact that "systematic theology" is a misnomer (see chapter 6, *E, (3)*). The "dogmatic" model has a number of weaknesses that, in my view, outnumber and outweigh its advantages.

(i) Those who see theology as a dialogue with tradition are in danger of lapsing into irrelevance—first, by becoming preoccupied with topics that once were of great interest but are no longer so (e.g., supralapsarianism, the relation of essence to existence in angels, etc.), and second, by overlooking topics of great concern today that were not explicitly discussed in the confessional tradition (e.g., crisis of meaningfulness, the nature of history, the nature of an "act of God," religious language, the functions of biblical language, presuppositions, racial justice, economic liberation). There is value, of course, in glancing, at least, at "obsolete topics." Obsolete topics have a way of coming back in new forms. (I used to list trichotomy as an "obsolete topic," but now I hear of a number of Christian teachers who give a very central role in their theology to trichotomy.) And I would not want to say that theology must be determined entirely by the questions modern people are asking. Still, if theology is application, it ought to be responsive to those questions, among others. Thus a twentieth-century theology ought to look very different from a nineteenth-century theology. It should not be the same thing, with another hundred years of tradition tacked on.

(ii) The "dogmatic" model may lead to a stifling of creativity in theology, to a slavish imitation of older methods of presenting theological ideas. "Theology as application" opens up much room for fresh approaches in form, style, models, and questions, as well as content. It allows us to use all the forms of teaching found in Scripture (poetry, narrative, letter, parable, song, object lesson, dramatization, as well as "theological treatise"), and, indeed, others besides—any form that does not contradict or obscure the message of Scripture.

(iii) Tradition-oriented theology also risks encouragement of an uncritical attitude toward the tradition of the church—a tradition that is sometimes deserving of criticism and that, even at its best, must be displayed as clearly subordinate to Scripture.

(iv) Such theology also runs a particular danger of falling into some of the logical fallacies discussed earlier. See especially the comparative *ad hominem* argument (chapter 8, *I, (3)*) and the causal fallacies (chapter 8, *I, (10)-(13)*). There is also the fallacy of confusing historical description with authoritative teaching. Often a writer will pose a theological problem and then try to resolve it, not by exegeting Scripture but by describing various historical responses to it. One sometimes gets the impression in some circles that we are to resolve theological issues by counting noses among the Puritans! G. C. Berkouwer, too, often leaves the reader in doubt as to whether he is arguing his own view or simply describing the history of a controversy. Expressions like "it was said," or "the question was discussed" abound in his writings, and one sometimes has to read between the lines to see what Berkouwer is actually advocating. And once one finds out, it is often difficult to see why he chooses one historical position rather than another. He seems to be doing systematic theology in the guise of historical theology.

That fallacy is related to what in ethics is called the "naturalistic fallacy," the fallacy of deducing ethical duties from facts about the world, of deducing "ought from is." To a Christian, this practice is not always a fallacy. Norms and facts are perspectivally related; one cannot know a fact without at the same time knowing some ethical "ought" (cf. Part One above, also Part Two, passim). But a non-Christian ethic, which sees the facts of the world as ethically neutral, is indeed in danger of committing this fallacy. It seeks to derive values from *value-free* facts, and that cannot be done. Now although Berkouwer's problem is related to the naturalistic fallacy, it is not the same thing. Berkouwer is a Christian, and he believes that the facts of history are value-laden. The problem in Berkouwer and in other writers is not that they derive norms from descriptions but that they fail to show *how* the norm arises from the description. Scripture needs, in these contexts, to be brought in more explicitly as the criterion for historical evaluation. If and when that is done, the method of historical theology can be of great value to systematics or dogmatics.

(v) Finally, the "dogmatics" model can mislead theologians and their readers about the nature of theology. It can suggest that theology is a body of information that has increased in more or less steady fashion from the first century until now and that must be passed on intact to the next generation, that is, theology as accumulation.

Thomas Kuhn in *The Structure of Scientific Revolutions*[5] has attacked that picture in regard to science in general. He argues that science does not progress by uniform accumulation. Instead, Kuhn argues that one "paradigm," or master model, gains ascendancy over others, accumulates detailed verification, and eventually is overthrown by a competing paradigm that rearranges all the data in the overthrown paradigm. Likewise, theology progresses by revolution (or cataclysm), as well as by accumulation. Origen's paradigm was replaced by Augustine's, which was replaced by the Aristotelian Christianity of Aquinas, which was overthrown by the Reformation paradigm, which has largely been supplanted (I trust not irreversibly!) by different forms of modernism.

But even apart from Kuhn's arguments, the accumulation model must be challenged. Theology does not progress by accumulation but by application. In one sense, it does not even need to accumulate truths, for the truths are given once and for all in Scripture. The task of theology, therefore, is not to say anything new but to apply what Scripture says to new sit-

5. Chicago: University of Chicago Press, 1970.

uations. Thus the "accumulations" of theology are at most accumulations of applications.

If I am right about that, it implies that *not* all past theology must be passed on to future generations. Our job as theologians is to apply the Scriptures to current situations. That must be the focus of our endeavor. If some past theological achievements are relevant to this purpose, then they ought to be mentioned. If not, we may legitimately leave them aside. It is not the case that one *must* learn Augustine's theology before he can understand Calvin's (however useful that may be) or that one must learn Calvin's before he can understand what God is saying today. Thus the theologian must make critical decisions about what is important for *his* audience to learn. (Of course, he must also distinguish between what they need to know and what they want to know, between what is important for them and what they *think* is important.) He may not simply and uncritically unload upon twentieth-century students the whole weight of past theology.

B. SCIENCE

We have already considered a number of theological tools that may be called sciences—language sciences, logic, and history (cf. also some general considerations on the relation of Christianity to science in chapter 3, *B*).

Here I wish to make the general point that like linguistics, logic, and history, all sciences help us to apply and therefore to interpret Scripture. It is true that many sciences, perhaps all, today are dominated by unbelieving presuppositions, and therefore we must spend a lot of effort in separating wheat from chaff. But once we are clearly operating on biblical ground, we can learn much from the sciences.

(1) Sciences will sometimes lead us to reconsider the truth, not of Scripture but of our *interpretations* of Scripture. Galileo and others led the church to reconsider its view that Scripture taught geocentrism. In my opinion, that was a good thing, something that the church should have done earlier, rather than disciplining the heliocentrists. Geologists who believe in an "old earth" have led theologians to reconsider their exegesis of Genesis 1-2, convincing some evangelical and Reformed scholars to interpret the temporal indications in these chapters figuratively. At this moment, I do not know where the truth lies on that matter. But the discussion is a proper one. The geologists may turn out to be wrong (as the Creation Research Society argues), but until that is proved to the satisfac-

tion of most Christians, we ought to consider at least the possibility of a revised exegesis.

Consider an example from psychology. Psychological interest in encouraging a "good self-image" has had some influence, I think, in a trend away from "miserable-sinner" theology. It is becoming more evident that the New Testament does not call believers "sinners," even though it recognizes that they do sin (1 John 1:8-10). Even at their worst, Christians are saints of God—washed, sanctified, and justified. Sin has no dominion over them. Thus older hymns in which saved people continue to confess that they are worms and wretches no longer seem as appropriate as they once were. This development has not come about as a "concession to secular psychology" but because of a rereading of Scripture in the light of questions raised by psychology. The process of rereading is, of course, always in danger of leading to compromise, but in many cases it is edifying and helpful. We need not at all accept everything the psychologists say about self-image (I certainly do not) to rethink our interpretation of Scripture in this way.

(2) Science also aids application by describing the situation to which Scripture is being applied. Medical science gives us important data about the unborn child that may well influence our thinking on abortion. We must know what the unborn child *is* to know how Scripture relates to him. (Of course, Scripture also has some things to say about what the child is.) Similarly, we must know what an IUD does before we know whether the use of it is biblically right or wrong. To know that, we must consult some medical specialists.

(3) Sciences also help in the communication of theology, not only in supplying technology for the publication and distribution of theological materials but also in helping us write and speak more helpfully. Sociological studies of various cultures can help us contextualize the gospel for those cultures. Such studies help us see what language is understood, what is not, what conveys the appropriate emotional content, what is offensive. Indeed, we *want* to offend with the offense of the cross; but we do not want to offend in unnecessary ways. Rather, we want to "become all things to all men that [we may] by all means save some" (1 Cor. 9:22). Such studies provide us with legends, traditions, images, and historical memories known to the people by which we may make fruitful contact—using these to illustrate, underscore, or contrast the gospel.

(4) Is theology itself a science? Over the years a lot of ink has been spilled on this question—an amount in my judgment disproportionate to its importance. Many theologians have been eager to show that theology is

an academically respectable discipline. I really don't care very much whether it is or not. If it's not, so much the worse for the academy!

Theology does use scientific methods, as we have seen above. I am uncertain whether there are any scientific methods that are distinctive to theology or whether the scientific aspects of theology are borrowed from other disciplines. Perhaps that is a question of encyclopedia, another area in which I have little interest (cf. Appendix B, after Part One).

In any case, it must also be said that theology is not *only* a science. It uses not only the methods of science but also those of art, literature, philosophy, law, and education. Indeed, since theology must be lived as well as spoken, it uses all of the methods by which human beings accomplish things in God's world (cf. my critique of Hodge's theology/science parallel in chapter 3, A, *(2)*).

(5) Is theology the queen of the sciences? Not in the sense that theologians are always more correct than other scientists. Theologians are as fallible as other people are. And often, as we've seen, astronomers and geologists and psychologists can alert theology to possible errors in its reading of Scripture. But there is another sense in which theology governs other disciplines. Theology expresses and applies the ultimate presuppositions of the Christian, which must take precedence over all our other ideas. In that sense, my theology must take precedence over my geology or my psychology.

A scientific discovery, as we've seen, may lead me to change my interpretation of Scripture at some point, though it cannot in itself *dictate* such a change. But if, after reflection, I determine that my original interpretation of Scripture was correct and that still conflicts with the apparent results of science, then I must follow Scripture. That, indeed, was Abraham's situation, according to Romans 4. He saw that humanly speaking the divine promise could not be fulfilled. He was too old to beget a son, and his wife was far to old to bear one. Thus he had every "scientific" reason to say that the promise was impossible. Yet he trusted God's Word, forsaking the obvious scientific conclusion. In that sense, Abraham's theology ruled his science; theology was "queen."

(6) On the one hand, most theologians are reluctant to claim such status for their discipline. Indeed, many have so little respect for it that they regularly capitulate to every scientific fad that captures their imagination. It is certainly proper to charge liberal theology with a fairly wholesale sellout of theology to unbelieving science.

On the other hand, most theologians are not devoid of conscience in this matter, and most—even the most liberal—would seek to defend themselves against the charge of sell-out. Bultmann, for example, denied that he was selling out to the "modern world view." At times, he even expressed his indifference on the question of whether that world view is true. Rather, he said, he used the modern world view as a tool of communication to reach modern man with the gospel. In his view, he was not denying the gospel at all, for the gospel, as he understood it, is neutral on the question of world view. Thus we can present the gospel *in faithfulness to the Scriptures* without affirming the existence of angels or the possibility of miracle.

Now in my judgment, Bultmann's point is absurd. Clearly, one may *not* be faithful to the gospel and leave open the possibility that Jesus did not rise from the dead. Still, it is interesting to note that Bultmann thought as he did. He believed that he had not only a scientific warrant for believing as he did but a scriptural warrant, a theological warrant, as well. And for him, as a Christian theologian, the theological warrant was far more important. If (Bultmann tried to convince his readers) Scripture did not permit his construction, then he would not hold it merely to agree with the scientists.

That kind of stance is pretty common among liberal theologians. Liberal theology, after all, succeeds only insofar as it can convince people of its fundamental allegiance to the Christian revelation. Once it loses its credibility in that respect, it becomes just another form of free thought, like Unitarianism or the humanist associations. Liberal theology succeeds only when it has some measure (however spurious) of Christian credibility. (In other words, it succeeds only to the extent that it can be mistaken for evangelical orthodoxy.)

That fact, I think, is important when we deal with liberal theology. We are often tempted (and are usually correct) to write the whole project off as capitulation to secular science. But we do not adequately refute liberals by making that point alone. It is also necessary to address the theologian's *theological* rationale, to show that his pretense of scriptural warrant is illegitimate. We must not only show that his view is wrong, but we must also remove his cloak of Christian credibility.

Theologians with little background in science often are, I think, more qualified to argue on that level than to debate the scientific questions head-on. (Often, I think theologians make fools of themselves by taking the latter course, even when they are basically right.) I hope to write a book someday about the inerrancy of Scripture, seeking to show not that science proves the Bible true at every controverted point but that the *theological rationale* of liberals and others for abandoning inerrancy is inadequate. In that book, I will try to show that the liberal's theological rationale is fundamentally anti-abstractionist in nature and is thus prey to all the confusions characteristic of anti-abstractionism (see chapter 6, A).

C. PHILOSOPHY

Again, the reader should turn to chapter 3, C for a definition and some general comments. The most important points about philosophy closely parallel those made about science in the last section.

If anything, philosophy is even more in need of reformation than the sciences are. Still, I am not convinced that everything said by non-Christian philosophers is false! There are points at which a discerning theologian, operating on biblical presuppositions, can profit from the insights of non-Christian philosophers. The reader will have noticed favorable references in this book to Ludwig Wittgenstein, Thomas Kuhn, Irving Copi, and others. I see no reason why we should not "spoil the Egyptians" by making use of these able minds.

From philosophy (both Christian and non-Christian) we can learn a number of useful things.

(1) The history of philosophy shows the futility of trying to find a solid basis for knowledge apart from the God of Scripture, whether through rationalism, empiricism, subjectivism, idealism, or some other method.

(2) Philosophers have argued well, nevertheless, that we need norms, facts, and subjectivity if anything is to be known.

(3) And they have presented good cases for the interconnectedness of knowledge, in particular for the interdependence of metaphysics (theory of being), epistemology (theory of knowledge), and the theory of value (ethics, aesthetics).

(4) They have shown (either by admitting it or by trying and failing to escape the conclusion) that human thought is dependent on presuppositions and thus on circular argument.

(5) They have developed useful systems of logic and mathematics.

(6) They have developed a number of distinctions that are useful in the analysis of language, causality, priority, experience, ethical values, and other matters of importance to theology.

From a Christian philosophy, theoretically, we could learn much more. I do not believe, however, that a Christian philosophy now exists that is reasonably adequate for the needs of the modern Protestant theologian.

CHAPTER TEN

The Existential Perspective—The Qualifications of the Theologian

In our discussion of method, we have focused on the Scriptures and on the tools of theology. Now we must pay attention to the theologian as a person.

A. THE PERSONALISM OF THEOLOGY

Those who draw a close analogy between theology and science, or who conceive of theology as a traditional academic discipline, often fail to do justice to the intensely personal nature of theology. That personalism is evident from a number of considerations.

(1) Theology is the expression and application of a person's deepest convictions, his presuppositions. Therefore it is inevitable that in his work the theologian shares *himself* with his readers at a level of some intimacy.

(2) Theology (*didache*) is a ministry of the church, practiced by all Christians to some extent, but also a full-time calling given to ordained officers. Qualifications for the teaching office include a knowledge of the gospel, as well as skills of communication and, especially, qualities of Christian character (see below, section C). Of course, the ungodly can do theology; they must, for all human actions constitute responses to and applications of the

Word of God.[1] These applications can be right or wrong, that is, good or bad theology, but they are theology nonetheless. But good theology, theology as it should be done, can be done only by believers. And it is done best by mature believers. Therefore the personal life of the theologian is highly relevant to the credibility of his theological work.

(3) The presuppositions that govern our thinking arise from many sources—reason, sensation, emotion, and so forth. The most ultimate presuppositions are religious in nature. If all of one's life contributes to the presuppositions that underlie one's theology, then all of life contributes to theology as such.

(4) Such presuppositions influence our reading of Scripture, by which, in turn, we seek to validate our presuppositions. That is called the "hermeneutical circle." Circularity of that sort, as we saw earlier, is inevitable. Under the leading of the Spirit, however, it is not a vicious circle. Contact with God's Word purifies our presuppositions. Then, in turn, when we use our purified presuppositions to interpret Scripture, we come to a clearer understanding of Scripture. Without the Spirit's work, however, the circle can be regressive: bad presuppositions distort the meaning of Scripture, that distorted meaning leads to even worse presuppositions, and so forth. Hence we should not be surprised when we see apparently sincere and intellectually sophisticated "seekers after truth"—often among the cults (and often among the ranks of professional theological scholars!)—whose conclusions seem *incredibly* far from the truth. This is one way that obedience and knowledge are closely linked (cf. Part One).

(5) The kind of knowledge we gain through theology is intensely personal in character—the knowledge of God himself. Since God cannot be seen, heard, or touched, this knowledge is not reached by the experimental methods of natural science. Ian Ramsey uses the illustration of a courtroom scene in which everything proceeds quite impersonally, persons being referred to by titles ("the Crown," "the accused," "the prosecution," "your honor"). To his amazement, the magistrate looks up and sees as "the accused" his long lost wife. Suddenly, the whole situation takes on a different tone. The new tone is due not to anything that can be seen or heard but to a whole range of memories, past histories, affections, disappointments.[2] Ramsey's illustration would be misleading if it were taken (as perhaps it is by Ramsey) to illustrate the *whole* nature of Christian truth. Christianity is not just an aura of personal relationships that surrounds

1. Remember that God's Word is known not only through Scripture but also through nature (Rom. 1:18-32) as discussed in Part One.

2. Ian Ramsey, *Religious Language* (New York: Macmillan, 1957), 20ff.

purely natural events. The Resurrection, for example, was not merely the disciples' recollection of Jesus' relationship with them before His death; it was a miracle in space and time. The risen Jesus could be seen and heard and touched. But Ramsey's illustration does indicate something that is present in all theology, even when theology speaks of the Resurrection and other great historical events. For all theology confesses a personal relationship with God—a covenant relationship. The Jesus who was raised from the dead is "my Lord and my God" (John 20:28). He is the one with whom we too are raised (Col. 2:12f.; 3:1).

For that reason, we tend to feel uncomfortable with certain attempts at theological talk. It doesn't seem quite right, for example, to speak of the resurrection of Jesus' body as the "resuscitation of a corpse." Some liberal theologians point that out in defense of the view that Jesus was raised only "spiritually" while his corpse remained dead. "Of course," they say, "the resurrection of Jesus has nothing to do with [note the fallacious use of negation] the resuscitation of a corpse!" But the Christian's hesitation about the phrase "resuscitation of a corpse" is not because of any doubt in his heart about the literal truth of the Resurrection or its physical character. The reason, I think, is rather that the phrase "resuscitation of a corpse" is not covenant language. It is not the language of personal relationship, the language of love. It does not connote all the theological richness of the biblical teaching. It "abstracts" (!) the Resurrection from its natural context.

Propositional language is important to theology. Theology conveys information about God. The argument of Brunner and others that propositional knowledge weakens the personal character of relations is absurd. Gaining information about someone often deepens our relationship with him. Good theological language, however, is never *merely* propositional; it is simultaneously an expression of love and praise. Preachers as well as theologians need to keep that in mind and to avoid language that encourages their people to speak of God in a kind of clinical jargon. It is not that such jargon is always wrong or sinful. Abstractions are necessary, we may recall! But lack of balance here can lead people (and preachers) into bad habits of thought and life. Personalism in theology is a means of edification. When we neglect it, we simply are not communicating the whole counsel of God.

I have known professors of theology who are so zealous to defend the scientific character of theology and its academic respectability that they actually forbid the use of personal references in theological writing. They forbid the author to refer to himself or to someone else (except, of course, to the *ideas* of another); they think that theology consists exclusively of ideas devoid of personalities. There are, of course, dangers that such professors are rightly seeking to avoid. There is the danger, for example, of taking *ad hominem* arguments as conclusive. There is also the danger of writing out of personal vindictiveness, rather than concentrating on the theological issues. But as we have seen, there is a legitimate place in theology even for *ad hominem* arguments, and "issues" are not sharply separable from "personalities." People's ideas are closely related to their reputations and to their character (as God's Word is one with God himself). Personal references can scarcely be avoided in theology. Even the most academic theology is an expression of a person's heart-relation with God. If a theology did avoid personal references, it would be a theology without a soul.

(6) Personalism is also evident in the nature of theology and apologetics as *persuasion*. As we saw in Part Two, the purpose of these disciplines is not merely to construct valid and sound arguments but to persuade people, to edify. And the goal is not merely to bring them to intellectual assent but to help them to embrace the truth from the heart in love and joy, to motivate them to live out its implications in all areas of life. Thus theology must be "personalistic," not only in expressing the personhood of the theologian but also in addressing the full personhood of its hearer.

B. THE HEART

The knowledge of God is a heart-knowledge (see Exod. 35:5; 1 Sam. 2:1; 2 Sam. 7:3; Pss. 4:4; 7:10; 15:2; Isa. 6:10; Matt. 5:8; 12:34; 22:37; Eph. 1:18; etc.). The heart is the "center" of the personality, the person himself in his most basic character. Scripture represents it as the source of thought, of volition, of attitude, of speech. It is also the seat of moral knowledge. In the Old Testament, *heart* is used in contexts where *conscience* would be an acceptable translation (see 1 Sam. 24:5).

The fact that the *heart* is depraved, then, means that apart from grace we are in radical ignorance of the things of God (Part One). Only the grace of God, which restores us from the heart outward, can restore to us the knowledge of God that belongs to God's covenant servants—the knowledge that is correlative with obedience.

One implication of this fact is that the believer's knowledge of God is inseparable from godly character. The same Spirit who gives the first in regeneration also gives the second. And the qualifications for the ministry of teaching (theology) in Scripture are predominantly moral qualifications (1 Tim. 3:1ff.; 1 Peter 5:1ff.). Thus the quality of theological work is dependent not only on propositional knowledge or on skills in logic, history, linguistics, and so forth (which, of course, believers and unbelievers share to a large extent); it is also dependent on the theologian's character. (We saw in Part One how knowledge and obedience are linked in Scripture.)

A second implication is that the knowledge of God is gained not only through one "faculty" or another, such as the intellect or the emotions, but through the heart, the whole person. The theologian knows by means of everything he is and all the abilities and capacities that have been given him by God. Intellect, emotions, will, imagination, sensation, natural and spiritual gifts of skills—all contribute toward the knowledge of God. All knowledge of God enlists *all* our faculties, because it engages everything that we are.

In the sections that follow, therefore, I shall discuss these two implications in turn and in more detail: the theologian's character and the theologian's capacities (or faculties).

C. THE THEOLOGIAN'S CHARACTER—THE ETHICS OF THEOLOGY

We saw in Part One how knowledge of God is closely linked with faith (John 11:40), love (1 Cor. 8:1ff.; 1 John 4:8), and obedience (Jer. 22:16). But do these qualities of the redeemed life have anything specifically to do with the *methods* of theology? That is, do these qualities *really* influence our knowledge of God, or do we just talk that way to sound pious? I believe that they do. Scripture doesn't link knowledge with obedience for no reason. The relation of knowledge and obedience is a meaningful one, and since it is *meaningful*, it has *applications* to the concrete work of theology.

Edward John Carnell, in his remarkable apologetic *The Kingdom of Love and the Pride of Life*[3] remarks, following Kierkegaard, that the attitude of detachment, so often prized in the sciences and philosophy, cannot adequately yield the unique inner secrets of a person. To learn something about a person's subjectivity, there must be a personal relation established so that communication—revelation of person to person—can take place. That is, of course, true in regard to our knowledge of God. God reveals His best secrets to those who love Him best. The same is true in our attempts

3. (Grand Rapids: Wm. B. Eerdmans Pub. Co., 1960), 44ff. Unfortunately, the book is now out of print.

to understand, evaluate, and apply the writings of other theologians (which, indeed, constitutes a large part of the work of theology).

Therefore the qualifications for teachers in Scripture are largely qualities of character (1 Tim. 3:2-7; 2 Tim. 2; 3:10-17; James 3; 1 Peter 5:1-4). Teachers are to be worthy of imitation, as was Paul (and ultimately, Jesus himself; 1 Cor. 4:6; 11:1; Phil. 3:17; 1 Thess. 1:6f.; 2:6; 2 Thess. 3:7-9; 1 Tim. 4:12; Tit. 2:7; Heb. 13:7; 1 Peter 5:3). Notice also the surprisingly strong emphasis on Paul's personal visits to the churches (Rom. 1:8-17; 15:14-33; 1 Cor. 4:14-21; 5:1-5; 2 Cor. 7:5-16; 12:14-13:10; Gal. 4:12-20; Eph. 6:21f.; Col. 4:7ff.; 1 Tim. 3:14f.; 2 Tim. 4:6-18; Tit. 3:12-14; Heb. 13:7f., 22f.; 2 John 12; 3 John 13f.). There is something important that the churches learned from those personal visits that could not have been taught by letter alone.

The meaning of Scripture is its use, and therefore teaching of it is best done by word and life (i.e., example) together. The apostolic example shows God's people how to use the Word, how to apply it. It is therefore an important aspect of teaching, of theology. Of course, not everything a teacher does will be worthy of imitation (not even every apostolic action was normative—Gal. 2:11-14). But a teacher's life must embody a level of godliness adequate to demonstrate the meaning of his teaching—a way of life dramatically different from that of the sinful world.

Thus the theologian's character gives him, by grace, that exemplary life that is requisite for the work of Christian teaching. But even if we seek to ignore that aspect and focus exclusively on verbal theology, we will find that that, too, is highly influenced by the theologian's character. Negatively, I believe that many of the ambiguities, fallacies, and superficialities that abound in theology are failures of character as much as (or more than) intellect. Many of these could be avoided if theologians showed a bit more love toward their opponents and their readers, a bit more humility about their own level of knowledge, a bit more indulgence in pursuing the truth, a little more simple fairness and honesty. Consider some of the worst theological practices from this perspective.

(1) First, the practice of taking an opponent's view in the worst possible sense, without first seeking to find a way of interpreting him so that his view is more plausible or even correct. Generally, this practice arises out of sheer hostility, blinding the theologian to more loving (and at the same time, more intellectually cogent) possibilities. This often leads to a "straw man" argument (i.e., an argument against a view that the opponent does not actually hold, which, perhaps, no one actually holds). It always weakens, rather than strengthens, the theologian's case against his opponent.

True, sometimes the "worst possible sense" is the correct way to interpret a theologian. But we should adopt such interpretations only as last resorts, only when all other possibilities fail. Love is not "easily angered" (1 Cor. 13:5). We are not to criticize others without careful attempts to ascertain the truth (Num. 35:30; Deut. 17:6ff.; 2 Cor. 13:1; 1 Thess. 5:21; 1 Tim. 5:19).

(2) Another theological evil is that of trying to appear more orthodox than you are by concealing, for certain readers, the more controversial features of your position. Cultists often pose as evangelical Christians when speaking to initial inquirers; only later does the inquirer discover that the cult is polytheistic or denies the deity of Christ or worships a cult leader or sanctions adultery. At the early stage, one learns only the best aspects of the cult. Only later, after some indoctrination, does he learn the distinctives. Well, that is what we expect from cults. The same sort of thing happens, however, in the theological mainstream. Theologians often go to great lengths to show how their views are more biblical than their opponents, saving until later (or passing over very rapidly) the disconcerting news that they reject the orthodox doctrine of biblical authority. Sometimes the controversial notions will be so subtly mixed in with traditional gospel truth that the reader will be taken completely off guard.

Much of Barth's writing, for example, is quite indistinguishable from evangelicalism, even from Reformed theology. Once one gets beyond his popular works, however, and into his *Church Dogmatics*, one learns that for Barth the Creator-creature distinction vanishes "in Christ," except that God maintains a kind of nominalistic "freedom" whereby He can renounce His very deity. A theologian, of course, does not have an obligation to include all his most controversial notions in his popular books; some of those notions are just too technical and difficult. But sometimes there almost seems to be a conspiracy (of the theologian in question and his supporters) to make a theology appear (to church courts, to beginning students, to supporters of educational institutions) more orthodox than it really is. Sometimes, indeed, there is the paradox that with one audience a theologian will make his work appear as conservative as possible, but with another he will try to show how radical, new, and different he is. It is often hard to avoid finding in such behavior a kind of "men-pleasing" of the sort that Scripture condemns.

(3) The inverse is also true. In expounding his opponent's views, the theologian may present only the most controversial or objectionable features of his opponent's position. Often in ethical literature, an author will attack a traditional position by presenting an extreme (often hypothetical)

case in which it is difficult to apply or even defend the traditional view. What goes unnoticed is that *all* ethical positions have difficulties. Any principle you choose (or any *un*principled position you take) will be hard to apply in some cases. The nontraditional ethicist will also have difficulties applying his approach in some areas.

Often, too, a theologian will attack the view of another by presenting objections to which the other has already replied, deliberately neglecting to deal with those replies. To unsophisticated readers, he conveys a false impression, suggesting that his opponent has no replies to his objections, when in fact he does. William Hordern charges that those who hold orthodox views of Scripture reject the possibility of God's giving guidance to people today.[4] He makes no mention of the obvious orthodox reply, one that has been made over and over again, that God continues to speak to us today *through* the infallible Scriptures, confirming and applying them to our needs by the work of the Holy Spirit. Thus Hordern gives to his readers the false impression that the orthodox have no reply to his point. This omission only makes his own discussion more shallow, since at this point he fails to deal with his opponent's position in its strongest form.

Like *(1)*, which dealt with one theologian's interpretation of another, this procedure violates the biblical exhortation "in humility [to] consider others better than yourselves" (Phil. 2:3). In these examples, one presents the position of another in the worst possible light. That is not exemplary of the love of Christ. We must remember that we will be judged by the standards with which we judge others (Matt. 7:1-5). We ought, therefore, not to demand of other theologians a kind of rigor to which our own thought would not measure up.

(4) A common form of unclarity occurs when the theologian states the traditional or orthodox view in untraditionally vague language, so that his own view, however radical or new, may appear to be within the bounds of orthodoxy. Paul Tillich, for instance, points out that the orthodox tradition recognizes some inadequacy in the symbols with which it describes God. To say that God is a "person" is to speak symbolically; God is more than what is connoted by the term *person*. From that fact, Tillich deduces that impersonal language about God is as appropriate as personal language, if not more so. But he neglects to point out that representatives of orthodoxy, such as Augustine, Luther, Calvin, and the church creeds (to say nothing of Scripture itself), uniformly prefer the personalistic language and

4. "The Nature of Revelation," in *The Living God*, ed. M. Erickson (Grand Rapids: Baker Book House, 1973), 178.

criticize as heresies some of the doctrines (like pantheism) associated with the impersonal language favored by Tillich. Often, too, the orthodox doctrine of Scripture is presented in such vague terms (for example, "Scripture is from God")[5] that it may coexist with almost any form of modern biblical criticism.

(5) Some theologians leave the impression that their view is the only alternative to another (or group of others) that is obviously objectionable (see chapter 8, *H*, *(4)*). Often such claims are so obviously false that it is difficult to believe that the theologian himself is unaware of their falsity.

(6) Sometimes, a theologian will attack the view of another simply by offering arguments for his own view, not even considering the arguments underlying his opponent's position. Such an approach is, of course, unfair to the opponent and puts his position in a worse light than it deserves (as in *(1)* and *(3)* above). To persuade someone of your view, you must not only argue your view, you must also refute the arguments by which your opponent arrived at *his* view. Without such consideration, your own argument will not be adequately persuasive. Note again how cogency and love go together.

(7) Often a theologian will correctly identify a weakness in the view of another but will play that weakness for far more than it is really worth. Thus minor differences are elevated to major differences, and theological disputes become church divisions. How contrary to the teaching of Scripture (see John 17:11, 22f.; 1 Cor. 1:11ff.; 3; 12; Eph. 4:3-6)! We have a responsibility before God not to exaggerate the importance of our differences. Some doctrinal differences (for example, over vegetarianism, observance of days, idol food—see Rom. 14; 1 Cor. 8-10) are treated very mildly in the New Testament, both parties being urged to live together in love, without any reference to formal discipline. Other issues (for example, Judaizing as Paul attacks it in Galatians) are much more serious, because they compromise the heart of the gospel. It is theologically and spiritually important to be able to recognize that difference and to behave appropriately.

Positively, we must learn to theologize in love (Eph. 4:15), a love that edifies and that promotes unity, not division. Theology ought to seek and promote *reconciliation* among brethren, even among denominations and theological traditions, as much as that is possible.

5. Cf., e.g., G. C. Berkouwer, *Holy Scripture* (Grand Rapids: Wm. B. Eerdmans Pub., Co., 1975), 142ff. "Scripture is from God" says very little about the Bible. All books are "from God" in one way or other.

Our "multiperspectival" approach offers some promising options in this regard. One suggestion (which I owe to Vern S. Poythress): build on the *strengths* of your opponent. Even the worst theology generally has some area of strength, some concern that is genuinely biblical. For example, Arminians (I am a Calvinist!) are strong in their concern for the importance of human decision, the fact that our choices have eternal significance. A Calvinist can build on that strength, seeking to show the Arminian that full justice can be done to his concern only within a Calvinistic framework. Yes, human decisions are eternally significant, he can say. But why are they so? Man is, after all, such a small creature in the universe. Why should his decisions have any important effects, even in his own life? The reason is that God has *declared* those decisions to be significant. (Up until this point, the Arminian would agree.) But God's declaration is a powerful one. He backs it up with deeds. He *makes* our decisions significant. *He sees to it* that everyone who believes is saved. Otherwise, a decision to believe is insignificant, a mere moment in human life that may or may not have any long-term significance whatever. Thus only a Calvinistic view of divine sovereignty enables us to take human decisions with full seriousness.

What is happening here? We have seen that all theological doctrines are interdependent (chapter 8, *F*). Each can be seen as a "perspective" on the whole of theology. Thus we can begin our theologizing with the doctrine of human responsibility, and once we understand that doctrine, we have understood all the rest. Therefore we begin there and use human responsibility as a "perspective" on the whole Reformed faith.

And, of course, we can make more obvious suggestions in our quest for a reconciling theology. We can analyze ambiguities, for often two positions that appear to be opposed are really compatible with one another, and we can see that compatibility once we express the positions more clearly. Also, we can be more self-critical. Self-criticism is a form of biblical humility that is necessary when we seek to rebuke others (Gal. 6:1; Matt. 7:1-5).

D. THE THEOLOGIAN'S CAPACITIES—THE SKILLS OF THEOLOGY

I drew two conclusions from the premise that the knowledge of God is a heart-knowledge. First, the theologian's character plays an important (and very practical) role in the work of theology. Second, the knowledge of God is a knowledge gained by the whole person as an integral unity—from his "center." I discussed the first implication in the previous section; now I must move on to the second.

To say that theological knowledge is a knowledge gained by the "whole person" raises questions about the relations of unity to diversity in the human personality. Traditionally, theologians and philosophers have distinguished various "faculties" within the human mind: reason, will, emotion, imagination, perception, intuition, and others. These distinctions have given rise to questions about which faculty is "primary." Some have argued for "the primacy of the intellect," reasoning that emotion, imagination, and so forth will lead us astray if they are not disciplined, corrected, and evaluated by intellectual processes. Others have said that the will is primary, for even intellectual belief is something that is *chosen*. Others have postulated the primacy of feeling, since everything that we believe or choose to do we choose or do because in some sense we *feel* like choosing or doing it. And arguments for the primacy of other faculties are similar.

Well, the alert reader can doubtless predict what is coming now. I think there is truth in all of those contentions and that they can be reconciled with one another, to an extent, if we see man's various faculties as perspectivally united. To speak of human "faculties" is to speak of diverse perspectives in terms of which we can look at the various acts and experiences of the human mind. None of the faculties, so understood, exists or acts apart from the others, each is dependent on the others, and each includes the others. Let us look at them one by one, noting some of these close relations among them.

(1) Reason

The term *reason* has a long history in western philosophy and has been used in a wide variety of ways. It can refer to logic, to those particular laws of logic called the "laws of thought"—particularly the "law of noncontradiction." Some philosophers have used *reason* to denote a particular *method* of thinking (defined, of course, by their philosophical schemes) or even to refer to their philosophy in general. (One is tempted to think that for Hegel *reason* was synonymous with *Hegelianism*.)

In this context (and in most others) I think it is least misleading to define *reason* in two ways. First, I think that *reason* should be defined as the human ability or capacity for forming judgments and inferences. So understood, reasoning is something that we do all the time (see chapter 8, A, *(1)*), not merely when we are pursuing academic or theoretical disciplines.

That is how *reason* is used in a *descriptive* sense. Second, I shall also use the term in a *normative* sense to denote *correct* judgments and inferences. In the first (descriptive) sense, an incorrect inference would be rational, for it is an exercise of reason as a human capacity. In the second sense, it would not be rational, for it would not measure up to the criteria of sound reasoning.[6]

Having defined *reason* in those ways, we can see that theology ought to be rational. Theology *is* the forming of judgments and inferences based on God's Word (applications being both judgments and inferences), and therefore it is a form of reasoning (descriptive), in the nature of the case. Furthermore, in the discussion of logic, I have already established that Scripture warrants making judgments and inferences (chapter 8, C). Theology that makes sound judgments and draws sound conclusions from Scripture would be rational in the normative sense.

To say that theology ought to be rational is really no different from saying that it ought to be scriptural or that it ought to be true. As we saw in our discussion of logic, when done properly, logic adds nothing to its premises but functions as a tool that helps us to see what is implicit in those premises, what they really say. That, indeed, is what logic is intended to do. When a deductive process changes the meaning of a set of premises, it is thereby defective. A system of logic that leads to such change is to that extent an inadequate system. The goal of logic is simply to set forth the premises as they really are. Similarly, the goal of theological reasoning is simply to set forth Scripture as it really is (including, of course, its applications, which constitute its meaning). Thus rationality in theology is nothing more or less than scripturality. It is not a separate set of norms to which theology must conform *in addition to* its conformity to Scripture.[7] Thus theologians ought not to feel threatened by the demand for rationality. Of course, if rationality is defined not as scripturality but as conformity to some theories of modern science, history, philosophy, and so forth, then conflict is inevitable.

Therefore when someone tells me that reason must be the judge of theological ideas, I can agree with him in a sense. My rational capacity is the capacity to make judgments, and so to say that theological judgments must be rational (in the descriptive sense) is a tautology. In the normative sense,

6. See, however, Appendix I for some additional questions bearing on the definition of *reason*.

7. And even if it were, for the Christian those norms would be subordinate to the ultimate norm, Scripture itself. Thus any demonstration of the rationality of Scripture would still be circular.

too, theology ought to be judged by reason, for that only means that inferences and judgments based on Scripture ought to be *sound* inferences and judgments, ones that really conform with Scripture. To speak of reason as a "judge," however, is rather strange. That may suggest to some (though not necessarily and not to all) that reason operates with some criteria independent of Scripture. Or such language may confuse my norm (Scripture) with one of my psychological capacities.

Must theology, then, conform to reason? Yes. But that means only that theology must conform with rigorous logic to its proper criterion, the inspired Scriptures.

Does reason have some sort of "primacy" over our other faculties? Well, all of our emotional inclinations, imaginative ideas, intuitions, experiences, and so forth must conform to reason, or they do not tell us the truth. But what does "conformity to reason" mean in this context? As we have seen, it means nothing more than "conformity to Scripture" or "conformity to truth." Thus to say that these must conform to reason to tell the truth is really a tautology. It is like saying you must be unmarried to be a bachelor. But we would not want to say that "being a bachelor" is a criterion or test of being unmarried. (The opposite would be equally plausible and equally implausible.) Thus there is circularity here.

Thus the *primacy of reason* in the above sense says very little. It does not even rule out a similar primacy for other faculties, even the emotions. Imagine someone who claims that he has come to know something through his emotions. If his claim is correct, then his emotions have led him into "conformity with truth." Given the definition above, that is the same as "conformity to reason." Emotion, in other words, as a way of attaining knowledge, is a form of reason. If his claim is not correct, one may still call his emotions a form of reason, for they are one of the capacities by which he makes judgments and inferences, even though they are not reliable in this case. In this case, then, we may say that his emotions are reason in a descriptive, not a normative, sense.

Indeed, it is possible that *reason* is only a name that we give to the inference and judgment-making capacities of the other faculties. Or, perhaps, it is a perspective on those other faculties, looking at them from the perspective of their role in discovering truth. (We shall see that when we look at them from that perspective, we must look at their other roles as well; thus reason would be a perspective on *everything* done by these faculties.)

In what follows, I shall try to clarify the foregoing discussion by looking at these relations from the other side, from the side of the emotions, imagination, and so forth. I shall try to show the role of these other faculties in forming judgments, as well as mention their other roles and the inseparability of the various roles from one another. If I am correct in my perspectival model, these subsequent discussions will also in effect be discussions of reason, enlarging upon what I have said in this section.

(2) Perception and Experience

Perception is associated with the sense organs, but it is not merely a synonym for sensation. *Sensation* refers to the operations of the sense organs, whether or not these operations yield knowledge. Perception, on the other hand, is a form of knowledge, the knowledge gained through the process of sensation. We say "I perceive x" when we see, hear, smell, taste, or feel x, when in our opinion the operations of the sense organs yield knowledge of x.[8]

Experience is a broader category than perception. It is possible to have an experience of something (for example, a prophet's experience of the divine Word) without perceiving it through the sense organs; at least that possibility is arguable. Following George Mavrodes,[9] however, we may understand experience in a way that is parallel to our account of perception. Mavrodes takes the x in "I experienced x" to refer not merely to a psychological state but to an object existing independently of the one who experiences it. Thus to say "I experienced x" is to claim that through my experience I have gained some knowledge of x.

Mavrodes also argues that experiencing x involves making some judgment about x.[10] The same is true of perceptual language (perceiving x, seeing x, hearing x, etc.) He adds,

> But . . . I do not know how to make more precise just how appropriate the judgment must be. It is fairly clear that a man may really see a wolf in the woods, though he takes it to be a dog. It seems, therefore, that the judgment need not be entirely correct. On the other hand, it also seems clear that a man may be in the presence of a wolf, in the sense that light reflected from the wolf stimulates his eye, etc., and yet make no judgment whatever, perhaps because he is preoccupied. In that case we would probably say that he failed to see the animal at all.[11]

8. I could say, then, that sensation is physical and perception is mental, but I don't want to get into the mind-body question in this book. That and the body-soul-spirit relationship will have to wait for another time, or, more likely, another writer.

9. *Belief in God* (New York: Random House, 1970), 50ff.

10. Ibid., 52.

11. Ibid.

Perceiving and experiencing, then, are not activities sharply different from reasoning. They are processes by which we reach judgments, even if those judgments are not always perfectly correct. Are they, like reason, means of *inference?* Of course, experiencing or perceiving something does not usually, if ever, involve going through a syllogism in the head. But if "reasoning" or "informal logic" is something that goes on in all of life, even when no conscious syllogizing takes place (see *(1)* above and chapter 8, A, *(1)*), then nothing prevents us from seeing experience or perception as a kind of inference. Data is presented to the senses. From that data, we infer the presence of objects or the existence of states of affairs.

Of course, as I indicated frequently in the earlier sections of this book, we have no access to uninterpreted data. "I see the tree" presupposes sense experience and a lifetime of conceptual learning by which I learn to place certain kinds of sensations in this particular category. "My father was here last night" may have been verified in part by sense experience, yet one cannot tell by sensation alone that a certain man is one's father. That judgment presupposes some historical knowledge beyond any possible verification by the direct experience of the individual. Thomas Kuhn's reports of anomalous card experiments, again, suggest that what we see is greatly influenced by what we expect to see, that expectation is influenced by a wide variety of factors.[12]

Reasoning, then, the capacity for making judgments and inferences, is present in all experience and perception as we have defined them. And as I indicated in my discussion of logic, logic is also dependent on perception and experience, since a logical syllogism must have premises, and premises are not usually, if ever, supplied by logic alone (see chapter 8, *D*). In any case, the use of logic is inconceivable without any experience at all, for we must at least experience the existence of logical principles if we are to perform any logical operations.

On the one hand, reasoning, then, involves experience, and experience involves reasoning. Epistemological attempts to build up the fabric of human knowledge from "pure experience" (corresponding to "brute facts"), untainted by any use of reason (empiricism), or from reason alone apart from experience (rationalism) cannot succeed. Attempts to account for knowledge in either of these ways are generally attempts to find some "bedrock" of truth, an "ultimate starting point" (either experience or reason) apart from God's Word. But God will not allow this. His creation is

12. See Thomas Kuhn, *The Structure of Scientific Revolutions* (Chicago: University of Chicago Press, 1970).

perspectival; all creatures are equally ultimate.[13] There is no bedrock except the divine Word.

Thus when Scripture speaks about "hearing," "seeing," and "touching" the Word of Life (1 John 1:1), it is not speaking about mere sensation, the mere workings of the sense organs apart from any rational thought. Such a concept of "sensation"—a philosophical abstraction—is not found in Scripture. To see, hear, or touch the risen Christ involves making a judgment about Him, an inference; it involves reasoning.

On the other hand, according to Scripture the knowledge of God does not come from mere reasoning apart from sensation, either. The verse cited above, and many others, make that fact evident.[14] Perception, rightly understood, is a legitimate means of knowledge. God has given us our sense organs (Exod. 4:11; Ps. 94:9; Prov. 20:12), and He assures us in His Word that though perception is fallible (so, of course, is reason), it is a means of knowledge (Matt. 5:16; 6:26ff.; 9:36; 15:10; Luke 1:2; 24:36-43; John 20:27; Rom. 1:20; 10:14-17; 2 Peter 1:16-18; 1 John 4:14).

Living between the apostolic age and the *parousia*, we are no longer in a position to see the risen Christ with the physical eye. But perception still plays a major role in theology. We perceive the biblical text through the senses, as well as other texts that serve as tools of theology. And by the senses we perceive the ancient manuscripts and artifacts of ancient culture that help us reconstruct the meaning of the text. And of course experience also reveals the present situation to which our theology will be applying the text.

And there is also that experience by which we grow in Christian maturity—the experience of living the Christian life, meeting challenges, succeeding, failing, praying, finding answers to prayer, persevering when answers aren't given, struggling against sin, and enduring hardship for Christ's sake. In many situations we live out those experiences described in Scripture; we experience what the Lord Jesus and His great saints experienced. Experience in this sense is important in showing us the meaning

13. The ultimate theological reality is the perspectival nature of God himself as a Trinity (see chapter 6, *B*). Everything in creation is related to everything else (see chapter 6, *A*), and thus everything in creation is a kind of vantage point in relation to which we may observe the rest of the universe. One or another of these vantage points may be more valuable to us than others on some occasions. But in principle any of them will serve this function, for all of them are equally created, equally placed by God in relation to the other creatures in the world. The ontological equality of created things insures that any of them may, on some occasions, be suitably used as a perspective.

14. On this point, see the discussion by Robert Reymond in *The Justification of Knowledge* (Nutley, N.J.: Presbyterian and Reformed Pub. Co., 1976).

of Scripture. Less experienced saints can always look things up in commentaries, but there is a special kind of insight that comes to those who have long had firsthand experience of the Christian warfare. (A young soldier may learn the rules, history, and techniques of warfare in the military academy, but there is much that he can learn only on the actual field of battle.) There is much, for example, in the Psalms that one cannot understand very well until he has undergone some of the same experiences as the psalmists and has understood the analogies between his experience and theirs.[15]

Christian teachers with that kind of experience have greater credibility, too, than those who have merely theorized about the gospel. A professor of mine once complained about a Sunday school program at his church, where his five-year-old son sang with other children a happy chorus about being "more than conquerors" in Christ. The professor thought that was somewhat silly; the kids hadn't conquered anything! I disagreed. I thought, and still do, that if the children were "in Christ," they had through Christ already conquered everything, in a significant sense. But my professor was not entirely wrong. He rightly sensed that when sung by the children, those words lacked the kind of credibility they would have on the lips of, say, the apostle Paul himself. Paul endured imprisonment, stoning, abandonment, treachery, loneliness, and the "thorn in the flesh" for the sake of Christ. When a man like that is still able to say "We are more than conquerors," his words carry a special kind of force. For him, the victory of Christ has been worked out in his life in a great many concrete ways. And that kind of life deserves and evokes a profound respect, giving his words a greater impact.

(3) EMOTION

a. *Emotions and Redemption*

Scripture doesn't discuss "the emotions" in any systematic way, any more than it discusses "the intellect." Yet Scripture has much to say about our emotions, about our joys, sorrows, anxieties, fears, and gladness. (Love, too, has a large emotional component, though it is best not to define it as an emotion.) Satan's temptation in the Garden appealed to Eve's emotions (Gen. 3:6), but also, importantly, to her intellectual pretensions, her desire to determine the truth autonomously, (3:1, 4, 5). Disobedience to God, however, did not lead to happy feelings but to shame (3:7). Fallen

15. I remember this point from a lecture by Pastor Albert N. Martin of Essex Falls, N.J.

man has a distinctively fallen complex of emotions: hatred of God, His Word, His creation, His people and love of the world, the flesh, the Devil. But redemption brings principial restoration: love of God, hatred of evil.

Redemption doesn't make us more emotional (as some charismatics might suppose) or less so (as many Reformed would prefer), any more than it makes us more or less intellectual. What redemption does to the intellect is to consecrate that intellect to God, whether the I.Q. is high or low. Similarly, the important thing is not whether you are highly emotional or not; the important thing is that whatever emotional capacities you have should be placed in God's hands to be used according to His purposes.

Thus intellect and emotion are simply two aspects of human nature that together are fallen and together are regenerated and sanctified. Nothing in Scripture suggests that either is superior to the other. Neither is more fallen than the other, neither is necessarily more sanctified than the other.

Greek philosophy traditionally presented a different picture: the human problem is a sort of derangement of the faculties. Whereas the reason ought to be in control, unfortunately the emotions often rule. Salvation comes (through philosophy, of course!) when we learn to subordinate emotions to reason. That idea is, of course, very plausible. We all know of people who get "carried away" by their feelings and do very stupid things. Such people are often rightly told by Christian counselors not to "follow their feelings."

But the Fall was not essentially a derangement of faculties within man. It was rebellion of the whole person—intellect as much as emotions, perception, and will—against God. My problem is not something within me; it is me. I must take the responsibility, unless Jesus Christ takes that responsibility in my place.

b. *Emotions and Decisions*

It is true, of course, that people sometimes "follow their feelings," rather than thinking responsibly. But it is also the case that people sometimes follow rationalistic schemes that run contrary to what they know in their "guts" (feelings) to be true. God gives us multiple faculties to serve as a sort of internal system of checks and balances. Sometimes reason saves us from emotional craziness, but emotions can also check the extravagant pretenses of reason.

Imagine someone from a Reformed background attending a charismatic meeting. He has been told that there is nothing good in the charismatic movement, and he has thought it all through intellectually. He thinks he has some pretty good arguments. Yet while at the meeting, he finds himself clapping, shouting "Amen," and rejoicing in the fellowship. Afterward comes time to give account! What should he do? Should he repent of having allowed his emotions to overrule his carefully wrought theory?

Well, he ought to think some more, obviously! Something is wrong somewhere, but it is not obvious *what* is wrong. Possibly, his emotions led him into a false path. Or, possibly, his emotions were leading him, properly, to reconsider the overly harsh judgments of his theoretical analysis. He must reason under the authority of Scripture. But that reason will have to take his new-found feelings into account. And he will not achieve complete "cognitive rest" until his intellect and emotions are somehow reconciled.

Here is another illustration. Writing book reviews is one of the more "intellectual" tasks that I perform. But it is interesting to see the role that emotions play even in that activity. After reading the first chapter of a book, I often have "a certain feeling" about the book: I like it or I don't like it or I have a reaction that is somewhere in between. I then try to think it through. Why do I have this feeling? My rational reflection may lead to a change in feeling, or it may enable me to defend and articulate the feeling. Still, the feeling plays a crucial role. I cannot imagine doing academic work at all without having some feelings of that sort. If I had no feelings about the book I was reviewing, I would simply set it aside. The feeling guides my reflection; my reflection refines my feelings. Those refined feelings provoke additional reflection, and so on. The goal is a satisfying analysis, an analysis I feel good about, one with which I have cognitive rest, a peaceful relation between intellect and emotion. That relation seems to me to be involved in all knowledge.

Scripture itself sometimes places emotion in the role that is often given to intellect or will. Psalm 37:4 says, "Delight yourself in the Lord, and he will give you the desire of your heart." And 2 Corinthians 7:10 says, "Godly sorrow brings repentance that leads to salvation and leaves no regret. . . ." It is not always wrong to "follow your feelings."

c. *Emotions and Knowledge*

The foregoing discussion suggests that emotions contribute to knowledge. When I experience joy, that joy is itself a datum that must be accounted for within the fabric of my knowledge. The joy does not just happen; it has a cause. It is a response of my mind and body to something or other. It may not be a proper response (any more than my reasoning and sensations always lead me to the truth), but it is a means by which truth reaches me. It is a means of knowledge.

In Part Two, chapter 5, C, we saw the importance of "cognitive rest" in human knowledge. That cognitive rest is something mysterious and difficult to describe. But it would not be wrong, I think, to describe it as a feeling—not a feeling like that of hot or cold that can be physically quantified, that is in fact a form of sensation, but a feeling like joy or sadness, the happiness at the completion of a task, the acceptance of the intellectual *status quo*, the confidence with which we entertain our idea. In other words, cognitive rest is something very much like an emotion.

Therefore (though my good friend and colleague Jay Adams balks at the suggestion), it is not entirely wrong to substitute "I feel" for "I believe." Of course, when people say "I feel that x is the case," they often seek to avoid responsibility for discerning objective truth. That is Adams's point and one that is quite true. But one may use the language of feeling without intending to flee responsibility. That language does, moreover, say something true about the nature of knowledge. Having a belief is, indeed, having a certain kind of feeling *about a proposition*. And when that feeling leads us rightly, that belief, that feeling, constitutes knowledge.

d. *Emotion as a Perspective*

Our previous discussions indicate that emotion is an important factor in knowing, one that interacts with reason in important ways. There is a mutual dependence between reason and emotion. But the considerations in the previous section (c) suggest that emotion is more than a mere "factor" in knowledge; it is a perspective on knowledge as a whole. "Feeling that p is true" *is* "believing that p is true," when that belief is viewed from a certain perspective. And a right (i.e., justified and true) feeling is a right belief, that is, knowledge.

Reasoning and feeling, then, are coterminous. To reason is to experience certain feelings concerning propositions; to emote is to draw from the data of experience certain logical applications to our subjectivity (which subjectivity is itself a perspective on the whole of reality).

Reasoning, perceiving, and feeling can be seen respectively as normative, situational, and existential perspectives on the human mind. We speak of reasoning when we want to focus on the mind's use of various principles and laws. We speak of perceiving when we want to focus on its access to the objective world. And we speak of feeling when we want to focus on the integrity of our subjectivity in the cognitive process.

e. *Emotion and Theology*

Thus emotion is unavoidably present in all theological work. It is important that we not stifle our emotional capacities by a too rigidly academic model of theology. We must be free in our theological work to make the proper emotional response to God's Word and to its applications. Otherwise, our theological knowledge itself will be in jeopardy.

Of course, the content of Scripture is not merely emotive. (The attempt by the logical positivists to classify all religious language as "emotive" seems rather silly today, even to those fairly sympathetic to the positivist movement.) But every part of it is emotive in the sense that every part is intended by God to generate a particular emotional response. He wants us to hate the evil, to rejoice in the good, to fear the threats, to embrace the promises.[16] That emotive content, as well as the conceptual content, must be applied to God's people. That, too, is the work of theology. If I read Romans 11:33-36 ("Oh, the depth of the riches both of the wisdom and knowledge of God! . . .") in a monotone, avoiding all trace of emotion, clearly I have not communicated the content of the verses very well, even if I have read every word perfectly. Similarly, if I expound those verses in a commentary or sermon, without somehow taking account of the depth of feeling there, I have obviously missed something enormously important. Systematic theology, too, must not ignore the emotive content of Scripture. That is not to say that theology must always be uttered, as it were, in an excited tone, but the theologian should *take account of* the Bible's emotive tone, as he would take account of any other biblical datum.

Romans 11:33-36, for example, makes it clear that the incomprehensibility of God is an *exciting* doctrine. It is a significant theological question to ask what generates this excitement and what can be done to restore it in our own time.

f. *Cultivating Godly Emotions*

A theologian, therefore, ought to have godly emotions. He ought to be the sort of person who rejoices in what is good and who hates what is evil. And he should be able to express and communicate that joy or hate infectiously.

To go into detail on how godly emotions are cultivated will take us afield. Some would argue that we cannot change our feelings per se. We can change feelings, they say, only by changing our behavior, our habits. I would reply that changing one's habits is important but that doing so pre-

16. See the *Westminster Confession of Faith*, XVI, 2.

supposes growth in knowledge, Christian rationality, perception, imagination, will, and so forth. Transformation of the emotions is part of the whole "package" of sanctification—transformation of the person as a whole. Growth in any one area can and will strengthen all the others.

In any case, it will not do to say that we "cannot" change how we feel. God demands change, and in one way or another, He will provide the means of change.

(4) IMAGINATION

Imagination has a rather bad reputation in some orthodox circles. *Imagination* in the KJV Old Testament generally refers to the inclinations of the rebellious heart (Gen. 6:5; 8:21; Deut. 29:19; 31:21; Jer. 3:17; 7:24; passim in Jeremiah). Although that is not the normal meaning of the word in modern English, some of the stigma from the older usage still colors the way some Christians understand the word. Nevertheless, I hope to rehabilitate *imagination*.

Imagination refers to our ability to think about things that are not. We can think about the past, though the past is by definition no longer present. We can think of possible or probable futures, though the future cannot be perceived. Or we can imagine mere alternate states of affairs, whether or not they have existed or could exist in the present or future. Thus our imaginations allow us to think of fantasy, of conditionals that are contrary to fact, of "what-if" scenarios.

Thus imagination has much to do with creativity, with art. (Recall what we said earlier about the inadequacies of the scientific model of theology.) Imagination has much to do with any attempt to do things in a new or different way.

In some theological circles, creativity itself has a bad name, perhaps being related in some minds to the "evil imaginations" of Jeremiah's prophecies or perhaps merely offending conservative sensibilities. Some intelligent people, however, have also objected to the presence of creativity in theology. Charles Hodge once said that at Princeton Seminary ("old" Princeton, of course) no new ideas had ever been advanced, and he hoped that none ever would be. Well, in a sense he was right. The work of theology is to proclaim the old ideas of Scripture and nothing else. But the work of theology is, indeed, to *proclaim* those old ideas to a new generation. This involves application, and that demands newness, since every new situation is somewhat different from its predecessors. This task involves interaction between Scripture and the subjectivities of human beings. But orchestrating that interaction requires art and creativity. And thus we are back to imagination; imagination is indispensable to theology.

We have seen that theology requires attention to its technical terms, models, order of topics, style and form, central focus, and applications to new audiences. In all of these areas, imagination obviously provides important assistance. But imagination is also involved in *every* case of theological concept-formation. Consider the concept of miracle, for example. The English *miracle* does not correspond precisely to any Hebrew or Greek term in the Bible. (That is, to a greater or lesser extent, the case with all English terms.) There are several Hebrew terms and three or four Greek terms that are translated "miracle," but these are also translated in other ways and can be used to denote events that from our point of view are not miraculous. Furthermore, there are events described in Scripture that are miraculous on nearly everyone's view but that are described without the use of miracle terms (e.g., 1 Kings 17:24). How, then, can we formulate a "biblical concept of miracle"?

If we cannot get our concept by studying the usage of miracle terms, perhaps we should try to study the miraculous events themselves as set forth in Scripture. But how do we know what events are miraculous until we have a concept of miracle? It seems that we cannot look for an answer unless we already know it!

That problem has philosophical ramifications that I will not try to deal with here. Practically speaking, the only answer seems to be that we must formulate some concept of miracle *before* we systematically investigate the biblical text. Here, then, is another form of the "hermeneutical circle." We seek a biblical concept of miracle from the Bible's own narrations and explanations of actual miracles. But to decide which narratives and explanations are relevant to our study, we must begin by looking at those passages that *seem to us* to be talking about miracles. In one sense, we must "begin with" our own idea of what a miracle is.

Are we now guilty of autonomous thought—of determining theological concepts "out of our own heads" and using those concepts to interpret Scripture? No. Consider this. (a) Even that initial concept of miracle that precedes serious Bible study is usually greatly influenced by Scripture. In Western culture, biblical miracles form a certain paradigm for the general concept of miracle. That is not to deny that Western thinkers often make serious errors in the definition of miracle, but they are usually at least in the right "ball park." (b) The initial concept, wherever it comes from, is just that—an initial concept. Our goal is, or should be, to refine it by continual interaction with Scripture. An initial concept should not be an "ultimate presupposition." It should be quite tentative, a hypothesis held lightly and open to the correction of Scripture, which, indeed, is our ultimate presupposition. (Many modern theologians make the mistake of using as ultimate presuppositions ideas that deserve only to be initial concepts, hypotheses open to scriptural verification or falsification.) For example, we might use as our initial concept Hume's view of miracle as a "violation of the laws of nature" and pick out as biblical examples only those narratives that seem to us to be violations of nature. In the course of our study, however, we would find that "natural law" is not a biblical concept, that events are never said to be miraculous by contrast with natural law, and that the notion of a "violation" compromises the freedom of our sovereign God to do what He pleases in the world. Thus our initial Humeanism must be revised in a more biblical direction. We will then use our "more biblical concept" to gain an even better understanding of the biblical teaching about miracles.[17]

We can see, in any case, the importance of imagination. The theologian must always set before himself, before he formally begins his study, one or more *possible* ways of answering his questions—possibilities that will guide his study of Scripture, and in conceiving of possibilities, imagination is crucial.

It is therefore important that imagination be *godly*. The imagination should be saturated in biblical teachings and thought patterns so that when an unanswered question is raised, the theologian will consider possibilities that are consistent with Scripture, those that are rendered likely by other biblical teachings.

Is imagination another epistemological perspective? Well, imagination is our faculty for knowing things that "are not"—the past and the future, the possible as opposed to the actual, the impossible as opposed to the possible, the fantastic. In one sense, then, it does not embrace all human knowledge. The point, however, has often been made that humans know what is only by contrast with what is not. You cannot know that a book is on the table unless you know what it would mean for the book *not* to be on the table. And the reverse is also true. So positive knowledge involves negative knowledge, and vice versa. And a perfect positive knowledge would include a perfect negative knowledge.

Furthermore, our concepts of possibility deeply influence our knowledge of actuality. Because Bultmann did not believe miracles are possible,

17. I hope to set forth that "more biblical concept" of miracle in my forthcoming *Doctrine of God*.

he did not believe that any actually happened. Knowledge that something is the case presupposes a knowledge that it *may* be the case.

And as I said earlier, imagination is important for remembering and for anticipating—for knowing the past and the future. But how can we know the present if we cannot relate that present to the past and future? If we have no knowledge of what has been happening, how can we make any sense out of what is happening now? And if we have no idea about the goal of events, where they are going, surely our knowledge of present events is at best highly defective. In fact, it is even difficult to conceive of the present merely as present. The moment we try to conceive of precisely what is "happening now," the events we are thinking about become past events. The present, as Augustine pointed out, can begin to look like an indivisible instant that cannot be characterized at all—for when we characterize it, it has become past. Perhaps, then, imagination as our road to the past and the future is also our only road to the present. Perhaps sensation, reason, and emotion are only different forms of and different perspectives on imagination. If imagination is not a "perspective," at least it comes close. It is involved in every act of belief or knowledge.

There is a great need for imagination among theologians today. There is a crying need for fresh applications of Scripture to situations too long neglected, for translating the gospel into new forms. The artistic gift may be well employed in the theological profession.

(5) Will

Will is our capacity to make choices, commitments, and decisions. Philosophers have often debated whether the intellect or the will is "primary." Do we make choices based on our knowledge, or does our knowledge arise from a choice to believe?

As you may guess, I think there is truth in both assertions. On the one hand, our choices do presuppose some knowledge—knowledge of the alternatives, knowledge of our own values, knowledge of data. On the other hand, all knowledge also presupposes choices—choices of how to interpret data, choices of values (criteria of truth and falsity, right and wrong), the choice as to whether to make a judgment or to suspend judgment, the choice to believe a proposition or its contradictory, the choice of whether to acknowledge or to suppress our beliefs, the choice of how strongly we will believe—that is, how much that choice will influence our lives. Every belief, then, is an act of will, and every act of will is an expression and application of our knowledge. Knowing and doing are one. (Recall the biblical equations of knowledge with obedience in Part One.)

Will is also involved in perception and emotion, which merely serves to underscore the preceding point. It is involved in perception: we *choose* to pay attention to sensations or to ignore them. (Remember Mavrodes's example of the wolf in the woods.) We choose to interpret sensations in one way, rather than another. (And remember, there is no sharp line between the interpretation of a sensation and the sensation itself—at least from our point of view.) It is also involved in emotion. The same event will move different people in different ways. A thief will be joyful over a successful heist; his victims will be mournful. The emotional difference results from different choices that have been made—differences in lifestyle, in values, in beliefs, in religious allegiance.

Will, then, is another perspective on knowledge in general and on reason, perception, and emotion as aspects of knowledge. Which of our three major perspectives does it fall under? Well, it doesn't much matter, since each perspective includes the others. But I would be inclined to make it another aspect of the existential perspective, alongside emotion. It could be argued that will is a function of an individual's strongest emotion: my choice is what I most feel like doing. (Advocates of free will, like H. D. Lewis and C. A. Campbell, would disagree, finding in will something radically mysterious, uncaused, and distinct from all emotions.)[18]

(6) Habits, Skills

Habits are those choices ((5) above) that we are accustomed to making, those choices that we make by force of habit, if not specifically moved to do otherwise. When those habits enable us to perform useful tasks, they are called skills.

Habits are important for knowledge. Presuppositions are habits—values that we customarily bring to bear on questions of truth and right. We develop habits of reasoning in certain ways, of interpreting data in certain ways, of feeling certain ways, of imagining certain kinds of possibilities rather than others, of making certain kinds of choices. Thus right or wrong choices in the past are reinforced by being repeated over and over. Godly decisions replicate themselves, leading to greater knowledge and sanctification (Rom. 12:1f.; Phil. 1:9f.; Heb. 5:11-14). Ungodly habits, on the

18. See H. D. Lewis, *Our Experience of God* (London: Allen and Unwin, 1959) and C. A. Campbell, *Selfhood and Godhood* (London: Allen and Unwin, 1957).

contrary, lead to worse and worse error, worse and worse sin (Rom. 1). Habits are hard to break; breaking them usually requires pain. The theologian must be prepared to endure that pain if necessary, even if that may include retracting earlier positions and suffering academic disrespect.

Skills in knowledge are called "wisdom" in Scripture. These are the good epistemic habits by which we are able to understand the truth and to put that truth to work in life. Wisdom comes through Christ by means of His Word and Spirit. Godly wisdom is sharply different from the wisdom of the world (1 Cor. 1-2), for it is based on the Word of God, not on man's autonomous thinking.

On the one hand, wisdom is the skill of "knowing how," rather than "knowing that." Both of these kinds of knowing are important. A football quarterback must master his playbook (knowing that), but he must also be able to do the things required by the playbook (knowing how). Lacking either form of knowledge, he will not do his job properly. At one level, it is possible to "know that" without knowing how. The quarterback might memorize the playbook but be unable to evade the oncoming tacklers. So someone might memorize the content of Scripture and the Reformed confessions but be hopelessly weak in the face of temptation.

On the other hand, even "knowing that" requires skills—in our examples, academic skills, skills of memorizing. And "knowing how" presupposes "knowing that." A skillful quarterback is one who "knows that," for example, he must move in a certain direction to avoid the tackler and who applies that knowledge to his life. Wisdom and propositional knowledge, therefore, are perspectivally related. Each is a help in remedying false concepts of the other.

Skills are important in theology (as in all disciplines)—skills with languages, in exegesis, in logic, in communication, and in dealing with people's needs. Scripture also has much to say about wisdom as the skill of godly living (James 3:13ff.; cf. Prov., passim). Without godliness, wisdom is of no value. Here again, God's Word correlates knowledge with obedience.

(7) Intuition

When we know something but don't know *how* we know it, we are inclined to say we know it "by intuition." Thus intuition is a kind of "asylum of ignorance." But I prefer to look at it as an index of the mysteriousness of knowledge. Knowledge, like God himself and like all of His creations, is incomprehensible. We can gain some insight into knowledge through His revelation, but we reach a place where our analysis ends, though all of our questions are not answered. Here, then, is another area in which knowledge requires faith.

Consider these specific mysteries. (a) The chain of justification cannot go on forever. If someone asks me why I believe that Sacramento is the capital of California, I can point to a reference work. If he asks how I know that reference work is telling the truth, I can (perhaps!) refer to the credentials of the authors or to the good reputation of the publisher. If he asks me how I know that those credentials or reputations are valid, I might be able to cite further grounds, reasons, or arguments that are based on perception, reason, emotion, and so forth. But if I am asked how I know that my reason is leading me in the right direction, it is difficult to answer except circularly, by offering another rational argument. At some point, we are forced into a corner where we say, "I just know." That is "intuition." Ultimate presuppositions, in that sense, are known intuitively, though they are verified by circular arguments of various sorts. This is true not only of Christianity but of all systems of thought. The human mind is finite; it cannot present an infinitely long argument and give an exhaustive reason for anything. It must, at some point, begin with a faith commitment, whether in the true God or in an idol.

(b) Not only at the beginning of the chain of justification but also at every point in the argument, we encounter God's mystery. Nothing physically forces us to draw logical conclusions. We draw them because we find ourselves agreeing with them, and we sense a moral demand upon us to affirm them (see chapter 8, A, *(3)*). At every point we make a choice, either in obedience to or in rebellion against those moral norms. What is our faculty for gaining knowledge of these imperatives? All the faculties are involved; it is the heart itself that makes the choice. But having integrated all of the data from different sources, if anyone asks what it is that reveals to us the final decision that we ought to make, I suppose the answer would have to be "intuition." Our "sense of when to stop investigating," our "cognitive rest," I said earlier, is like a feeling. But the term *intuition* may also be properly used for it, if we hesitate to sound emotionalistic!

CHAPTER ELEVEN

Method in Apologetics

Often when people think of apologetic method, they think of a series of steps that one should go through in every apologetic encounter—a series of questions or topics or "spiritual laws" that must be treated in a fixed order. I tend to be suspicious of that sort of approach, though I will not deny that such methods have done some good. When Christians are timid about evangelism, it is often helpful for them to have some "canned" material on the tip of their tongues, material that is usable with a variety of people. Still, that sort of approach has its limitations. Many people resent being confronted with "canned" material, feeling that they are not being respected as individuals. Furthermore, many people are able to raise objections or topics that the rigid method has not anticipated, leaving the apologist-evangelist in the lurch.

In fact, it is impossible to set forth in detail one method that will be successful in every situation. Indeed, there are as many methods in apologetics as there are apologists, persons needing Christ, and topics of discussion. Apologetic confrontations are "person-variable," to use Mavrodes's term (see chapter 5, C, *(2)*). Some concrete suggestions that can be used by *some* apologists with *some* people will be found in my *Doctrine of God* (forthcoming, God willing). In that book, I present some sample discussions of the existence of God, the problem of evil, miracles, and the deity of Christ—perhaps the most commonly discussed areas of difficulty within Christianity.

Still, some more general points can be made about apologetic method, points that are applicable to a wide range of situations, and I wish to formulate some of them in what follows. Since apologetics is a branch of theology, much of the earlier material on theological method is relevant here, and of course much of Part One and Part Two is also of importance to apologetic method. Apologetics will employ the three perspectives in broadly circular arguments to justify its contentions, using the Scriptures, extrabiblical tools, and the apologist's own gifts of godly character and skillful faculties. I would, however, also like to list some things that tend to happen in actual apologetic encounters, and that is the purpose of this section.

In this discussion, I will mention a number of strategies that the apologist may use, strategies warranted by Scripture. I will discuss them in two general categories: "defensive" apologetics, the defending of the Christian faith against the objections of unbelief, and "offensive" apologetics, the Christian's own attack on unbelieving thought and life.[1] Within each of these general categories, I shall list specific strategies under normative, situational, and existential perspectives.

The reader should not mistake this outline for a "method" in the sense of a step-by-step evangelism outline. I would not claim that *all* of my strategies must be used on every occasion or even that most of them ought to be used. And certainly I would not claim for a minute that these approaches must be used in the precise order listed. Questions about which strategy to use on which occasion or about the order of presentation are problems for practical theology, and my gifts are not of the practical sort (much as I seek to glorify practice in my theories!). I shall merely set forth some strategies that can and may be used in some situations. More than that I will not claim for the following discussion.

A. DEFENSIVE APOLOGETICS

Let us begin with defensive apologetics, which presupposes an initiative on the part of the unbeliever. The unbeliever raises an objection, the believer responds. George Mavrodes, in the book that I have frequently cited,[2] distinguishes three ways of helping a "doubtful" inquirer to share in the experience of God—ways that are similar, in his view, to the ways that we seek to help people share in other sorts of experiences. First, when we

1. These are not sharply distinct. Theistic proofs, for example, can be seen either as defensive (answering the atheist's attacks) or as offensive (directly attacking the atheist's own world view.)

2. *Belief in God* (New York: Random House, 1970), 82ff.

want someone to see something that we see, we often say, "Come over here"; we seek to place the other person in circumstances that are similar to our own. Second, we "tell the person what to look for." And third, we try to provide the other person with a "conceptual framework that exhibits the meaning of the particular experience . . . by integrating it with a large range . . . of other experiences." Mavrodes points out that these methods are generally presented together and that no one of them will likely be successful without the other two. These methods correspond pretty closely to my existential, situational, and normative perspectives. The unbeliever needs to be put in new circumstances (existential regeneration), he needs to be told the facts (situational), and he needs to have a system (inevitably involving norms) in terms of which the meanings (i.e., the applications, the significance, importance, and normative content) of those facts can be apprehended. Let us, then, look more closely at this methodological triad.

(1) The Normative Perspective

a. The "conceptual framework" or "system" in terms of which the meanings of facts are apprehended is, of course, the teaching of Scripture (applied to all the relevant circumstances). It is important that the apologist have a good grasp of the Scriptures and be able to use them appropriately and creatively. By that I do not mean that the apologist should merely recite proof texts for an inquirer, though sometimes that is precisely the thing to do (see chapter 6, C, *(3)*). Proof texts are not to be used without sensitivity to the inquirer's level of understanding and the relevance of the texts to the topics at hand.[3]

b. Many objections of unbelievers against Christianity concern the Scriptures themselves: the historicity of events described in Scripture, the morality of biblical law, alleged contradictions, and so forth. The apologist must have a sound knowledge of biblical backgrounds, as well as of the text itself. Preferably, he should know the texts in the original languages, though ignorance of these ought not to deter the believer from carrying out his apologetic responsibility (1 Peter 3:15). If he doesn't know the original languages, doubtless he can find a pastor or professor who does, or he can consult a reference work. Often it is sufficient to direct the unbeliever

3. Sometimes, however, it is not wrong to "change the subject" when the "topic at hand" is unfruitful. Jesus often did this—for example, in John 3:3. Spiritual sensitivity is needed to know when and how.

to look at the questioned passage in context; many objections are based on easily correctable misunderstandings of the text.

c. Frequently, when objections are raised, Christians fail to do the most obvious thing—to ask whether that problem is treated in Scripture itself and, if so, how Scripture handles it. There is, for example, a wealth of material in Scripture on the problem of evil (Gen. 3; 22; Ps. 73; Job; Hab.; Matt. 20:1-16; Rom.; Rev.) that is often neglected in arguments about this topic. This is not to say that extrabiblical considerations may not be used, but we should not, however, neglect our chief resource (the only offensive weapon in the Christian arsenal, Eph. 6:17), the Word of God itself.

d. It is always important to make clear to the unbeliever what our ultimate source of authority is. If he is epistemologically sophisticated, this may involve explaining the concept of a presupposition and the honest admission that our arguments are "broadly circular." (Of course, it is also important to show the unbeliever that *he too* has presuppositions and that *he too* cannot avoid circularity. See B, below.) Is it necessary to make this admission in every apologetic encounter, or even to make it the centerpiece of our argument? Some presuppositionalists evidently think so, but I don't.

Of course, we certainly should not be ashamed of our presuppositions. If the question comes up, we ought to be honest about it. Presuppositionalism is not a weakness but a strength of our position. Furthermore, the goal of an apologetic encounter is conversion, which is nothing less than presuppositional change. An apologist must present the biblical demand for repentance in all aspects of life, including thought. And that is, implicitly, a demand for a change in presuppositions.

But we can make that demand, and make it clearly, without ever using the *presupposition* and thus without getting into the rather technical philosophical discussions that inevitably accompany the term. Many people will not understand such philosophical terminology and will find philosophical talk distracting. The important thing is not to *talk* about our presuppositions but to *obey* them in our thought, speech, and life. Our apologetic must always be an *obedient* apologetic—subject to God's revealed Word and thus governed by our own ultimate presuppositions. But whether we talk about presuppositions or not will depend on the situation. If an unbeliever is willing to accept statements we make on biblical presuppositions, and if he does not challenge the believer on epistemological grounds, there is no need explicitly to raise the issue. But if, as often happens, the believer's authority, his justification for his assertions, is questioned, then something will have to be said about Scripture as our presupposition.

e. It is clear, in any case, that the believer ought not to accept or pretend to accept an unbelieving criterion of truth or value. Scripture does teach, to be sure, that God is revealed to everyone in nature (including human nature) and to many people (both believers and unbelievers) through miraculous deeds, signs, and wonders. Scripture never suggests, however, that these revelations are properly evaluated on the basis of unbelieving criteria (or "neutral" criteria, which, as we have seen, do not exist). See *(2)*, below, on this question and Thom Notaro, *Van Til and the Use of Evidence*.[4]

f. How, then, can we communicate with unbelievers if we cannot accept their presuppositions? Van Til suggests that we ask the unbeliever to accept our criteria "for the sake of argument," to exhibit to him the content of the Christian revelation, which is, of course, its own best argument. The unbeliever will then have the opportunity to use a *reductio ad absurdum* (see chapter 8, *H, (3)*) to try to derive absurdities from the Christian premises, and the Christian may request a similar privilege of the unbeliever. (I will say more about this in *B*, below.)

g. Finally, when objections are raised against Christianity, it is important to remember that we don't always *have* to have answers for them. First Peter 3:15 does urge believers always to be ready to give an answer to everyone who asks a reason of the hope that is in them. We do have reasons for our faith, and we ought to be prepared to share them; but that does not entail that we have, or ought to have, answers to every conceivable objection. Many objections can be fully answered only by probing into the "secret things" of God (Deut. 29:29), the things that God has chosen to leave unrevealed. (I believe that the problem of evil is one such example.) Also, objections will often be raised that are simply beyond the technical competence of a particular believer. Most high school students will not be able to deal with objections based on the differing textual traditions of the biblical manuscripts, for instance. The Christian mind is a finite mind. There are many things that we do not know or understand, but that fact is nothing to be embarrassed about. It is, in fact, a confirmation of Christianity (albeit something of a "throwaway argument," see chapter 8, *H, (6)*), for Scripture teaches us exactly that. If we *could* answer all objections to Christianity, we would be God. God would not be incomprehensible, and Christianity, therefore, would be false.

Thus we do not believe in Christianity because we have found answers to all possible objections. We believe in Christianity because God has re-

4. Phillipsburg, N.J.: Presbyterian and Reformed Pub. Co., 1980.

vealed himself in Scripture, the world, and ourselves. He has revealed himself with such clarity that we are obligated (and able, by grace) to believe in Him, *despite* unanswered questions, just as Abraham did.

That fact is one we ought to be honest about, and in an apologetic encounter, it is appropriate to share it with an unbeliever. It saves us embarrassment when we are unable to reply to his attacks, and, more importantly, it helps him to see what the basis of faith really is. And that, of course, is something he must come to know (at least subconsciously) if he is to become a believer. That underscores the presuppositional thrust of our apologetic; we walk by faith in God's Word, not by our autonomous ability to answer all the difficulties therein.

(2) The Situational Perspective

We have seen that it is entirely proper to use extrabiblical evidence in arguments for Christianity, if that extrabiblical evidence is interpreted biblically. The unbeliever has no *right* to demand evidence, for he already has all the evidence he needs in God's clear revelation in nature, Scripture, and in himself. But an apologist has the obligation to underscore that evidence, to show the unbeliever "what to look for" (Mavrodes), as well as how to look for it and how to look at it. As he presents the evidence, he simultaneously applies Scripture, for he interprets the evidence biblically, thus expounding the meaning of Scripture to the unbeliever in a fresh way. And that, in fact, is just the way that Scripture itself uses evidences in presenting the truth (see chapter 5, *B, (3)-(5)*).

Unfortunately, there has been very little actual analysis of evidence in the Van Tillian presuppositionalist school of apologetics. Van Til's *Christian Theistic Evidences*[5] presents a philosophy of evidence and a critique of non-Christian or sub-biblical approaches but no actual survey of the evidences themselves. Thom Notaro's *Van Til and the Use of Evidence* is an excellent defense of Van Til against the charge of fideism. It too formulates important principles for the use of evidence, but it does not present actual evidence within that perspective, except in illustrative examples. I hope this gap in the Reformed apologetic literature will soon be filled, though I cannot fill it, at least not here and now. Like most of my presuppositionalist brethren, my gifts and training are "abstract" and philosophical.

5. Unpublished syllabus, 1961.

There is a great deal of literature on Christian evidences, however, written from other viewpoints that is of use to the Reformed apologist. Books that advocate the use of "traditional" or "evidentialist" methodology (McDowell, Montgomery, Hackett, Pinnock, Gerstner, Sproul) are wrong in many ways, as we have seen, but they also have some positive value.[6]

a. Books by those "evidentialists" provide a great deal of *information* that when analyzed according to biblical presuppositions, can help us. For example, when we speak to unbelievers about the Resurrection of Christ, we may very well use arguments similar to some of those used by McDowell, Montgomery, Gerstner, and Sproul. It is quite proper to point out that the resurrection of Christ is as well attested as any other historical fact. It is legitimate to ask why the apostles were willing to die for the belief that Christ had risen. It is legitimate to examine the alternate (unbelieving) explanations of the resurrection reports and to show how implausible they are. Using those sorts of arguments does not, in itself, compromise our biblical presuppositions. Indeed, though the evidentialists themselves would not grant this point, those arguments presuppose a Christian world view—a world of order, logic, and value. They are intelligible only within the "broad circle" of Christian argument. Outside of that circle, the arguments can be evaded easily. To David Hume, for example, *any* alternative explanation of the events was preferable to a miraculous explanation, simply because miracles are inherently incredible. On that basis, mass delusion, for instance, psychologically unlikely though it may be, is preferable to an actual resurrection as an explanation of the events. Of course, we differ with Hume's criteria of probability. When we expound these arguments, we are presupposing different, Christian criteria. Thus when we assert the credibility of the resurrection on the basis of the biblical testimony, we are at the same time expounding a Christian epistemology and world view.

b. For some unbelievers, in fact, that sort of argument may be sufficient. Not all are as epistemologically sophisticated as David Hume. And the

6. Some of the more recent titles in this genre include Josh McDowell, *Evidence That Demands a Verdict* (San Bernardino, Calif.: Here's Life Publishers, 1979), *The Resurrection Factor* (San Bernardino, Calif.: Here's Life Publishers, 1981), *More Than a Carpenter* (Wheaton, Ill.: Tyndale House, 1977); Stuart Hackett, *The Reconstruction of the Christian Revelation Claim* (Grand Rapids: Baker Book House, 1984); John W. Montgomery, *Where Is History Going?* (Grand Rapids: Zondervan Publishing House, 1969), *Faith Founded on Fact* (Nashville and New York: Thomas Nelson Publishers, 1978); R. C. Sproul, John H. Gerstner, and Arthur Lindsley, *Classical Apologetics* (Grand Rapids: Zondervan Publishing House, 1984); Clark Pinnock, *Reason Enough* (Downers Grove, Ill.: Inter-Varsity Press, 1980).

Holy Spirit has granted faith to many through the presentation of the kinds of arguments mentioned above. To such persons, we do not need to *talk* about presuppositions; the message about presuppositions is *implicit* in the argument itself. To accept the kind of argument that presupposes a Christian world view and epistemology is at the same time to accept that world view and epistemology; it is to accept the whole gospel. It should not surprise us, then, to find God working through "traditional" apologists. The traditional apologetic contains much truth, much of which contradicts the *theory* of evidentialist apologetics. Evidentialist apologetics is not cogent and persuasive because it is based on unbelieving or "neutral" presuppositions but because it is (insofar as it is sound) based on Christian presuppositions.

c. With other unbelievers, more may be needed. The Spirit may not choose to work through traditional arguments. If the inquirer, like Hume, is philosophically sophisticated, his continuing unbelief may manifest itself in epistemological objections. He may ask what basis we have for preferring a miraculous explanation of the events following Jesus' death to a naturalistic one. In that case, we must get into epistemology—presuppositions, circularity, perspectivalism, whatever is necessary. And most likely our argument will not be complete unless there is an attack on the inquirer's own epistemology (see *B*, below). But even with inquirers of that sort, the traditional arguments can be a way to start the conversation.

d. The traditional apologists often reason on a presuppositional basis, despite their lack of a fully adequate presuppositional apologetic *theory*. Defenders of miracle often point out that Hume's definition of miracle expresses an unbelieving presupposition and thereby begs the relevant question. R. C. Sproul, an "evidentialist," has developed a pretty good account of Romans 1, though rather inconsistent, I would say, with his antipresuppositional apologetic theory. Montgomery and Gerstner advocate presuppositional argumentation—argumentation based on biblical authority—*after* the authority of Scripture has been proved by "neutral" argument. Much of their defense of presuppositionalism is sound, even if we dismiss the neutralist prologue, as I hope we all will. Montgomery speaks helpfully about the need to integrate data into a *gestalt* or system of thought, but he fails to see how this necessity is inconsistent with his radical empiricism. In all of these ways, traditionalist apologists contribute positively to the sort of apologetic I am advocating.

e. Finally, the neutralist apologists often point out effectively some errors of unbelieving thought—factual, logical, and so forth—and these accounts are often helpful.

(3) The Existential Perspective

Here, several matters demand our attention.

a. *Proof and Persuasion*

We have seen (chapter 5, C, (2)) that the goal of apologetics is not merely to produce sound arguments but to persuade people. Because not every sound argument is persuasive with a particular individual or group, it is all the more important to deal with inquirers as individuals and in a loving way to try to understand each of their particular needs and to develop arguments directed toward those needs. In effect, then, there will be a different "apologetic method" for every inquirer, though in some respects all of our methods should be alike.

The objection has often been raised that since only God can change a person's heart, we should not seek to effect such change, lest we confuse our own work with that of the Spirit. Instead, the argument goes, we should simply present sound arguments and leave it to the Spirit to convince people. Scripture, however, rejects the idea that divine sovereignty and human responsibility are incompatible. God sovereignly acts through human agency, and human agency—human actions—are made effective because God is sovereign. It is right, then, that we should seek the same ends that God seeks—nothing less than conversion, a fundamental change of heart, in those to whom we witness. And that, indeed, is what we find in Scripture. Paul, for example, "reasoned in the synagogue, trying to persuade Jews and Greeks" (Acts 18:4; cf. v. 28; 19:8). Paul's goal was not merely to cover subject matter but to persuade, to change the opinion of his hearers through a change of heart. Apologetics, therefore, can never be far removed from evangelism, and vice versa. The two are perspectivally related, apologetics focusing on the means (godly reasoning based on Scripture) and evangelism focusing on the goal (the conversion of sinners).

b. *The Mystery of Persuasion*

I have spoken earlier of the mysteriousness of that "cognitive rest" that marks the moment of persuasion. There is no rational argument that infallibly or inevitably leads to that point, which is the result of the work of God's Spirit (above, *a*) and of many created means. Both argument and the influence of Christian love (below, *c*) are important.

Other means have been recommended to inquirers who have heard arguments for Christianity and yet who languish in indecision. One of the most famous of those arguments is Pascal's "wager,"[7] which goes like this: Even if we do not know that Christianity is true, we should "wager" that it is, for if we wager against Christianity and it turns out to be true, we have lost everything, but if we wager for Christianity and it turns out to be false, we have lost nothing; therefore we should choose Christianity. Pascal's wager has been subject to many objections. Consider these. (A) What if Islam or some other religion or philosophy is true? In that case, it would seem that believing in Christianity could be a substantial loss indeed—a loss of the truth at least and possibly a loss of eternal salvation as well. Pascal seems to have considered only two options: Christianity and irreligion. But we have seen that in fact Pascal is right. There are only two options that really matter, and inquirers often recognize that fact at one point or another of their search. For those who do not accept that premise, of course, Pascal's wager will not be persuasive (though it will still reflect the truth); but for those who do, it may be persuasive. (B) Is the wager a blatant appeal to selfishness? Well, it does appeal to self-interest, but Jesus and Scripture frequently do the same thing. Although Christianity teaches self-sacrifice, it is a self-sacrifice that leads to long-term blessing. Loving God is not incompatible with seeking the best for oneself. In fact the two are inseparable (cf. Matt. 6:33; 19:28-30; 1 Tim. 4:8). (C) Does the wager assume that Christianity cannot be known with certainty to be true? No. It assumes that the inquirer, at this point, is unwilling to *grant* the certainty of Christianity. (D) Does the wager urge the inquirer toward hypocrisy, toward a commitment in something that he does not believe with confidence? Pascal does urge inquirers in this situation to *act* as Christians—to go to church (mass, in his case), to confess their sins, to use the holy water, and so forth—as a *means of arousing* true faith.

But Pascal is a writer with great sensitivity to the subtleties of persuasion—those "reasons of the heart that reason cannot know." When someone decides on the basis of the wager to attend church, for example, he is not necessarily being hypocritical, though he may be. Rather, he may be following the dictates of his reason (and therefore of his conscience), taking the course that seems most prudent. If he wrongly believes that Christianity is uncertain, well, so do many Christians. His decision may nonetheless show marks of regeneration. His decision to attend church may be a decision to obey God, and that decision, though it cannot save the soul, may be an early expression of true faith. True faith may well exist before it

7. Pascal formulated this argument in his *Pensees*. It was defended by William James in his famous essay, "The Will to Believe."

is professed, before the believer even feels ready to profess it. (Consider the case of regenerate children.) Acts of faith may precede the verbal profession of faith, and those acts may make it easier for the inquirer to profess faith later on.

Faith is a lot like wagering, after all—not that Christianity is uncertain or like a throw of the dice! But the Christian's certainty is not the kind of certainty envisaged by rationalist philosophers, either (see chapter 5, A, (8)). It is not the certainty of those who have had all their problems answered, to whom the truth is exhaustively understood. Think again of the example of Abraham, who ventured in faith, though many objections to God's promise stared him in the face. In the midst of questions and unresolved difficulties, we follow God. We are uncertain in the sense that we cannot explain all the difficulties, but we are certain enough to stake our lives on Christ, certain enough to walk the path of obedience, certain enough to accept Him as our standard of certainty. There is, therefore, something like wagering in true faith.

In a practical apologetic situation, it might not be wise to make explicit use of Pascal's wager. If it can be defended, it nevertheless can also be easily misunderstood. Yet it is important in apologetics to urge an inquirer toward a decision. That does not mean manipulating him or encouraging hypocrisy. It does mean, however, making clear to him the nature of faith. It means making clear that faith does not—indeed may not—wait on the resolution of all intellectual difficulties and that faith is expressed not only in intellectual or verbal confession but also in all of life's activities. If the inquirer is not ready to verbalize a confession of faith, he should nevertheless be encouraged (not discouraged, as in some circles) to seek after godliness and to make such use of the means of grace as the church (under Scripture) will permit.

c. *The Character of the Apologist*

In apologetics it is especially important that teaching be by life as well as word (chapter 10, C). One of the strongest (i.e., *most persuasive*) arguments is Christian love. Remember 1 Peter 3:15 and verse 16, which is often neglected in this context.

> But in your hearts set apart Christ as Lord. Always be prepared to give an answer to everyone who asks you to give the reason for the hope that you have. But do this with gentleness and respect, keeping a clear conscience, so that those who speak maliciously against your good behavior in Christ may be ashamed of their slander.

Our apologetics must be pervaded by a sense of Christ's lordship (see Part One), and this demands *diligent preparation* so that we may be able to obey our Lord's Great Commission, being prepared to answer inquirers—not only with proclamation, but with answers and reasons. And it requires *boldness* so that we may take advantage of these opportunities. And it also requires *gentleness* and *respect*. The inquirer is to be treated neither as a statistic nor as someone to be manipulated into a verbal commitment; nor is he to be treated with contempt, though his unbelief is loathsome to God. He is a human being, made in God's image, and is to be loved and treated with dignity. The work of the Schaeffers at L'Abri will be an enduring example to us in that regard, for they labored to present thoughtful answers in a context of love and respect.[8]

B. OFFENSIVE APOLOGETICS

Apologetics is sometimes defined as the "defense of the faith," but that definition can be misleading. Apologetics is not only defense but also offense—an attack by Christians against unbelieving thought and action.[9] As the apostle Paul puts it, "We demolish arguments and every pretension that sets itself up against the knowledge of God, and we take captive every thought to make it obedient to Christ" (2 Cor. 10:4f.). Indeed, as is true in some other fields, "the best defense is a good offense." In fact, it could be argued that offense is the *primary* function of apologetics. After all, God has nothing to defend, to "apologize" for. Jesus Christ is the mighty ruler of heaven and earth, the invincible warrior on the march to bring in His kingdom, putting down all powers and authorities that are opposed to Him (Col. 2:15). Apologetics is one of His tools for putting His enemies under His feet.[10]

So it is not enough for the Christian merely to respond to the unbeliever's objections. The Christian is called to turn the attack against God's enemies. This, in fact, is the role that the Lord himself took as the prosecuting attorney of God's covenant lawsuit against His unfaithful people,

8. See Edith Schaeffer, *L'Abri* (Wheaton, Ill.: Tyndale House, 1969) and *The Tapestry* (Waco, Tex.: Word Books, 1981).

9. Obviously, when I speak of "offense," I am not urging the apologist to be "offensive," i.e., nasty or rude. The apologist ought to avoid giving offense, except for the offense of the cross of Christ itself. I am using "offense" as it is used in sports and war: our attack on the enemy.

10. Van Til was once criticized for using military imagery. Without forgetting what I said in the last section about gentleness and love, I must reply as he did: That language is biblical.

Israel, and the role He will assume when He returns.[11] When Satan or his human associates bring accusations against God's people, God regularly refuses to answer the charge and brings accusations against the accusers (see Gen. 3:18-25; Job 38-42; Matt. 20:1-15; Rom. 3:3f.). Similarly, after refuting several questions intended to entrap Him, Jesus turns on His critics (Matt. 22:41-45), as does Paul, after an extended attempt at defensive apologetics (Acts 28:23-28). Note also the element of solemn warning found in so many divine utterances—1 Samuel 8:9; Psalm 81:11f.; Isaiah 28:17; 44:25; Jeremiah 1:10; Lamentations 2:14; Hosea 2:9—particularly against false claims to wisdom in opposition to God's Word. Unlike many today, God is not afraid to be negative.[12]

Of course, such negative criticism will not do much good unless at the same time we cogently present a positive Christian alternative. Therefore defense and offense cannot long be separated. I shall, however, focus in this section on offense, trusting the reader to keep the two aspects in proper balance.

Van Til's method of apologetic offense is the second step in his apologetic method. The first step is to ask the unbeliever to assume the truth of the Christian position "for the sake of argument" so that the believer might present that position to him with its inherent rationale. That is Van Til's defensive strategy. His offensive strategy, the second step, is for both parties to assume the unbeliever's presuppositions—again only "for the sake of argument"—so that the believer can present a *reductio*, a demonstration that the unbeliever's premises lead to total unintelligibility. This second step, however, needs some more analysis. In what sense can a believer accept an unbeliever's position "for the sake of argument"? How much of it are we to accept in this way? All of it? Then we will be accepting everything the unbeliever says—all his rebuttals to our position and all his arguments for his own. That way we will never refute his position. What Van Til evidently means here is that the believer accepts "for the sake of argument" certain fundamental premises of the unbeliever's system—atheism or "pure chance," for example—and then from those premises he deduces chaos and meaninglessness, completing the *reductio*. But in that deduction, of course, he is thinking as a Christian. At that point, he is no longer presupposing unbelief, even "for the sake of argument." The moral of this discussion is that the Christian never really abandons his own

11. Meredith G. Kline, *Images of the Spirit* (Grand Rapids: Baker Book House, 1980). See Job 38; Isa. 1:18ff.; 3:13; Jer. 1:16; Hos. 4:1; John 16:8 (the Holy Spirit).

12. Many of the texts noted in this paragraph were drawn to my attention by Os Guinness (in a series of taped lectures).

presupposition, even for a moment. Even when accepting the unbeliever's principles "for the sake of argument," he still is thinking as a Christian. What really happens in this second step, then, is that the Christian is telling the unbeliever how the unbeliever's principles look to him as a Christian.[13]

With these clarifications, let us look at "offensive" apologetics under our three perspectives.

(1) Normative Perspective—Scripture Versus Dialectic

a. When the unbeliever attacks Christianity for being based on "faith" as opposed to "reason," it is important to reverse the complaint. The unbeliever, too, has presuppositions that he does not question and that govern every aspect of his thought and life. Thus in a relevant sense, he too has "faith." He too argues in a circle. It is not as if the two are equal, however, for the non-Christian has no basis for trusting reason, except his blind faith. If this world is ultimately the product of chance plus matter, of space and time, why should we assume that events in our heads will tell us anything reliable about the real world? The Christian, though, knows that God has given reason to us as a reliable tool for knowing Him, the world, and ourselves. Thus the shoe is on the other foot. The Christian perspective is rational; the unbeliever's is based on blind faith.

b. It is also appropriate for the apologist to point out to the unbeliever what Scripture says about him. Although he is made in God's image and surrounded by God's clear revelation, he has refused to acknowledge and obey God, exchanged the truth for a lie, and sought to suppress the truth, to hinder its functioning.

c. Something also can be said about what the unbeliever seeks to substitute for the truth—the rationalist-irrationalist dialectic (see chapter 1, A and C, (3)). We may recall that the non-Christian rationalist claims an autonomous criterion of truth apart from God's revelation; the non-Christian irrationalist denies the existence of truth and rationality. These are the only two possibilities if one rejects the God of Scripture: idolatry or nihilism.

Rationalists and irrationalists are not found only among professional philosophers. Ordinary unbelievers also demonstrate these commitments, though not in such epistemologically self-conscious ways. The rationalist

13. The point of this paragraph was suggested to me by my colleague Vern S. Poythress of Westminster Theological Seminary in Philadelphia.

could be the self-made businessman who sees himself as the master of his fate or the local politician who thinks that by careful government planning we may overcome all of our social woes or the bartender who has an opinion on everything or the neighbor who thinks that "modern science" has utterly disproved Christianity. (He could also be the Pharisee, the church elder who thinks that because of his good works or doctrinal knowledge he deserves God's favor, or the "black sheep"—actually a Pharisee in another garb—who thinks that he must become a much better person before he will have the right to seek God.) The irrationalist could be the town drunk who couldn't care less about anything or the happy milkman who lives on sentimentality and seems bewildered when anyone asks him his basis for living or the angry teenager who hates all authority and seeks to destroy everything he sees.

Rationalists and irrationalists are often at odds with one another, but under the skin they are the same, united in unbelief.

(i) *Rationalism is irrationalistic.* The non-Christian has no right to have faith in reason. He accepts it only by an irrational leap. The rationalist's rational scheme never gives him the divine knowledge that he claims. Since this is God's world, the facts never fit into his godless system. Faced with this problem, three courses are possible to the unbeliever: become an irrationalist, compromise with irrationalism (admitting that the scheme is not fully adequate), or cling to his scheme and deny the existence of any discrepancies. The latter course is the most consistently rationalistic, but it too has pitfalls. It pulls the rationalist farther away from reality and isolates him in a world of his own. The farther he goes in this direction, the more he is isolated, the more he comes to know only his own system, the less he comes to know the world. And what do we call it when someone is locked in a fantasy world, knowing only his own thought processes, ignorant of reality? Well, we could call him an irrationalist! Thus the rationalist is forced to become an irrationalist—either directly or by way of some compromise with irrationalism as a middle ground. The middle ground, however, is unstable. Where do we draw the line between the competence of reason and its limitations? The Christian has the guidance of revelation to do that, but the non-Christian has no basis for making any decision. He can only follow his inclinations—irrationalistically. In all of those ways, then, rationalism must lead to irrationalism.

(ii) *Irrationalism is rationalistic.* (A) Irrationalism can only be asserted on a rationalistic basis. How can one know that there is no truth or meaning?

To know that, he would have to know the whole universe. It is that difficult to prove a negative. (B) Irrationalism is self-refuting. It claims to know that there is no knowledge; it believes it to be true that there are no truths, thus asserting rationalism and denying it at the same time! (C) Irrationalists generally compromise their irrationalism in the way they live. Remember Schaeffer's example of John Cage, who preaches irrationalism through his music but who assumes an orderly world when he grows mushrooms (chapter 5, C, *(1)*). Short of the lunatic asylum, such inconsistency is inescapable. But irrationalism, once compromised, is refuted. Once one concedes the existence of *any* meaning or order, he is no longer able to deny the existence of meaning or order.

(iii) *Rationalism and irrationalism are parasitic on Christianity*. Of course, rationalism and irrationalism are both radically opposed to Christianity, yet they depend on Christianity in some ways for their plausibility. (Recall our "square of opposition" from Part One, particularly the horizontal lines denoting verbal similarity.) It is, after all, the Christian revelation that informs us that human reason has both powers and limitations. Rationalism and irrationalism build on those notions of powers and limitations, respectively, but they do so independently of God, and neither is able to specify what those powers and limitations are. Thus rationalists and irrationalists have no principle to keep them from the extremes of sheer irrationalism and sheer rationalism.

In those ways, both rationalism and irrationalism (as well as the various compromise positions) are vulnerable to Christian attack. None of these positions is really distinct from the others, and thus each is subject to all the difficulties mentioned. These positions would have no plausibility at all if it were not for their resemblance to Christianity.

Those analyses can guide our witness to many different kinds of people. Of course, people may not be willing to listen to us. They may lose interest and walk away—at that point becoming irrationalists, abandoning the search for truth. Or an inquirer may become so irrationalistic that he will not be moved by *anything* you say to him. If you charge him with inconsistency between his irrationalism and his life-decisions, he may answer, "So what? Who cares about consistency?" Once a person's thinking gets that far from the truth, there isn't much you can say to him as an apologist, except to witness to him by your life and proclamation. A person like that is much like someone who is catatonic or otherwise withdrawn from reality. With my colleague Jay Adams, I agree that in such cases you should keep talking but don't expect (at first, anyway) to carry on any rational arguments.

This discussion has been a bit philosophical, and the reader might well wonder if any of it will help in witnessing to "ordinary people." Well, remember what I said earlier: we find rationalists and irrationalists not only among philosophers but also among all sorts of people. Consider the fellow who has "dropped out" of life. In a rare sober moment, he confesses to you that he sees no meaning in life. Ask him why he drinks. His answer will reveal that he does value *something*, whether that is drunkenness itself or freedom from pain or whatever. Further questions will reveal additional contradictions with his irrationalist perspective. Ask him why he values what he values, and you will be able to show him how arbitrary his values are. Point to Jesus as the only one who can give lasting peace and comfort in a harsh world. Of course, at some point, he may lose interest or be unwilling to talk any further. No apologetic method can guarantee that that won't happen. We can only do our best and pray for God to work.

(2) SITUATIONAL PERSPECTIVE—THE ERRORS OF UNBELIEF

In attacking an unbelieving position, it is also appropriate simply to point out errors of various sorts, other than the fundamental error of a false presupposition (above, *(1)*). These are of different types.

a. *Unclarities*

Unclarities abound in discussions about God and Christianity. Often Christians themselves are unclear, as we saw earlier, and we need to guard against that. Still, remembering our own weaknesses (Gal. 6:1; 1 Peter 3:15f.), it is proper for us to point out unclarities in non-Christian systems, if only to facilitate communication and understanding.

The non-Christian, then, shares with the Christian a tendency toward unclarity. But there are also special reasons for unclarity in unbelief that stem from the very nature of unbelief itself. We have seen in the last section that non-Christian rationalism and irrationalism depend for their plausibility on their resemblance to similar Christian concepts. Rationalism feeds on the Christian premise that the world is governed by a fully rational plan, that nothing can be known unless someone knows everything. Irrationalism feeds on the Christian premise that human beings do not know everything, that much of the world is mysterious to us, beyond the capacity of our reason. Thus non-Christian rationalists and irrationalists borrow Christian terminology and ideas to express their very anti-Christian positions. The result is unclarity.

Similarly, modern theologians depend on concepts of divine transcendence and immanence (again, see Part One on this issue) that contradict the biblical teaching but that can be made to *sound* very biblical. God is exalted, high above us, yet near to us through Christ. With such biblical language, these thinkers express the notions that God is so far from us that He never speaks clearly in written revelation and never acts unambiguously in miraculous deeds and that God is so near that He cannot be clearly distinguished from the creation, so that in effect the creation is deified and God becomes creaturely.

That sort of unclarity, especially, must be exposed, for it is a great barrier to communication of the gospel, and it reveals very sharply the nature of the unbeliever's distortion of the truth.

b. *Factual Errors*

Factual errors, too, may be exposed. Again, Christians also make factual errors, and so we ought not to give the unbeliever the impression that we think we are infallible! It is important that we admit when we are wrong, not just to be nice to an inquirer but also because the Christian's fallibility is a teaching of Scripture—part of the biblical message!

The human tendency to make such errors, however, is accentuated by the dynamics of unbelief, for at heart, the unbeliever hates the truth and wants to suppress it. Thus unbelievers often fail to grant what to Christians are very obvious facts. We should point out such errors, and we should point out their origin in unbelief itself, when we are able to do so.

Here again, the writings of our "evidentialist" brethren are helpful, along with standard works in Bible, archaeology, art, modern culture, history, and so forth. The more we can learn about God's world, the better we will be at refuting factual errors.

c. *Logical Errors*

Similar points can be made here. Everyone makes logical errors, but unbelievers have special reasons for making them. It is important for the apologist to know enough logic to refute unsound arguments and to show the influence of unbelief in producing that unsoundness. When Bultmann says that we cannot believe in angels because we live in a world that uses radio, we must reply that this is a total *non sequitur*. But why would an intelligent man use such an obviously fallacious argument? Because he is determined to be "modern," rather than to be faithful to God's Word.

(3) Existential Perspective—Points of Contact

a. The apologist should also seek to know the people he is addressing. He should seek to know individuals. Each inquirer is different, though all have essentially the same problem and need. We should, therefore, try to speak in a way that each will understand and to address each peculiar situation. We do this out of love, respecting each person as the image of God, and also because of the very nature of communication. It is usually important for us to ask questions to find out where the inquirer is in his thought and life. The dialogue must be a two-way street. Do not only preach; spend as much time listening as time permits. The concepts of rationalism and irrationalism will help us here. Guinness[14] uses the categories of "dilemma" and "diversion" to describe what I have called rationalism and irrationalism. Some unbelievers are aware to some extent of their situation, wrestling with the issue of how they can live in God's world while maintaining their unbelief. Such persons are sensitized to their "dilemma" and are still trying to work it out on their own terms (rationalism). Others seek to flee from the problems, either sometimes or all the time. David Hume was often bothered by the implications of his skeptical thoughts, but he said that a good game of backgammon could banish such worries for a while. That's irrationalism, the attempt to escape from truth. We should try to find where our inquirer is on this scale.

There will always be some inconsistency in the unbeliever, not only in his theorizing but particularly between his theorizing and his life. Recall John Cage again, who presupposes an orderly world when he grows mushrooms but preaches chaos through his music. Every unbeliever is like that, for every unbeliever is an irrationalist who nevertheless needs to live in a rational world. The drunkard who "doesn't care about anything" at least cares enough about drink to purchase it and swallow it. The philosopher who thinks that "all is relative" at least believes that his relativism is absolutely true. Many who attempt suicide write notes, thus indicating that they have not entirely despaired of meaning.

Apologetics is addressed not only to individuals but also to families, to groups, to nations (as in the Old Testament), and to the world. The apologist is often called on to present his message, not only one-on-one but in speeches, publications, and media appearances. To do that effectively, it is important to know something of the mentality of the groups being addressed. What are the distinctive characteristics of modern culture? Of

14. In the taped lectures mentioned earlier.

present-day American society? Answers to such questions can also improve the effectiveness of our witness to individuals.

Books and articles by the Schaeffer group (Francis, Edith, and Franky Schaeffer, Os Guinness, Donald Drew, Udo Middelmann, and Hans Rookmaaker) and by the the Rushdoony group (R. J. Rushdoony, Gary North, Greg Bahnsen, Jim Jordan, David Chilton, and others—especially Herbert Schlossberg's fine *Idols for Destruction*[15]) are among the most helpful sources within the Reformed community for this purpose. Also, we should not neglect another group that is difficult to define, yet remarkably cohesive, that consists mostly of Anglicans and Catholics (most of whom are British), who have produced much good literature that challenges the complacency of modern culture (e.g., books by G. K. Chesterton, George MacDonald, Charles Williams, Dorothy Sayers, C. S. Lewis, J. R. R. Tolkien, Harry Blamires, Malcolm Muggeridge, Thomas Howard, Michael Novak, James Hitchcock, and Peter Kreeft). In some ways, even William F. Buckley, Jr. must be counted in this tradition, as should Alexandr Solzhenitsen! These authors paint a picture of a world taken up with secularization, pluralization, privatization of religion (which I think is now gradually being overcome), psychological truth (what feels good—subjectivism), the lessening respect for life, and overconfidence in government (perhaps not as prominent in the 1980s).

The apologist may disagree with these generalizations, but it is important that he form some responsible (scripturally based) opinions in these areas if he is to speak effectively to knowledgeable people in modern society.

The matters discussed in this section are sometimes called "points of contact" between believers and unbelievers. I have avoided using the term "point of contact," though it is very commonly used in apologetics, because I find it very ambiguous. It can mean (as in the present context) a mere commonness of interest (e.g., in abortion, in Reagan, in nuclear disarmament) that can open the way for a testimony. Or it can refer to some neutral criterion of truth that presupposes neither belief nor unbelief. (In that sense, I would say that there is no point of contact between believers and unbelievers.) Or it can refer to some facts or norms that both the believer and unbeliever know. (In that sense, there are many points of contact. The unbeliever suppresses this knowledge, but his suppression does not necessarily render it unconscious. See chapter 1, C, *(2)*). Or it can refer to some psychological faculty (perhaps the heart itself) that can be reached

15. Nashville: Thomas Nelson Publishers, 1983.

by a gospel presentation or apologetic argument, if God wills. (Yes, there is point of contact in that sense.)

b. Having come to some understanding of his audience, the apologist must, like all theologians, decide on the form in which to present his message. Here there are many possibilities, and a good imagination will help the apologist to visualize them. Dialogue, lecture, fantasy tales, visual aids (see Jer. 27:1-7; Ezek. 4:1-3; Isa. 8:18), dramatic actions (Ezek. 4:4-17), various kinds of media presentations, letters to editors, books, and many other approaches are legitimate vehicles of apologetic content. Flexibility here is important. The apostle Paul became all things to all men that he might by all means save some (1 Cor. 9:22). Following that principle may mean enduring discomfort or loss of dignity or even being persecuted for the sake of our ministry. Tradition and personal comfort must be pushed into the background.

The important thing is to present the message as clearly as possible. That implies that we must "identify" as closely as possible with those whom we seek to win. We may not, of course, identify with their unbelief. But we must seek to look at the world through their eyes as much as possible so that our message is not obscured by cultural or traditional factors that are irrelevant to the gospel. References to the history, customs, literature, and even religion[16] of those whom we are trying to win are valuable tools.

Nor are we required always to disagree with the prophets, the customs, and the ideas of the unbeliever. The unbeliever's suppression of the truth does not entail that everything he says is false (see chapter 1, C, *(2)*). It simply means that he is opposed to the truth and resists it, even when he finds it within him, as he must.

Thus the presuppositional apologist need not be embarrassed by Acts 17:16-34. In that passage Paul does not appeal to some "neutral" criterion of truth but to the revealed knowledge of God that even pagans (unbelievers) are unable to escape. In the Acts passage, contrary to their own inclinations, Paul's pagan audience admits two truths of the Christian faith: their own ignorance (v. 23) and God's immanence (v. 28). But as in Romans 1, Paul condemns them for having *resisted* this revelation. Their idolatry is ignorant, is sinful (v. 30), and must be repented of. Far from endorsing their religion, Paul condemns and corrects it (vv. 23ff.). He teaches an immaterial, personal, and sovereign God, contrary both to the pagan worship and to the sophisticated philosophical concepts of the Epicureans and

16. Guinness urges apologists to "use their prophets," citing Acts 17:28.

Stoics (v. 18). His proclamation of resurrection and final judgment by the man Jesus (v. 30f.) evoked mockery. Paul's perspective is wholly biblical, as evidenced by his allusions to the Old Testament (Exod. 20:3f.; Deut. 32:8; 1 Kings 8:27; Ps. 50:9-12).[17]

There is no reason why the apologist cannot agree with certain elements of unbelieving thought, as long as he takes account of the fact that unbelievers seek to suppress the truth that they know. Such agreements, then, are not appeals to common or neutral criteria; they are appeals to the truth that Scripture warrants (though it be found on unbelieving lips).

17. Stephen R. Spencer's unpublished article "Is Natural Theology Biblical?" drew a number of these Old Testament parallels to my attention, pointing out that Paul's Athenian address is really a continuation of his reasoning in the synagogue—see Acts 17:17.

APPENDIX E

EVALUATING THEOLOGICAL WRITINGS

In Appendices E, F, and G, I intend to restate some of the principles of the book that are particularly relevant to "young theologians," seminarians writing their first theology papers. I hope that they will also be helpful to a few older ones, too! Although many of these points are made in the book, I hope here to put them in what may be a more convenient form: checklists against which students may compare their own theological writings and those of others.

The first checklist is a list of ways in which theological articles, lectures, and books may be evaluated.

1. *Scripturality*. Are the ideas teachings of Scripture? Are they at least consistent with Scripture? This is, of course, the chief criterion.

2. *Truth*. Even if an idea is not found in Scripture, it may be true—for example, a theory about the influence of Bultmann on Pannenberg.

3. *Cogency*. Is the author's case adequately argued? Are his premises true, his arguments valid?

4. *Edification* (Eph. 4:29). Is it spiritually helpful? Harmful? Hard to say?

5. *Godliness*. Does the text exhibit the fruit of the Spirit, or is it blasphemous, gossipy, slanderous, unkind, and so forth?

6. *Importance*. Is the idea important? Trivial? Somewhere in between? Important for some but not for others?

7. *Clarity*. Are the key terms well defined, at least implicitly? Is the formal structure intelligible, well thought out? Are the author's positions clear? Does he formulate well the issues to be addressed and distinguish them from one another?

8. *Profundity*. Does the text wrestle with difficult, or only with easy, questions? (Robert Dick Wilson, the great Old Testament scholar, used as his motto, "I have not shirked the difficult questions"—a good motto for all theologians to remember.) Does it get to the heart of a matter? Does it note subtle distinctions and nuances that other writers miss? Does it show extraordinary insight of some kind?

9. *Form and Style*. Is it appropriate to the subject matter? Does it show creativity?

The most important of these is *1*, of course. In seminary teaching, I tend to grade papers mostly on clarity *7*, cogency *3*, and profundity *8* because of the difficulty of applying doctrinal and practical tests in an academic setting.

The following criteria are *unsound*, for reasons discussed in the book. Do *not* use these in evaluating theological works.

10. *Emphasis*. See chapter 6, *A*. In this kind of criticism, one theologian attacks another for having an improper "emphasis." But there is no such thing as a single normative emphasis. An emphasis becomes a problem only when it leads to other sorts of problems, those mentioned in *1-9* above.

11. *Comparability*. See chapter 8, *I, (3)-(5)*. Here a work is criticized because it resembles another work that is poorly regarded. Such resemblance, however, is never sufficient ground for criticism. The strengths and weaknesses of each work must be evaluated individually.

12. *Terminology*. See chapter 6, *C, (1)* and chapter 7, C and *D* (especially *D, (5)*). Criticizing the terminology of a work—its metaphors, "motifs," and definitions—is never sound unless the terminology causes some of the problems listed above in criteria *1-9*. The terminology itself is never the problem. This sort of criticism falls under our condemnation of "word-level," rather than "sentence-level," criticism.

APPENDIX F

HOW TO WRITE A THEOLOGICAL PAPER

What follows is *my* method of theological research and writing. There are, of course, many others, and I would not dream of imposing my approach on anyone else. Still, you have to start somewhere, with some sort of model in your head; and after some years of work in the field, I still think the following plan has some merit.

Every theological paper, even those wholly devoted to the author's original ideas, will involve some research. (This is the case even for papers and other presentations that are not written in a traditional academic style.) At the very least, it will involve exegetical research and intelligent interaction with biblical texts. Otherwise, the theological work can hardly make any claim to scripturality; and if it is not scriptural, it is simply worthless. Additionally, there should usually be some interaction with other orthodox theologians to guard against individualistic aberration. There may also be interaction with nonorthodox theology, secular science, politics, economics, philosophy, cultural trends, and the like, by way of contrast, critique, and "point of contact" (see chapter 11, *B*, *(3)*).

Furthermore, every paper should contain something of the theologian himself. It is rarely sufficient simply to tell the reader what someone else says (an "expository paper," as I call it). Nor, in seminary level papers, is it adequate to write down a series of "standard" arguments on an issue—arguments that have been used time and time again. I describe papers of that sort as "party lines." Party lines are often useful; it is good to have at your fingertips the standard arguments for infant baptism, for example. I myself use this kind of argument frequently in talking with inquirers. But generally, party-line arguments do not belong in theological papers. Expositions, summaries, surveys, party lines—all of these are essentially regurgitations of ideas obtained from other sources. They involve little analytical or critical thinking. But such thinking is precisely what is needed, if the paper is to represent an *advance* in the church's knowledge.

Integration between research and one's own creative thought, then, is the goal—or rather an important means to the ultimate goal of edification. To achieve this purpose, I work according to the following steps (more or less).

1. Choose a topic with care, one that will be helpful to people, one that you can handle adequately in the time available to you and in the length of document you intend to write (or size of nonwritten presentation).

2. Understand your sources. Scripture texts ought to be fully exegeted. With other sources, I generally write out complete outlines of the ones that are most important. If I am reviewing a book (at some length, at least) I usually outline the entire volume, seeking to understand precisely the structure of the arguments, what is being said and how it is being said. Those sources which are less important, that is, those which will be referred to only in passing or of which only small portions are of interest, can be treated with proportionately less intensity; but the theologian is responsible to make *correct* use even of incidental sources.

3. Write down what you find interesting. After I outline my sources, I usually go back and read them again (it goes faster the second time, for the outline helps) to discover things that interest me. I write down (with page references) anything that seems to be especially useful, anything especially bad, anything confusing or perplexing, any tidbit that might add spice to my writing. This is the beginning of real theological creativity (though creativity of a sort is not entirely missing even from stages *1-2*).

4. Ask questions about your sources. What is the author's purpose? What questions is he trying to answer, and how does he answer them? Try to paraphrase his position as best you can. Is his position clear? Analyze any ambiguities. What is he saying on the best possible interpretation? On the worst? On the most likely? If you come across anything especially interesting, add it to the notes mentioned in step 3.

5. Formulate a critical perspective on your sources. How do you evaluate them? Use criteria *1-9* under Appendix E. There must always be some evaluation, positive or negative; if you don't know what is good or bad about the source, you cannot make any responsible use of it. With a scriptural text as a source, of course, the evaluation should always be positive.

With other texts, there will generally be some element of negative evaluation (see chapter 7, *E*).

6. Organize your notes according to topics of interest. I generally go through my notes and write down everything that bears on a particular topic. A computer can be of assistance here.

7. Ask, then, What do I want to tell my audience on the basis of my research? Determine one or more points that you think your readers, hearers, viewers (etc.) ought to know. The structure of your presentation should be fully determined by that purpose. Omit anything extraneous. You do not need to tell your audience *everything* you have learned. Here are some things you might choose to do at this point. (a) Ask *questions*. Sometimes a well-formulated question can be edifying, even if the theologian has no answer. It is good for us to learn what is mysterious, what is beyond our comprehension. (b) *Analyze* a theological text or group of them. Analysis is not "exposition" (above) but "explanation." It describes *why* the text is organized or phrased in a certain way—its historical background, its relations to other texts, and so forth. (c) *Compare* or *contrast* two or more positions. Show their similarities and differences. (d) Develop *implications* and *applications* of the texts. (e) *Supplement* the texts in some way. Add something to their teaching that you think is important. (f) Offer *criticism*—positive or negative evaluation. (g) Present some combination of the above. The point, of course, is to be clear on just what you are doing.

8. Be self-critical. Before and during your writing, *anticipate objections*. If you are criticizing Barth, imagine Barth looking over your shoulder, reading your manuscript, giving his reactions. This point is crucial. A truly self-critical attitude can save you from unclarity and unsound arguments. It will also keep you from arrogance and unwarranted dogmatism—faults common to all theology (liberal as well as conservative). Don't hesitate to say "probably" or even "I don't know" when the circumstances warrant. Self-criticism will also make you more "profound." For often—perhaps usually—it is objections that force us to rethink our positions, to get beyond our superficial ideas, to wrestle with the really deep theological issues. As you anticipate objections to your replies to objections to your replies, and so forth, you will find yourself being pushed irresistibly into the realm of the "difficult questions," the theological profundities.

In self-criticism the creative use of the theological imagination is tremendously important. Keep asking such questions as these. (a) Can I take my source's idea in a more favorable sense? A less favorable one? (b) Does my idea provide the only escape from the difficulty, or are there others? (c) In trying to escape from one bad extreme, am I in danger of falling into a different evil on the other side? (d) Can I think of some counter-examples to my generalizations? (e) Must I clarify my concepts, lest they be misunderstood? (f) Will my conclusion be controversial and thus require more argument than I had planned?

9. Decide on an audience. Children of a certain age? Unbelievers? New Christians? Educated? Uneducated? Theologically trained? Professional scholars? Americans? Other nations? The audience chosen will have a great effect on the format and style of the presentation.

10. Decide on a format and style. Again, flexibility is important. Consider various possibilities: (a) academic research paper, (b) sermon, (c) dialogue form (valuable for many reasons, not least that it encourages you to be more self-critical), (d) drama, (e) poetry, (f) fantasy, (g) allegory, (h) mixed media, (i) popular article. There are many others.

11. Produce your formulation—on paper or use whatever medium you choose. Outlining beforehand is helpful, but I generally find myself changing the outline as I see where the text seems most naturally to be going. More helpful is *rewriting*. A word-processor can be immensely helpful at this point. If you have problems with sentence structure, paragraph organization, and so forth, it is often helpful to read your work aloud, preferably to someone else.

The thrust should not be a summary of your research (that would be an "expository" paper) but your own creative response to your research. Do not spend ten pages in exposition and only one in evaluation or analysis. Include only enough exposition to explain and justify your own conclusions.

The whole work ought to be undergirded with prayer. We have seen the importance of God's sovereign working to the success of theology and apologetics. Who else can bring about the knowledge of God but God himself?

APPENDIX G

MAXIMS FOR THEOLOGIANS AND APOLOGISTS

In this next checklist, I would like to enumerate for theologians and apologists some "do's" and "don'ts," based on the discussions in the book. This list will be, in effect, a summary of the book's proposals.

1. Do all to the glory of our covenant Lord (chapter 1).

2. Do not draw facile epistemological conclusions from the doctrines of God's incomprehensibility and knowability (chapter 1, *B*, *(1)*).

3. Do see all theology as an exposition of God's lordship attributes (chapter 1, *B*, *(2)*, *a*).

4. Do recognize the dependence of the theologian and apologist on divine illumination (chapter 1, *B*, *(2)*, *b*).

5. Do theology—indeed, all your thinking; indeed, all your living—in obedience to God (chapter 1, *B*, *(2)*, *b*; chapter 10, C and *D* [esp. *(5)* and *(6)*] ; chapter 11, *A*, *(3)*).

6. Do not seek to do theology without a personal knowledge of God as your friend through Christ (chapter 1, *B*, *(2)*, *b*).

7. Do recognize that unbelievers seek always to avoid, suppress, and hinder the truth (chapter 1, C). Thus their theological perception, though informed by God's revelation, is not dependable.

8. Do not, however, draw simplistic conclusions from the unbeliever's depravity, for example that everything he says is false (chapter 1, C, *(2)*; chapter 11, *B*, *(3)*).

9. Do trace, in non-Christian thought, the dynamics of rationalism and irrationalism—hopeless positions necessarily connected with unbelief (chapter 1, *A*, *(2)*; chapter 1, C, *(3)*; chapter 11, *B*, *(1)*).

10. Do not try to isolate facts, laws, or subjectivity as "prior" to the others or as having more authority than the others. Recognize the interdependence of these as "perspectives" (chapter 2).

11. Do not think of theology merely as an expression of feeling (chapter 3, *A*, *(1)*).

12. Do not think of theology as mere scientific theory-making (chapter 3, *A*, *(2)*; chapter 9, *B*), or as seeking some "purely objective" truth.

13. Do think of theology as "the application of the Word of God by persons to all areas of life" (chapter 3, *A*, *(3)*).

14. Do not distinguish meaning from application (chapter 3, *A*, *(3)*; Appendix C; chapter 7, *A*).

15. Do seek to justify your assertions, but remember that on some occasions we may believe something without being able to give a justification (chapter 4, *A*; chapter 10, *D*, *(7)*; Appendix I).

16. Do not seek any justification deeper than the self-attesting authority of Scripture (chapter 4, *A*; chapter 5, *A*).

17. Do not seek to make one of the "three perspectives" on justification more ultimate than the others (chapter 4, *B-D*; chapter 5, *D*; chapter 6, *B*). Cf., maxim *10*, above.

18. Do reason in a "broad," rather than a "narrow," circle. Include in your arguments as many facts, as much data, as you can (chapter 5, *A*, *(6)* and *B*, *(5)*).

19. Do reason circularly, even if it seems absurd. Have faith that Scripture is right when it says that the unbeliever really knows God, and that, indeed, a God-honoring circle is the only proper, the only rational, way to reason (chapter 5, *A*, *(6)* and *E*; chapter 11, *A*, *(1)*). Cf., maxim *16*, above.

20. Do let your presuppositions and your faith work in you a sense of certainty; don't resist the process. But remain teachable, also out of faith (chapter 5, *A*, *(8)*).

21. Do offer that same certainty to those to whom you witness (chapter 5, *B*, *(3)*).

22. Do present the facts together with their scriptural interpretations. Do not be embarrassed about using extrabiblical information in theology, if you are interpreting it within a scriptural framework (chapter 5, *B*, *(4)*; chapter 9; chapter 11, *A*, *(2)* and *B*, *(2)*); cf. maxim *18*, above. Do not give the impression that you have reached the "brute facts," or the truth, apart from Scripture's interpretation of it (above references, also chapter 10, *D*, *(2)*).

23. Do present your witness with a goal of nothing less than leading the inquirer to full saving faith (chapter 5, *B*, *(5)* and C; chapter 11, *A*, *(3)*).

24. Do relate your witness to the individual, personal needs of your inquirer, as well as to those needs he shares with everyone (chapter 5, C; chapter 11, A, *(3)* and B, *(3)*).

25. Do point out inconsistencies between the unbeliever's life and his doctrine to show that his unbelief cannot meet his real needs (chapter 5, C, *(1)*; chapter 11, B, *(2)*).

26. Don't be ashamed to admit that from one perspective, belief is a feeling; but don't let that perspective make you irresponsible to the norms and the facts (chapter 5, C, *(3)*; chapter 10, *D*, *(3)* and *(7)*).

27. Do seek holiness as a means to theological maturity. Realize that some theological disputes cannot be resolved until one or all parties achieves greater spiritual maturity (chapter 5, C, *(4)*). Cf. maxims *1* and 5 above.

28. Do use artful presentations to help people see facts in biblical patterns (chapter 5, C, *(5)*).

29. Do seek renewal of groups and institutions as well as individuals, recognizing that individual and group renewal are inseparable (chapter 5, C, *(6)*; chapter 11, *B*, *(3)*).

30. Do not regard abstraction as an unmitigated evil (chapter 6, *A* and *E*, *(2)*; chapter 7, *A*, *D*, *E*, *F*; chapter 8, *E* and *I*, *(8)*).

31. Do not criticize someone for "having the wrong emphasis," unless you can show that that emphasis does harm according to criteria *1-9*, Appendix E (and chapter 6, C, *(3)* and *(6)*; chapter 8, *I*, *(17)*).

32. Do not speak about "the context" of something, unless you have some clear idea of which context you are talking about (chapter 6, *A*, *B*, C).

33. Do remember that the "central message" of Scripture is relative to all of its particular messages, and vice versa (chapter 6, *B*).

34. Do not demand that the "central message" of Scripture be formulated in only one way. Recognize the diversity of the biblical formulations (chapter 6, *B*).

35. Do not use "word-level" criticism: do not criticize a theologian's terminology (metaphors, distinctions, comparisons) unless you can show that that terminology does harm according to Appendix E, criteria *1-9* (also see chapter 6, C, *(1)*; chapter 7, C, *D*, *E*, *I*). Do not attack terminology merely because of the etymology or past historical usage of that terminology (above references; also see chapter 8, *I*, *(3)* and *(6)*).

36. Do use biblical characters as examples for the Christian life, after having ascertained the proper evaluation of the characters' actions in the light of all Scripture (chapter 6, C, *(4)*).

37. Do not be ashamed to use biblical texts allegorically or in other unusual ways, if they are fitted to those tasks (chapter 5, C, *(5)*).

38. Do use a text according to its purpose, recognizing that that purpose may be very rich and complex (cf. *37*, above; chapter 6, C, *(6)* and *D*).

39. Do engage in biblical theology, but not with a cultic spirit. Look at it as one of many ways to bring out the applications of Scripture (chapter 6, *E, (2)*).

40. Do not regard your theological system as superior in any way (materially or formally) to Scripture itself. Make sure your emotional attachments and attitudes are consistent with this resolution (chapter 3, *A*, *(2)*; chapter 6, *E, (3)*; chapter 7, C; chapter 9, A, *(2)*, *b-f*).

41. Do seek clarity, remembering, however, that some vagueness is unavoidable because of the nature of language and the vagueness of Scripture itself (chapter 7, *A*; chapter 8, *I, (14)-(17)*; chapter 9, *A, (2), d*). Be equally critical both of unnecessary vagueness and of false precision.

42. Do not be ashamed to be negative, where necessary (chapter 7, *E*). Avoid, however, careless disjunctions (cf. chapter 8, *I*).

43. Do not offer criticism of a theological formulation based only on the "sound" or the "feel" of that formulation (chapter 7, *I*).

44. Do make lists: write down all the possible things that might be meant by an expression you are seeking to analyze. Determine its best sense, its worst sense, its most likely sense (chapter 7, *I*).

45. Do point out the systematic ambiguity of nonorthodox theology (chapter 7, G).

46. Do use logic as any other tool of theology—with an awareness of your own fallibility, but without irrational fear (chapter 8; chapter 10, *D, (1)*). The same is true for language, history, science, and philosophy (chapters 7-9).

47. Do anticipate objections (chapter 8, C).

48. Do be suspicious of claims concerning "logical order," either among theological realities or within the presentation of theological truth. Be open to the possibility of *interdependence* among these realities and teachings (chapter 3, A, *(2)*; chapter 6, *B*; chapter 8, *E* and *F* and *I, (13)*; chapter 10, *D*). Cf. maxim *10*, above.

49. Do ascertain the burden of proof (chapter 8, G and *I, (6)*).

50. Do not think that you have refuted someone's position merely by offering arguments for an alternative view (chapter 8, *D*).

51. Do be aware of possible argument forms and fallacies, remembering that arguments that are strictly fallacious often have some value (chapter 8, *H* and *I*).

52. Do be loyal to your confessional tradition, being aware, however, of its fallibility (chapter 9, A, *(2)*). Do not, therefore, subscribe to "every statement" in any human confession.

53. Do not think of theology as an accumulation of discoveries from one generation to the next (chapter 9, A, *(2), h*; maxim *13*, above).

54. Do not demand that theology be impersonal or academic (chapter 10, A and *D (3)*).

55. Do be fair. Show love even to your opponents (chapter 10, C).

56. Do use all your human faculties (reason, perception, emotion, imagination, will, habits, intuition) as you use the "tools" of theology (maxim 44)—without embarrassment, but with an awareness of your own fallibility (chapter 10, *D*).

57. Do avoid any attempt to give one of your faculties (above, *52*) primacy over the others (chapter 10, *D*). Cf. maxims *10, 17*, and 48, above.

58. Do reason with unbelievers only on the basis of Scripture, using Scripture itself in the argument where appropriate (chapter 5, *E*; chapter 11, A, *(1)*). Cf. maxim *19*, above.

59. Do admit it when you don't know the answer; such ignorance is a *strength* of our apologetic (chapter 11, A, *(1)*).

60. Do make judicious use of evidentialist works in apologetics, presenting their facts together with the biblical interpretations of those facts (chapter 11, A, *(2)*). See maxim *22*, above.

61. Do "use the prophets" of unbelievers to bring to their attention the truth that they have been suppressing (chapter 11, *B, (3)*).

62. Do be flexible in the form you use to communicate (chapter 11, *B, (3)*; cf. Appendix F, *10*).

APPENDIX H

REVIEW OF GEORGE LINDBECK'S
The Nature of Doctrine[1]

I have submitted the following review for publication in the *Presbyterian Journal*. It seemed good to include it here as well, since it discusses some metatheological matters not explicitly brought out in the present volume and also makes another application of my triadic perspectives. Here is the review.

* * * * *

This volume is highly technical and difficult, but it describes a theory of the nature of religion and theology that could become influential in coming years.

Lindbeck teaches at Yale, where a number of professors have made interesting contributions in "metatheology," the theory of theology itself. He does not appreciate "fundamentalist" views of Scripture, and he urges a faith that is reconcilable with modern world views. At the same time, he has a certain "conservative" bent. In 1975 he was one of the signers of the *Hartford Declaration* which, in effect, said "enough is enough" to the "secular theologies" and "radical theologies" of the time. He has brought both of these concerns into the context of Lutheran-Roman Catholic ecumenical dialogue. He believes, like a liberal, that these doctrinal traditions are

1. Philadelphia: Westminster Press, 1984.

reconcilable; but, like a conservative, he believes that these traditions are to be taken seriously and maintained.

Lindbeck believes he can resolve this apparent contradiction by a particular theory of the nature of doctrine. In the past, he says, doctrine has been understood as propositional truth (orthodoxy) or as the articulation of religious experience (liberalism). There is, however, a third alternative: doctrine is a kind of *language*. Language is a system of symbols that we use to do different jobs in our common life. So, says Lindbeck, doctrine provides the religious community with a set of "rules" by which many things can be done and said. Thus the *conservative* Lindbeck can insist that doctrines are central and in some cases irreplaceable; without language, we can say nothing. But the *liberal* Lindbeck can insist that the language itself entails no propositional truths but only gives us tools by which we may (among other things) formulate such truths. He believes that creeds, for example, make no positive truth claims but exclude some doctrinal formulations and permit a range of others. Creeds are not to be simply repeated but to be used as tools for saying other things; we learn the Latin conjugation *amo, amas, amat* not to repeat it endlessly but so that we may learn to say other things, like *rogo, rogas, rogat*. In all of this, Lindbeck makes much use of modern anthropologists (e.g., Geertz), linguists (e.g., Chomsky), and philosophers (e.g., Wittgenstein, Kuhn) who have been moving in similar directions.

Lindbeck tries very hard to show that on his theory some doctrines may be regarded as superior to others, even infallible. I don't think he succeeds. Lindbeck offers us "rules," but doesn't offer us any adequate means of judging which ones we ought to use. I do think, however, that once we accept (as Lindbeck does not) an orthodox view of Scripture, then we can learn much from his theory. He has, in effect, presented what is to most of us a new, and in any case interesting, *perspective* on the nature of doctrine that in my view complements, rather than replaces, the other two that he mentions. Doctrine is all three things: propositional truth-claims, expressions of the inner experience of regeneration, and rules for the speech and conduct of God's creatures. No one of these is prior to the others. Lindbeck's book is an excellent exploration of the third perspective, which is, undoubtedly, the one most neglected in present-day theology. We can learn from Lindbeck that, indeed, the purpose of doctrine is not to be simply repeated, but also to be "applied"—to be *used* for all of God's purposes in the world. And if we cannot *use* it, we cannot in any serious sense claim to "understand" it.

APPENDIX I

THE NEW REFORMED EPISTEMOLOGY

Recently, there has been much discussion of the book *Faith and Rationality: Reason and Belief in God*, edited by Alvin Plantinga and Nicholas Wolterstorff (henceforth *FR*).[1] Since the concerns of this book definitely overlap those of my *Doctrine of the Knowledge of God* (henceforth *DKG*), I thought it would be best to add an appendix in which I commented on the relations between the two volumes.

I did not read *FR* until after I had finished writing *DKG*,[2] but *DKG* was influenced somewhat by some earlier articles and books that foreshadowed *FR*. In *DKG* I made considerable use of George Mavrodes's *Belief in God*,[3] especially his concept of "person-variable" proof that is prominent in *FR*. I also commented briefly (and favorably) on Wolterstorff's critique of "foundationalism" in *Reason Within the Bounds of Religion*.[4] And though I did not cite them directly, I was very much aware while writing *DKG* of Plantinga's "Is Belief in God Rational?"[5] and the articles of Wolterstorff, Alston, and Plantinga in *Rationality in the Calvinian Tradition*, edited by Hendrick Hart, Johan Vander Hoeven, and Nicholas Wolterstorff,[6] in which my "Rationality and Scripture" also appears. The latter volume consists of papers delivered at a conference I attended that was held at the

1. Notre Dame and London: University of Notre Dame Press, 1983.

2. *FR* was published in 1983, but the first printing evidently sold out quickly. I was unable to get a copy until early 1986, but *DKG* was finished in December 1984. Thus I was unable to take account of the book directly in the text of *DKG*.

3. New York: Random House, 1970.

4. Grand Rapids: Wm. B. Eerdmans Pub. Co., 1976.

5. In *Rationality and Religious Belief*, ed. C. F. Delaney (Notre Dame and London: University of Notre Dame Press, 1979), 7-27.

6. Lanham, Md., and London: University Press of America, 1983.

Institute for Christian Studies in Toronto during the summer of 1981, at which these matters were a central topic of discussion. I might, indeed, have structured *DKG* as a response to those writings, but I had my own agenda that, as I shall indicate, was significantly different from theirs.

In general, I approve of their approach, but there are some areas of difference, both of emphasis and of viewpoint. Here I shall summarize their argument and then present my evaluation.

(1) Some Broad Comparisons

First, I will make a few introductory comments. *FR* "arose out of a year-long project of the Calvin (College) Center for Christian Studies on the topic of 'Toward a Reformed View of Faith and Reason'."[7] Contributors were philosophers Alvin Plantinga (formerly of Calvin, now of Notre Dame), Nicholas Wolterstorff (Calvin), George Mavrodes (University of Michigan) and William P. Alston (Syracuse University), historian George Marsden (Calvin), and theologian David Holwerda (Calvin). This is a group of very well known thinkers, highly regarded in secular academia as well as in Christian circles. The philosophers are arguably the *most* highly respected American thinkers in the field of the philosophy of religion. Plantinga was written up in *Time Magazine* some years ago for his work on the theistic arguments, and that popular acclaim was not out of keeping with his professional reputation. The others are equally prominent and impressive thinkers.

The evangelical Christian commitment of these philosophers, though certainly genuine, has not always been evident in their writings. They have a tendency (even in *FR*) to write as if they were neutral observers, merely interested in the logical analysis of religious propositions for its own sake, without any particular religious stake in the outcome of the argument. That stance is the common one among modern philosophers of religion, whatever their personal convictions may be, though it is quite opposite to the stance of Cornelius Van Til and, indeed, of *DKG*. Nevertheless, in *FR* the philosophers let down their guard just a bit, even inching slightly toward theology.[8] One gets the impression (well, I do, anyway) that in these essays they are trying not merely to clarify concepts (though they do that admirably) but also to counsel fellow-believers who are struggling with real challenges to their faith.

7. *FR*, 9.

8. The definitions of philosophy and theology presupposed in this comment are, of course, not those advocated in *DKG*!

And these authors seem to want to give distinctively *Christian* counsel. There is almost no interaction with Scripture itself (though see pages 10-15 of the Introduction), but there are genuinely biblical concerns expressed. Plantinga and Wolterstorff want us to regard belief in God as a "basic" belief, one that is, in some sense, "prior" to other beliefs. (Holwerda sharpens this point: *contra* Pannenberg, faith in God's revealed promise is prior to the interpretation of history.[9])

And Plantinga and Wolterstorff, at least (together with historian Marsden), even express a sense of responsibility to the Reformed theological tradition. Wolterstorff considers it an advantage that his viewpoint has some affinity with the Continental Reformed tradition,[10] as do Plantinga[11] and Marsden.[12] Wolterstorff is even willing to describe his view ("admittedly not very felicitously") as "Calvinist epistemology" or "Reformed epistemology."[13] All of that, of course, is very similar to the stance of *DKG*.

Also similar to *DKG* is *FR*'s focus on the *ethical* dimension of epistemology. These authors, like me, see epistemic acts (believing, knowing, understanding, reasoning) as subject to ethical evaluations, as are other human actions. This focus, I think, adds to the "theological" flavor of both books. Here, however, an important difference also emerges. In *DKG*, the emphasis is on epistemic *obligations*, but in *FR* the emphasis is on epistemic *rights*. I am concerned about what we *should* believe; *FR* is concerned about what we *may* believe. The difference is not sharp; *DKG* occasionally reflects on permissions and *FR* occasionally on obligations. But there is a difference of emphasis.

A bigger difference concerns the *source* of epistemic ethical value, whether permission or obligation. I believe that the authors of *FR* would, as evangelical Christians, locate that source ultimately, somehow, in divine revelation. But *FR* does not refer to that fact.[14] *DKG*, on the contrary, is concerned above all to expound the relations between revelation—specifically Scripture—and human knowledge.

These differences partially explain a difference in *tone* between the two books. Like Van Til's writings, mine is homiletic, or just plain "preachy." I am expounding God's authoritative Word as I understand it to bear on

9. *FR*, 304-11.
10. Ibid., 7f.
11. Ibid., 63-73.
12. Ibid., 247-57.
13. Ibid., 7. Cf. Plantinga, 74-91.
14. Wolterstorff admits this in his Introduction, 9.

epistemological questions. Though my book is, I trust, philosophically informed, it is probably more like theology than philosophy, as those terms are usually understood. I do, however, inch toward a more philosophical presentation than Van Til employed, just as the authors of *FR*, as I said earlier, inch toward theology. Thus the two books, I think, improve the potential for communication between Christian thinkers of the Van Tillian tradition and those of the tradition of logical analysis.

Related somewhat to the above is the fact that *FR* is more rigorous, elegant, and cogent in arguing its conclusions than is *DKG*. *FR* takes more time to establish each detail of its case. I am capable of using a more logically rigorous style of argument than I used in *DKG* (though probably not nearly as skillfully as the philosophers in *FR*), but I decided against it because I believe that such a style would alienate many potential readers, would make the book too long and, more importantly, would detract from the impact of *DKG as a sermon*.

(2) The Argument of *Faith and Rationality*

a. *The Evidentialist Challenge*

But now we must survey the argument of *FR*. Perhaps its main theme is its attempt to answer what it calls the "evidentialist challenge to religious belief."[15] The "evidentialist" (who may be either a believer or a nonbeliever) maintains that it is not rational to accept a religious belief unless that belief is based on evidence and argument—on reasons of some sort. John Locke, David Hume, W. K. Clifford, Antony Flew, Michael Scriven, and even Thomas Reid (whose position is cited as in other respects congenial to that of *FR*) are described as being evidentialists in this sense.[16] On the one hand, a non-Christian evidentialist may then argue that it is irrational to believe in Christianity, for Christianity is not adequately supported by evidence. On the other hand, a Christian evidentialist may take up the challenge and argue that the weight of evidence does support Christianity after all.

15. Ibid., 5-7, 24-39, 137-40.

16. Plantinga cites Aquinas as another example (44-48). Wolterstorff, however, appears to disagree, maintaining that Aquinas (and Anselm) seek only to demonstrate by evidence or argument what is already believed without any evidence or argument (140f.). On Wolterstorff's view, the "evidentialist objection" is "peculiar to modernity" (140).

b. *Classical Foundationalism*

FR's approach, however, is to reject the evidentialist objection as illegitimate. In the first place, the authors argue, this objection is based on a discredited epistemological theory that they call "classical foundationalism."[17] This theory teaches that our beliefs may be divided into two categories: beliefs that depend on other beliefs and beliefs that do not and which therefore can be called "basic" or "foundational." Beliefs of the first sort are justified by their relation to basic beliefs. A nonbasic belief, if it is to be rational, must be deducible from a basic belief or at least be rendered probable by a basic belief. The basic beliefs usually are said to include such beliefs as "1 + 1 = 2," "I feel dizzy," "I see a tree," (or, more modestly, "I *seem* to see a tree")—beliefs that may be described as self-evident, a priori, incorrigible, or evident to the senses. These are thought to warrant such a degree of certainty as to require no evidence or argument.

Now in classical foundationalism, religious belief is excluded from the foundation, since it is thought to lack the certainty associated with the other types of foundational beliefs. Since, then, religious beliefs cannot be "basic," they must be demonstrated or rendered probable by beliefs that are "properly basic." Hence, religious beliefs (as opposed to "basic" beliefs) require evidence, proof, argument, if they are to be held rationally. Thus classical foundationalism requires evidentialism. And Plantinga argues that the converse is also true: evidentialism presupposes classical foundationalism.[18]

But according to these authors, classical foundationalism is false. In *Reason*, Wolterstorff argued that it is impossible to derive all human knowledge from foundational propositions: you cannot find enough propositions to make up the "foundation," and from the foundation, however construed, you cannot derive the sum-total of your knowledge. In *FR*, Plantinga points out that many of our everyday beliefs (such as "I had breakfast this morning," "The world has existed for more than five minutes") cannot plausibly be shown to be derivable from self-evident or incorrigible propositions. Furthermore, he asks, what is the ground for the classical foundationalist's *criterion* of "proper basicality"? What is his reason, for example, for excluding religious beliefs from the foundation? His criterion, argues Plantinga, cannot itself be justified on a foundationalist basis; for neither is it a "basic" proposition nor may it plausibly be argued

17. Ibid., 1-5, 47-63, also Wolterstorff's *Reason*, cited earlier.
18. Ibid., 47f.

to be derivable from basic propositions.[19] Foundationalism, then, is a self-defeating position, since the theory cannot justify its key criterion of "proper basicality."

Since, then, classical foundationalism is faulty, the evidentialist objection lacks force. There is no reason why belief in Christianity should not itself be "properly basic," included in the "foundation" of our noetic structure. And if it is, then we are within our rights (epistemically permitted) to believe in Christianity without any evidence or reasons at all.

c. *Christian Experience*

Alston adds a careful argument to the effect that to believe in Christianity on the basis of "Christian experience" is no less rational than to believe in physical objects on the basis of sense perception.[20] His argument supports Plantinga's by suggesting, in effect, that Christian experience has as much right as sense perception to being accepted as foundational or basic.

d. *Wolterstorff's Alternative Criterion*

Wolterstorff's contribution is to suggest a positive alternative to the discredited foundationalist criterion of rationality.

> A person is rationally justified in believing a certain proposition that he does believe unless he has adequate reason to cease from believing it. Our beliefs are rational unless we have reason for refraining; they are not nonrational unless we have reason *for* believing. They are innocent until proved guilty, not guilty until proved innocent.[21]

On this criterion, a three-year-old child might be rationally justified in believing there are birds outside his window even if, when asked, he is unable to supply anything like a reason for this belief. That, of course, accords well with common sense, in contrast with the evidentialist position, which would, in effect, require the child to abandon his belief until he is able to produce a respectable argument for it. And this criterion, like Plantinga's arguments, warrants one's right to believe in Christianity without being able to offer any reasons for so believing.

19. Ibid., 59-63. This is the sort of argument that has been effectively used to refute the logical positivist verification principle.

20. Ibid., 103-34.

21. Ibid., 163. Wolterstorff does recognize some exceptions to this rule, and on the following pages he formulates a more technical version of it that takes account of those exceptions. Those qualifications need not detain us here.

e. *The Great Pumpkin*

We must note, of course, that although our beliefs are "innocent until proved guilty" on this view, it is indeed possible for them to be proved guilty. To say that a belief is "basic" is not to say that it is infallible or even incorrigible. The "justification" accorded to our basic beliefs is only a *prima facie* or "defeasible" justification. I am rationally justified in giving up a basic belief, even belief in God, if I find some good reasons for disbelieving.[22]

Thus we are not bound to accept just any belief as "properly basic." Plantinga discusses the "Great Pumpkin objection," which is to the effect that if it is rational to accept the existence of God as a basic proposition, it should also be rational to accept the existence of the Great Pumpkin, or any other belief, as properly basic. No, he says, we may reject such beliefs if there are reasons for disbelieving them.[23] Wolterstorff adds that if we adopt the practice of just believing anything arbitrarily, we are adopting a "most unreliable 'mechanism' of belief formation"[24] and that is good reason to reject that practice and not to adopt beliefs based on it.

f. *Grounds for Believing*

There are, then, negative grounds, grounds for rejecting beliefs, even when the beliefs are proposed as basic. But are there any positive grounds, grounds for believing those propositions that I take to be basic? Or are they "groundless"? Plantinga replies that indeed positive grounds do exist. He compares religious beliefs to beliefs based on perception.

> Then my being appeared to in this characteristic way (together with other circumstances) is what confers on me the right to hold the belief in question; this is what justifies me in accepting it. We could say, if we wish, that this experience is what justifies me in holding it; this is the *ground* of my justification, and, by extension, the ground of the belief itself.[25]

He also makes comparisons with beliefs about states of the minds of others and beliefs based on memory. In the former case he says:

> If I see someone displaying typical pain behavior, I take it that he or she is in pain. Again, I do not take the displayed behavior as *evidence* for that belief; I do not infer that belief from others I hold; I do not

22. Cf. Plantinga, 75-78, 82-87; Alston, 111-13.
23. Ibid., 73-87.
24. Ibid., 172.
25. Ibid., 79.

> accept it on the basis of other beliefs. Still, my perceiving of the pain behavior . . . forms the ground of my justification for the belief in question.[26]

Note the distinction: our basic beliefs have "grounds" but not "evidence." He later elaborates (in relation to perceptual beliefs),

> What justifies me in believing there is a tree present is just the fact that I am appeared to in a certain way; it is not necessary that I know or believe or consider the fact that I am being appeared to.[27]

Plantinga does not, however, want to say that argument is entirely irrelevant to basic belief. For one thing, an argument may persuade me that a potential refutation of my basic belief is faulty. An argument that refutes a refutation is certainly relevant to the justification of my belief when it is being challenged. Such an argument does not prove the truth of my belief, but it removes an impediment to my holding it.[28] Nor does he wish to concede that belief in God's existence as basic is based on "faith" as opposed to "reason" (i.e., that it is "fideistic"). Rather, he means to put belief in God's existence among that class of beliefs which are traditionally described as "deliverances of reason"! Self-evident propositions, perceptual propositions, and so forth are commonly accepted as properly basic because they are "deliverances of reason." That is, it is generally agreed among philosophers that such propositions should be believed simply because it is rational to believe them. We believe in the external world, in other minds, in the past, because we have a natural *rational* tendency to do so. Plantinga finds this similar to Calvin's treatment of God's existence, where he warrants belief in God on the basis of a divinely implanted *sensus deitatis*, a natural tendency to believe in God. In Plantinga's brand of Calvinism, belief in God is by reason, not by faith! (And that implies, interestingly, that "theists and nontheists have different conceptions of reason, since a nontheist would not accept theism as a deliverance of *his* reason."[29]

g. *Situated Rationality*

It is also important to observe that on this view the justification of beliefs is *person variable*. Wolterstorff says:

26. Ibid., 79, emphasis his. He mentions other "justification-conferring conditions," including *testimony* on 85f.

27. Ibid., 86.

28. Ibid., 82-87.

29. Ibid., 87-91; the quotation is on page 90.

> When I was young, there were things which it was rational for me to believe which now, when I am older, it is no longer rational for me to believe. And for a person reared in a traditional tribal society who never comes into contact with another society or culture, there will be things rational to believe which for me, a member of the modern Western intelligensia, would not be rational to believe. Rationality of belief can only be determined in context—historical and social contexts, and, even more narrowly, personal context. It has long been the habit of philosophers to ask in abstract, nonspecific fashion whether it is rational to believe that God exists, whether it is rational to believe that there is an external world, whether it is rational to believe that there are other persons, and so on. Mountains of confusion have resulted. The proper question is always and only whether it is rational for this or that particular person in this or that situation, or for a person of this or that particular type in this or that type of situation, to believe so-and-so. Rationality is always *situated* rationality.[30]

Thus for Wolterstorff, it is no longer

> of much interest to spend time pondering whether evidentialism is false. It seems highly likely that it is. But the interesting and important question has become whether some specific person—I, or you, or whoever—who believes immediately that God exists is rational in that belief. Whether a given person is in fact rational in such belief cannot be answered in general and in the abstract, however. It can only be answered by scrutinizing the belief system of the individual believer, and the ways in which that believer has used his noetic capacities.[31]

Even if God exists, Wolterstorff thinks, it may be rational for some people not to believe in His existence.[32] If someone hears arguments against the existence of God and is unable to refute them, then for him belief in God's existence is not rational. It may, however, still be right for him to believe in God, even if such belief is irrational!

> Perhaps, in spite of its irrationality for him, the person ought to continue believing that God exists. Perhaps it is our duty to believe more firmly that God exists than any proposition that conflicts with this and/or more firmly than we believe that a certain proposition

30. Emphasis his. Cf. his comments on Chisholm (147). Plantinga argues that even the classical foundationalist cannot avoid thinking of reality as "situated." He points out that for Aquinas a proposition may be self-evident to one person and not to another (56f.).

31. Ibid., 176.

32. Ibid., 177.

does conflict with it. . . . May it not . . . be that sometimes the nonrationality of one's conviction that God exists is a trial, to be endured?[33]

(3) MAVRODES'S EMENDATIONS

a. *Positive Apologetics: Why Not?*

At this point, it is appropriate to bring Mavrodes's article into the discussion. Mavrodes dissents somewhat from the consensus position of Plantinga, Alston, and Wolterstorff. Although he grants that these three have shown Christian belief to be rational in terms of their definition of "rational," he suggests that something more is needed. "Convincing someone that it would be rational for him to believe in God does not amount to giving him a reason for believing in God."[34] Thus an atheist might be convinced by Plantinga et al. that believing in Christianity is rational, while (rationally!) maintaining his atheism. The Plantinga argument does eliminate one possible reason for *not* believing in Christianity, but it does not give a reason *for* so believing.

Mavrodes questions why these men accept the validity of negative apologetics (refuting refutations) but deny the value of positive apologetics (giving reasons). The most likely answer, he notes, is that to the Plantinga group, these beliefs do not need reasons, since they are "properly basic." He points out, however, that in a review of Clark Pinnock's *Reason Enough*, Wolterstorff (strangely) takes a different tack: evidence is not needed because unbelievers already have sufficient evidence but resist it. "Maybe," Mavrodes comments, "[this inconsistency] represents a deep ambivalence in Reformed thought, a tendency to oscillate between holding that belief in God is backed by plenty of evidence and holding that it involves no evidence whatever."[35] He seems to think, however, that it is more likely that the remarks in Wolterstorff's review were merely a slip and that his actual position is not that Christian belief is warranted by evidence but that such facts as the design of the world activate in us a natural disposition to believe, one that the unbeliever sinfully resists.[36]

Still, Mavrodes persists, Wolterstorff does acknowledge the legitimacy of *negative* apologetics. If the unbeliever's sinful rationalization militates against the use of positive arguments, why should it not militate against

33. Ibid.
34. Ibid., 195.
35. Ibid., 198.
36. Ibid., 199

negative ones as well? Positive underscoring of evidence is certainly one way to combat rationalization. And if Wolterstorff (and his colleagues) are willing to use positive as well as negative arguments to defend the *rationality* of Christian belief, why should they not permit the same variety of arguments for the *truth* of such belief?[37] Is it because such arguments are person-variable that no argument will be effective for every unbeliever? But what, then, would be wrong with tailoring arguments to fit particular individuals?[38]

Most of us, after all, are interested in truth, not only in rationality (defined in the Plantinga sense).[39] Mavrodes suggests that there are procedures that bring us closer to truth than the procedure of merely accepting every rational belief that occurs to us. One cannot *prove*, perhaps, that these procedures (perception, logical reasoning, and so forth) are reliable, but in fact we do have a "natural disposition" to rely on them. One could, then, reconstruct natural theology as the attempt to show that there are beliefs produced by natural belief-forming mechanisms that imply or render probable the truth of Christian beliefs. Since Wolterstorff and Plantinga urge us to trust in these "natural mechanisms" and indeed allow us to ground our "basic" beliefs in them, what objection could they have to such a procedure?[40]

They might object that beliefs thus accepted on the basis of evidence will not be held with the full certitude of faith but only tentatively and weakly. But Mavrodes questions whether this is necessarily the case. Why cannot people hold beliefs with full certitude even though they came to believe in them by means of argument? Is it because those arguments are only probable and thus deserve only partial acceptance? But according to Wolterstorff and Plantinga, it is legitimate to give full credence to beliefs based on *no evidence at all*! Why, then, ought we to assume that an argument based on partial evidence deserves less firm credence than one based on no evidence at all?[41]

37. Ibid., 199-202, 204f.

38. Ibid., 204-8.

39. Remember that in the Plantinga-Wolterstorff sense, beliefs may be rational but untrue, and vice versa. In his article in the volume that I cited earlier (the one edited by Delaney), Mavrodes distinguishes between "rationality-oriented" and "truth-oriented" approaches and makes the uncharacteristically blunt comment, "If push comes to shove, I think I would opt for truth over rationality every time," (33).

40. Ibid., 208-14.

41. Ibid., 214-17.

b. *Are "Basic" and "Nonbasic" Beliefs Sharply Distinct?*

Thus Mavrodes concurs with the Plantinga-Wolterstorff view that we can believe in Christianity without reasons, but he disagrees with their rejection of positive apologetics. He also offers another important suggestion. He notes that Wolterstorff and Plantinga, critical as they are of classical foundationalism, still operate within a foundationalist framework to this extent: they see all of our beliefs as either "basic" or "derived." But is it really that simple?

> Readers of this volume who are theists might usefully try the following experiment on themselves. Pause for a moment and consider your own belief that God exists, just as it stands right now. . . . Is that belief . . . based on some other beliefs that you hold? And if so, what are those other beliefs, and *how* is the belief in God's existence based on them? (Do they entail it, for example, or render it probable, or what?)[42]

Mavrodes suspects (and I think rightly so) that for most of us there will be no clear answer to these questions. This fact suggests that the contrast between "basic" and "derived" beliefs oversimplifies the epistemic situation.

(4) My Response

In general, my own response is to applaud the "Reformed epistemology" of *FR*, especially with the Mavrodes emendations. Its account of epistemic rights supplements usefully my own account in *DKG*, which focuses on epistemic obligations (and, I trust, vice versa). I would, however, also like to submit some comments by way of additional analysis of the issues.

a. *Grounds and Reasons*

Plantinga's assertion that basic beliefs have "grounds" but not "reasons" has a paradoxical ring to it, suggesting that there are some problems of definition here. My dictionary lists *evidence* and *sufficient reason* as synonyms for one meaning of *ground* and *ground* as a synonym for *reason* in one sense of that term. Plantinga evidently wishes to take *reason* exclusively in the sense of "consciously articulated reasons" or "arguments." However, I don't think it is necessary to define the term so narrowly. Ordinarily, we speak of someone's having a reason for a belief or action even in

42. Ibid., 203.

cases where that person does not, even cannot, articulate his reason. And it is not absurd to speak of animals as having reasons for beliefs, as in, "My dog thinks the ball is somewhere in the bush, because she thinks I threw it in that direction," for example.

And there is value in *not* defining *reason* as narrowly as Plantinga does. For the line between articulated and nonarticulated reasons is not a sharp one.[43] When I ask a child why he thinks it is morning and he points outside to the rising sun, is that an articulated reason or a nonarticulated one? When my dog behaves as if she thinks there is a ball under the bush and sniffs (indicating, if you will, that the ground of her belief is an odor), is that articulate or nonarticulate reasoning? Furthermore, I suspect that our articulations of reasons (including the science of logic) grow organically out of our inarticulate sense of what is reasonable. As I discuss in *DKG*, formal logic is based on informal logic; formal logic attempts to systematize, facilitate, and evaluate the results of our "natural disposition" to hold rational beliefs.

Plantinga and Wolterstorff seem to think that there is an important difference between accepting the deliverances of our natural dispositions and accepting conclusions on the basis of argument. In the case of perceptual knowledge, they argue, it is not that our perceptual experience implies or renders probable the existence of physical objects, but rather that we have a natural disposition to believe in such objects when confronted with such experience. And the same is true, they argue, for Christian belief. But what is an argument if it is not an attempt to put into words the deliverances of such natural dispositions? And is not reason itself (considered now as the human capacity for drawing conclusions from premises) such a natural disposition? Do we not accept the logical implications of our beliefs because of a natural disposition to do so? Responding to evidence is a natural disposition, and *evidence* refers to data that engages that natural disposition. Thus Wolterstorff's "slip," to which Mavrodes referred, is not surprising. It is often perfectly natural and proper for us to refer to what stimulates our belief-forming dispositions as "evidence." (I say "often," for not *all* such stimuli constitute evidence. See Mavrodes's counter-example

43. Perhaps the reason why Plantinga et al. think it is (or write as if this were the case) is their own high standards of articulate reasoning. If I had to write a philosophical paper as rigorous and as cogent as those in *FR* to give an explicit argument for a belief, then I too would be tempted to say that Christianity does not require argument. Surely, at least, it does not require *that kind* of argument. If my standards were that high, I would be much more tempted to say that the justification of Christian beliefs is by something entirely different from argument.

on page 199. But though not all such stimuli constitute evidence, all evidence, when it produces belief, constitutes such a stimulus.)

If we use *reason* as I am suggesting, the Plantinga-Wolterstorff thesis in question becomes this: Christian belief is grounded not in articulated but in nonarticulated reasons. Put that way, their thesis loses plausibility. I cannot think of any good reason (!) for holding it. Christian faith is surely grounded in reasons (my definition), whether those reasons are expressed or not.

Of course their broader point will still stand, reformulated, somewhat, in this way: we are within our epistemic rights in believing in God, even if we cannot produce any (relatively!) explicit or articulate reasons for doing so. Mavrodes, I think, provided the best formulation of this in *Belief in God* (1970),[44] with his distinction between "having a reason" and "giving a reason." Rather than saying that we have "grounds but not reasons" for Christian belief, it would be clearer to say that we can "have" reasons even when we cannot "give" them. I am surprised that this distinction did not play a major role in *FR*, for it expresses (much better than the terminology used in that book) what I think the authors wanted to say.

The evidentialist, then, is not wrong to insist that belief be based on adequate reasons, that we "proportion belief to the evidence." His error is to insist that these reasons be formulated, perhaps even that they be formulated in a way that makes them acceptable to the objector.

b. *Situated and Objective Rationality*

Once we eliminate Plantinga's sharp distinction between grounds and reasons, the door is open for a somewhat more "objective" concept of rationality. We will recall that Wolterstorff, especially, advocates a concept of "situated" rationality. It is wrong, he says, to ask "in the abstract" whether it is rational to believe a certain proposition; we can only ask whether it is rational for a particular individual in a particular situation (or, somewhat more liberally, for a particular *type* of person in a particular *sort* of situation) to believe it.

Now the concept of situated rationality is important. Each individual's epistemic rights and obligations are somewhat different from those of every other individual. I have, for example, an obligation to find out when my classes at Westminster Seminary are to be taught and where they will meet. My week-old son Justin has no such obligation. But there are also epistemic obligations and rights that are the same for everyone: all are re-

44. Cited earlier.

quired to know God, to know His will for them, to know that they have sinned and need God's forgiveness. All of us, furthermore, have an obligation to live wisely, which involves being faithful to God in our epistemic activities, and thus, I would say, presupposing the truth of His revelation in all of our thinking. Wolterstorff, let us recall, allows for the possibility of such an obligation: "Perhaps it is our duty to believe more firmly that God exists than any proposition that conflicts with this. . . ."[45] Would that obligation, if it exists, pertain only to some individuals? I believe I have shown in *DKG* that it does exist and that it pertains to everyone. And if everyone has an *obligation* to believe in God, surely that obligation justifies them in doing so. So there are some beliefs that are obligatory and justified for all persons, as well as some that are obligatory and/or justified only for some.

The epistemic obligations and rights that differ from individual to individual depend on those obligations and rights that we all share. The ultimate authority in all areas of human life, epistemic included, is Scripture. All human actions and beliefs are, if justified, justified by Scripture in various ways, as I discussed in *DKG*. In one sense, then, rationality is the same for everybody: a belief is rational if it conforms to the norms set forth in Scripture. In another sense, rationality varies from person to person, for the norms of Scripture *apply* differently to different persons and situations, as I explain by using the ideas of situational and existential perspectives. But rationality in the individual sense depends on rationality in the universal sense. It is Scripture that ultimately determines how rationality is to be used in particular situations. Thus when we are faithful in carrying out our unique callings, forming our individual beliefs according to the norms of God's Word, we are in one sense only carrying out the dictates of universal rationality. Situated rationality, then, is an individual's application of universal rationality.

Do rationality and truth coincide on this basis? On the *FR* approach, of course, a false belief can be rationally justified, and a true belief can fail to be. It would not be absurd simply to define "rational beliefs" to mean "true beliefs," perhaps acknowledging differences of degree so that the "most rational" beliefs would be those that are closest to the truth. The *FR* authors should, I think, have recognized that there are other legitimate uses of *rationality* besides their own. But we cannot really solve the problem simply by redefining *rationality*. That would only be playing with words. In

45. *FR*, 177.

fact what they call *rationality*, situated rationality, is a fact with which we must deal, whether we want to call it "rationality" or not.

I think that what we need is to distinguish different levels of justification and thus different levels of rationality. A primitive tribesman who believes that the earth rests on the back of an elephant is, we may say, justified in his belief at one level, given that he has never heard anything to the contrary or encountered any reason for doubting his belief.[46] But this "justification" is, of course—as the *FR* writers admit—justification in a "weak" sense. That the tribesman is justified in his belief will not make that belief at all credible to a sophisticated modern astronomer. And since Scripture urges us to live wisely, to prove all things, to walk in truth, we have an obligation, in general, not to remain complacent with such weakly justified beliefs. I say "in general," because other obligations may, as Wolterstorff says, take precedence. My beliefs about Eskimo culture are probably mostly false at the moment, but other duties presently outweigh my *prima facie* duty to improve the quality of my beliefs in that area. Until I do, however, I would be wise not to seek to address a congress of sociologists on the subject of Eskimo culture. And my reason for not addressing them may be put this way: my beliefs in this area are not sufficiently justified, meaning that I do not have beliefs in this area that I can defend with sufficient competence and cogency for such a gathering. So talk about justification (and hence rationality) presupposes a context of discussion. The tribesman's belief is justified in the context of tribal life, but the astronomer may well characterize this belief as unjustified, since his universe of discourse is different. Also, we can say that the belief is rational from one perspective, nonrational from another. So we must distinguish between low-level rationalities and higher-level rationalities, and indeed we ought, other things being equal, to seek the higher levels.

The highest level of justification-rationality for the human mind exists when a person has attained truth through the use of reliable belief-forming mechanisms that are in keeping with biblical norms. At this level, all true beliefs, and only true beliefs, are justified and hence rational. This is, of course, the goal of human knowledge. Therefore, although the *FR* discussions of situated rationality are helpful and interesting, I must dissent from their rejection of any other kind of rationality. Wolterstorff, as we have seen, explicitly denies the legitimacy of asking in general whether it is rational to believe something. On the contrary, to ask (yes, "in the ab-

46. In *DKG* I stated that even unfallen Adam may have erred in his beliefs, though he could not have erred in discerning his present responsibilities to God.

stract"!) whether it is rational to believe, say, in the existence of physical objects is usually to ask whether that belief meets the higher (or highest) standards of justification. (I say "usually," for of course this question may be a shorthand way of asking about "situated rationality" for a definite group, such as modern analytic philosophers.)

Is it ever rational, either in the "situated" sense or in the "objective" sense, to disbelieve God's existence or irrational to believe it? Obviously not, in the objective sense, granted that God exists. In regard to the situated sense the question becomes: Is anyone ever in a situation where he lacks a ground for believing that God exists? I would say no on the basis of Romans 1, which teaches that all persons not only have grounds for believing in God (epistemic permission if you will) but that all actually know Him at some level of consciousness.

c. *Ultimate Presuppositions*

It should be evident that the "basic beliefs" of *FR* are *not* the same as the "ultimate presuppositions" of *DKG*. Plantinga notes that the distinction between basic and nonbasic beliefs is only one of the distinctions relevant to a description of someone's "noetic structure." Other distinctions are between different degrees of belief (strength, firmness) and between beliefs of different "depths of ingression." He explains the latter concept this way:

> Some of my beliefs are, we might say, on the periphery of my noetic structure. I accept them, and may even accept them firmly, but I could give them up without much change elsewhere in my noetic structure. . . . So (the) depth of ingression (of such beliefs) into my noetic structure is not great.[47]

His example of a belief with a low depth of ingression is his belief that "there are some large boulders on the top of the Grand Teton." A belief with a great depth of ingression would be his belief that other persons exist.

The "ultimate presuppositions" of *DKG* are, first of all, commitments of the heart either for or against God. This heart commitment for God entails trust in God's Word and therefore ultimate trust in the truth of what God says. To presuppose God's Word, therefore, involves a belief in the truthfulness of God's Word, which has "dominion" over our other be-

47. Ibid., 50f. Cf. 82f. Cf. also Wolterstorff, 174. On strength of belief, see Wolterstorff, 143f., 156, and Mavrodes, 214ff.

liefs.[48] In Plantinga's terms, then, my belief in the truth of Scripture will, among all my beliefs, have the greatest depth of ingression into my noetic structure. It will also be that in which I believe most firmly. Of course, this is complicated by continuing sin, noetic as well as other kinds, in the life of the believer. At times, sinful, that is, unbelieving, thought will temporarily overcome my godly presuppositions. But my life as a whole, over the years of my regeneracy, will indicate (at least to God who sees the heart) that God's revelation is my firmest and most "deeply ingressed" commitment.

Are ultimate presuppositions also "basic" in Plantinga's sense? Well, I share Mavrodes's suspicions about the whole attempt to divide all of our beliefs into "basic" and "nonbasic" categories. God's existence is a presupposition of mine; but I am willing to argue for it, as noted in *DKG*. And since I don't distinguish as Plantinga does between "grounds" and "reasons," I would not want to characterize my belief in God as lacking reasons, for that would be to admit that my belief is groundless.

I would agree with Plantinga, however, that it may be rational for someone to believe in God's existence even if he cannot "give a reason" for that belief. We may "have reasons" even when we cannot "give reasons." If that is a sufficient basis for saying that this belief is "basic," then I don't object to calling it that. And the expression "properly basic" may also be useful in communicating the point that God's revelation is not subject to attestation by something else more authoritative than itself. The evidential attestation of Scripture is really an application of Scripture's own self-attestation, as I have argued in *DKG*. I would say, then, that the "ultimate presuppositions" of *DKG* are, in Plantinga's terms, beliefs that (1) are held with the highest degree of firmness, (2) manifest the greatest depth of ingression, and (3) are basic.

Frankly, I consider it a weakness in *FR* that the concept of an ultimate presupposition is not systematically discussed, a weakness that *DKG* may help to remedy. *FR* does occasionally allude to *something like* ultimate presuppositions. Recall, for example, Wolterstorff's suggestion, "Perhaps it is our duty to believe more firmly that God exists than any proposition which conflicts with this. . . ."[49] Perhaps indeed! And there is Plantinga's recollection from his former professor of the statement that "theists and

48. I continue to maintain that Romans 6:14 presents the most basic difference between believer and unbeliever: the unbeliever is under the dominion of sin; the believer is not. Here I am applying this distinction to the noetic area.

49. Ibid., 177.

nontheists have different conceptions of reason."[50] Belief in God is ultimately, of course, the presupposition that controls even one's concept of reason itself. And George Marsden's historical article reinforces the presuppositional flavor of the book. He argues that the nineteenth-century evangelicals in America failed to challenge the prevailing scientific methodology, trying instead to use it to vindicate Christianity. Here Marsden, former student of Van Til, is making essentially a presuppositionalist point: our belief in God's revelation must govern our thinking about everything else. But it is not a point that could be made about Plantinga's "properly basic" beliefs, because those beliefs may or may not be held firmly or be deeply ingressed; they may be maximally defeasible, and so they are not necessarily of sufficient weight to overturn allegedly scientific methods in the name of Christ.[51] Holwerda's article on Pannenberg also requires a concept of presupposition stronger than Plantinga's "properly basic beliefs." For Holwerda argues that God's revelation must govern our thinking about history. That is possible only if our beliefs about that revelation are not only properly basic but presuppositional in character.

FR, notwithstanding some unclarity in the matter, certainly seems to be leaning in a presuppositionalist direction, and I am happy for that. Perhaps there will now be, as Van Til has always hoped, a renewal of communication between Westminster and Calvin, between Van Tillian presuppositionalists and the philosophers of the Christian Reformed establishment. I do believe that both groups can learn much from each other.

50. Ibid., 90.

51. It would be unfair, too, not to refer here to Wolterstorff's account of "control beliefs" in his *Reason Within the Bounds of Religion* (cited earlier), which approaches what I want to say about presuppositions.

APPENDIX J

AN ONTOLOGICAL CLARIFICATION

This book is about epistemology (theory of knowledge), rather than ontology (theory of the nature of things); but of course the two cannot be sharply separated. One's view of reality will determine, to a great extent, his view of knowledge, and vice versa.

It occurs to me, as I reread what I have written, that my epistemological formulations may pose an ontological problem for some readers. I have written that norm, situation, and self are "perspectivally" related, which suggests that the three are really identical. Yet elsewhere I have insisted that the three are distinct and are not to be confused.[1] The apparent contradiction deserves comment.

When I say that the three are "perspectivally related," I mean to call our attention to the fact that "everything is normative," "everything is object," and "everything is subject." "Everything is normative" means that God's laws are revealed in all of our experience and that therefore all our experience of reality is intended in some way to help us govern our lives. "Everything is object" simply means that everything can be an object of our thought (even the "secret things of God" can be thought of as secret). "Everything is subject" means that all our knowledge is a knowledge of our own experience, our own thoughts, and so forth.

But if everything is norm, subject, and object at the same time, then how, one might ask, can the norm actually *govern* our subjectivity and our understanding of the objective world? Does the very *meaning* of normativity (and similarly of objectivity and subjectivity) become lost in this

1. See especially chapter 5, A, *(9)*, *a* and B, *(1)*.

construction? Does "norm" become indistinguishable from "object" and "subject"? Do the three terms simply become synonymous?

This problem, I think, can be overcome once we recognize that there are different *levels* of normativity. "Everything is normative," but everything is not *equally* normative. There is a "hierarchy" of norms. For example, God expects us to obey civil rulers. They have a genuine authority; their words are genuinely normative. But when they require disobedience to God, then God's Word takes precedence. Science, too, has a certain authority, but it is a "defeasible" authority, one that can be overcome by special revelation. Similarly, we can generalize by saying that all reality imposes demands on us but that some forms of revelation take precedence over others. The reason for this is not that natural revelation is in itself less authoritative than special but because our perception of natural revelation is obscured by sin, and special revelation is precisely the means God uses to correct our sinful misunderstandings of nature.

Thus we need never confuse God's Word with nature or with our own subjectivity. Although "everything is normative," the hierarchy of norms enables us to distinguish clearly between God's Word and the promptings of our own hearts. It is this distinction that leads us to say that "norm" is *not* the same thing as "object" and/or "subject." The difference between norm and subject is the difference between levels of normativity on the hierarchy.

And it is also a difference in *function*. "Norm," "object," and "subject" all refer to the same reality; they cover the same territory. But each attributes a different function to reality. "Norm" attributes to reality the capacity to govern intelligent subjects. "Object" attributes to reality the property of being *knowable* by intelligent subjects. "Subject" indicates that reality is inseparable from the subject himself and is to be found in and through his own experience.

Bibliography

Alston, William P. *Philosophy of Language*. Englewood Cliffs, N.J.: Prentice-Hall, 1964.

Armstrong, Brian. *Calvinism and the Amyraut Heresy*. Milwaukee, Wisc.: University of Wisconsin Press, 1969.

Austin, J. L. *How to Do Things With Words*. Cambridge, Mass.: Harvard University Press, 1962.

Barr, James. *Old and New in Interpretation*. London: SCM Press, 1966.

______. *The Semantics of Biblical Language*. London: Oxford University Press, 1961.

Barth, K. *Church Dogmatics*. New York: Charles Scribner's Sons, 1936.

Bavinck, H. *Doctrine of God*. Grand Rapids: Wm. B. Eerdmans Pub. Co., 1951.

Berkouwer, G. C. *Divine Election*. Grand Rapids: Wm. B. Eerdmans Pub. Co., 1960.

______. *Holy Scripture*. Grand Rapids: Wm. B. Eerdmans Pub. Co., 1975.

______. *The Providence of God*. Grand Rapids: Wm. B. Eerdmans Pub. Co., 1952.

Bloomfield, Leonard. *Language*. London: Allen and Unwin, 1935.

Buber, Martin. *I and Thou*. New York: Charles Scribner's Sons, 1958.

Campbell, C. A. *Selfhood and Godhood*. London: Allen and Unwin, 1957.

Carnell, Edward John. *The Kingdom of Love and the Pride of Life*. Grand Rapids: Wm. B. Eerdmans Pub. Co., 1960.

Clark, Gordon H. *Faith and Saving Faith*. Jefferson, Md.: Trinity Foundation, 1983.

______. *Johannine Logos*. Nutley, N.J.: Presbyterian and Reformed Pub. Co., 1972.

______. *Religion, Reason and Revelation*. Philadelphia: Presbyterian and Reformed Pub. Co., 1961.

Clowney, Edmund P. *Preaching and Biblical Theology*. Grand Rapids: Wm. B. Eerdmans Pub. Co., 1961, 1975. Reissued by Presbyterian and Reformed Pub. Co.

Copi, Irving M. *Introduction to Logic*. New York: Macmillan, 1961.

De Graaf, S. G. *Promise and Deliverance*. 4 vols. St. Catherines, Ont.: Paideia Press, 1977.

De Graaff, A., and C. Seerveld, eds. *Understanding the Scriptures*. Hamilton, Ont.: The Association for the Advancement of Christian Scholarship, 1968.

Delaney, C. F., ed. *Rationality and Religious Belief*. Notre Dame and London: University of Notre Dame Press, 1979.

Dooyeweerd, Herman. *In the Twilight of Western Thought*. Nutley, N.J.: Presbyterian and Reformed Pub. Co., 1968.

Downing, F. Gerald. *Has Christianity a Revelation?* London: SCM Press, 1964.

Ebeling, G. *The Nature of Faith*. Philadelphia: Fortress Press, 1961.

Farrer, Austin. *The Glass of Vision*. Westminster: Dacre Press, 1948.

Frame, John M. *The Amsterdam Philosophy: A Preliminary Critique*. Phillipsburg, N.J.: Harmony Press, 1972.

______. "God and Biblical Language." In *God's Inerrant Word*. Edited by John W. Montgomery, 159-77. Minneapolis: Bethany Fellowship, 1974.

______. "The Problem of Theological Paradox." In *Foundations of Christian Scholarship*. Edited by Gary North, 295-330. Vallecito, Calif.: Ross House, 1976. Also published as *Van Til the Theologian*. See below.

______. "Rationality and Scripture." In *Rationality in the Calvinian Tradition*. Edited by Hendrick Hart, Johan Vander Hoeven, and Nicholas Wolterstorff, 1-15. Lanham, Md.: University Press of America, 1983.

______. Review of Brian Armstrong's *Calvinism and the Amyraut Heresy* (Milwaukee, Wisc.: University of Wisconsin Press, 1969) in *WTJ* 34 (1972): 186-92.

______. Review of David Kelsey's *The Uses of Scripture in Recent Theology* (Philadelphia: Fortress Press, 1975) in *WTJ* 39 (1977): 328-53.

______. "The Spirit and the Scriptures." In *Hermeneutics, Authority, and Canon*. Edited by D. A. Carson and John Woodbridge, 213-35. Grand Rapids: Zondervan Publishing House, 1986.

______. *Van Til the Theologian*. Phillipsburg, N.J.: Pilgrim Publishing, 1976.

Gaffin, Richard B. *Perspectives on Pentecost*. Phillipsburg, N.J.: Presbyterian and Reformed Pub. Co., 1979.

______. *Resurrection and Redemption*, formerly *The Centrality of the Resurrection*. Grand Rapids: Baker Book House, 1978. Reissued by Presbyterian and Reformed Pub. Co., 1987.

Geehan, E. R., ed. *Jerusalem and Athens*. Nutley, N.J.: Presbyterian and Reformed Pub. Co., 1971.

Greidanus, Sidney. *Sola Scriptura*. Toronto: Wedge, 1970.

Hackett, Stuart. *The Reconstruction of the Christian Revelation Claim*. Grand Rapids: Baker Book House, 1984.

Halsey, James S. "A Preliminary Critique of 'Van Til: the Theologian'." *WTJ* 39 (1976): 120-36.

Hart, Hendrick, Johan Vander Hoeven, and Nicholas Wolterstorff, eds. *Rationality in the Calvinian Tradition*. Lanham, Md., and London: University Press of America, 1983.

Hempel, Carl. "The Empiricist Criterion of Meaning." In *Logical Positivism*. Edited by A. J. Ayer. Glencoe, Ill.: The Free Press, 1959.

Hick, John. *Philosophy of Religion*. Englewood Cliffs, N.J.: Prentice-Hall, 1963.

Hodge, Charles. *Systematic Theology*. Grand Rapids: Wm. B. Eerdmans Pub. Co., 1952.

Hordern, William. "The Nature of Revelation." In *The Living God*. Edited by M. Erickson, 177-95. Grand Rapids: Baker Publishing House, 1973.

Kelsey, David. *The Uses of Scripture in Recent Theology*. Philadelphia: Fortress Press, 1975.

Kline, Meredith G. *Images of the Spirit*. Grand Rapids: Baker Book House, 1980.

______. *Treaty of the Great King*. Grand Rapids: Wm. B. Eerdmans Pub. Co., 1963.

Klooster, Fred. *The Incomprehensibility of God in the Orthodox Presbyterian Conflict*. Franeker: T. Wever, 1951.

Kuhn, Thomas. *The Structure of Scientific Revolutions*. Chicago: University of Chicago Press, 1962. Second revised edition 1970.

Kuyper, Abraham. *Principles of Sacred Theology*. Grand Rapids: Wm. B. Eerdmans Pub. Co., 1965.

Lee, Francis Nigel. *A Christian Introduction to the History of Philosophy*. Nutley, N.J.: Craig Press, 1969.

Lewis, H. D. *Our Experience of God*. London: Allen and Unwin, 1959.

Lindbeck, George. *The Nature of Doctrine*. Philadelphia: Westminster Press, 1984.

McDowell, Josh. *Evidence That Demands a Verdict*. San Bernadino, Calif.: Here's Life Publishers, 1979.

———. *More Than a Carpenter*. Wheaton, Ill.: Tyndale House, 1977.

———. *The Resurrection Factor*. San Bernadino, Calif.: Here's Life Publishers, 1981.

Mavrodes, George. *Belief in God*. New York: Random House, 1970.

Miller, Randolph C. *Education for Christian Living*. Englewood Cliffs, N.J.: Prentice-Hall, 1956.

Montgomery, John W. *Faith Founded on Fact*. Nashville and New York: Thomas Nelson Publishers, 1978.

———. *Where Is History Going?* Grand Rapids: Zondervan Publishing House, 1969.

Morris, Charles W. *Foundation of the Theory of Signs*. Chicago: University of Chicago Press, 1938.

Murray, John. "The Attestation of Scripture." In *The Infallible Word*. Edited by Ned Stonehouse and Paul Woolley, 1-52. Grand Rapids: Wm. B. Eerdmans Pub. Co., 1946. Reissued by Presbyterian and Reformed Pub. Co.

———. *Collected Writings*. Edinburgh: Banner of Truth Trust, 1977.

———. *The Epistle to the Romans*. Grand Rapids: Wm. B. Eerdmans Pub. Co., 1960.

———. *Principles of Conduct*. Grand Rapids: Wm. B. Eerdmans Pub. Co., 1957.

Notaro, Thom. *Van Til and the Use of Evidence*. Phillipsburg, N.J.: Presbyterian and Reformed Pub. Co., 1980.

Partee, Charles. "Calvin, Calvinism and Rationality." In *Rationality in the Calvinian Tradition*. Edited by Hendrick Hart, Johan Vander Hoeven, and Nicholas Wolterstorff. Lanham, Md.: University Press of America, 1983.

Pinnock, Clark. *Reason Enough*. Downers Grove, Ill.: Inter-Varsity Press, 1980.

Plantinga, Alvin. *God and Other Minds*. Ithaca, N.Y., and London: Cornell University Press, 1967.

Plantinga, Alvin, and Nicholas Wolterstorff, eds. *Faith and Rationality: Reason and Belief in God*. Notre Dame and London: University of Notre Dame Press, 1983.

Poythress, Vern S. "A Biblical View of Mathematics." In *Foundations of Christian Scholarship*. Edited by Gary North, 159-88. Vallecito, Calif.: Ross House, 1976.

______. *Philosophy, Science and the Sovereignty of God*. Nutley, N.J.: Presbyterian and Reformed Pub. Co., 1976.

Pratt, Richard. "Pictures, Windows and Mirrors in Old Testament Exegesis." *WTJ* 45 (1983): 156-67.

Quine, W. V. "Two Dogmas of Empiricism." In *From a Logical Point of View*. Edited by W. V. Quine, 20-46. New York: Harper and Row, 1961.

Ramsey, Ian. *Religious Language*. New York: Macmillan, 1957.

Reymond, Robert. *The Justification of Knowledge*. Nutley, N.J.: Presbyterian and Reformed Pub. Co., 1976.

Ridderbos, Herman N. *The Coming of the Kingdom*. Philadelphia: Presbyterian and Reformed Pub. Co., 1973.

______. *Paul: An Outline of His Theology*. Grand Rapids: Wm. B. Eerdmans Pub. Co., 1975

Ryle, Gilbert. "Formal and Informal Logic." In Ryle, *Dilemmas*, 111-29. London: Cambridge University Press, 1954.

Schaeffer, Edith. *L'Abri*. Wheaton, Ill.: Tyndale House, 1969.

______. *The Tapestry*. Waco, Tex.: Word Books, 1981.

Schaeffer, Francis. *The God Who Is There*. Downers Grove, Ill.: Inter-Varsity Press, 1968.

Schleiermacher, F. *The Christian Faith*. Edinburgh: T. and T. Clark, 1928.

Schlossberg, Herbert. *Idols for Destruction*. Nashville: Thomas Nelson Publishers, 1983.

Spier, J. M. *An Introduction to Christian Philosophy*. Philadelphia: Presbyterian and Reformed Pub. Co., 1954.

Sproul, R. C., John H. Gerstner, and A. Lindsley. *Classical Apologetics*. Grand Rapids: Zondervan Publishing House, 1984.

Tillich, Paul. *Systematic Theology*. Chicago: University of Chicago Press, 1951.

Toulmin, Stephen. *The Uses of Argument*. London: Cambridge University Press, 1958.

Traina, Robert A. *Methodical Bible Study Methods*. Wilmore, Ky.: Asbury Theological Seminary, 1952.

Urmson, J. O. *Philosophical Analysis*. London: Oxford University Press, 1956.

Van Til, Cornelius. *Christian Theistic Evidences*. Unpublished syllabus, 1961.

______. *Common Grace*. Nutley, N.J.: Presbyterian and Reformed Pub. Co., 1972.

______. *Common Grace and the Gospel*. Nutley, N.J.: Presbyterian and Reformed Pub. Co., 1972.

______. *Defense of the Faith*. Philadelphia: Presbyterian and Reformed Pub. Co., 1955.

______. *Introduction to Systematic Theology*. Unpublished.

______. "Why I Believe in God." Philadelphia: Great Commission Publications, n.d.

Vander Stelt, John. *Philosophy and Scripture*. Marlton, N.J.: Mack Publishing Co., 1978.

Vos, Geerhardus. *Biblical Theology*. Grand Rapids: Wm. B. Eerdmans Pub. Co., 1959 and Edinburgh: Banner of Truth, 1975.

______. *The Pauline Eschatology*. Grand Rapids: Wm. B. Eerdmans Pub. Co., 1972. Reissued by Presbyterian and Reformed Pub. Co., 1986.

______. *Redemptive History and Biblical Interpretation*. Phillipsburg, N.J.: Presbyterian and Reformed Pub. Co., 1980.

Warfield, B. B. *The Plan of Salvation*. Grand Rapids: Wm. B. Eerdmans Pub. Co., 1942.

Wittgenstein, Ludwig. *Philosophical Investigations*. New York: Macmillan, 1958.

______. *Tractatus Logico-Philosophicus*. London: Routledge and Kegan Paul, 1961.

Wolterstorff, Nicholas. *Reason Within the Bounds of Religion*. Grand Rapids: Wm. B. Eerdmans Pub. Co., 1976.

Young, E. J. *Thy Word Is Truth*. Grand Rapids: Wm. B. Eerdmans Pub. Co., 1957.

Index of Proper Names

Index of Topics

Index of Scripture References